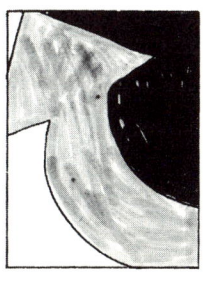

**Experimental
Contributions
to Clinical
Psychology**

Core Books in Psychology Series
Edward L. Walker, *Editor*

PSYCHOLOGY: A STORY OF A SEARCH
W. Lambert Gardiner, *Sir George Williams University*

THE UPTIGHT SOCIETY: A BOOK OF READINGS
Howard Gadlin, *University of Massachusetts*
Bertram E. Garskof, *Federal City College*

HUMAN SOCIALIZATION
Elton B. McNeil, *The University of Michigan*

READINGS IN HUMAN SOCIALIZATION
Elton B. McNeil, *The University of Michigan*

COMPARATIVE ANIMAL BEHAVIOR
Richard A. Maier, *Loyola University, Chicago*
Barbara M. Maier

AN INTRODUCTION TO COGNITIVE PSYCHOLOGY
Melvin Manis, *The University of Michigan*

EXPERIMENTAL CONTRIBUTIONS TO CLINICAL PSYCHOLOGY
Erasmus L. Hoch, *The University of Michigan*

Experimental Contributions to Clinical Psychology

Erasmus L. Hoch
The University of Michigan

**Brooks/Cole
Publishing Company**

A Division of Wadsworth
Publishing Company, Inc.

To C. A. W.

© 1971 by Wadsworth Publishing Company, Inc., Belmont, California 94002. All rights reserved. No part of this book may be reproduced, stored in a retrieval system, or transcribed, in any form or by any means, electronic, mechanical, photocopying, recording, or otherwise, without the prior written permission of the publisher: Brooks/Cole Publishing Company, a division of Wadsworth Publishing Company, Inc.

L.C. Cat. Card No: 70-157431
ISBN 0-8185-0011-5
Printed in the United States of America
1 2 3 4 5 6 7 8 9 10 — 75 74 73 72 71

This book was edited by Adrienne Harris and designed by Linda Marcetti. The technical illustrations were done by John Foster. The book was set in Linofilm Helvetica; it was typeset, printed, and bound at Kingsport Press, Kingsport, Tennessee.

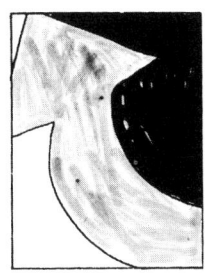

Preface

This book rests upon the premise that communication among psychologists of *every* persuasion will help the whole field of psychology to grow faster than if each of us were but tending his own scientific patch. It attempts to show the interdependence of clinical psychology and other areas of psychology and to illustrate the advantages of attacking a particular problem in psychology from several different directions.

My earlier, briefer introduction to the field (Hoch, 1971) attempts to tell interested readers what clinical psychology is about. This second book, which encompasses the previous one, assumes that the reader is already converted and would like to know more fully what this field entails.

Part One of the book is devoted to some methodological considerations. Part Two presents some of the dilemmas faced by the investigator who carries on research with human subjects. Part Three, on research and theory, is intended to illustrate the variety of resources from which clinical psychology may draw in its quest for broader understanding. Part Four, on theory and practice, deals both with answers that *seem* to have been found and with questions that continue to be asked.

I hope that, in reading this book, the student with predominantly clinical interests will gain a healthy respect both for the clinician as a behavioral scientist and for the nonclinician as a contributor to the clinical enterprise. In emphasizing the similarities rather than the differences between the schizophrenic and ourselves, Harry Stack Sullivan (1947) reminded us poignantly that ". . . above all else, we are all much more human than otherwise." I would like to suggest in this book that, regardless of our areas of specialization within psychology, we are all much more psychologists than otherwise.

For their helpful reviews and suggestions, I would like to thank my colleagues of The University of Michigan who read portions of the manuscript: Professors Benno G. Fricke, Harry F. Gollob, Jesse E. Gordon, Ralph W. Heine, E. Lowell Kelly, John E. Milholland, Warren T. Norman, James D. Papsdorf, J. E. Keith Smith, Stephen B. Withey, and Research Associate Frank M. Goode, as well as former colleagues, Professors George L. Geis of McGill University, Irwin Katz of the City University of New York, Sarnoff A. Mednick of the New School for Social Research, Harold L. Raush of the University of Massachusetts, and Sherman Ross of the National Research Council. Special thanks are due Professor Edward L. Walker of The University of Michigan, whose editorial support was much appreciated, and Louise H. Kidder of Northwestern University, who offered the kind of critical comments on the entire manuscript that only a student can. I am very grateful to Adrienne Harris, who offered her invaluable editorial talents with delicacy and therapeutic consideration for an author's feelings. For her painstaking secretarial efforts in the preparation of the manuscript, I am indebted to Ruth Rowry.

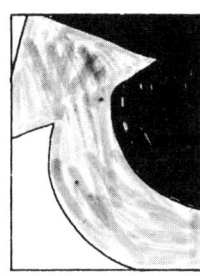

Contents

Part One: Methodology 1

  1. The Nature of the Problem 3
      On Observation, Labeling, and Inference 3
      Psychodynamics and Levels of Abstraction 5
      The Clinical Psychologist's Dilemma 7

  2. Methodological Convergence 11
      The Study of Sleep and Dreaming 11
      The Problem of Behavior Modification 33

Part Two: Psychology and Human Subjects 49

  3. Ethical Dilemmas in Research 51
      A Socioclinical Study 53
      A Field Study of Clinical Relevance 56

  4. Methodological Considerations 60
      Problems of Design 61
      Artifacts Involving Human Subjects 67

Part Three: Research and Theory 77

  5. Animal Research and Clinical Analogues 79
      Traumatic Avoidance Learning 80
      The Study of Aggression 95

  6. The Analysis of Conflict 114
      Clinical Data-Gathering 115
      The Study of Natural Events 115
      Experimental Manipulation 121
      Humor as a Mechanism of Defense 127
      Interpersonal Conflict and Conflict Resolution 130

7. Research on Levels of Awareness 136
   - Pupillometrics 136
   - Hypnosis: Another Royal Road to the Unconscious? 141
   - Conscious-Unconscious Control of Behavior 153

8. Research in Clinical Assessment 161
   - Clinical Prediction 163
   - Prediction in the Form of Postdiction 167
   - Effect of Background Training and Fund of Information on Prediction 169
   - The Other Side of the Coin 172

9. The Hospital as a Social System 182
   - Communication Processes 182
   - Theoretical Models of Social Interaction 185

10. Psychopathology: Real and Experimental 193
    - The Study of Schizophrenia 195
    - Experimental Clinical Diagnosis 225

Part Four: Theory and Practice 239

11. The Observation of Behavior 241
    - Psychological Constructs 241
    - Psychopathology 254

12. The Prediction of Behavior 264
    - General Ability 265
    - Personality Dynamics 289
    - Some Methodological Dilemmas 302
    - Extracurricular Problems of Prediction 310

13. The Control of Behavior 314
    - The Issues 315
    - Psychotherapeutic Approaches 315
    - Behavior Modification Approaches 324

14. The Continuing Dialogue 340
    - Psychotherapy: Pro and Con 340
    - Behavior Therapy: Pro and Con 344
    - Rapprochement 348
    - Reorientation 349

15. Theory and Practice: Two Sides of the Coin 352
    - Theory: A Guide to Practice 352
    - Practice: The Implementation of Theory 358

References 363

Index 379

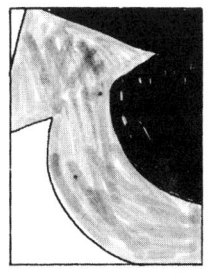

**Experimental
Contributions
to Clinical
Psychology**

Part One
Methodology

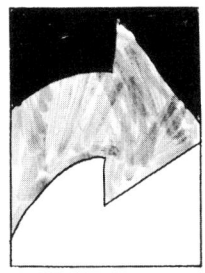

1
The Nature of the Problem

Few people would venture to diagnose a neighbor's chest pains as an incipient heart attack. But should he complain that his wife is hard to get along with or that his children are out of hand, most are ready to offer advice, if not to prescribe solutions. People-watching is a universal hobby and every man a self-proclaimed expert, unfortunately. The road to amateur psychology is paved with good intentions and, alas, with bad theories, as the following story will attest.

On Observation, Labeling, and Inference

Several years ago, after sitting with a group of colleagues in weekly committee meetings over the period of a year, I was struck by the sudden realization that one could divide this group of ten people in a very simple way. In the comfortable atmosphere of the conference room, some members of the committee *invariably* put their feet on the conference table while others *never* did! And, as it happened, of the ten people involved, five fell into each group, so that the box score for the year looked like this:

"Tablefooters"	"Non-tablefooters"
B – –	F – –
H – –	Ho – –
M – –	K – –
N – –	Ma – –
W – –	Wy – –

In mildly scientific fashion, several members of the committee were independently asked to list names in each category. The result was 100 percent agreement. The

4

layman, acting as self-styled psychologist, might now be tempted to proceed from this observation to fancier efforts, first using conventional labels (for example, "inhibited" versus "uninhibited"), and then moving with zeal to further inferences, perhaps even toward a miniature theory. Let us imagine for a moment where this could lead.

Someone might assume, for example, that putting one's feet on the table represents a kind of carefree abandon, an easygoing, relaxed temperament, the ability to translate inner peace into corresponding outer behavior. It would not seem farfetched, therefore, to hypothesize that the "tablefooters" (the uninhibited, by this token) were the product of a permissive, accepting, tolerant early environment, in which freedom, mental health, and other good things prevailed.

That's fine (although the facts would have to be checked). But what is interesting, yet vexing, about this psychological enterprise is that someone else might proceed along quite different lines to quite different conclusions. This latter, more pessimistic "theorist" might begin by assuming that one does not usually put one's feet on the table. Such behavior, he would argue, represents not an easygoing nonchalance but rather a defiance of social convention. Therefore he might hypothesize differently about the two groups. He would see the tablefooters as rebellious rather than uninhibited. Their early upbringing, the "theorist" speculates, must have been rigid and authoritarian; their present behavior must represent defiance of authority, whether blatant or subtle, conscious or unconscious. Again, such speculation would have to be checked against the facts, insofar as they can be determined.

The same observation, then, can lead to two equally plausible lines of theorizing. This makes "psychologizing" at once intriguing and frustrating, especially when some skeptic suggests that, lest we proceed too blithely, we should first investigate some more prosaic facts. Is it perhaps true that the non-tablefooters are aged 25–35 and the tablefooters 48–63, so that the latter, as senior citizens, can afford to take more liberties than the former, who, as assistant professors on trial, need to be on their good behavior? Or is the age distribution the other way around, with the young men being the tablefooters, so that perhaps the older, feebler group does not put its feet on the table for reasons that are arthritic rather than psychological?

Most discouraging of all for the amateur psychologist would be to have someone point out that, with such a high conference table, it becomes uncomfortable for the non-tablefooters (all of whom prove to be under 5'6") to put their feet on the table, in contrast with the tablefooters (the shortest of whom is 6'1"). The committee in this case did not happen to consist of giants and dwarfs, but it could have.

Methodology

This is not exactly an example Freud might have chosen. It is, however, the stuff of which the layman's collective wisdom is sometimes made as he ventures into the realm of psychological conjecture. For this is an area in which the untrained can often sound very interesting but turn out to be very wrong! The intellectual hop-skip-and-jump from observation to hypothesis to theory can easily wind up as a technical flop.

Without getting overly prophetic, let us look for a moment at another way in which the untrained or the careless can leap at psychological inferences and end up in an awkward position.

Psychodynamics and Levels of Abstraction

We cannot go too far wrong if we stick closely to observed fact (although even here some classic experiments on testimony [Münsterberg, 1908] make one wary). If a woman wears a dress that comes to five inches above her knees, we can safely state that (by definition) she wears miniskirts. That is correct, but not particularly interesting in itself. However, we may conjecture about the "psychodynamics" of her choosing this mode of dress, particularly when the woman, although comely, is 40 years old. Such speculation becomes more interesting; unfortunately, it also becomes more risky. Let us follow the process.

We can observe, although perhaps not as directly or as objectively, that the woman is a rather shy, or at least a somewhat reserved, person. Others who know her agree that she speaks softly, is very polite, and tends not to assert herself in a group. We cannot measure such attributes as readily as the length of her skirts, but at least there is a consensus among several observers that this is so.

We have, then, departed a little from the more objectively determinable facts, but not much. We are now at the more interesting point of contrasting the seemingly modest makeup of the woman with her somewhat sexy appearance. We learn, however, that we have paid a small price, inasmuch as one of our colleagues doubts that she is really as reserved as she appears on the surface. He has, for example, observed on her desk a catalog of high-priced bathing suits, featuring mainly the bikini type. Putting two and two together, then, our colleague is willing to move yet another step up the abstraction ladder—that is, to make an additional inference that this outwardly modest person is really unconsciously seductive. Now the situation becomes decidedly more interesting psychologically; it becomes at the same time more shaky scientifically. In fact, of six people who know the woman well, three are willing to countenance such a hypothesis, while three are not. Thus, we pay a price for moving from a clear but dull fact (she wears miniskirts—defined operationally as dresses five or more inches above the knee) to an interesting but possibly erroneous inference (the shy lady is a temptress).

Intrigued by the process of psychological inference and where it might lead, the most widely read and imaginative of the six observers suddenly gets a burst of clinical intuition that a new complex has been discovered. In a poetic flash he even coins a name for it—the "sea anemone syndrome"! This woman, so modest in her demeanor, yet dressed in attire quite risqué for a 40-year-old, is more complicated than she herself suspects. Like the beautiful sea anemone that coyly attracts unsuspecting prey, she is unconsciously bent upon seducing and destroying men. Bravo!—says the proud theorist. Nonsense!—say four others. It occurs to the remaining member of the group of six that the price of inference might be pictured as shown in Figure 1.

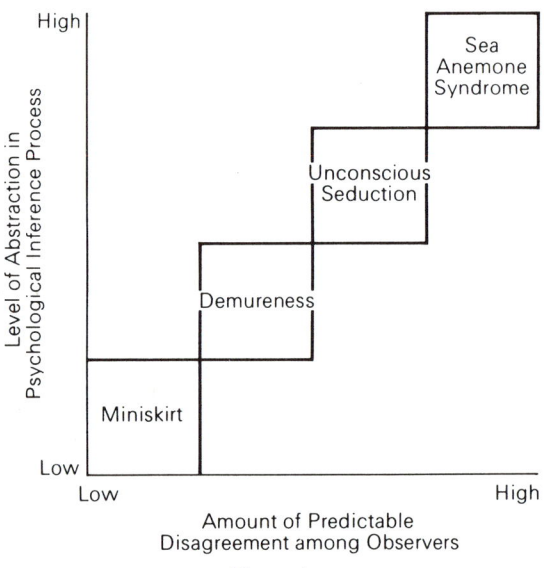

Figure 1

This hypothetical example represents a fanciful but not atypical situation. The amateur "psychologist" indulges in inferential speculation as a pastime; the clinical psychologist does so of necessity. There is a difference. The former proceeds with temerity, the latter with caution, fully cognizant that the price of psychodynamic theorizing is sometimes error but hopeful that he can minimize error by seeking data that will confirm or disconfirm his hunches.

The Clinical Psychologist's Dilemma

One's image of a clinical psychologist might well be that of someone who administers projective (personality) tests to mental hospital patients or spends his professional life in a private office helping neurotics cope better with life—both worthy objectives. Indeed, a dictionary of psychological terms (English & English, 1958) defines clinical psychology as "... that branch of psychology which deals with the psychological knowledge and practice employed in helping a client who has some behavior or mental disorder to find better adjustment and self-expression. It includes training and actual practice in diagnosis, treatment, and prevention, as well as research for the expansion of knowledge" (p. 90).[1]

Apt as the definition is, it needs elaboration. The clinical psychologist of today is concerned with adjustment as well as with maladjustment. His interest lies in behavior modification generally, rather than in treatment specifically. He shows less concern with testing *per se* and more concern with the general problem of assessment. In short, he is interested in observing carefully and measuring accurately, to the end that clearer description, better prediction, and more adequate control of behavior may be attained. In clinical psychology this is more easily said than done. The strength of a phobia (an irrational fear) is not indexed as readily as the strength of the connection between words such as "light-dark" versus "light-heavy" (although some [Lang & Lazovik, 1963] do not see the former as such an impossible task). Nor is the degree of gain from psychotherapy measured as easily as the reaction time on a visual-motor task (for example, pressing a button as soon as a light goes on). And constructs like "repression" (unconsciously excluding something from awareness) are not as readily specified as the hunger of a rat that has been carefully kept at 80 percent of normal body weight for a month and run in a maze 22 hours after its last meal.

The above discussion is not to imply, however, that the usual principles of inquiry do not apply in clinical work, nor that methodological ground rules can be waived. Clinical problems may be different in character, but they merit rigorous study nonetheless. Techniques for their analysis are sometimes relatively new, and often still awaiting development, so that the clinician may often have to take on an unenviably difficult task. Nevertheless, as a behavioral scientist, he is held to the same canons of evidence that govern his colleagues in other areas.

There are some interesting ironies in this picture. When an unmanned space vehicle landed on the moon, scientists were able to learn something about the moon's com-

[1] Used by permission of David McKay Company, Inc.

The Nature of the Problem

position by noting how many inches the craft had sunk into the lunar surface. In contrast, although we spend as much as 40,000 hours in dreams during our lifetime, psychologists still know relatively little about this phenomenon, which is certainly much closer to home.

Indeed, the behavioral scientist in general, and the clinical psychologist in particular, may be tempted to conclude that the more personally and socially meaningful problems of life (such as conflict and stress, interpersonal relations, group interaction, or marital compatibility) are precisely those with which scientists find it hardest to come to grips. It is possible to predict with reasonable confidence whether John Smith can become a good airplane pilot; it is not so easy to predict how happy he will be in his forthcoming marriage.

At the risk of oversimplification, the situation might be outlined as shown in Table 1.

Table 1

		Personal-social meaningfulness of problem under study	
		More	Less
Rigorousness of research design available	More	A	B
	Less	C	D

The problems in cell *D* of Table 1 cause us little concern. We do not really know how to tackle them, but then they hardly seem worth the effort. No one is really interested in studying whether mosquitoes have attitudes toward each other. It is the problems in Cell *A* on which we would like to be spending our time—the quest for psychological solutions to interracial crises, achievement of world peace, accurate prediction of marital compatibility, or maximization of educational effectiveness, for example. Unfortunately, behavioral scientists are often forced to work either in cell *B,* where their research techniques are relatively unimpeachable but the problems under study unmoving, or else in cell *C,* where the problems are undeniably profound but the techniques for their study are at best unsophisticated.

Perhaps the dilemma arises, in part, from the fact that the field of clinical psychology has broadened since two decades ago when clinical psychologists usually worked in medical settings and were understandably absorbed in psychopathology *per se.* Today it is not unusual to find them interviewing residents of a racial ghetto after a civil disorder, or questioning policemen after a wild political convention. Here they are working on problems allied to social psychology or perhaps sociology. It therefore behooves them to have more than a passing acquaintance with current developments in these areas. It is not unusual in this day of psychopharmacology, with its tranquilizers, energizers, and antidepressants, to find a physiological psychologist on the staff of a mental hospital. And he may well be working beside an experimental psychologist who knows a good deal about the laws of learning and has the job of teaching psychotic children to talk. In addition, they may be joined by a social psychologist, who, as an expert on organizational structure, conducts research on how interactions among the psychiatrists, social workers, nurses, and psychologists affect the patients' progress.

For each of these specialists to make the most meaningful contribution in the clinical setting, he also needs to be a generalist of sorts. That is, he needs to know something about the most pertinent developments in psychology *generally* while remaining thoroughly conversant with progress in clinical psychology *per se*.

My thesis, then, is that the more a clinical psychologist knows about what is going on in the rest of psychology, the better a clinical psychologist he is. Conversely, the more a physiological, experimental, social, or other kind of psychologist knows about significant developments in clinical psychology, the more consummate a psychologist he is.

When a surveyor stakes out a piece of land, Nature does not always make it convenient for him. Trees may stand in his direct line of sight, so that, with the help of his sextant, he has to sight around them; he has to triangulate—establish several other fixed positions—in order to plot a line to his goal. The answers to the many intriguing, but complex problems that the clinician sets himself may well require a kind of triangulation—taking fixes on what the rest of psychology knows that is applicable to the problem at hand.

For example, it may turn out that a schizophrenic is not only the product of a miserable family situation but also the victim of certain biochemical anomalies. In such a case, the physiological psychologist will have much to offer. Similarly, when one examines closely the reward-and-punishment contingencies that existed in a patient's nuclear family, it is reasonable to hope that the general experimental psychologist, sometimes called the "rat psychologist," may have some enlightening ideas about how pathological behavior is shaped and maintained. Clinicians have become increasingly interested, too, in the extent to which the bizarre behavior of a chronic patient (who may have spent 18 years or so in a woefully understaffed state hospital with few treatment facilities) is really a product of his schizophrenia. To what extent might he be reflecting the consequences of this stultifying institutionalization? Here it is not unreasonable to assume that the social psychologist will have some relevant theoretical concepts and research findings to contribute.

In this book I do not presume to merge the many facets of psychology into one kaleidoscopic image. I will, however, try to document the thesis that much of what is happening in the nonclinical areas of psychology is grist for the clinician's mill and that, in turn, psychologists in such areas as motivation, learning, perception, attitude change, problem-solving, and decision theory would do well to acquaint themselves with the latest developments in clinical psychology, the better to give a third dimension to their research and theory.

The old saw about the right hand needing to know what the left is doing is particularly applicable in clinical psychology, where diverse methodological roads lead to knowledge. Clinical inference is one road, statistical analysis another, experimental manipulation a third. Here, then, is a kind of methodological triangulation, or *convergence,* which is particularly needed in an area of science whose problems are always intriguing but often intractable.

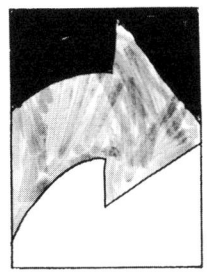

2
Methodological Convergence

The Study of Sleep and Dreaming

Ironically, some of the most widely shared and deeply meaningful experiences of man have been less systematically studied than the movements of celestial bodies that are light-years away. Sex is one of these experiences; it had to wait for Kinsey and his colleagues in the 1940s to produce data that could be trusted. Dreaming is another. As old as man himself, the dream process has, until recently, proved far less amenable to rigorous study than we might have wished.

Part of the problem lies in its inaccessibility, the rest in its complexity. In a brilliant *tour de force,* Freud (1900) established a whole body of theory, elaborated upon by his successors, that conceptualized the dream process in a unique way, offering an original and defensible rationale for its phenomena and for its role in the "psychic economy." Clinical psychologists have made, and will continue to make, fruitful use of such creative insights in the realm of both theory and application.

Thanks to psychoanalytic theory, dreams offer the skilled clinician some fertile hunches in the understanding and treatment of problems of adjustment. Typical is an oft-cited example of how an experienced psychoanalyst (Reik, 1948) cuts through symbolism, whether of waking or sleeping origin, to decode the "language of the unconscious." Consider Reik's description of an encounter with a patient:

> Our session at this time took the following course. After a few sentences about the uneventful day, the patient fell into a long silence. She assured me that nothing was in her thoughts. Silence from me. After many minutes

she complained about a toothache. She told me that she had been to the dentist yesterday. He had given her an injection and then had pulled a wisdom tooth. The spot was hurting again. New and longer silence. She pointed to my bookcase in the corner and said, "There's a book standing on its head." Without the slightest hesitation and in a reproachful voice I said, "But why did you not tell me that you had had an abortion?" (p. 263).[1]

To an accomplished clinician like Meehl (1954), this is an example of clinical skill at its best (for, as it turned out, Reik had inferred correctly). To Cronbach (1960), an expert on the subject of assessment, such skill is ". . . compounded of theory, imagination, experience, and willingness to make (and verify or discard) rash guesses" (p. 605). We shall not, for the moment, concern ourselves with whether this was such a rash, although skillful, guess, whether Reik himself was unconsciously responding to other cues (perhaps from his patient's previous sessions), how often such hunches on his part proved misses rather than hits, or other considerations that might be raised. The fact is that the data of dreams serve very useful purposes when analyzed by skilled clinicians. What is often frustrating, however, is the lack of systematic opportunities to confirm or disconfirm the correctness of the interpretations of dream content. Fortunately, there are other options open to the clinician-scientist who feels that such data merit detailed analysis. Let us, therefore, take a look at the three-pronged attack on analysis of the dream process, which clinicians are now in a position to launch.

A Three-Pronged Attack

In their presentation of psychological methodology, Scott and Wertheimer (1962) point out that psychological knowledge is obtainable from three sources—naturalistic observation, systematic assessment (statistical calculation of relationships among variables), and experimental manipulation (laboratory research). In an address to the American Psychological Association, Cronbach (1957) developed a related theme, characterizing one wing of psychology as "experimental psychology" and the other as "correlational psychology," and regretting the fact that there have been times when the two have gone their separate ways.

Cronbach urged a unification of "the two disciplines of scientific psychology"; we shall explore all three of the methodologies that Scott and Wertheimer describe—clinical, statistical, and experimental—using the study of dreams as an example.

[1] From *Listening with the third ear* by T. Reik. New York: Farrar, Straus & Giroux, Inc., 1948. Reprinted by permission.

Clinical Analysis

When Freud proposed that dreaming was as fitting a subject for psychological study as the more observable behavior of everyday life, the notion was at most tolerated and hardly advocated. Yet to refuse to deal with unique kinds of behavior merely because one had no readily available methods for their analysis might well have been to throw out the baby with the bath. The solution lay not in denigrating the data but in learning to analyze them. The problem was not with the dreamer but with the clinician.

In the belief that the material of dreams might contribute as much to the understanding of behavior as the data of waking life, creative clinicians like Freud proceeded to develop distinctive methods for such analysis. The interested reader can follow the historical development elsewhere. (See, for example, Blum, 1966.) Let us, however, examine some general principles that characterize this approach.

First, it seems clear that one-to-one types of interpretation are far too simple. That is, while certain dream symbols may well have a higher probability of representing particular themes than others—our cultures do, after all, have some universal elements—it is generally assumed that the same symbol may have multiple meanings, perhaps as many as there are dreamers. In the following passage, Bonime (1962)[2] illustrates this thesis well, discouraging those whose superficial knowledge of Freud leads them to conclude fearlessly, for example, that "snake equals penis."

> If a woman were dreaming of a snake which associatively became established as a penis [that is, it reminds her of the latter in waking life], it would still be necessary, if one is to achieve insight into her personality through her dream symbol, to establish the quality of experience with a penis which was symbolized by that snake. If she were a professional dancer largely preoccupied by a desire to be seductive, and if she had performed the dance of a snake charmer, then the penile snake could symbolize her desire to charm men or to control them by her sexual allure. The problem, however, would then be the characterological one of desire for control and manipulation. Such pathology, furthermore, would not be confined to the sexual sphere, but would be an aspect of her total personality, a determinant in her relations with men, women, and children, even though the penis symbol appeared to focus exclusively upon the manipulation of men. . . .
>
> If a woman had been made pregnant before a promised marriage by a man who later deserted her, the penile snake in her dream might represent the quality of deceit or poisonousness, or both, not only in men but

[2] From *The clinical use of dreams* by Walter Bonime, M.D., Basic Books, Inc., Publishers, New York, 1962. Reprinted by permission.

Methodological Convergence

also in any human being who offered intimacy. If she had had a puritanical upbringing and yet indulged in a sexual affair, the penile snake might represent hidden sinful desires or actual secret activities of a sexual nature.... By still further extension, the snake could refer... even to yearnings for other types of self-indulgence, self-gratification, even of a nonsensual, esthetic, intellectual, or material nature. For a puritanically raised woman who had healthily rebelled, emancipated herself, and fulfilled not only her sexual desires but also her artistic and intellectual inclinations, that penile dream-snake might be a symbol for a healthy self-fulfillment in any of a variety of totally nonsexual spheres. In other words, by analogy with sexual emancipation, the snake, originating for this woman as a penis symbol, could come to be a broader symbol for self-emancipation....

The snake in another woman's dream might represent fear of sexual attack from men, or a related desire to castrate them in the manner of killing a snake. Or the penis might represent a pervasive contempt for men...

In many patients, however, a dream snake may not in any manner refer to the phallus. A woman patient (this would be equally true of a man), during her childhood, while walking with other children, might have overcome her fear of being bitten by snakes by picking one up. For this patient, a snake in a dream could symbolize courage—a courage utterly unrelated to sexuality. If she had been laughed at on that walk because, unlike the other children, she had failed through fear to pick up the snake, a snake in her adult dream might symbolize humiliation.

Another woman, deceived by her closest female friend, might dream of the friend as a snake, with no penile implications whatever.

It is obvious at this point that the meanings of the dream symbols, as I view them, neither derive from a collective unconscious nor conform to the requirements of a theory of a universal pattern of psychosexual ontology (pp. 36–37).

Returning to our general principles, it seems reasonable to assume, secondly, that the dream and its contents are best understood as part of a larger whole—that whole being the particular personality that is under study. As a corollary, then, the elements of a dream—its symbols, events, and similar features—can be understood meaningfully only in terms of other information known, or to be discovered, about a person.

Third, in order to deal with all of the variables, it seems necessary to enlist the dreamer himself in the interpretation of his dream—that is, to get *his* reactions to and feelings about the dream as a whole and its components. For this purpose, one might have him "associate" to the dream and its elements—that is, to reflect on, divulge, and discuss ideas, memories, and feelings that occur to him in connection with it.

Methodology

Finally, a proper analysis of the total data—that is, the dream as reported and the dreamer's associations thereto—requires the confirmation or disconfirmation of the hypotheses that have emerged from the conjoint efforts of dreamer and analyst.

In one sense, we are talking here of the "naturalistic observation" of Scott and Wertheimer (1962). With the help of the dreamer, the analyst looks at what happened, notes as much of the action as he can, and records his interpretations and conclusions. In the hands of experienced clinicians the process leads to fertile hypotheses for further exploration. The following dream and a part of its accompanying analysis, as reported by Breger (1967), will help give the reader an understanding of the procedure and its possibilities.[3]

> My mother and I were living in the woods . . . we were walking down a highway and there were lots of deer running around. And the people on the highway kept stopping, ah, there were business stands along the highway like service station operators, and they kept asking us if we would like to buy one of the deer that was standing around. And so I went over to this jewelry store with one of these people following us. My mother kept trying to explain that we couldn't afford it and they never would understand. We went into this store and were looking for, I can't remember the article we were looking for. Anyway, we went into this place, and it was very, very small and ah . . . my mother would, this was pretty important, she slipped behind the counter along with the lady and I was still sitting on a big stool on the other side of the counter. And I tried on several of whatever it was I was looking for. And we all decided to go up, the three of us decided to go up, to a house to have some coffee and some cookies. And so, we, they were saying, I said "do you think I could get through this space to get behind the counter," because we were going to go out the back door, or, "do I have to go around the house." They kept kidding me and said that I would probably have to go around the house. Apparently, I was fat or something, I don't know. Anyway, as a matter of fact, I couldn't get through the space. So I had to go around the house. The house was this very primitive looking wooden cabin. And for some reason or other we all sat down and started reading a paper. And we were also drinking tea or something . . . and some horrible tasting cookies. They were just totally tasteless and looked like honeycomb, apparently some specialty of the woods. And we were reading the paper, the paper was a New York City paper and it was talking about, I was reading about the advertisements for insurance companies and for undertakers and things like that. They were all just horrible. They were saying things like, ah, "so what if you die, ah, let's snap it up and get rid of them" and all these funny things. And you know, really strange peculiar things, like "throw them in the ground real fast and they will forget tomorrow." And, ah, with smiling undertakers standing there. And then one kind of cute

[3] Reprinted by permission of the author and the American Psychological Association.

thing from a camera company saying something about, "for the kids who peeked away." And there was a picture of two little children who were skating, standing there looking, ah, ostensibly looking at the camera, both of them, when you examine them a little closer one was peeking to the right and one was peeking to the left just as the shutter was open. And ah, the next picture was, these same two kids and it's saying they are standing there on the street on an ice-skating rink, even though the subway down below is being renovated. So I thought for a while about the whole ice-skating rink falling into the subway station. I'm trying to remember some more advertisements, I don't think I can, I just know they were all pretty gruesome, except those pictures of the little kids (p. 20).

The dreamer in this case was a young female graduate student serving as a subject in Breger's dream laboratory. During this period she was struggling with the decision of whether to marry her boyfriend of two years' standing. She had just recently decided to go through with the marriage despite her fear that it might interfere with her continuation in graduate school and thereby snuff out the chance for a career. On the other hand, her boyfriend, who also was trying to make up his mind about the marriage, was still vacillating.

What, then, might the dream of this young woman "mean"? On the basis of extensive personality assessment, and with the help of the subject's associations to her dream (and a related one of the succeeding night), the following were some of the speculations, as reported by Breger:

Initially, she had no associations to the "woods" nor to being "fat" (she is, in fact, a petite, attractive girl who has never had any problem with her weight). The unpleasant affect of the dream was quite prominent and when asked to associate to it she very rapidly went from the "undertakers" who smilingly deal in death to "abortionists" who do the same. Suddenly, some light was shed on the dreams. She reported having had an abortion a year previously when she had been pregnant by the same boyfriend. She also spoke with some regret about having lost the child and expressed concern over what her mother would think if she found out about it. . . .

The pregnancy, abortion, and her feelings about it are portrayed in several ways. Her own "fatness" in both dreams probably symbolizes pregnancy. . . . The "ugly" aspects of the fatness probably symbolize the guilt she experiences . . . her nostalgic feeling about the lost child . . . is alluded to as the kids who "peeked away" when the shutter was open. The abortion itself is kinesthetically represented as children falling through a hole in the context of death, that is, the "undertakers" who say "throw them in the ground real fast and they will forget tomorrow."

The abortion is also symbolized in both dreams as something that costs a lot of money, reducing her ugly fatness in one, and the insistent salesman who wants a lot of money for the deer (perhaps a fusion of her lost "dear" and an innocent uncivilized creature). . . .

> Finally, there is the contrast between the country (the "woods") and the big city (the newspaper from New York). . . . At one level, she describes her mother as very unsophisticated—a simple country girl—while she has made a much more sophisticated life for herself—as an outstanding student, fashion model, and graduate student. At the same time, several of her dreams portray her dissatisfaction with her sophisticated big-city way of life. . . . Here, she is drawn toward a similar life . . . There remains however, the possible barrenness of this life (the tasteless cookies, "a specialty of the woods") which relates to her view of her mother's life and the possibility that being a wife and mother herself would be very dull . . . (p. 21).

Given as he is to this type of creative, and reasonably plausible, psychodynamic speculation, the clinician is the first to urge caution in the too-ready acceptance of such hunches. Indeed, he has learned to regard them as hypotheses for further exploration rather than as findings *per se*. For, as Bonime illustrated in the passage cited on p. 13, the data lend themselves to multiple hypotheses; it is in the confirmation or disconfirmation of those hypotheses that the clinician finds further guidelines to the interpretation of particular dreams and a subsequent fuller understanding of the person who dreamed them.

Let us turn next to the second, and quite different, method of analysis that one might use in understanding the relationship between dreaming and behavior.

Statistical Analysis

As Cronbach (1957) points out, the experimental psychologist arranges situations to his liking and, insofar as he can, exercises tight control over all but the dependent variable (that is, the outcome measure). He orders research *à la carte,* as it were. The "correlational psychologist," to use Cronbach's term, studies situations as he finds them in nature, situations that we either have not yet learned to control or never will. He gathers data already given but brings to their analysis a variety of statistical techniques in order to note relationships of interest, or to discover others we may not even have surmised.

The data of dreams are natural events of the kind to which the correlational psychologist might profitably devote attention. All he need do is collect them systematically, conjecture about variables with which these data may share interesting connections, and then bring his statistical wizardry to bear on the relationships.

To some, this approach to the understanding of dreams may seem practical but not very creative. Meehl (1954) has, in another connection, spoken of "clinical" versus "actuarial" (statistical) approaches in clinical psychology, suggesting that the latter approaches may prove to be at least as fruitful as the former. Indeed, some clinical psychologists are willing to exchange the satisfaction of making clinical inferences for the certainty that comes from more straightforward calculation of relationships. Let us look for the moment at some of these "actuarial" possibilities.

It is not difficult to think of variables that could conceivably be related to the content and process of dreaming. Children's dreams may differ in interesting respects from those of adults. The dreams of men may be unlike those of women. Are artists' dreams different from construction workers' dreams? Are the dreams of a practicing homosexual significantly different from those of a normal married male? Are there dimensions along which the dreams of the *same* person shift as he moves from childhood through adolescence into adulthood? The reader can doubtless add questions of his own.

The clinician finds no shortage of relationships to investigate statistically. One could wonder, for example, to what extent the element of color figures in dreams and, where it does, to which psychological variables it is related. Do certain people usually have pleasant dreams, while others have consistently unpleasant dreams? If so, what are the personality variables that differentiate them? Assuming that one can establish indices of how hostile or fearful given dream episodes are, to what other variables might these indices be related? In short, there is no end of speculation concerning the relationship between characteristics of the dream and the dream process on the one hand and personality, intellectual, social, or related variables on the other.

Let us imagine that a correlational psychologist is interested in the relationship between the degree of hostility contained in a sample of dreams from 25 randomly selected persons (assuming that a valid index of hostility is derivable) and the degree of hostility ascribed to these persons by others (assuming a reasonable consensus among the judges—be they acquaintances, clinicians examining test responses, or others). He would be interested in discovering whether the relationship turns out to look like *A, B,* or *C* in Figure 1.

If the results (shown in hypothetical form) turned out to be those of relationship *A,* then subsequent theorizing would take a different course than if the situation proved to be that of relationship *B.* Given the results in relationship *C,* however, the clinician would be thrown back upon other theoretical leads. Whatever one may think about such a statistical approach, it is clearly different in character from the foregoing clinical analysis. What the clinical approach gains in freedom to formulate conclusions, it loses in the degree of certainty about their validity. On the other hand, while the statistical approach stays as close to its data as possible and thereby gains confi-

Methodology

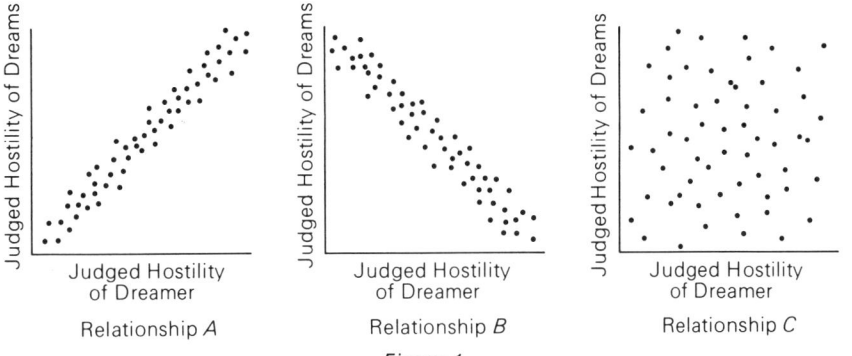

Figure 1
Hypothetical relationships between personal hostility and dream content.

dence in the conclusions reached, the conclusions may often be several steps removed from any implementation in clinical practice.

Proponents of the third method of analysis employ quite another strategy. Resorting to experimental manipulation, this group attempts to intrude into the dream process itself. Monitoring dreams on the spot—that is, while they are actually occurring—recording the data as close to the moment of awakening as possible, and actually manipulating the process systematically, the clinician who takes to the dream laboratory values tight experimental control. Let us look at some of his efforts.

Experimental Analysis

In science, as elsewhere, one seldom gets something for nothing. The psychologist interested in the study of stress and conflict, for example, has the choice of either observing the problem *au naturel,* knowing that he is studying the real thing—as in the Detroit riots of 1967—or of arranging situations that are intended to produce stress and conflict that can be studied more systematically. The former situation has the advantage of genuineness but the disadvantage of lack of control. Looters making off with TV sets are not likely to stand around answering interviewers' questions, while police are equally disinclined to take time out to explain why they shot someone rather than arresting him. The alternative situation—the one in which the experimenter fabricates a conflict situation in the laboratory—has the advantage of tight control over the variables of interest but suffers somewhat from artificiality.

Mindful of this dilemma, the laboratory-oriented clinician is likely to entertain reservations about a strictly clinical approach to the analysis of dreaming. For one thing, he argues, a dreamer usually brings his data (that is, the dream as remembered or recounted) to his analyst a day or so after it has taken place, so that he has remembered and reported some dreams, or parts of dreams, but forgotten (or "repressed" or "suppressed") others. Furthermore, in the usual situation the analyst has little, if any, direct control over the subject's (or patient's) dreaming. Skillful as the clinician may be at interpretation, he is not in a position to manipulate the dream process actively in order to understand better what might be influencing it. Hence, the newer laboratory techniques and experimental methodology have proved welcome to the clinician intent on studying more rigorously the dynamics of dream production.

Specifically, the "hardware" involved in these new techniques consists of the electroencephalograph (EEG), the electrooculograph (EOG), and the electromyograph (EMG). By means of electrodes taped to the subject at various places and connected to recording devices, each of these instruments yields characteristic information. The EEG, with its wires leading from several places on the skull, records the ongoing pattern of waves (electrical activity) emitted by the brain. The EOG, recorded through wires taped to the subject's eyelids, provides tracings of the movements of his eyeballs (the importance of which will be explained shortly). And the EMG, through similar recording techniques, registers muscle tension at whatever point on the subject's body its leads are attached. Together, the three instruments provide a running account of the overt and covert behavior of the laboratory subject.

Data-gathering now becomes a straightforward procedure for the clinician who is fortunate enough to have a dream laboratory at his disposal. He gets subjects who are willing to sleep nightly in the laboratory (usually for pay), hooks them up to the recording devices, observes the tracings, and then has objective data gathered at the scene of the dream, as it were. After the pioneering discoveries of Aserinsky and Kleitman (1953), it became clear that the various wave patterns (EEG tracings, for example) provide a veridical moment-by-moment account of what is going on in the "inner life" of the subject as he sleeps.

The findings are revealing. As shown in Figure 2, sleep is neither a uniform state nor a state in which nothing happens. Note that the EEG tracings of a typical sleeping subject take at least four distinct forms—commonly called Stages 1, 2, 3, and 4 of sleep. A variety of neural activity seems to be going on while the subject seems to be sound asleep. What is more, the action is marked by characteristic electrical tracings, so that, with reasonable objectivity, it can be noted when the subject proceeds from one stage of sleep into another in the course of the sleep cycle. As shown in Figure 3, a night's sleep consists of a number of such cycles (6 to 8, on the average) during which the sleeper passes progressively from one stage of sleep to another, although with individual differences appearing from person to person.

Granted that the EEG tracings tell us something we might otherwise not have known about the process of sleep, what do they add to our knowledge of the nature of

Methodology

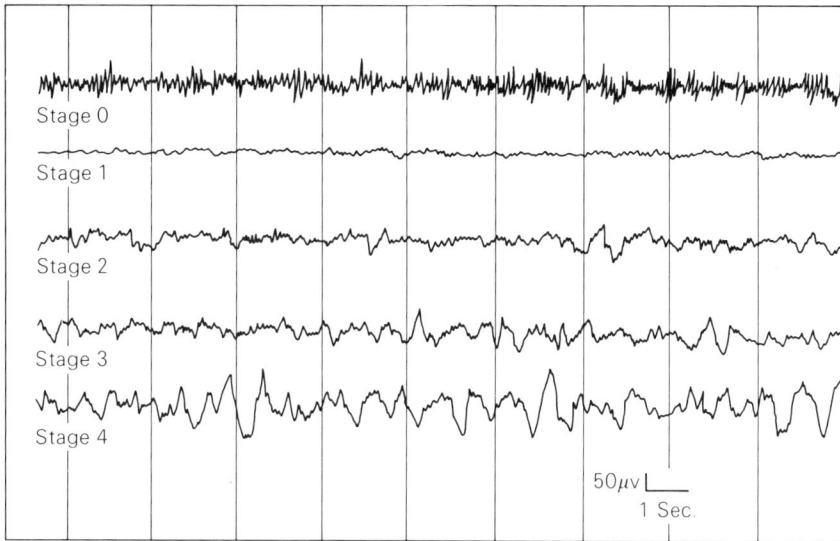

Figure 2
Sample EEG tracings during various stages of sleep. (Figure 1 from *Sleep: An experimental approach* by W. B. Webb. Copyright 1968 by The Macmillan Company and reprinted by permission.)

dreaming? Here the electrooculograph (EOG) makes its contribution. As Aserinsky and Kleitman discovered, the EOG, like the EEG, shows distinctive patterns — sometimes slow, smooth, asynchronous, at other times fast, jerky, or conjugate (that is, both eyes moving in the same direction). And, more significantly, when a certain EOG pattern — rapid eye movement (REM) — coincides with a certain EEG pattern — Stage 1 sleep — dreaming seems to be going on.[4]

How do we know this? It's very simple, thanks to the laboratory techniques. We awaken sleeping subjects at certain points — that is, during times when they are showing the various tracings — and ask them what was going on. In a typical experiment (Aserinsky & Kleitman, 1953) 20 of 27 subjects awakened during Stage 1–REM sleep reported that they had been dreaming; awakened during Stages 2, 3, or 4, with no REMs showing on the EOG tracing, only 4 of 23 subjects reported dreaming. The rest described the sleep experience that preceded awakening as "thinking." Car-

---

[4]This is not the case during the initial Stage 1 EEG when the subject is in the process of falling asleep. It is the case, however, during the other Stage 1 periods of the sleep cycle (see Figure 3), when the subject emerges from Stages 2, 3, or 4 to pass into Stage 1 — the so-called "emergent" Stage 1 — where the Stage 1–REM sleep combination indicates that dreaming is taking place.

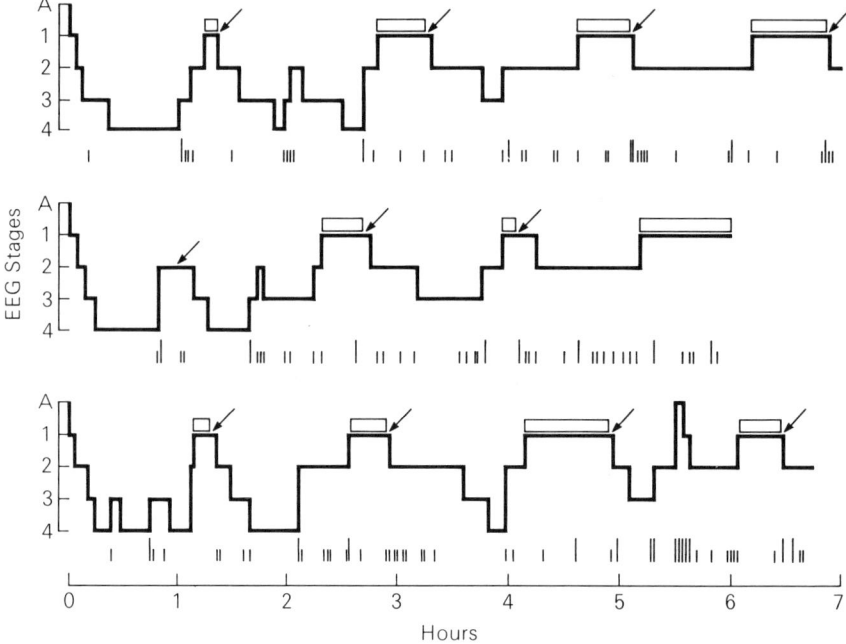

Figure 3
Continuous plots of the EEG stages of a subject during three representative nights. The dark bars represent the rapid eye movement (REM) periods that characteristically occur during Stage 1 sleep, in contrast to the non-rapid eye movement (NREM) periods of Stages 2, 3, and 4. The vertical lines below the graphs indicate body movements; the longer lines represent gross body shifts, the shorter lines represent smaller movements. (Figure 3 of Dement and Kleitman, 1957. Reproduced by permission of Elsevier Publishing Company, Amsterdam, 1957, from the *Journal of Electroencephalography and Clinical Neurophysiology*.)

ried out on a large scale, such experimentation (Dement, 1965), involving 2,240 Stage 1–REM awakenings, yielded reports of dreaming in 83 percent of the cases.[5]

As a result of these technological developments, we are in a position to know with reasonable accuracy when a sleeping subject is undergoing the experience of dream-

---

[5] With REM awakenings, subjects recall dreams from 60–93% of the time; with non-REM (NREM) awakenings they recall dreams from 0–54% of the time. The latter range is attributable in part to how dreaming is defined and in part to the manner of awakening (that is, whether sudden or gradual). Further evidence for REM as an index of dreaming during emergent Stage 1 sleep comes from several studies that show an impressive relationship between the length of the rapid eye movement period (REMP) and the number of words used to report the dream; the relationship is equally good between the length of the REMP and the time required by a subject to act out the dream in real life.

ing. It is possible, therefore, to awaken him at the time to get an on-the-spot, relatively uncontaminated, account of his dream content—an "instant replay," so to speak—which can be tape-recorded immediately for later analysis.

Such methodological advances allow us to talk with considerably greater confidence about the nature of the sleep and dream cycle. How does it look, for example? Figure 3 showed the relationship between REM and NREM sleep for a typical subject. There are, to be sure, significant inter-subject differences; but there is, as Webb (1968) points out, even more remarkable intra-subject consistency. In any case, we now have some idea of the parameters of sleep and dreaming. Assuming a 7- to 8-hour sleep period, these parameters include such general findings as the following:

1. The first dream of the night takes place about 60 to 90 minutes after the onset of sleep.
2. From 10 percent to 30 percent of sleep time shows REMPs.
3. About 4 to 6 REMPs occur per night, some marked by 2 or 3 dreams, so that a person may experience 10 to 20 dreams during the 1 to 2 hours of the sleep cycle that are spent in dreaming.

These figures provide a clearer, more detailed picture of the sleep–dream cycle. More important for the clinician, however, is the newfound opportunity to study the dream process as it takes place. It now becomes possible to manipulate relevant variables in order to note their effect. A whole new set of questions becomes accessible to investigation, while many old, but previously unanswerable, questions can be raised anew. In short, the clinician as experimenter is now in a position to manipulate such variables as he deems relevant to the nature and process of sleep and dreaming. The experimental paradigms that thus become available are interesting ones, as shown in Figure 4.

The dream researcher might pre-program his subjects before they retire for a night of sleep in the laboratory. That is, before the subjects go to bed (at point *A* of Figure 4), they would be exposed to particular pre-sleep experiences—watching a harrowing movie, reading a sexy novel, being engaged in a heated argument, to name only a few. The investigator would be interested in how such pre-sleep experiences are reflected, if at all, in the dreams of the subjects when awakened at point *C*—that is, at the immediate conclusion of a Stage 1–REM period. In other words, the researcher, would be interested in the *A–C* relationship.

Or the research could focus on how inputs planted at subawakening levels in the course of the dream (at point *B*) manifest themselves when the dream is recounted at point *C*. Here the *B–C* period might hold the key to a fuller understanding of the

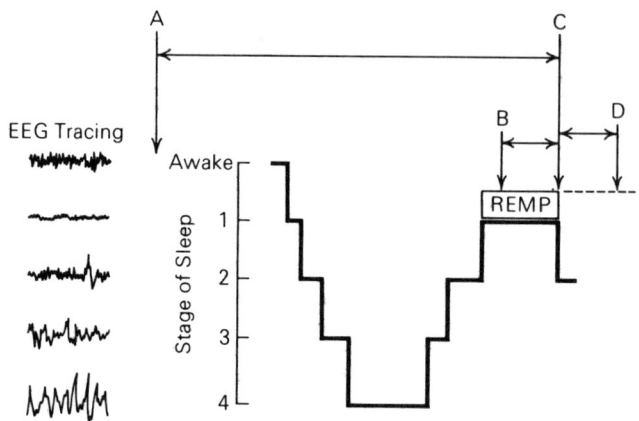

Figure 4
Some technologically feasible research paradigms in the study of sleep and dreaming.

nature of "dream work," as suggested by Freud—that is, the variety of symbolic transformations and related disguises that dream content is said to represent.

Again, another investigator might be particularly intrigued by the fact that dreams, however elaborate in process, are so evanescent even only a short time after awakening. His concern would be with the *C–D* period, and he might well be an experimental psychologist with a special interest in short-term memory, who finds it hard to accept a construct such as "repression" as an explanatory principle.

These new possibilities have hardly unraveled all the unknowns of sleep and dreaming. They promise, however, to make the process less mysterious. It falls to the ingenuity of experimenters to ask the right questions and to translate them into testable hypotheses. Studies can be relatively simple and still enlightening. Are our dreams, for example, only the disguised representation of an external event (which can be identified objectively)? Do they take place in a few seconds, as the oft-cited account of Maury's (1861) famous dream of the French revolution would have us believe (his falling bedpost was presumably represented in the dream as the guillotine blade), or do they occur in "real time"?

The new laboratory techniques open such questions to investigation. Experiments in which subjects were allowed to dream for varying lengths of time and then were asked to guess how long they had been dreaming show that dreams are by no means split-second occurrences. Other experiments have introduced external stimuli at subawakening levels (a flashing light or a spray of water, for example) during a Stage

1–REM period to see how these might get woven into the subsequent dream account. The findings suggest that, while such stimuli can be incorporated to some extent, they seem to account for only a small part of the variability of dream content.

While such general findings are of interest to the clinician, he is more concerned with the significance of the individual differences that the new techniques help reveal. Some people, for instance, claim they never, or almost never, dream; others assert that they dream almost constantly when asleep. Is it true that certain people are really "nondreamers"? Or are they simply "nonrecallers"? If the latter, are they "repressing" the recall of what they have dreamed? And, if so, are such people significantly different from dreamers on important psychological variables? Such questions are now open to empirical investigation, given the methodology and technology at hand.

We can, for example, compare the accounts we hear immediately after the dreamer is awakened with the next morning's report of the same dream, noting the degree of congruity between the two. If the two versions differ appreciably, is simple decay of the memory trace or interference from waking activity responsible, or have the individual's defense mechanisms actively distorted the dream?

The questions now accessible to empirical investigation are intriguing. Theoretical notions long held may now be susceptible to proof, disproof, or modification. Others can be tried on for size. The following are typical of the questions that present themselves as one thinks about the possibilities:

1. To what extent, and in which ways, are the real events of the preceding day represented in the dreams of the night?
2. Can the course of the dream in progress be affected by the introduction of specific subawakening external stimuli of psychological significance beyond the simple sensory inputs described above?
3. Is it possible to "prefabricate" dreams—that is, to influence dream content by regulating the experiences of a person during the day or evening preceding the dream night?
4. What happens as one arbitrarily deprives a person of the opportunity to dream (by awakening him every time his EEG–EOG recordings indicate that he is starting to dream)?
5. Do the new laboratory techniques provide means for testing the validity of some, or all, of the theoretical notions customarily held about the psychological significance of dreaming—wish-fulfillment, disguised gratification, censorship, and the like?

The raising of such questions in no way minimizes the value of the substantial body of theory already formulated by psychoanalytic theorists. Certainly, their extended contacts with patients constitute a rich repository of information, which lends itself to fertile hunches that can be elaborated into complex theory when confirmed by repeated experience. Freud's *Interpretation of Dreams* (1900) constitutes such an effort; succeeding analysts have either built on his groundwork or erected theoretical structures of their own.

These earlier basic beliefs about the nature and purpose of dreaming can now be combined with the recent laboratory techniques to look anew at such major assumptions as the following:

1. Dreams serve a "wish-fulfilling" function. That is, certain of our needs and wishes that strongly seek expression cannot be granted or satisfied in real life, often because they are not sanctioned by the prevailing mores. Such satisfaction becomes possible in the unreal world of dreams.
2. Were satisfactions achieved in dreams too obviously, the dreamer might find his sleep disturbed. Hence, psychoanalytic theory holds that gratification of needs often proceeds in disguised, symbolic form, with the manifest (overt) dream content serving to camouflage the latent (real) meaning of the dream experience, thus allowing the person to sleep relatively undisturbed. As Freud put it, the dream is the guardian of sleep.
3. Where the "dream work" has not sufficiently disguised the expression and gratification of certain impulses of the sleeper, he may not only wake up but later find himself unable to remember the dream or parts of it at all ("repression").[6]

Our purpose at this point is to consider how present laboratory research focuses on the creative hypotheses of the psychoanalytic theorists in order to broaden our understanding of the nature of dreaming. Let us, therefore, look at some typical efforts of investigators to subject some of these interesting notions to empirical test.

Dreaming as Wish Fulfillment

If dreams do, indeed, serve the purpose of gratifying needs that are not being met in real life, an analogue of such a situation might be created by depriving subjects of gratification of certain needs in order to note the influence of such deprivation on the content of their dreams. As a first step toward studying the most significant psycho-

[6] The student interested in further reading can find ample material on the subject in Blum (1966) or in such treatises as those of Freud (1938), Fromm (1957), and Hall (1966).

logical needs in the long run, one can begin with simpler needs, like the satisfaction of thirst. It is quite possible, for example, to deprive laboratory subjects of fluids for a substantial block of time (say 24 hours), in order to study the influence of such deprivation on dream content. The investigator would first establish a baseline for each subject during a number of nights prior to the deprivation by calculating the proportion of themes of thirst-quenching and related activities appearing in his dream narratives; then he could compare the dreams on the night following deprivation with those of preceding nights.

Dement and Wolpert (1958) did such a study. Fifteen dream narratives of three subjects deprived of fluids for 24 hours showed ten of the fifteen narratives to be unrelated to the deprivation experience and none of the fifteen to involve drinking as such. The five dreams containing elements that might conceivably have reflected the influence of deprivation are reported by Dement (1965) as follows:

> a. "I was in bed and was being experimented on. I was supposed to have malabsorption syndrome."
> b. "I started to heat a great big can of—a great big skillet of milk. I put almost a quart of milk in it."
> c. "Just as the bell went off, somebody raised a glass and said something about a toast. I don't think I had a glass."
> d. "While watching TV I saw a commercial. Two kids were asked what they wanted to drink and one kid started yelling, 'Coca-cola, orange, Pepsi' and everything."
> e. "I was watching a TV program and there was a cartoon on with the animals that are like those in the Hamm's beer advertisement" (p. 224).

Of this study, Dement (1965) remarks:

> The dehydrated state undoubtedly exerted some influence on the content of the dreams, but it is puzzling, in view of the wish-fulfillment theory of dreaming and the subjects' suffering and overwhelming preoccupation with their thirst, that none were able to slake their thirst directly as did Freud who, after eating anchovies, frequently dreamt of "swallowing down water in great gulps, and it has the delicious taste that nothing can equal but a cool drink when one is parched with thirst" (p. 224).

We are for the moment not concerned with whether such simple small-scale studies undermine elaborate large-scale theories. Our purpose is simply to indicate how one interested in testing certain aspects of dream theory now has at his disposal techniques for subjecting questions of clinical import to closer and reasonably objective scrutiny.

Sleep Preservation

Freud's notion of dreams as the guardian of sleep was an intriguing one, and one for which he made a very plausible case. Were he alive today, he would doubtless be engaged in interesting dialogue with his contemporaries. Among them he would find some asking whether it is really true that we dream in order to sleep, or whether, indeed, the situation is possibly the reverse, namely, that we sleep in order to dream. Lerner (1967) and Breger (1967) have recently raised the latter possibility, while Foulkes (1966) and Webb (1968) pose such interesting considerations as the following:

1. Judging from the data derived from normal subjects in laboratory sleep research, people spend, on the average, about 20 percent of the night in Stage 1–REM sleep — that is, in dreaming. If dreams serve special psychological purposes, one might expect considerably more variability, differing as people do in quality of psychological adjustment.
2. Animals, as well as people, show such Stage 1–REM patterns. Hence, either dreams are not just psychologically sleep-protective in character, or else animals, too, have their problems of adjustment.
3. Even the newborn infant shows REM–sleep. Indeed, infants spend a greater proportion of time in REM–sleep than do adults. If we assume that infants do not engage in dreaming as we know it, or at least that their dreams do not serve the same purpose as adult dreams, then perhaps, suggest Roffwarg and his colleagues (1966), REM–sleep serves a physiological rather than a psychological function. As they put it:

> We have hypothesized that the REM mechanism serves as an endogenous source of stimulation, furnishing great quantities of functional excitation to higher centers. Such stimulation would be particularly crucial during the periods *in utero* and shortly after birth, before appreciable exogenous stimulation is available to the central nervous system. It might assist in structural maturation and differentiation of key sensory and motor areas within the central nervous system, partially preparing them to handle the enormous rush of stimulation provided by the postnatal milieu, as well as contributing to their further growth after birth. The sharp diminution of REM sleep with development may signify that the mature brain has less need for endogenous stimulation. Proof that the critical function of the REM sleep mechanism during development is the one of 'autostimulation' of structural and responsive capacity in the central nervous system must await future experimentation (p. 617).

4. Perhaps there are arguments to be made on both physiological and psychological grounds. It is true that when people are purposely deprived of REM time (by being awakened in the laboratory whenever their tracings show them to be in that state),

they will exhibit more REM–sleep on "recovery" (that is, undisturbed) nights than had been shown in their baseline sleep pattern. The phenomenon does not apply exclusively to REM–sleep, however. Consistently deprive a subject of NREM–sleep time, and, if not artificially awakened, he will exhibit longer NREM (for example, Stage 4) sleep periods than he did during the period when his baseline was being recorded. Thus, to regard dreaming as serving solely psychological purposes may be to gloss over some important physiological functions.

Yet to subscribe to a totally physiological position would be equally in error. REM-deprived subjects not only tend to spend more time in REM–sleep on recovery nights; while awake they also (presumably as a consequence of REM deprivation) begin to show signs of psychological disturbance—restlessness, irritability, delusions, and hallucinations. Too, when awakened repeatedly before their dream sequences are completed, subjects who have a high degree of "dream continuity" in their dream narratives begin to show psychological effects—frustration, hostility, delusional trends—that suggest a need to complete sequences started, as if to serve a definite psychological purpose. Thus, the psychological and physiological functions of sleep and dreaming seem to be of a "both–and" rather than "either–or" character.

Repression

The dynamic-nondynamic controversy over the nature of dreaming has much fuel to keep it burning. The phenomenon of repression, for example, figures prominently in both psychoanalytic theory and in speculation about some aspects of dreaming and dream recall. And, on the basis of some of the empirical findings, the concept seems to fare well.

As pointed out earlier, on the whole, awakenings during REMPs produce immediate dream recall about 83 percent of the time; if the investigator waits only a few seconds before requiring the subject to narrate his dream, however, the recall rate drops to 69 percent. Most surprising is the finding that, if an interval of a few minutes ensues before the subject is asked for his narrative, recall becomes virtually zero! Learning theorists can argue about whether the phenomenon represents decay of memory traces, as in short-term memory, interference from waking activity, or related phenomena. The clinician, on the other hand, can, with equal persuasiveness, suggest that the mechanism of repression is at work.

The clinician can find research support for the repression argument. Although most people will admit that they dream, some will represent themselves as nondreamers—that is, they feel they dream rarely, if at all. Yet, take such people into the laboratory, as Foulkes (1966) reports, involve them in the sleep studies described above, and it turns out that the alleged "nondreamers" do show REMPs and, when awakened during them, report dreams. True, according to one study (Antrobus et al., 1964) the "nondreamer" group show slightly less REM time than do admitted dreamers (19 percent versus 24 percent respectively), yet, strangely enough, "nondreamers" have been found to have greater EEG activity as well as EOG activity during their REMPs than do dreamers. Does this suggest greater psychological arousal during the dreams of "nondreamers" and, accordingly, a greater need for repression of what was dreamed, hence, a lower rate of laboratory dream recall and a real-life insistence that one has not dreamed?

Many people report dream-like fantasies during the hypnagogic period (the period of falling asleep); others do not. The nondreamers, Foulkes (1966) reports, when administered the California Psychological Inventory, "responded favorably to a set of individual CPI items expressing a rigid, moralistic, and repressive outlook on life, to wit:

> "I set a high standard for myself and I feel that others should do the same."
> "I would disapprove of anyone's drinking to the point of intoxication at a party."
> "I am in favor of a very strict enforcement of all laws, no matter what the consequences."
> "I feel sure that there is only one true religion."
> "I would rather be a steady and dependable worker than a brilliant but unstable one" (pp. 190–191).

It is difficult to judge to what extent such findings substantiate the role of repression in the dream process, but they should nonetheless give one pause for thought. Meanwhile we turn to another area that figures prominently in psychoanalytic theory.

The Role of Sex

The nature and process of sexual adjustment play a significant role in psychoanalytic theory. Therefore, it is not surprising to find dream content and symbolism regarded as valuable sources of insight into this area. It is instructive to look at some of the current laboratory findings, now that new techniques have made empirical evidence available.

Fisher (1967) has recently made the role of sex in dreaming a central subject of some research. Having at hand the laboratory techniques and facilities described earlier, he needed comparable indices of sexual aspects of dreaming. It seemed logical to regard penile erection during sleep as a realistic index of sexual involvement in the dream process.

Under suitable conditions, the phenomenon could simply be observed in sleeping subjects and recorded by the researchers. Better for scientific purposes, however, was a more objective measure. By fitting subjects with various devices (a so-called strain gauge being the most sensitive), Fisher and his co-investigators were able to synchronize the usual EEG and EOG tracings with the additional objective data coming from the measures of erection—that is, degree of tumescence and detumescence during the course of sleep. Some interesting findings emerged.

First, manifestations of erection during NREM periods were conspicuous by their absence. Even moderate erection was rare during these times. In contrast, erection was almost invariably registered during REMPs; it was absent in only 5 percent of 86 REM periods studied by four methods of measurement. Indeed, the nature of erection followed a characteristic pattern. According to Fisher (1967): "On an average, erection begins about two minutes before the beginning of the REM period, full erection is attained about five minutes after the REM period begins, detumescence sets in about a minute before the termination of the REM period, and full detumescence is reached about ten minutes after the termination" (In Witkin & Lewis, 1967, pp. 110–111).

The so-called "morning erection" or "bladder erection" is, according to some, simply the erection that occurs during the last REMP of the night. What is more interesting, however, is that the phenomenon of erection seems correlated with general dream content. For, as Fisher reports: "It was found that dreams with aggressive content associated with anxiety or other negative affect either brought about inhibition of erection or produced rapid detumescence in ongoing erection. On the other hand, dreams with manifest erotic content or with latent sexual content were associated with tumescence" (in Witkin & Lewis, 1967, p. 113).

Perhaps the above simply suggests that cognitive and affective aspects of the dream process are reflected in the broader physiological state of the dreamer—erection being one such manifestation. In recent work with animals, however, Dement (1965) found that cats deprived of REM periods showed marked disturbances in sexual and eating behavior. As Fisher interprets the significance of these findings, ". . . dreaming normally permits drive discharge, and when such discharge is prevented from taking place, substitute discharge occurs during waking behavior in the form of gross hypersexuality and hyperorality. These results also reinforce Freud's contention that the majority of dreams have a sexual component, using the term sexual in its broad psychoanalytic meaning to include pregenital and genital aspects" (in Witkin & Lewis, 1967, p. 116).

In sum, while the foregoing does not substantiate everything the psychoanalytic school says about the erotic character of the dream process, it certainly lends support to the notion that dynamics of a sexual nature seem to play a significant role in the process of dreaming.

In closing this section, I do not want to leave the impression that the dream laboratory is the new fountain of knowledge from which all wisdom flows. The recently developed techniques, while refreshingly objective, are hardly foolproof, and the relationships that have been discovered (for example, the correspondence between Stage 1–REM sleep and dreaming) do not hold invariably. The results are sometimes equivocal, and moot questions abound.

Perhaps, then, the reader is best left with a conceptual model proposed by Stoyva and Kamiya (1968) that may help him pull together some of the loose ends which further reading in this area will undoubtedly unravel. For these investigators "... dreaming — in the sense of any mental activity during sleep — is a hypothetical construct, not directly accessible to public observation. This hypothetical construct is indexed, but indexed in an imperfect way, by both REMs and verbal report" (p. 199). Accordingly, the model they suggest is represented in Figure 5.

As described by Stoyva and Kamiya (1968), the numbered areas represent the following states of affairs:

> *Region 1* . . . the ideal case where the hypothesized dream activity, the verbal report of dreaming, and Stage 1 REMs occur congruently.
> *Region 2* . . . the valid dream reports occurring from awakenings outside REM periods (e.g., non-REM reports, hypnagogic reports).
> *Region 3* . . . the dream experience that neither indicator detected; in other words, S [the subject] forgot his non-REM dream.
> *Region 4* . . . the occurrence of no dream reports despite the occurrence of both the dream experience and REMs.
> *Region 5* . . . the possibility that there are invalid dream reports from non-REM sleep.
> *Region 6* . . . the possibility that invalid dream accounts may be reported from REM awakenings.
> *Region 7* . . . the possibility that REMs may occur in the absence of any dream experience and not be followed by dream reports (pp. 199–200).

Ideally, a nicely elaborated dream account would invariably be produced when, and only when, a subject is awakened from Stage 1 EEG sleep accompanied by REMs. This is usually the case, but the congruence is by no means perfect.

Methodology

If the clinical analysis of dreams has its problems, so does experimental analysis. Much as they might want to, scientists can seldom march swiftly and in orderly ca-

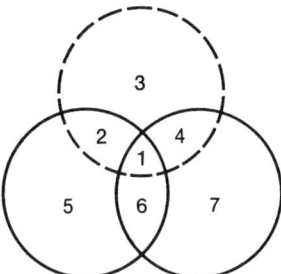

Figure 5
Possible relationships among the hypothetical dream experience, the verbal report of dreaming, and Stage 1-REMs. (Figure 1 of Stoyva & Kamiya, 1968. Copyright 1968 by the American Psychological Association and reproduced by permission.)

dence straight from hypothesis to proof. As Bachrach (1962) good-naturedly puts it in his "Second Law" relating to the planning of research, "Things take more time than they do."

In turning to our second example of the benefits to be reaped from a joining of hands across specialties, the reader is therefore reminded that we are speaking of the promise that lies ahead, not of any millennium that has been reached. Let us, then, look at the general problem of behavior modification in this spirit.

The Problem of Behavior Modification

The phenomenon of behavior change is hardly the exclusive province of the clinician. The developmental psychologist, for example, is intrigued by the manner in which children gradually learn to form concepts, as revealed in the dramatic series of experiments by Piaget (Inhelder & Piaget, 1958). Show a 4-year-old a cylinder of water, then before his eyes pour it into a second cylinder of greater height but equal diameter, and ask him what happened. He will typically say there is now less water. On the other hand, if the water is poured from the original cylinder into a cylinder of equal diameter but shorter height, he will feel there is now more water. Two or three years later the same situation poses no problem. How and when, the developmental psychologist asks, are such changes accomplished?

The experimental psychologist, for his part, is equally concerned with behavior change—witness his many experiments involving both animals and humans. And certainly the social psychologist is interested in the dynamics of change, as he studies shifts in attitudes when people move into an interracial housing project.

Perhaps what differentiates the clinical psychologist from his colleagues is the fact that he is so frequently engaged in the attempted modification of "deviant" behavior. Such situations are plentiful. A patient walks about the hospital grounds with wads of paper stuffed in his ears, the better to keep out "the voices." A young man seeks help for his irresistible impulse to steal and collect women's handkerchiefs. An executive is in danger of losing a well-paying job because of alcoholism. A 7-year-old boy repeatedly runs away from home. An intelligent college student is contemplating suicide because he is making a "B" rather than an "A" average.

Quite properly one thinks of psychotherapy in connection with such problems. We shall turn to its methods later. For the moment, however, let us survey some more recent developments for bringing about behavior change—techniques growing out of knowledge contributed by other areas of psychology. Shouldn't it be possible, for example, to borrow from the body of knowledge called "learning theory" principles which, translated into clinical terms, might yield effective new techniques for changing behavior? Might such approaches supplement, or in certain cases even replace, some of the techniques of psychotherapy?

We are not concerned here with whether psychotherapy has fallen short. Others have engaged in argument and counterargument on that subject. Our interest is rather in exploring how knowledge gained in the nonclinical areas might suggest techniques that produce effects in a relatively short time, achieve results that are lasting, and prove effective in treating some classes of maladjustment that our present methods find difficult to handle. That, at any rate, is what their protagonists promise. Let us, then, note some efforts to translate theory into practice—that is, to adapt principles of learning discovered by the general experimental psychologist to the treatment of problems confronted by the clinical psychologist.

The new methods have a history. Early in the century, in their classic experiment with 11-month-old Albert, Watson and Rayner (1920) found they could get the youngster to show unmistakable signs of fear (crying, screaming, making avoidance responses) at the sight of a rabbit that he had previously approached with interest and apparent pleasure. By simply using a loud noise as a conditioning stimulus and pairing it several times with presentation of the rabbit, they soon produced the conditioned emotional reaction noted above (see Walker [1967] for a description of conditioning procedures). It also became evident that, because of "stimulus generalization," Albert now showed the same (though somewhat milder) avoidance behavior toward objects that resembled a rabbit—a kitten or his mother's fur piece, for example.

Some time later, Mary Cover Jones (1924) demonstrated the converse—namely, that learned fears could, in a similar systematic way, be extinguished. Using counter-conditioning, she proceeded over a period of days to introduce the rabbit into the situation at "safe" (that is, far) distances and under circumstances that were pleasant for the child—eating, in this case. In this situation the boy showed, at most, mild disturbance. Hence, it was feasible to bring the rabbit progressively into closer range during meals of the following days and, since the child continued to remain relatively calm under the circumstances, to close the gap between the rabbit and the boy. It was not long before he could bear having the animal close by him and, indeed, actually ate with the rabbit in his lap.

Given such possibilities, it is not difficult to understand why interested clinicians have felt it worthwhile to explore the feasibility of adapting the techniques and principles of general psychology to the treatment of some clinical problems—phobias, sexual perversions, compulsive stealing, cigarette addiction, stuttering, delusional talk, obsessions, alcoholism, fetishism, and others.

To some the "behavior therapy" movement, as it has come to be called, seems the dawn of a new era; others regard it as an oversimplified attempt to achieve dramatic results that may not last; still others continue to keep an open mind. We shall try the third approach, citing the arguments of protagonists and antagonists, presenting some typical studies, and leaving the reader to form his own opinion on the subject. As a prelude one might look at a study which has a slightly cynical note but points up the need for caution, whatever position one takes.

At issue is an effort by Ayllon et al. (1965) to demonstrate how a psychotic patient may readily be "shaped" into showing symptomatic behavior, using the same reinforcement procedures one might employ in getting a pigeon to peck a disc. In this case the investigators were interested in having a 54-year-old schizophrenic woman engage regularly in an arbitrarily selected behavior—"holding a broom while in an upright position"—a response she had not been seen to perform during a year's observation. That is, the baseline for this particular behavior was zero. In a total of approximately 12,000 two-minute time samples she had not once shown the broom-holding behavior the investigators wished to establish. Instead, her total behavior consisted of lying in bed about 60 percent of the time, sitting and walking about 20 percent of the time, and eating and toileting during the remainder.

36 It was also noted that, while she did little else, she did smoke. Cigarettes, then, might serve as an appropriate reinforcer for whatever behavior one wanted to establish—even as meaningless a behavior as broom-holding. Using operant conditioning techniques, the experimenters were able to establish and increase dramatically the frequency of broom-holding behavior by the patient. Further, they were able to maintain the behavior by means of a conditioned reinforcer (a poker chip that could later be exchanged for a cigarette) and to extinguish the behavior as reinforcement was withdrawn. The course of the rise and fall of the behavior of "holding the broom while in an upright position" is shown in Figure 6.

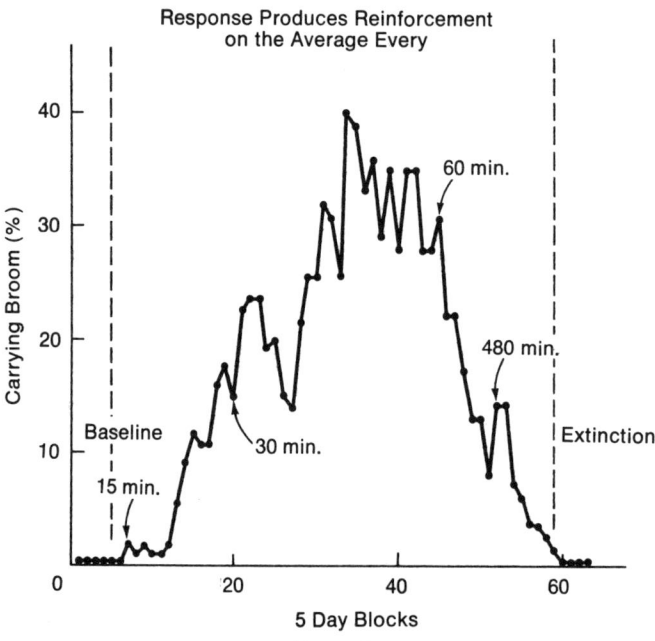

Figure 6
Shaping, maintenance, and extinction of broom-holding behavior. (The percentage is obtained by dividing the number of observed responses by the total number of 160 observations collected in a 5-day period.) (Figure 5 of Ayllon et al., 1965. Copyright 1965 by Pergamon Press and reproduced by permission.)

But the investigators added an extra twist. Two psychiatrists, neither of whom had had previous contact with the patient or knew of the research being conducted, were asked to observe the patient and comment on her behavior. Their reactions follow:

Methodology

> *Psychiatrist A:* "The broom represents to this patient some essential perceptual element in her field of consciousness. How it should have become so is uncertain; on Freudian grounds it could be interpreted symbolically, on behavioral grounds it could perhaps be interpreted as a habit which has become essential to her peace of mind. Whatever may be the case, it is certainly a stereotyped form of behavior such as is commonly seen in rather regressed schizophrenics and is rather analogous to the way small children or infants refuse to be parted from some favorite toy, piece of rag, etc." (p. 3).

Another psychiatrist was less cautious in his appraisal. To him the behavior appeared as follows:

> *Psychiatrist B:* "Her constant and compulsive pacing holding a broom in the manner she does could be seen as a ritualistic procedure, a magical action. When regression conquers the associative process, primitive and archaic forms of thinking control the behavior. Symbolism is a predominant mode of expression of deep seated unfulfilled desires and instinctual impulses. By magic, she controls others, cosmic powers are at her disposal and inanimate objects become living creatures.
>
> "Her broom could be then:
> 1. a child that gives her love and she gives him in return her devotion;
> 2. a phallic symbol;
> 3. the sceptre of an omnipotent queen. . . . this is a magical procedure in which the patient carries out her wishes, expressed in a way that is far beyond our solid, rational and conventional way of thinking and acting" (p. 3).[7]

We are not interested here in the subterfuge, except as it helps dramatize the fact that behavior is to be interpreted with caution, especially when psychodynamic formulations involve abstractions and inferences. Good clinicians prefer to work from a maximum rather than a minimum of information, making as few inferential leaps as necessary.

The fact is that behavior, whether normal or pathological, is maintained by its consequences. Thus, the actions of even the most chronic patient should be somehow amenable to modification. Clearly, one would not ordinarily choose to shape such a relatively meaningless activity as broom-holding. One might, however, use the same systematic approach in developing desirable, or extinguishing undesirable, behavior patterns, as Ayllon and Michael (1959) have in fact done with such problems as delusional talk, hoarding behavior, and refusal to feed oneself.

---

[7] The comments of the two psychiatrists, as cited in Ayllon et al., 1965, have been completed by reinserting passages from the same set of comments quoted in Haughton & Ayllon in Ullmann & Krasner, 1965 (pp. 97–98).

What is different in the approach of behavior therapists is that they are not concerned—at least not primarily concerned—with the psychological functions such behavior may serve for the patient. Their interest is the more immediate one of eliminating or modifying the disadvantageous behavior and replacing it with more adaptive behavior. If a patient refuses to eat unless fed by the nurse, the behavior therapist worries less about the psychodynamic meaning of such behavior than about correcting it—a task not quickly accomplished by usual psychotherapeutic means.

By way of bringing about more desirable patient behavior (desirable at least in terms of freeing valuable nursing time), one might look to certain reinforcement contingencies intended to produce or eliminate behavior of various kinds. Table 1 shows how a set of such contingencies might be represented.

Table 1

		Reinforcing stimulus	
		Appetitive (e.g., approval)	Aversive (e.g., shock)
Reinforcement contingency	Presentation following response	A	B
	Removal following response	C	D

Assuming a behavior therapist did not know (and was for the moment not really concerned with) the psychodynamic meaning of the refusal of a patient to eat by herself, how might he choose among the alternatives in arranging a treatment program? His choice can be made somewhat easier if he takes into account additional information. The patient of Ayllon and Michael, for example, was a particularly neat person. According to ward personnel, she was fastidious about her appearance. Cleanliness, one could assume, was for her positively reinforcing, slovenliness aversive. It was also evident that she did eat when spoonfed by the nurse. Thus, something about the situation of being fed by the nurse, or of being in the company of the nurse, presumably constituted positive reinforcement. How, then, might such observations lead to a treatment plan?

Ayllon and Michael chose to rely on a combination of contingencies represented by Table 1. If some food happened to drop on the neatly dressed patient while the nurse presumably did her best to feed her, such an event would involve an aversive stimulus. (The nurses were in fact instructed to have such "accidents" take place in the course of spoonfeeding the patient.) If, on the other hand, there was something the patient could do to lessen or prevent such spillage—that is, if the aversive stimulus

Methodology

(food dropped on the patient) could be escaped or avoided by some action of the patient (feeding herself, for example), one would be making use of the principle of negative reinforcement. In other words, the object is to increase the frequency of a certain behavior (in this case, feeding oneself) by making removal of an aversive stimulus (in this case, food spillage) contingent upon a particular response (self-feeding).

However, the concern here was not simply with removing disadvantageous behavior (refusal to feed oneself), but also with replacing it by more appropriate behavior (usual habits of eating). Here positive reinforcement had a role to play. Since the patient apparently found the presence of the nurse rewarding, the nurse was instructed not to leave as soon as the patient started feeding herself during a meal but rather to remain with her for several minutes thereafter, conversing or simply sitting beside her.

While the patient's refusal to eat had in this case originally been based on claims that her food was being poisoned, it is interesting to note that, although Ayllon and Michael had made no attempt to deal with this delusion, such statements disappeared as the patient began eating under the above regimen. The effectiveness of the treatment plan can be judged from the results shown in Figure 7.

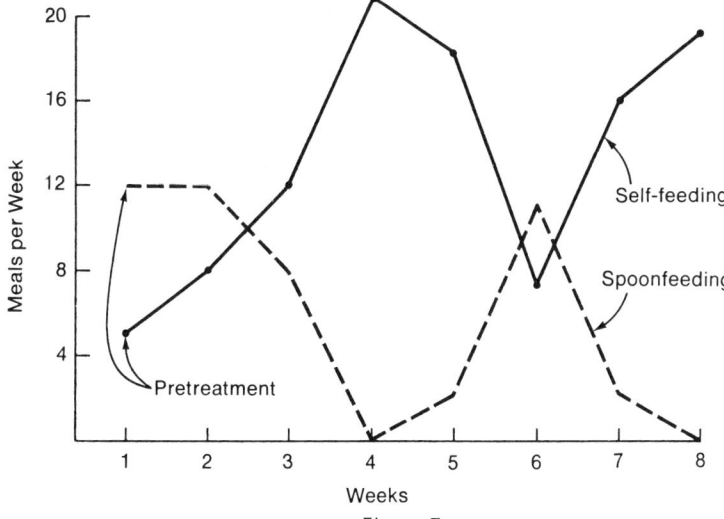

Figure 7
Record of a patient's eating behavior while under treatment by conditioning procedures. (Figure 4 of Ayllon & Michael, 1959. Copyright 1959 by the Society for the Experimental Analysis of Behavior, Inc., and reproduced by permission.)

The behavior therapist tends to play down, or even rule out, the need to infer what underlies symptoms—that is, what psychodynamic meaning symptoms may have. He is not alone, however, in the conviction that understanding the background and significance of deviant behavior is not a necessary precondition to its modification. Indeed, some theorists (Hobbs, 1962; Saslow, in Krasner & Ullmann, 1965) would argue that, even in psychotherapy, insight does not necessarily precede change but may actually follow it.

Most psychotherapists would nevertheless advance objections, stating that the removal of symptomatic behavior, without corresponding insight into its meaning and consequent correction of its underlying causes, would simply result in replacement of the original symptoms by others—"symptom substitution." There are several sides to the argument, but for the moment let us focus on clinical efforts to explore the feasibility of making certain consequences contingent on behavior with a view to its modification. Ayllon and Michael, in the self-feeding experiment, employed an operant conditioning paradigm (see Walker, 1967). Lang and Lazovik (1963) used a respondent conditioning paradigm (discussed in the next section). Still others see good reason to combine respondent and operant techniques (as exemplified in the treatment of a case of school phobia by Lazarus et al., 1965).

In the last analysis, evidence speaks louder than argument. Let us therefore turn to the efforts of some who keep an open mind on the subject while resting their case on the results of carefully designed studies.

A Program of Research

The discerning student may well find some of the behavior modification studies reported in the literature less rigorous in execution than one might wish. In such cases, weaknesses in the studies are often due to the difficulty of doing research under "field conditions"—for example, on a hospital ward—where the investigator does not have as much control over his variables as he would in the laboratory. Lang and his colleagues have made a commendable attempt to design and carry out a series of interlocking studies in the area of behavior modification, paying close attention to methodological considerations, as the following generalized analysis attests.

As their target behavior, Lang and Lazovik (1963) chose a specific phobia—a pathological fear of snakes. Few people relish the thought of getting close to a live snake; a harmless garter snake is enough to make some strong men step back. Most of us, however, find little difficulty in walking through the woods or in looking at snakes, even with some fascination, in the reptile house of the zoo. For a few people—the "snake-phobic"—the latter would be a disturbing experience; in fact, for some in this group the mere sight of a snakeskin belt could be traumatic.

To Lang and Lazovik and to Wolpe (1958) before them, the previously described procedure of Jones (1924), somewhat elaborated and applied systematically, represented a ready-made method for the treatment of phobias. If, as in Jones' case of the rabbit-phobic boy, one could get "a response antagonistic to anxiety [for example, relaxation] to occur [repeatedly] in the presence of anxiety-evoking stimuli" (Wolpe, 1958, p. 71) [that is, snake-related situations], there would be reason to believe that the symptomatic behavior would lessen, if not disappear. How to do this? Here Wolpe had set the stage, using as his therapeutic principle the construct of "reciprocal inhibition": "If a response antagonistic to anxiety can be made to occur in the presence of anxiety-evoking stimuli so that it is accompanied by a complete or partial suppression of the anxiety responses, the bond between these stimuli and the anxiety responses will be weakened" (p. 71).

Lang and Lazovik devised a Fear Survey Schedule, which they used to select appropriately phobic subjects from a pool of college students claiming to have a snake phobia; they then set up the treatment situation accordingly. The "responses physiologically antagonistic to anxiety" were insured by teaching students a special method of achieving total relaxation (Jacobson, 1938). The "anxiety-evoking stimuli" were introduced by having the patient visualize a series of snake-related situations, which he himself had previously ranked in a hierarchy from least disturbing (for example, seeing the word "snake") to most disturbing (for example, visualizing stepping on a live snake). This latter "item hierarchy" (differing from person to person) represented, in effect, a gradient of generalization (as in Albert's fear reaction to his mother's fur piece as well as to the actual rabbit). The experimenters originally hypnotized each subject in order to help him visualize the particular scenes in his hierarchy more vividly; however, later research has shown that merely imagining the scenes vividly is sufficient.

The subject, achieving complete relaxation at the beginning of the session, was first asked to visualize the least anxiety-provoking scene in his hierarchy while trying to remain completely relaxed. Having succeeded, he was told to visualize the next least anxiety-provoking scene in his hierarchy, again attempting to maintain relaxation. If he achieved this second step, he was asked to move on to the third scene. Needless to say, the typical subject soon arrived at a scene he found difficult to visualize while remaining relaxed. When this happened, he signaled the experimenter as previously instructed, and he was then asked to revisualize the preceding scene. The goal of the treatment procedure was to enable the subject, over the course of a number of sessions, to visualize the most anxiety-provoking scene in his original item hierarchy while still remaining calm. This accomplishment, the researchers hoped, would generalize to real life, leaving the subject considerably less (or not at all) handicapped by his earlier phobia.

The experimental plan, then, was to select subjects (students in this case), who by their own testimony were snake-phobic, so that the symptom could be treated by this "systematic desensitization." But suppose the subjects were only *saying* they were terrified of snakes? Clearly, there was need for behavioral confirmation. This was accomplished by means of an "Avoidance Test," in which the subject was encouraged to approach, as closely as he dared, the glass case of a nonpoisonous live snake kept in the laboratory. The experimenters created a graded series of tasks, such as approaching the case, standing by it while the experimenter removed its cover, remaining there (if possible) while he lifted the snake from the case, and so on. Here, in a simple, objective way one could presumably measure the subject's anxiety in terms of the distance he maintained between himself and the snake.

As thorough investigators, Lang and Lazovik required still further evidence, however. While the subject's overt behavior could be regarded as an objective index of the strength of his phobic reaction, it was possible that his behavior on the Avoidance Test might reflect his tendency to respond to social pressure more than the strength of his phobia. Something further was therefore needed to insure that subjects were not merely saying what they thought was expected (on the Fear Survey Schedule), nor simply doing what they were being asked to (on the Avoidance Test). This further evidence took the form of physiological measures taken on the subjects in the test situation. Only after all three indices—verbal, behavioral, and physiological—had confirmed the presence of a full-fledged phobia, was a subject taken into the experiment.

But these were only the preliminary measures. To Lang and Lazovik, it was clearly not enough to run the experiment as follows:

Design A

Pretest ——— Relaxation ——— Systematic ——— Post-test
(measures of   training   desensitization   (measures of
strength of phobia   strength of phobia
prior to treatment)   following treatment)

[Treatment: Relaxation training — Systematic desensitization]

If the phobia turned out to be weaker or nonexistent following the treatment period, such an experimental design would leave one uncertain whether the treatment had been responsible for the outcome, whether the mere passage of time accounted for the change, or whether perhaps the pretest was responsible. Clearly a control group was necessary. Thus, the design would need at the very least to look like this:

Design B

Experimental Group (EG)	Pretest —— Relaxation training —— Systematic desensitization —— Post-test
Control Group (CG)	Pretest —— * —— * —— Post-test

Clearly, the control group added new information to the experiment, subjects having been chosen from the pool of phobic students and randomly assigned to the experimental group (EG) or control group (CG). With two such presumably comparable groups, one could compare the results of the treatment and nontreatment conditions. This additional dimension would still leave some important questions unanswered, however. For example, assuming that the subjects in the EG emerged better adjusted (that is, with their phobia weakened or eliminated) than those in the CG, how could one tell whether the systematic desensitization procedure had accomplished the results? Might the second procedure have been just so much window dressing, the relaxation training itself having actually achieved the "cure"?

Lang and Lazovik had also asked themselves these questions prior to the experiment, so their preliminary design had to include at least the following additional features:

Design C

EG	Test 1 —— Relaxation training —— Test 2 —— Systematic desensitization —— Test 3
CG	Test 1 —— * —— Test 2 —— * —— Test 3

Suppose neither group had shown any difference in the strength of its phobic tendencies as measured on Test 1 and Test 2 (and both groups had initially been comparably phobic). Suppose, further, that the CG showed results on its Test 3 equal to those on Test 2, while the EG showed significantly less phobic behavior on its Test 3 than on Test 2. One could now feel considerably more confident about ascribing the gains to the systematic desensitization procedure itself.

It had taken at least Design C to satisfy Lang and Lazovik that systematic desensitization did, indeed, appear to be an effective procedure in the treatment of phobias. Nevertheless they still hesitated to jump to conclusions too quickly, and in subsequent research Lang, Lazovik, and Reynolds (1965) pursued additional unexplored factors that could have entered to confound the results. Might it still be possible, they asked, that it had been not the systematic desensitization procedure but a "placebo effect" (see Part Two, Chapter 4) that had accomplished whatever results had been achieved — that is, that the mere expectation of being "cured" had done the trick? After all, a good deal of interaction between experimenter and subject had been involved. True, customary psychotherapeutic trappings were absent — there had been no delving into past history, no interpretation of subjects' behavior on the part of the experimenter. But there were other features incidental to the procedure that could either be regarded as aspects of an unintended psychotherapeutic relationship or else as evidence of the "perceived demand characteristics" that Orne (1962) has described (see Part Two, Chapter 4). How, then, might one strengthen the research design so that one could be more confident it was the systematic desensitization technique itself that was accomplishing results?

Here Lang and his colleagues hit upon the notion of "pseudotherapy." If there were a second control group that received something that only *resembled* systematic desensitization, then this group would find itself exposed to the therapist-client relationship without actually receiving the experimental treatment (that is, the systematic desensitization procedure). And if it were really the placebo effect that was at the root responsible for the results, then this second CG should show gains comparable to those of the EG. Thus, the design finally evolved as the following:

Design D

EG	Test 1	—Relaxation training—	Test 2	—Systematic desensitization—	Test 3
CG$_1$	Test 1	— * —	Test 2	*	Test 3
CG$_2$	Test 1	—Relaxation training—	Test 2	Pseudotherapy	Test 3

As in the case of the EG, prior to the treatment procedure a second control group (CG$_2$) also constructed an anxiety hierarchy of items relating to snakes. Unlike the subjects of the EG, however, the subjects of CG$_2$ underwent a process of "pseudotherapy," which consisted of discussion between experimenter and subject of scenes from the subject's hierarchy. In such "therapy," however, the experimenter led discussion away from the snake theme itself and into more neutral areas. For example, if the subject mentioned snakes on his uncle's farm, the "therapist" would steer him into a discussion of farms, rural life, and relatives rather than snakes. If then, a simple placebo effect had accomplished the results in the earlier experiment, the subjects of CG$_2$ could be expected to do as well on the pseudotherapy regimen as those of the EG on systematic desensitization.

As it turned out, the subjects of CG_2 fared no better than those of CG_1, who had received no treatment whatever. Subjects of the EG emerged significantly less phobic (as measured by verbal, behavioral, and physiological indices) than those of either CG_1 or CG_2. Also, when subjects were followed up some months later, their gains were shown to have persisted.

It should not be thought that Lang and his colleagues then shouted a psychologist's "Eureka!," feeling they had a sure cure for what ails people with phobias. On the contrary, the moral of the story is that, as scientists intrigued by new possibilities, they strove painstakingly to subject those possibilities to careful test, lest anyone make premature, rash pronouncements to the psychological world.

Indeed, the story does not end there. Davison (1968), for one, has proceeded to carry the investigation to its next step. Concerned with the temporal contiguity of the stimulus events in subjects' imaginal hierarchies, he investigated whether the treatment procedure represented a genuine counterconditioning process, "... according to which the neutralization of aversive stimuli results from the evocation of incompatible responses which are strong enough to supersede anxiety reactions to these stimuli ..." (p. 92). Indeed, he found that the regular desensitization procedure was more effective than one in which irrelevant stimuli were paired with relaxation, or than one in which subjects were exposed to graded imaginal aversive stimuli without relaxation.

Yet, more recently, Krapfl and Nawas (1970) have questioned whether this settles the issue. They point out that Davison neglected to include in his design the treatment procedure in which relaxation is paired with relevant (rather than irrelevant) stimuli that are not in the usual ascending order of increasing aversiveness. They found, interestingly, that when the aversive stimuli are arranged in *descending* order—that is, when the imaginal sequence proceeds from the most aversive item in the series to the least aversive—treatment is equally successful. At the very least, such developments should help underscore for the reader the conviction of Krapfl and Nawas that ".... the processes underlying systematic desensitization are still far from understood" (p. 337).

Were it possible simply to borrow a few leads from the laboratory, transport them into the therapy situation, and produce long-lasting cures in short order, the ghost of Sigmund Freud might well rise to haunt us. At this point there is little fear of that. Results are not achieved so easily. We are not talking here of a new order of technician who, with benefit of some gadgetry and a handful of techniques, aims to put psychotherapists out of business.

Our concern is with the clinician interested in aiding people to replace disadvantageous behavior with more satisfying forms of behavior and helping well-adjusted persons maximize their potentialities. If these ends can be realized effectively by existing or still-to-be-discovered methods of psychotherapy, that is all to the good. If additional methods of behavior modification—such as the conditioning therapies, for instance—can be added to the clinician's armamentarium, so much the better. In short, there is no unbridgeable gulf between psychotherapy and behavior therapy.

The possibilities by no means begin and end with the principles of conditioning, whether classical or instrumental. Bandura et al. (1967), for example, have explored the use of "modeling" in achieving behavior change. In a carefully controlled experiment, they assessed the relative effectiveness of four treatment conditions for dealing with children's fear of dogs, two of which used a peer model (a child of the same age who was unafraid of dogs) and two of which did not. The area of behavior therapy has room not only for such additional procedures as modeling but also for other principles derived from research on learning that can be adapted to clinical situations—practice trials (in learning to make assertive social responses, for example), stimulus satiation (as when a patient who hoards towels is purposely given a profusion of towels to hoard), and other principles one is capable of using.

In Part Four I will try to effect a rapprochement among present methods of achieving behavior change, be they psychotherapy or behavior therapy. The examples I have cited have illustrated that (a) controversial areas of clinical theory and practice are amenable to rigorous experimental test, and (b) only by attempting to cover one's tracks methodologically, as did Lang and his colleagues, will clinical psychologists be able to resolve many open questions. Improperly practiced, behavior therapy could amount to a potpourri of treatment gimmicks, superficially applied by some with little theoretical background and even less methodological sophistication. In the hands of competent investigators, who respect both people and science, behavior therapy holds promise for enlarged understanding of the complex problems that clinicians confront.

The province that has come to be known as clinical psychology is a rugged one. The problems it is asked to solve are tough, and the methodological and technological tools needed for the job remain to be forged in many cases. One might well feel that, for this reason, clinicians need to be correspondingly tough-minded, lest untested assumptions breed unfruitful theory. Accordingly, Part Three on research and theory is intended to illustrate the variety of sources from which clinical psychology can draw in its relentless quest for broader understanding. Part Four on theory and practice subsequently deals with answers that seem to have been found as well as with

Methodology

questions that continue to be asked. Clearly, the job of the behavioral scientist is never finished.

We turn first, however, to a variety of dilemmas with which the clinical psychologist needs to reckon as he takes on the formidable task of studying and dealing with the interesting and complex human organism.

Part Two
Psychology and Human Subjects

3
Ethical Dilemmas in Research

In a cartoon from the *New Yorker* of a few years ago a callow youth is shown riding his bicycle timidly past the austere gates of an estate labeled "Crile Research Foundation" and bearing a sign reading "Trespassers Will Be Experimented Upon." Interestingly, at about the same time, the Surgeon General of the U.S. Public Health Service issued directives (1967) declaring that henceforth no research would be supported by Public Health Service funds unless a duly constituted panel had decided the study would be conducted so as to safeguard the welfare and protect the rights of any human subjects involved.

Why the fuss? For good reason, some (including psychologists) would argue. In fact, two special issues (November 1965 and May 1967) of the *American Psychologist*, house organ of the American Psychological Association, were devoted to the respective themes of "Ethics of Research with Human Subjects" and "Testing and Public Policy." The latter featured verbatim congressional testimony on the use of psychological tests (especially with government employees). The climate in which the hearings took place can be gauged from a series of representative headlines:

> *The Washington Post* (June 11, 1965): Pupils Given 'Offensive' Personality Test
>
> *Saturday Review* (June 19, 1965): Calipers on the Human Mind
>
> *Wall Street Journal* (February 9, 1965): Personnel Tests Win Widening Business Use Though Critics Fume
>
> *The Washington Post* (June 20, 1965): Psyching Out—You Can't Flunk This Test But It Tattles on Your Id
>
> *The Washington Post* (June 10, 1965): Shriver Defends Even Personality Tests for Peace Corps

Cartoonists, too, lost no time. Herblock, for example, turned his critical eye on the subject, picturing a psychological questionnaire in the presumptuous role of Napoleon.

Obviously some of the tests used by psychologists and some of the research conducted on the basis of the tests had raised not only the qualms of the public but the hackles of congressmen. Indeed, some psychologists themselves had uneasy feelings about certain developments in their field. Consider, for example, the reaction of the clinical psychologist, who works hard to help clients in individual psychotherapy, when he comes upon the following ad of a scientific-instrument company in one of the psychological journals:

> *The Wireless Shocker.* By using radio control you can deliver a shock to a patient up to 1000 feet away with no connections. Now behavior modified in the laboratory or office situation may be subjected to generalization and discrimination training more closely approximating the situations to which the behavior must be transferred. This device has been effectively used with head bangers and other autistic behavior [*Journal of Applied Behavior Analysis,* Fall 1968, **1** (5)].

Taken out of context, such procedures may sound outlandish, if not sadistic. But, their protagonists ask, is it more humane to allow a maladjusted child to bang his head incessantly against any available object (unless constantly restrained) to the point of sustaining brain damage? The use of harmless shock to eliminate such behavior, they contend, is by far the lesser of the evils, especially since it is difficult to reduce or eliminate such self-destructive behavior by more conventional means.

If psychologists sometimes seem perverse (as the foregoing notoriety would suggest), it is only because transactions involving human subjects are easily so construed. The physicist gets into less trouble with magnets and the epidemiologist with chicken eggs (though they too have their detractors—the former about the nuclear age, the latter about the Hong Kong flu).

The psychologist gets a full measure of critical attention. In the area of clinical practice he is faulted on not being able to "cure" people fast enough (as in psychotherapy) and looked on with some suspicion when he tries to learn more about them (as in personality testing). One might expect that turning to basic research would be the safest way out. Hardly. Here, too, knowledge has its price. Clinical research, by nature, cannot easily avoid getting into areas of privacy and confidentiality, such as studying personal conflict, or assessing and measuring traits and abilities people hold dear.

But let us get down to two cases on subjects of interest to clinicians, although the cases themselves originate from nonclinical areas. In the first example a social psychologist studies the conditions under which people can be made to behave in ways alien to their nature; the clinical manifestations become clear in the process. In the second case, an experimental psychologist studies behavior under stress—a central problem in clinical theory. In both cases, despite the best of intentions, the investigators could not escape involvement in debate on the ethics of research involving human subjects.

A Socioclinical Study

Milgram (1963) called his research effort "a behavioral study of obedience." Others before him had been appalled by the protestations of leading Nazis that they had carried out concentration-camp atrocities because, as soldiers and members of the party, they could only *obey*. Gilbert (1947), a clinical psychologist on the scene at the time, had, in fact, administered extensive batteries of psychological tests to the leading figures. His *Nuremberg Diary* is both a clinical and a sociopolitical document.

Milgram was moved to study the phenomenon of obedience in milder form, but under more rigorous control. He intended to set up an experimental analogue in which no one would lose (that is, get hurt), while science would gain. That was his object. But, as it turned out, he got more than he bargained for.

Milgram was interested in the extent to which one person would obey the orders of another, more prestigious person when such orders involved meting out punishment, in a presumably legitimate cause, to someone else. The pretext in this case? The experiment was ostensibly being conducted to study the effectiveness of electric shock in facilitating learning; this explanation was an effective guise, since the scene of the experiment was Yale University.

The procedure was straightforward. A subject was instructed to administer an electric shock to another "subject" (who was actually a confederate of the experimenter) whenever the bogus subject made a mistake in attempting to learn a task—in this case, associating word pairs. In fact, the real subject was to administer shocks of progressively *higher* voltage with each mistake made by the learner. He administered this "punishment" by pressing, in turn, buttons marked in 15-volt intervals from 15 volts to over 450 volts, and plainly labeled "slight shock" through "danger: severe shock."

No effort had been spared to make the apparatus look authentic. Buzzing, spark-throwing antics occurred whenever a shock button was depressed. Yet, although the real subject did not know it, the apparatus actually delivered no shocks to the learner, who was in an adjoining room. The learner's answers appeared on a screen in the real subject's room. Hence, the real subject had every reason to believe that his fellow subject was being shocked. By prearrangement with the experimenter, at the point when the 300-volt shock was (presumably) received, the pseudosubject began to pound on the wall. From then on, the learner's answers no longer appeared on the screen. Human nature having some redeeming features, the subjects at that point characteristically turned to the experimenter for help. They were told to regard the absence of an answer after 5–10 seconds as a wrong answer, one punishable by the next higher level of shock. The wall-pounding of the learner was again heard after the 315-volt shock button had been pressed; thereafter no further sound came from him, nor did any answers appear on the screen. Subjects hesitating to go on, or protesting the procedure, were urged to continue by the experimenter, who used a standard set of four verbal prods to get them to go on, if possible (for example, "The experiment requires that you continue").

There was ample deception—the counterfeit subject, the fake shocks, the presumed suffering on the part of the learner. The data should nonetheless provide significant information on the extent to which one person (the subject) would obey a more prestigious person (the experimenter) in the proper setting (a reputable university research laboratory) for an ostensibly good cause (the study of the efficacy of punishment in facilitating learning).

Little had Milgram anticipated the results. Not a single subject stopped before the 300-volt level was reached. What is more, 26 of 40 subjects actually were persuaded to go the limit, that is, to continue on to the highest level of shock—450 volts! But at great psychological cost. As Milgram (1963) describes it: "Many subjects showed signs of nervousness in the experimental situation, and especially upon administering the more powerful shocks. In a large number of cases the degree of tension reached extremes that are rarely seen in sociopsychological laboratory studies. Subjects were observed to sweat, tremble, stutter, bite their lips, groan, and dig their fingernails into their flesh. These were characteristic rather than exceptional responses to the experiment" (p. 375).

But had the subjects really felt the shocks were all that painful to the learner? (All had, incidentally, been given a look at the "electric chair" before the experiment began and had been asked to sit in the learner's seat to experience a sample of 45 volts—in this one instance, real.) To assess how painful the higher-level shocks must have been to the learner, the subjects were later given a rating device. On a scale ranging from 1 (not at all painful) to 14 (extremely painful), the modal judgment of the subjects was between 13 and 14!

Milgram had intended (and achieved) a well-controlled study in an area of great interest to both social and clinical psychologists—the dynamics of the relation between people in superior and subordinate roles, be it experimenter and subject, teacher and student, parent and child; some would add therapist and client. No punishment had been administered, yet some astounding behavior had been observed. The data opened up new lines of theory to be pursued and tested in further studies.

However, Milgram opened up as much area for criticism as for praise. The critics included not only reporters for the major newspapers but Milgram's colleagues as well. The study was attacked not as poorly designed but as almost too effective. Although he had used voluntary subjects who were paid regardless of the nature of their performance, and who could have quit at any point and kept their earnings, his experiment had proved to turn some of them temporarily into "a twitching, stuttering wreck." The experimenter had simply urged, not forced, them to go on; they themselves had done so. In self-defense, Milgram (1964a) pointed out that his research report had described how he had subsequently "debriefed" each subject, by revealing the deception and assuring him that no shocks had actually been administered. In fact, the "learner" actually met the real subject again to reassure him that no harm had been done.[1]

By way of reaffirming the reader's faith in human nature, it should be added that, in further studies involving additional variables, Milgram (1964b, 1965) found that subjects were not as readily susceptible to such untoward behavior. More recently, Tilker (1970), using an experimental procedure patterned after Milgram's, has found that when subjects are made to feel responsible for the safety of the other person and when they receive maximum feedback on his presumed condition, most of them exhibit socially responsible behavior in that they attempt to do something about the situation.

History adds an interesting footnote. After the dust of controversy had settled, Milgram received an award in recognition of his efforts from the American Association for the Advancement of Science, a society respected for its dedication to the promotion of knowledge.

---

[1] We leave the reader to make up his own mind on the issues, encouraging him to turn to such further writings on the subject as: (a) a study by a group of psychologists at the University of Minnesota (Walster et al., 1967) intended to assess the psychological effectiveness of debriefing procedures; (b) a dialogue between Milgram and his critics (Baumrind, 1964; Milgram, 1964a); and (c) the report of a special Panel on Privacy and Behavioral Research (1967) appointed by the President's Office of Science and Technology.

56 A Field Study of Clinical Relevance

Critics have faulted Milgram's study on methodological as well as ethical grounds, for, despite its ingenuity, his investigation took place in the inevitably artificial surroundings of a laboratory. Some psychologists would rather study stress where it occurs naturally—in real life. According to Selye (1956), life consists of a succession of stresses, each of which leaves its physical, physiological, and psychical marks. Why not study stress in the raw? Assuming this could be done without harm to anyone, clinical psychologists would be the first to welcome the findings—whether gathered by themselves, other psychologists, or fellow professionals—for the dynamics of stress and the modes of coping with it are at the heart of clinical theory and practice.

It is true that some approximation of behavior under stress can be obtained in a laboratory situation. The task a subject is required to perform can be made progressively more taxing to the point where his performance inevitably begins to show signs of deteriorating. Or, reports on his performance (regardless of its merits) can be worded to give an unflattering impression, which will be stressful to the subject. Again, the subject can be told that, during his attempts to learn a given task, his errors will be punished by the delivery of an electric shock. Ingenious as such efforts may be, however, the stress they induce might nonetheless seem somewhat synthetic. How might one proceed to study behavior under circumstances as real as possible?

Several years ago, Berkun et al. (1962) attempted such a study for the military, which has an obvious interest in how servicemen will tolerate stress. Clearly, the person who goes to pieces under fire is not a potential Medal of Honor winner. For the benefit of all concerned, it becomes important to identify him early and defer him. The investigators exposed servicemen, ages 18–24, to a variety of conditions, one of which involved flying in a twin-engine DC-3 military aircraft. Performance was to be measured via two paper-and-pencil tests, one of which (the Emergency Data Form) pertained to disposition of the recruit's belongings in case of death, the other (Emergency Instructions Test) being a 12-item, multiple-choice test on procedures to be followed in case a plane needed to "ditch" in the water in an emergency. The subjects were assigned randomly to three groups—an Experimental Group, a Flying Control Group, and a Grounded Control Group. The reader can judge from the following how real the situation may have seemed to the subjects.

Psychology and Human Subjects

Once aloft, at 5,000 feet Ss completed one irrelevant test and then waited for the plane to reach a higher altitude. In the case of the Experimental

Group flights, the aircraft lurched while changing altitude. Ss saw that one propeller had stopped turning and heard about other malfunctions over the intercom; they were then informed directly that there was an emergency. A simulated pilot-to-tower conversation was provided to the Ss over their earphones to support the deception. As the aircraft passed within sight of the airfield, Ss could see fire trucks and ambulances on the airstrip in apparent expectation of a crash landing.

After several minutes the pilot ordered the plane steward to prepare for ditching in the nearby ocean, since the landing gear would not function properly. This was a prearranged signal for the "steward" to administer the questionnaire both to Ss and to the overt experimenter, to make it appear to Ss that this experimenter was in the same emergency situation in which they found themselves. The Emergency Data Form was given first, on a straightforward basis, because requesting information of this sort would seem plausible under the circumstances. The Emergency Instructions Test was given under the pretext that this would furnish proof to insurance companies that emergency precaution had been properly followed. These papers were supposedly to be put in a waterproof container and jettisoned before the aircraft came down on the ocean.

While Ss worked on both of these pencil-and-paper tests, the pilot-to-tower communication was cut out from their earphones to permit them to work without distraction. At no time was there any inter-communication among Ss, since both the aircraft noise and the seating arrangement made any contact impossible. After a specified time period, the aircraft made a safe landing at the airport. Ss were taken to a nearby classroom, where, after individually responding to the SSS [Subjective Self-Report Scale] . . . , they were thoroughly informed as to the true nature and purpose of the experiment (p. 5).[2]

As their designations imply, neither the Grounded Control Group nor the Flying Control Group was exposed to the presumed emergency, the former taking its paper-and-pencil tests on the ground, the latter taking them in the air in the course of a routine flight.

How effective was this "real" situation in inducing stress that could be studied under controlled conditions? The investigators had incorporated three types of measures: verbal, behavioral, and physiological. As judged from the postflight interview, five subjects of the Experimental Group had apparently seen through the deception and thus were excluded from the data analysis. How, then, did the Subjective Self-Report Scale scores of the three groups compare? The results are shown in Table 1 (where the higher the score, the greater was the stress experienced):

[2]Copyright 1962 by the American Psychological Association. Reprinted by permission of the authors and publisher.

Table 1
Subjective Self-Report Scores of the groups in the various conditions.

Treatment Group	N	M[a]	SD[b]	p
Experimental	15	60	20	
				<.05[c]
Flying Control	20	45	17	
				ns[d]
Grounded Control	26	41	16	

Note: The higher the score, the greater the stress reported.

[a] Mean score.

[b] Standard Deviation (for this and other statistical measures, see Hays, 1967).

[c] Probability of occurrence by chance. Thus, $p < .05$ means that less than 5 times in 100 would one expect a difference as large as this or larger to have occurred just by chance; in other words, there was a statistically significant difference between the Experimental and the Flying Control groups.

[d] Not significant (that is, the two control groups did not differ significantly in the amount of stress reported).

(Adapted from Table 2 of Berkun, Bialek, Kern, & Yagi, 1962. Copyright 1962 by the American Psychological Association and reproduced by permission.)

The Experimental Group reported having experienced significantly more stress than did either of the control groups, the latter two not being significantly different from each other.

The situation on the physiological indicator paralleled the psychological findings. Using urinary 17-hydroxycorticosteroids as a physiological index of experienced stress, the investigators found, as shown in Table 2, that the experimental situation had, indeed, been more stress-producing for the experimental group than for its flying counterpart control.

The experimental group also showed significantly impaired performance (as compared with that of the control groups) on both tests taken during flight, while the two control groups did not differ significantly from each other.

Here, then, was a chance to study the real thing—not the more synthetic stress produced under laboratory conditions. All kinds of functional relationships of potential

Table 2
Physiological measures (urinary 17-hydroxycorticosteroids) in experimental and control conditions.

Treatment Group	N	M	SD	p
Experimental	15	577	136	<.01[a]
Flying Control	10	389	128	

[a] *Note:* less than 1 time in 100 would one expect a difference as large as this or larger to have occurred just by chance. (Table 4 of Berkun, Bialek, Kern, & Yagi, 1962. Copyright 1962 by the American Psychological Association and reproduced by permission.)

clinical significance could thus become accessible to direct and reasonably well-controlled study under "real" conditions. But again there were problems.

Some problems were methodological. For example, despite the elaborate efforts to make the situation as realistic as possible, there were still a few subjects who saw through the ruse. While one can omit the data provided by such subjects, there is always the possibility that such omission might bias the results. One wonders, too, whether still other subjects might have doubted the situation. There are ways of handling such problems statistically; however, there are other problems not solved as readily.

Does the scientist have the right to exploit as subjects men who have been drafted to serve as soldiers? Couldn't a terrifying experience, even one that involves only imagined rather than actual danger, leave lasting psychological effects (despite the experimenters' attempts to debrief subjects after the study)? Is it right to subject people to traumatic experiences without their knowledge and consent?

4
Methodological Considerations

Bachrach (1962) has remarked: "People don't usually do research the way people who write books about research say that people do research" (p. vii). In a delightful little book, he illustrates aptly how the investigator often gets more than he bargained for; the course of research does not always run smooth.

It is tempting to think that some areas come off better than others. One might envy a colleague like the engineering psychologist, for example, in the belief that this expert in the study of "human factors" (as his field is sometimes called) probably has everything under control at all times. Not quite, as an experimental psychologist has reminded us (Versace, personal communication, 1968) with the following illustration.

Engineering psychologists working for major automobile manufacturers engage in considerable research on the characteristics of drivers. Conveniently, the steady stream of visitors to automobile plants provides a readily accessible and presumably representative population. If requested, many of them participate willingly in experiments measuring driver behavior under various conditions. Thus, the researchers may be interested in determining how quickly a subject can pull a lever of a certain kind, step on a pedal in a particular position, and so on. Such behavior can be tested under very standardized conditions, timed precisely, even photographed—experimental conditions that should satisfy the most fastidious of researchers.

There happen, however, to be a few "extraneous" features in the situation. Often the visitor willing to serve as an experimental subject is female, and, in the mode of the day, frequently dressed rather skimpily. She finds herself asked, on signal, to reach for a lever in a variety of compromising positions, while a male experimenter stands by to observe closely (perhaps even to photograph the action). One suspects that, under the circumstances, there may be more variables determining her reaction time than the experimenter had intended. It would not seem farfetched to imagine the subject devoting part of her attention to continuing to look reasonably ladylike under the circumstances. At least Versace is convinced that even in such an otherwise objectively researchable area, there are more uncontrolled variables than meet the eye.

If such a situation exists in engineering psychology, it is compounded in clinical research. Two classes of examples will illustrate the problem—one dealing with experimental design, the other with some interesting artifacts that creep into research with human subjects.

Problems of Design

Constraints of Field Research

A little study by Chapman (1963) teaches a big lesson. Like many others, he was interested in investigating schizophrenic thought processes. As is often the case, the hospital patients he wished to use as subjects were on drugs (tranquilizers and other psychopharmacological agents). In order to avoid having drug effects confound performance, it was necessary to "dry out" the subjects—that is, to remove them from drugs for 6–8 weeks, by which time the pharmacological effects would presumably have worn off. This is accepted procedure, but what is not always recognized, as Chapman helped show, is that it may lead to misleading interpretations of experimental results.

Taking patients diagnosed as schizophrenic, Chapman selected those who met certain criteria (of sex, race, age, length of hospitalization, treatment history, and the like). One hundred eleven patients turned out to be potential subjects, all of them on drugs at the time. Of these, however, only 52 were able to deal with the initial screening task, half of them taking a Homonym Test, the other half a Breadth of Concept Test (described in the footnote of Table 1). Thus, more than half the original subjects were lost at the outset. Nevertheless 52 patients were still available to be taken off drugs for 6 weeks for testing during the additional drug-free weeks 7 and 8.

Further problems characteristic of clinical research soon appeared. The hospital management refused to allow 14 of the 52 patients to participate (12 because they were considered too disturbed, the other 2 because they were due to leave the hospital shortly). Still undaunted, the investigator decided to proceed with the remaining 38 subjects, who were now taken off drugs. It was not long, however, before ward personnel began to complain—the psychological condition of some of the 38 was getting worse, they were growing harder to handle, their symptoms were becoming exacerbated. Consequently, at the behest of exasperated nurses, 18 more patients were returned to drugs by their physicians, leaving only 20 to continue on the drying-out regimen (as compared with the previous 38 to which the earlier 52 of the original 111 had been reduced!).

A less enterprising researcher might, at this point, have dropped the study in despair, and an unsophisticated one might have fretted a bit, then proceeded routinely with the remaining 20. To Chapman, however, there was now an interesting question. What might have happened had he studied these 20 during weeks 7 and 8 and generalized to the population of schizophrenics? Inquisitively, he looked back at the larger group of 38 patients whose test results were available, wondering to what degree those who had been returned to drugs were similar to those left in the study. The findings, shown in Table 1, proved instructive.

Table 1
Mean error test scores of groups of patients kept off drugs and returned to drugs.

Patient Group	Test	
	Homonym[a]	Breadth of Concept[b]
Kept off drugs (20 of 38)	3.0	11.2
Returned to drugs (18 of 38)	18.5	20.0

[a] Encircle the word that most nearly means "Sea": See   Ocean   Idol
[b] In the following set of (30) words, encircle those that represent fruits (in another set, tools, etc.); cross out those that do not.
(Adapted from Table 1 of Chapman, 1963. Copyright 1963 by the American Psychological Association and reproduced by permission.)

It was plainly evident that the test performance of the remaining 20 patients differed significantly from that of the 18 patients who had been lost when returned to drugs by their physicians. Differences as large as these or larger would have occurred fewer than 5 times in 100 just by chance. Had Chapman proceeded and then used the test performance of the remaining 20 during weeks 7 and 8, his generalizations about schizophrenics could have been seriously in error. Clearly, the study was dealing not only with subjects labeled schizophrenic but also with nonsubjects called nurses, psychiatrists, and hospital administrators. Consider, then, a second and related problem.

The Confounding of Variables

In one's eagerness to gain knowledge in the area of psychopathology, it is tempting to attribute whatever deficiencies are found to the disorder under study. Schizophrenics as a group may show certain difficulties in concept formation; therefore, one is led to conclude that the difficulties are characteristic of the schizophrenic process. Not necessarily, caution Silverman and his colleagues (1965). Like Chapman, they were concerned lest one ascribe to a psychological disorder attributes that might be a function of some concomitant of hospitalization. Again, curiosity paid off.

Is it conceivable, Silverman and his group wondered, that some of what we associate with certain disorders (for example, schizophrenia) might represent the effects of institutionalization rather than of the disorder itself? The possibility led them to compare the performance of groups institutionalized for short and long periods of time.

For the purpose, Silverman et al. chose San Quentin prisoners, all of whom were serving time for felonies. They divided the prisoners into short-term and long-term groups and studied their respective performances on a perceptual (Titchener Circle Illusion) and a cognitive (Pettigrew Category Width) task. The research team was already familiar with how schizophrenics perform in these areas. The question was whether "such perceptual differences were peculiar to the schizophrenics or whether comparable differences would be found in nonschizophrenics who were institutionalized for relatively short and long periods of time" (p. 657). The results led to the following conclusion: "Analysis of their perceptual performance indicated that: (1) significant perceptual differences existed between early-term and long-term prisoners and (2) differences in styles of perceptual and cognitive response within the two groups were comparable to those found within acute and chronic schizophrenic groups" (p. 657).

Such a finding gives pause for thought. So does a third feature of the study of human behavior — placebo effects.

Placebo Effects

Given a certain drug whose pharmacological properties are known, we can expect an animal subject to behave in a certain way, once the drug has been administered and given time to take effect. With people, the situation is not nearly so simple. A woman with an acute asthmatic attack gasps desperately for air, shouts to the physician who is passing the door of her hospital room, pleading for an injection that will terminate the attack. Knowing her from past contacts, he obliges; shortly after the injection, she is able to breathe normally and thanks him profusely for his help. However, the fact may be that, although the patient thinks otherwise, the physician has given her an injection of saline solution (plain salt water) rather than a drug. Yet it has apparently served its purpose.

Evidently where human subjects are involved, variables in addition to the drug itself influence the effects of its administration (or nonadministration)—psychological variables such as the patient's expectation, his perception of the drug-giver, his needs to be viewed as "sick," or the prestigiousness of the setting in which drugs are administered (or nonadministered). In short, a person may show a certain response to being injected not only because of the pharmacological properties of the drug (that may or may not have been administered), but because of a "placebo effect." The mere fact of getting attention, the entertaining of expectations about what is going to happen, or perhaps an unconscious motivation to react in a certain way can all play a role.

Let us look for a moment at how such factors may influence results in a state psychiatric hospital which is woefully understaffed and hopes for anything that will make management of patients easier. Each psychiatrist has, let us say, 300 patients under his care. Obviously, little close personal contact is possible, there being so many patients to so little staff. Under the circumstances, the hospital administration might well have welcomed the advent of the tranquilizing drugs and begun dispensing them on a large scale (assuming a penurious state legislature had voted funds for this purpose).

If after four months the patients show improvement according to before-and-after rating scales filled out by ward personnel, even the layman might hesitate to conclude that "miracle drugs" had been discovered. He would doubtless ask further questions. How much of the improvement might have come from the increased attention shown the patients, who are now called to the nurses' station, given a pill, perhaps even greeted with an unaccustomed "How are you feeling?" Did it matter that the nurses who made the before-and-after ratings were the same nurses who dispensed the tranquilizer? Was the rating scale a reliable one—that is, would Nurse A, rating Patient B now, rate similar behavior on his part in the same way an hour from now? Was the measure a valid one—that is, was it really measuring mental status, or perhaps something else?

At the very least, one would see the need for a control group (a group of comparable patients who did not receive the drug over the four-month period but were treated like the patients on drugs in other respects), because variables other than the drug might have played a role in the improvement of patients—the arrival of a new superintendent with a modern philosophy of hospital administration, for example. Even then one might wonder about allowing the nurses who make the ratings know who is and who is not getting the drug. Could the control patients perhaps receive a pill that contained only an inert ingredient (a placebo) but looked and tasted like the drug pill? For, as noted above, the mere belief that one is receiving a helpful medication might in itself produce alleviation of symptoms.

The experienced clinical investigator is, of course, well aware of such problems and has ways of handling them. The double-blind design, for example, in which neither staff nor patients know who is receiving a drug and who a placebo, has become standard practice in drug research. But even with due precautions such research with human subjects has its pitfalls, as Chassan (1967) has shown in a book intended to keep psychologists and psychiatrists from framing poor designs and even poorer conclusions.

Ross et al. (1962) have pointed out that a central problem is to separate the pharmacological effects of the drug under study from whatever placebo effects may enter to confound the findings. For this purpose, they suggest the simple, yet effective, design shown in Table 2.

Table 2
Paradigm for drug research using 4 groups (A, B, C, D).

	Drug	No Drug
Pill	A	B
No Pill	C	D

The subjects in cell A would show the combined pharmacological and placebo effects, those in cell B the placebo effects alone. The subjects in A are correct in the belief that they are receiving medication; subjects in B think that they are too, but theirs is only a "sugar pill" (a placebo). The subjects in cell C should show the pharmacological effects of the drug itself without the placebo effect; they would be receiving the drug but not be aware that they were—the so-called "silent administration" of the drug. The subjects in cell D could constitute a control group, because they are subject to neither pharmacological nor placebo effects. The problem now becomes one of implementing the design.

Ross and his colleagues resorted to a simple procedure using three media—the drug, a placebo (sodium bicarbonate in a form resembling the drug pill), and orange juice. Their procedure for the four conditions is shown in Table 3.

Table 3
Experimental procedure involving 4 groups (A, B, C, D).

	Drug	No Drug
Pill	A Drug in form of pill, followed by orange juice	B Placebo (sodium bicarbonate) in form of pill, followed by orange juice
No Pill	C Drug dissolved in orange juice (without subject's knowledge)	D Plain orange juice

There was, of course, the possibility that the subjects of cell C might have sensed that their orange juice had been "spiked." (Although these were geriatric patients in a domiciliary home, they were still in good shape mentally.) Therefore, as a precaution, the research team had, in as natural a way as possible, enlisted the subjects' help in a survey ostensibly being conducted for the Florida State Growers of Tallahassee. Asked to judge the flavor of the orange juice on a 5-point scale from Excellent to Very Poor, the subjects in cells C and D showed no significant difference in their ratings. Presumably, then, the taste of the orange juice in which the drug had been dissolved did not tip the subject off.

With a suitable design at hand, Ross et al. conceived some interesting studies intended to disentangle pharmacological from placebo effects. Working with a drug known to have a depressive effect on mood, they presented the situation to the geriatric patients in a neutral way. Thus, subjects in the Pill group were told: "This is a study from which we hope to gain information about the effects of this drug upon mood, the way that you feel . . ." Subjects in the No Pill group were simply told: "This is a study from which we hope to gain information about mood, that is, the way an older person feels . . ." In other words, in the latter group there was no reference to a drug.

The design shown in Table 3 was used as part of a detailed experimental procedure. After obtaining the data on comparable groups of subjects in the four conditions, the investigators found the situation pictured in Table 4.

Ross and his co-investigators suggest an interesting explanation of the results. Subjects in cell B have a double advantage. They experience the positive placebo effect

Table 4
Effect of experimental conditions on mood.

	Drug	No Drug
Pill	A Moderately comfortable	B Most comfortable
No Pill	C Most uncomfortable	D Moderately comfortable

(Adapted with permission of author and publisher: Ross, S., Krugman, A. D., Lyerly, S. B., & Clyde, D. J. Drugs and placebos: A model design. *Psychological Reports,* 1962, **10**, 383–392, Table 4.)

(that is, they think they are getting medicine) yet not the depressive effects of the drug (since they are getting none). By contrast, subjects in cell C suffer the worst of both conditions; they are without the placebo effect (having received no pill) and, in addition, suffer the negative effect of the depressive drug (dissolved in their orange juice without their knowledge). The mood scores of subjects in cells A and D prove to be almost identical, but for different reasons. Subjects in cell D constitute a neutral control group, having received plain orange juice. Subjects in cell A, on the other hand, have been subjected to the depressive effect of the drug but presumably have received the psychological lift of the placebo; the two effects cancel each other out, according to Ross et al., with the result that the A subjects show almost the same mood as the D subjects.

Clearly, the placebo effect needs to be reckoned with. And there are further complications that throw the unwary researcher off the scent while challenging the well-trained investigator to capture and control them. Let us look at a few.

Artifacts Involving Human Subjects

Orne (1962) has made the following observation:

> A number of casual acquaintances were asked whether they would do the experimenter a favor; on their acquiescence they were asked to perform five push-ups. Their response tended to be amazement, incredulity and the question "Why?" Another similar group of individuals were asked whether they would take part in an experiment of brief duration. When they agreed to do so, they too were asked to perform five push-ups. Their typical response was "Where?" (p. 777).

The simple illustration makes an important point. People seem unusually willing to cooperate in an experiment. Orne was not the first to make the observation, however, as he readily admits in prefacing his article with a statement made by Pierce (1908):

> It is to the highest degree probable that the subject['s] . . . general attitude of mind is that of ready complacency and cheerful willingness to assist the investigator in every possible way by reporting to him those very things which he is most eager to find, and that the very questions of the experimenter . . . suggest the shade of reply expected . . . Indeed . . . it seems too often as if the subject were now regarded as a stupid automaton . . . (Orne, p. 776).

Orne has dubbed the phenomenon the "perceived demand characteristics" of the experimental situation. That is to say, the subject is not without expectations, hunches, and suspicions about the experiment or what the experimenter hopes to find. Further, he seems generally quite willing to help the latter confirm the hypothesis—that is, to prove a "good" subject.

That the experimenter has some preconceptions about how things will turn out cannot be denied; research studies proceed from specific hypotheses. One is entitled to one's hunches. What would be disturbing, though, would be to find him unwittingly influencing the outcome of the very investigation that is designed to test them. And this, according to Rosenthal (1963), is precisely what can happen. Just as Orne is concerned about the effect of "perceived demand characteristics" on the subject's part, so Rosenthal is distressed by what seems to be unwitting "experimenter bias"—that is, the tendency of the experimenter to unintentionally influence the results.

Give a group of experimenters sets of pictures of human faces wearing neutral expressions (as evaluated by independent judges), and ask each to have his subjects rate the people according to success or failure in life on a scale from minus 10 (extreme failure) through zero (average) to plus 10 (extreme success). Tell each experimenter beforehand that subjects tend to rate the pictures in a certain way. (Some experimenters are told subjects tend to see people largely as failures; other experimenters are told that subjects tend to see people largely as successful.) Subsequently have each test his particular group of subjects. What did Rosenthal and Fode (1963), who did the experiment, find?

Although each experimenter gives identical instructions to those in his group (as prescribed by the experimental procedure), the subjects seem to behave in accordance with the experimenter's (unexpressed) expectation! That is, experimenters who have been told most people tend to rate faces on the success side find their subjects doing just that; experimenters who have been led to believe most people tend to see such faces as those of unsuccessful people find their subjects rating the pictures significantly less positively than does the other group.

In short, the experimenters are getting what they expect to get, although no observable communication of the expectation seems to have taken place between experimenter and subject. Having obtained such results, Rosenthal has not only followed up and confirmed the phenomenon of "experimenter bias" to his satisfaction in many subsequent studies (in some, even animals seem influenced by experimenters' expectations) but has taken it almost as his mission to make researchers in general conscious of this artifact.

In his article on the experimenter as a stimulus object, McGuigan (1963) has raised the problem in more general terms. It happens, as he points out, that many studies involve not one experimenter but several. This raises a question: ". . . does the fact that two experimenters differ only in regard to a single characteristic affect the performance of subjects in two otherwise identical experiments?" (p. 423). If so, this is something not to be suffered lightly. True, it could happen that the particular characteristic may not influence performance in terms of the dependent variable, in which case there would be no problem. Or it may prove to influence performance, but in the same direction for all subjects. Two experimenters may differ in degree of anxiety, for example, and the less anxious experimenter may be getting higher scores from his subjects than the more anxious from his. However, in the case of both experimenters, the experimental group may be performing significantly better than the control group. Here again, there would be no great problem.

McGuigan reminds us, however, that there may be an interaction between particular characteristics of the experimenters and the independent variable. Where this is the case, one may find the situation shown in Figure 1, which presents the results obtained by nine experimenters, each of whom was assessing the relative effectiveness of the same four methods of learning.

This clearly presents a problem of interpretation. When one is reminded that clinical psychology is often faced with such situations—as when several methods of psychotherapy are being compared—it is obvious that, whether such phenomena are called facts or artifacts, they deserve close attention.

The experimenter, then, is more than an experimenter. He is apparently also a variable in any interaction with human subjects—be it in the relationship of subject to experimenter, examinee to examiner, or client to therapist. Presumably, the results

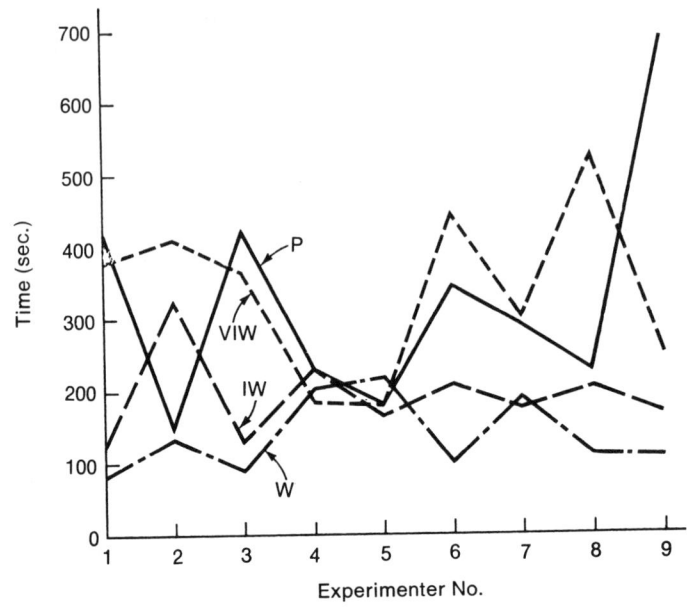

Figure 1
Scores for four methods of learning, plotted as a function of experimenters. (Figure 1 of McGuigan, 1963. Copyright 1963 by the American Psychological Association and reproduced by permission.)

of experimentation are primarily a function of the independent variable under study. They are, however, also influenced to some extent by the expectations the human subject brings to the situation and by the expectations held by the psychologist himself.

The latter finding is strikingly illustrated in another study by Rosenthal et al. (1966). Nineteen male experimenters participated in a verbal conditioning experiment involving 60 female subjects. The experimenters were told that their subjects had been allotted to them on the basis of personality characteristics matching their own. (Actually subjects had been assigned randomly to experimenters.) Each experimenter was further given (a) one of two expectations—that his subjects would condition well or that they would condition poorly—and (b) one of two impressions of conditionability—that it was related to general learning ability or that it represented susceptibility to manipulation.

Thus, before running his subjects in the experiment, a given experimenter might have been led to expect that his particular subjects would condition well and that such conditionability was related to general learning ability. Since subjects assigned to him were allegedly similar to him in personality, such would be a "congruent" situation. Thus, his subjects (and, therefore, he) were presumably smart. In contrast, another experimenter might have been led to expect that his subjects would condition poorly. If it had been suggested to him that conditionability was correlated with susceptibility to manipulation, he too would face a congruent situation; that is, his subjects would prove by their poor conditionability that they were not the type of people who could easily be manipulated—they had minds of their own.

For those experimenters who had been told conditionability was a good thing (was correlated with general learning ability), but that their subjects would not condition well, the situation was "incongruent." Their subjects (and, hence, they themselves) were presumably not smart. A condition of incongruence existed also for the experimenter who had been told conditionability was a bad attribute (that is, that it represented susceptibility to manipulation), but that his subjects would probably prove readily conditionable. Thus, they (and he) were presumably putty in the hands of others. In short, the "master experimenters" had set up the four conditions shown in Table 5 for the group of 19 experimenters before the latter ran their respective subjects.

Table 5
Relationships between different combinations of experimenter expectation and belief.

		Expectation	
		Subjects would condition well	Subjects would condition poorly
Belief	Conditionability is related to general learning ability.	A Congruent	B Incongruent
	Conditionability is related to susceptibility to manipulation.	C Incongruent	D Congruent

After each experimenter had run his subjects in the same way in the verbal conditioning procedure, conditionability scores were calculated for the respective groups of subjects. The results are pictured in Figure 2.

Interestingly, the subjects of experimenters for whom the situation was congruent conditioned significantly better than did the subjects of experimenters for whom the situation was incongruent. Yet every effort had been made to standardize the procedure. The lesson is clear. If experimental results are peddled by someone mindless of these eventualities, let the buyer beware.

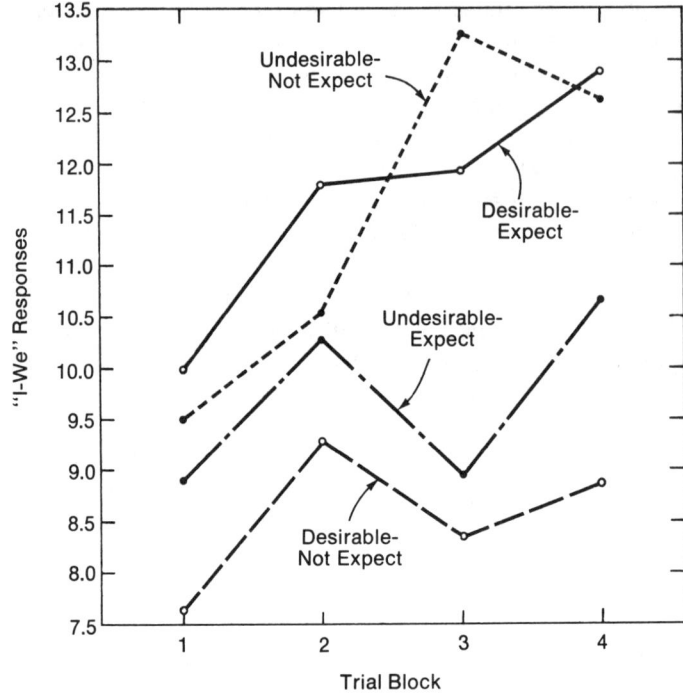

Figure 2
Frequency of conditioned response as a function of experimenter expectancy, outcome desirability, and number of trials. (Figure 1 of Rosenthal, Kohn, Greenfield, & Carota, 1966. Copyright 1966 by the American Psychological Association and reproduced by permission.)

Up to this point, then, we have noted three types of artifacts.

1. Subjects come to experiments not as blank slates or passive guinea pigs. They have, on the one hand, some hunches (whether correct does not matter) as to what the experiment is about and what the experimenter hopes to "prove." At the same time, they seem disposed to help him prove it; that is, they seem to cooperate in fulfilling what they consider to be the experimenter's expectations.
2. Experimenters do — as subjects believe — have hypotheses they hope to confirm. What is disturbing is the preliminary, if not conclusive, evidence that such expectations may influence subjects' performance despite the experimenters' best efforts to prevent it.
3. As the last-mentioned experiment by Rosenthal et al. demonstrates, there seems to

be an interaction between what the experimenter expects to find and the desirability of the outcome (as he sees it) with a consequent influence on the results he gets from his subjects.

But, to use the term "experimenter bias" in a different sense, it is also possible for the experimenter to (mis)interpret findings in a way that confirms his hypothesis. Barber and Silver (1968a), in an article entitled "Fact, Fiction, and the Experimenter Bias Effect," suggest that such bias appears in Rosenthal's work. Skeptical about the alleged prevalence of this phenomenon, they analyzed 31 studies in which the experimenter-bias effect was said to have been evident. They emerged unconverted. In their judgment, the findings had not been properly analyzed in many of the studies, so that Rosenthal and his colleagues could be blamed for inadequate statistical checks rather than praised for having discovered an important phenomenon. As a result, Barber and Silver not only doubted the pervasiveness of the experimenter-bias effect but also advanced less esoteric explanations for it where it seemed to appear—research assistants might have had poor work habits, subjects might have been getting reinforced verbally for "expected" responses, or experimenters might have been providing other kinds of cues as to how they expected subjects to behave.

In his rebuttal, Rosenthal (1968) undertakes a detailed reply to the specific objections raised by Barber and Silver, adding an appendix in which he comments on their "many serious omissions of fact." They, in turn, offer a counter-rebuttal (Barber & Silver, 1968b), so that at this point psychologists as a whole are probably as divided on the subject as are those who have argued the matter in print.

The situation is perhaps complicated further by the fact that subjects not only have expectations about what the experimenter is after; they also have expectations as to how they will be affected by the experimental procedure. A recent study by Weil et al. (1968) on the effects of marihuana smoking illustrates the phenomenon.

In view of the prevailing concern about the growing use of this drug, Weil and his colleagues attempted a well-controlled study of its effects. Previous investigations had suffered notable limitations—the absence of placebo control groups, oral administration of the drug, and other methodological flaws. Most of all, however, Weil et al. were concerned with another feature that had received scant attention. As they put it: "All indications are that the form of marihuana intoxication is particularly dependent on the interaction of drug, set, and setting. Because of recent increases in the extent of use and in attention given this use by the mass media, it is difficult to find subjects with a neutral set toward marihuana" (p. 1236).

Whether one conceives of the above as a variable to be controlled or as an artifact to be watched, the investigators in this case paid careful attention to this feature, as the following indicates:

> Greatest effort was made to create a neutral setting. That is, subjects were made comfortable and secure in a pleasant suite of laboratories and offices, but the experimental staff carefully avoided encouraging any person to have an enjoyable experience. Subjects were never asked how they felt, and no subject was permitted to discuss the experiment with the staff until he had completed all four sessions. Verbal interactions between staff and subjects were minimum and formal. At the end of each session, subjects were asked to complete a brief form asking whether they thought they had smoked marihuana that night; if so, whether a high dose; and how confident they were of their answer (p. 1237).

Clearly, as far as these experimenters were concerned, much more was involved than the pharmacological effect of a particular drug on the nervous system. The attitude, expectations, and stereotyped beliefs of the subject could, it was felt, determine their reaction to the marihuana-smoking situation as much as, or more than, the chemical effects of the drug itself.

The experimenters were concerned with such features as order of treatment (that is, balancing of the sequence in which subjects smoked high, low, and placebo doses), performance and mood measures, and physiological parameters (heart rate, pupil size, etc.) among others. Interesting findings emerged: (a) on high doses of marihuana (2.0 grams), all of the subjects who were chronic users became "high"; by contrast, only one of the nine naive subjects did; and (b) following high doses, the performance of naive subjects on perceptual-motor tasks suffered a decrement; that of chronic users actually improved slightly.

Weil and his co-workers were not ready to rule out the possibility that physiological sensitization to the drug might account in part for the differences between naive and chronic users (even though, unlike alcohol drinkers, chronic marihuana users suffer "reverse tolerance"—that is, they require successively smaller doses for getting high). They were at the same time, however, equally impressed by the possibility that a psychosocial factor might be at work. In their words:

> Indirect evidence makes the psychological hypothesis attractive. Anxiety about drug use in this country is sufficiently great to make worthy of careful consideration the possibility of an unconscious psychological inhibition or block on the part of naive drug takers. The subjective responses of our subjects indicate that they had imagined a marihuana effect to be much more profoundly disorganizing than what they experienced. . . .

> As anxiety about the drug is lessened with experience, the block may decrease, and the subject may permit himself to notice the drug's effects (p. 1241).

In a series of interesting speculations on the effects of drugs upon their users, Becker (1967) has elaborated considerably on this and related points. While he grants that the physiological action of drugs such as marihuana and LSD contribute "in some part" to their effect, he stresses even more the role played by the expectations the user has and the interpretations he places on the sensations he experiences. The latter, according to Becker, may be to a considerable extent a function of the subculture of which the drug user is a part. Thus, he points out: "If others whom the user believes to be knowledgeable single out certain effects as characteristic and dismiss others, he is likely to notice those they single out as characteristic of his own experience. If they define certain effects as transitory, he is likely to believe that those effects will go away" (p. 165).

Even with drugs used in general medical practice, where side effects are to be expected, the physician may be an important determinant of how the patient reacts to what he experiences, Becker feels. In short, he theorizes that social and psychological factors may contribute as significantly to the phenomena experienced by drug users as do the pharmacological properties of the drugs themselves. As he puts it: "The three-way link between history, culture and social organization, and the person's subjective state may point the way to a better understanding than we now have of the social bases of individual experience" (p. 176).

On the face of it, evaluating the effect of a given drug on performance, mood, and physiology seems straightforward. Where human subjects are involved, however, it turns out to be not nearly so simple a proposition.

In short, it is as if clinical work always has to reckon with at least three classes of variables: the independent variables under study; experimenter variables in the form of expectancies and their concomitants; and subject variables as represented by set, beliefs, and related cognitive, affective, and motivational predispositions. The consequent interaction of the three classes of variables makes clinical psychology, whether in theory, practice, or research, at once intricate and intriguing.

With such a set, we concern ourselves in Part Three with research and theory, in Part Four with theory and practice.

Methodological Considerations

Part Three
Research and Theory

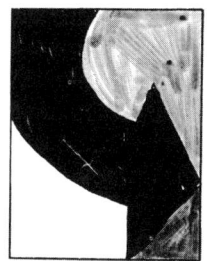

5
Animal Research And Clinical Analogues

Any visitor to some of Europe's famous old cathedrals will probably remember how his guide explained why the bell tower had sunk or the transept arches were sagging. The architects, it seems, either had created their masterpieces before the physicists had clearly specified the rules of stresses and strains, or else had not bothered to consult such research-minded colleagues. The situation in clinical psychology and psychiatry is not much different. People need help with problems of living, and clinicians try to supply that help. Few clinical principles have as yet been spelled out as clearly as the laws of thermodynamics, but a parent seeking help in bringing up his child can hardly be put off until that happy day arrives.

This section has a dual purpose. It attempts to sample research efforts going on in some major areas of clinical concern and, at the same time, it emphasizes the need for clinical psychologists to "look sideways." It behooves one to keep a watchful eye on what one's colleagues in other areas are finding that may be pertinent to clinical interests, sometimes directly, sometimes by extrapolation. Thus, we will begin with animal research, something that is hardly the stock-in-trade of the clinical investigator. We will try to translate some sample findings into clinical terms.

Probably many more scientific discoveries than one would expect are stumbled upon serendipitously. That is, in the course of studying a problem in which an investigator is particularly interested, he unexpectedly runs across another phenomenon and finds that it is more intriguing than his original problem. Indeed, the new phenomenon itself often becomes the object of a whole new line of research. Such has been the case a number of times as experimenters working with animals were struck by the implications of their findings for the clearer understanding of human behavior.

The clinical psychologist is not generally given to studying how pigeons learn to discriminate among colored disks. Nor is he usually found running experiments on how monkeys perform after parts of their brain have been removed, or how hungry rats behave when their foodbox is wired for shock. Such animal research is usually left to his colleagues, whether experimental, comparative, or physiological psychologists. Lately, however, even some experimental social psychologists have taken to studying animals in the hope of shedding further light on human social interaction. Zajonc (1965), for example, found that the performance of the lowly cockroach, with and without an audience (of other cockroaches), offers some fruitful leads to the understanding of the phenomenon of social facilitation in general.

Whether many clinical psychologists will join the animal researchers remains to be seen. What is clear is that much of what "rat psychologists" and others are discovering in the laboratory has clinical implications. In order to start the reader thinking along these lines, we shall turn for illustrative purposes to some early work by Solomon and his colleagues, followed by some recent work by Seligman, one of Solomon's students. The animals used in this case were dogs, and the primary area of interest was the effect of punishment on behavior.

Traumatic Avoidance Learning

It is difficult to find any book on clinical problems that does not at some point touch on the effects of punishment as either a determinant of some behavior to be explained or as a method of modifying some behavior to be changed. Let us look at the degree to which punishment, especially drastic punishment, may produce deviant behavior and result in its perpetuation, even when such behavior no longer makes sense. Solomon et al. (1953) must have been as surprised as anyone else at the behavior of the dogs they submitted to traumatic shock in their study of the effects of punishment.

The problem seemed simple. A dog put into one compartment of a two-compartment "shuttlebox" and submitted to an intense electric shock simply had to learn that by jumping over the partition that separated the two boxes he could terminate the shock. In fact, he was even given prior warning (by a buzzer) that shock was to come, so that, if he learned to jump to the opposite compartment in time, he could avoid shock altogether. Specifically, the experimental procedure was as follows.

With the dog in one compartment of the shuttlebox, a gate was lowered alongside the partition that separated the two compartments, restricting the dog temporarily to the one section. As a trial began, a buzzer sounded, and one second later the gate was raised, allowing access to the other compartment; it was now possible for the dog to jump over the barrier that separated the two. The buzzer continued for a total of 10 seconds, at which point very intense electric shock was applied continuously to the floor grid on which the dog stood. His reaction was not unexpected—he dashed about the compartment, shrieking, even losing control of his bodily functions. In the course of this agitated behavior, the animal eventually scrambled over the partition, an act which immediately terminated the shock, since the floor of the compartment into which the dog jumped was not electrified at the time.

After a 3-minute interval, a second trial began. The procedure was identical, except that the animal was now starting from the second compartment. Its floor grid was subsequently electrified, as in the procedure above, and this time escape lay in jumping back into the first compartment, which was now free of shock. After another 3 minutes the alternation was repeated, running through a planned number of trials per day.

As the reader may suspect, while the dogs continued some of the same frantic behavior noted above during the early trials when shock was turned on, they managed to scramble over the barrier sooner on successive trials. By about the fifth trial most dogs were jumping before the 10-second buzzer warning period was over, which meant they received no shock on the particular trial. In other words, what had begun as escape behavior (that is, experiencing shock and then escaping from it) had soon turned into avoidance behavior (jumping in less than 10 seconds, thus avoiding shock altogether). After a dog had learned to avoid shock on a given number of consecutive trials, the experimenters discontinued shock altogether. Thus, regardless of how long a dog now remained in a particular compartment, he received no shock at all.

The findings themselves were shocking. In the complete absence of shock, the dogs nevertheless continued to jump within the original 10-second time limit. Indeed, they tended, on the average, to jump within 1.0–1.2 seconds after the warning buzzer had sounded on each trial—even though they would never have received shock no matter how long they had remained in either compartment. In fact, when 13 dogs were given a total of 2,582 extinction trials (that is, trials without any shock at all), on only 11 (of the 2,582 trials) did a dog fail to jump in less than 10 seconds! Thus, the experimenters found a typical behavior: a dog would meet the acquisition criterion of avoidance learning within 11 trials, and then would continue through a sequence of as many as 490 trials (with shock turned off) without showing any signs of extinction detectable from either its response latencies (that is, the time it took the dog to jump after the buzzer had sounded) or its behavior.

Looked at more closely, this behavior showed many interesting features. As mentioned above, with shock turned off altogether, the dogs typically continued to jump within 1.0–1.2 seconds after the buzzer began sounding. Their behavior became quite stereotyped, almost ritualistic. Even more noteworthy was the fact that, although they continued jumping on each trial, there were no signs of overt anxiety. All things considered, since it required some effort for dogs to jump the shoulder-high barrier, one would expect the jumping behavior to extinguish spontaneously after a while in the absence of any further shock experience.

To clinicians, who are frequently confronted by "senseless" behavior on the part of patients, there is an interesting parallel here. The compulsive hand washer, for example, who may wash his hands 30 times a day because he becomes intolerably anxious when he does not, seems similar to the dog who jumps for hundreds of effortful trials when jumping actually serves no purpose. When it turns out that the hand washer has a superior IQ and has read widely, yet still remains an unwilling victim of his compulsion, the problem becomes all the more complex. Let us look at further efforts of Solomon and his fellow investigators for some additional parallels of clinical interest.

If the jumping behavior of the dogs, which made no sense under the shockless conditions, was not going to extinguish spontaneously, could extinction be promoted through various experimental procedures? Since shock no longer followed the buzzer, and jumping was thus "irrational," what would happen if one electrified the compartment *into which* jumps were made? The experimenters described the results as follows:[1]

> An attempt was then made to discourage the 490-trial dog from jumping by electrifying the opposite compartment on each trial, so that the dog jumped *into* shock. The gate was immediately lowered after each jump to prevent retracing, and the shock, at just subtetanizing level, was continued for three seconds and then terminated. The dog became more upset, and at subsequent presentations of the CS [conditioned stimulus] jumped more vigorously. His latencies were maintained at their already extremely fast level of 1.0–1.2 seconds. After 100 additional trials under this shock-extinction procedure, the dog was still jumping regularly into shock and gave no signs of extinguishing. As he jumped on each trial he gave a sharp anticipatory yip which turned into a yelp when he landed on the electrified grid in the opposite compartment of the shuttlebox (Solomon et al., 1953, pp. 291–292).

[1] Copyright 1953 by the American Psychological Association. Reprinted by permission of the authors and publisher.

In one of the experiments involving thirteen dogs, the above procedure extinguished the jumping behavior in only three of the subjects. Once the three animals had stopped jumping, they never jumped again; there was no spontaneous recovery of the response. The other ten, however, showed entirely different behavior.

As the experimenters described it:

> These dogs jumped *faster* and *more vigorously* into the shock than they had jumped previously under the ordinary extinction procedure . . . they often slammed into the far end of the compartment into which they were jumping. In addition, they all developed anticipatory reactions prior to jumping, which indicated that they knew they were to be shocked. The most common reaction was to yelp at the CS, jump vigorously, and then yelp at the shock, barking rapidly when the shock was terminated (p. 295).

The reader may wish to speculate on his own about what might have led the dogs to persist in their jumping behavior in the face of such odds. At any rate, the situation began to look more complicated than it had seemed at first. Solomon and his team consequently explored further possibilities. If discouragement of jumping had had little extinction effect, one might try to actually *prevent* it. What would happen, for example, if a tangible barrier to jumping—a plate of glass—were placed between the two compartments? Again, the treatment was not without its complications, as noted in the following description:

> We placed a plate of glass in the opposite compartment, flush against the barrier and gate so that it blocked the passage between the two compartments. The plate of glass could not be seen by the dog until the gate was raised and the buzzer was sounded. . . . On the first glass-barrier trial, [the dog] jumped forward immediately at the CS and smashed his head against the glass. He drew back and was fairly quiet, and the gate was lowered after two minutes. On the subsequent trials, on which he did not strike the glass, he barked furiously, panted very rapidly, quivered, and drooled while the CS was present, but quieted down after the gate was lowered, and remained quiet during the minute before the next trial was started (p. 292).

The persistence of the jumping behavior even under such conditions is evident from the investigators' report that it required 647 extinction trials before this dog stopped jumping in the presence of the CS alone. Only when the researchers used a *combination* of treatments—shock and glass-barrier conditions in various sequences—did extinction begin to materialize. Even here there were some remaining problems. Nonetheless such combinations eventually led most of the dogs to stop jumping, as shown in Table 1.

Table 1
Proportion of animals extinguishing the jumping response under various extinction procedures.

Experiment	Special Procedure Used	After 200 Trials Ordinary Extinction Procedure	After 10 Trials Ordinary Extinction Procedure	Total
2	None	0/13*	0/10	0/23
3	Glass-barrier procedure only	1/5	1/4	2/9
4	Shock procedure only	1/7	2/6	3/13
5	Combined procedure, glass-barrier procedure first	4/4	2/2	6/6
5	Combined procedure, shock procedure first	5/6	3/4	8/10

*Represents none out of 13 dogs.
(Table 2 of Solomon, Kamin, & Wynne, 1953. Copyright 1953 by the American Psychological Association and reproduced by permission.)

The persistence of this conditioned emotional response (CER) to the sound of the buzzer, leading to the jumping response, continued to hold the attention of the investigators. What interested them particularly was the fact that, while the dogs made their hundreds of jumps during the shockless period following the original conditioning experience, they showed no overt anxiety. Yet if a dog was restrained from jumping on any trial as the buzzer sounded, clear signs of anxiety at once became evident. In other words, anxiety had not actually disappeared but had merely gone underground.

Might it simply be, then, that the jumping behavior was being reinforced by anxiety reduction? It seemed not. For autonomic feedback to occur, a period of 2.4–3.1 seconds would have to elapse. However, as mentioned previously, jump latencies stabilized at about 1.0–1.2 seconds. Consequently it could hardly be argued that the dogs were responding to their own emotional reactions, for anxiety would not have had time to be aroused.

According to the Law of Effect (see Walker, 1967), the dogs might have been expected to jump for a while following the elimination of shock in the original conditioning sessions. Thereafter, however, the latency of jumping could have been expected to increase and, as a result, eventually become long enough for autonomic feedback of the CER to occur, at which point the dogs would presumably jump again, strengthening the connection between the CS and jumping. The experimenters therefore advanced the following explanation: "A cyclical mechanism of this sort, with the emotional reaction being elicited only rarely, but, when elicited, giving renewed strength to the CS-jumping bond, would account for the high resistance of the jumping response to the ordinary extinction procedure. The final extinction of jumping would begin only when the emotional reaction had been elicited often enough to be itself extinguished, or at low strength" (p. 299).

For present purposes, we are less concerned with the further dialectical argument and the interesting technical speculations Solomon et al. offer than with the implications for human behavior. As the experimenters themselves suggest: "The picture is surprisingly akin to the clinical picture in compulsive neurosis. It contains the possibility of the organism 'frightening itself' by remaining in the presence of the CS long enough for the CS to be effective, while no emotionality will be elicited with *short* latencies for *instrumental* acts" (p. 299).

In other words, the latter behavior prevents any possibility for its own extinction. Whatever effectiveness the glass-barrier treatment had had, according to the researchers, was due to its "reality testing" function. That is, by keeping the animal in the situation after anxiety had been aroused, so that it could "see" that nothing happened when it did not jump, the strength of the jumping response should gradually diminish over repeated experiences of this kind. The problem with the compulsive hand washer is, of course, that he is *not* kept from performing the instrumental act. With respect to effective treatment of learned avoidance responses in general, then, Solomon et al. conclude: "Of course, the best way to produce extinction of the emotional response would be to arrange the situation in such a way that an extremely intense emotional reaction takes place in the presence of the CS. This would be tantamount to a reinstatement of the original acquisition situation, and since the US [unconditioned stimulus] is not presented a big decremental effect should occur" (p. 299).

The Concept of "Learned Helplessness"

It was this remarkable resistance to extinction that drew the attention of Seligman, one of Solomon's students. The dogs in the traumatic avoidance situation had learned their lesson all too well. They continued almost incessantly to practice an act which had originally served a purpose but no longer did so. What would happen, Seligman and his colleagues wondered, if *prior* to such shuttlebox training, dogs had experience with *inescapable* shock (that is, shock from which they had *no* way of escaping)?

Using a harness in which the dog was hung hammock-style, with its four legs protruding, Overmier and Seligman (1967) subjected animals to a number of intense, inescapable shocks. In this situation, regardless of its behavior, the dog could not escape shock. Twenty-four hours later the dogs were put in a shuttlebox situation, under conditions described in the preceding section. The results were dramatic. Like the dogs used by Solomon et al. (1953), the dogs with prior inescapable shock experiences scrambled about frantically at first. But, *unlike* Solomon's dogs, they soon stopped running, stood, and took the shock until it terminated! Seligman, Maier, and Geer (1968) describe the behavior:

> The dog does not cross the barrier and escape from shock. Rather, it seems to "give up" and passively "accept" the shock. On succeeding trials, the dog continues to fail to make escape movements and thus takes 50 seconds of severe pulsating shock on each trial. If he makes an escape or avoidance response, this does not reliably predict an occurrence of future responses, as it does for the normal dog. Pretreated dogs occasionally escape or avoid shock by jumping the barrier and then revert to taking the shock (p. 256).

Since clinicians are interested in how the prior history of persons can determine present functioning, this experiment opened up some important considerations. Seligman and Maier (1967) present some relevant data. They were interested not only in the effects of inescapable shock prior to shuttlebox training but also in the effects of *escapable* shock prior to shuttlebox training. Suppose, for example, conditions were such that the dog in the harness could prevent the otherwise inescapable shock from continuing by making a certain response. The experimenters arranged the situation in just this way. By pressing a panel on either side of its head, a dog could terminate any of a series of 64 unsignaled, intense shocks. In other words, escape learning (though not avoidance learning) was possible for this group of dogs.

How would such a group compare with a "yoked" control group of dogs whose experiences in the harness had been solely with inescapable shock—that is, without the opportunity to terminate shock through panel pressing? "Yoking" in this case refers not to being restrained in the apparatus but to the procedure whereby every dog in the control group was paired (yoked) with a dog in the experimental group, so that each control-group dog could be administered precisely the sequence and duration of shock that his experimental group counterpart had received as a result of the latter's panel-pressing behavior.

Under this arrangement some of the dogs—the experimental group—had control over what happened in the harness; by pressing the side panels with their heads these dogs could terminate shock. By contrast, the yoked controls could do nothing about the situation, for their behavior and the receipt of shock were independent of each other. Seligman and his colleagues speak, therefore, of the "learned independence of events." A third group, the normal controls, were not faced with the inescapable shock situation at all, since they were subjected solely to shuttlebox training under the usual shock conditions. Did the groups vary in their shuttlebox behavior as a result of their prior experiences? Indeed they did, as shown in Table 2.

Table 2
Indexes of shuttlebox escape/avoidance responding.

Group	Mean Latency (in sec.)	% Subjects Failing to Escape Shock on 9 or More of the 10 Trials	Mean No. of Failures to Escape Shock[a]
Escape[b]	27.00	0	2.63
Normal control	25.93	12.5	2.25
"Yoked" control	48.22	75	7.25

[a] In 10 trials.
[b] Escape group: panel-pressing group.
(Table 1 of Seligman and Maier, 1967. Copyright 1967 by the American Psychological Association and reproduced by permission.)

Clearly the yoked controls fared significantly worse in the shuttlebox than the dogs in the other two groups. The escape group, in fact, did just about as well as the normal controls. Apparently the shock experience in the harness, over which they had had some control—by performing the correct response they could terminate it—had left no lasting effects, judging from these dogs' ability to handle the shuttlebox situation as well as dogs that had had no experience with inescapable shock (the normal controls). The yoked controls, however—the dogs that had learned that their behavior was *independent* of what happened to them (that is, they had no control over their fate)—seemed to have suffered a drastic impairment of performance. When they did escape from shock by jumping the barrier, they took significantly longer to do so than the dogs of the other two groups, and, in fact, 75% of them did not escape in 9 or more of 10 trials in the shuttlebox. Apparently they too had learned something from the prior inescapable shock experience—that they were helpless! At least, they behaved as though they were helpless in the shuttlebox.

Thinking about the prior life history of patients he has seen, the clinician might well become interested in having these promising leads pursued by further empirical study. Seligman and Maier (1967) had the same intention and sought in a later experiment to refine the research design in such a way as to compare other possibilities. Suppose, for example, that several groups of subjects had various combinations of shuttlebox and harness experiences—a situation that might more adequately represent the complicated life histories of people. How would the respective groups behave? The more complex design now consisted of the sequence of conditions shown in Table 3.

Table 3
A design for the evaluation of effects of prior experience.

Group	Day 1	Day 2	Day 3
Pre-escapable	Shuttlebox (E/A)	Harness (Inesc)	Shuttlebox (E/A)
No Pre-escapable	– –	Harness (Inesc)	Shuttlebox (E/A)
No Inescapable	Shuttlebox (E/A)	Harness (– –)	Shuttlebox (E/A)
Pre-inescapable	Shuttlebox (*)	Harness (Inesc)	Shuttlebox (E/A)

(*): Shuttlebox condition in which shock was programmed independently of jumping.

(E/A): Shuttlebox condition in which escape or avoidance were contingent on jumping.

Harness (Inesc): Inescapable shock administered in the Pavlovian harness.

Number of Trials: Day 1, 10 trials in each shuttlebox condition.
Day 2, 64 trials in each harness condition.
Day 3, 30 trials for the Pre-escapable and No Inescapable groups; 40 for the other groups.

Before looking at Figure 1 the reader may wish to try to imagine several human subjects whose life histories are analogous to the four conditions shown in Table 3 and then make some prediction as to which group would fare better, which worse. One dependent variable in which Seligman and Maier were interested was the failure to escape in the shuttlebox situation on Day 3, given differing prior experiences on Days 1 and 2. The results are shown in Figure 1:

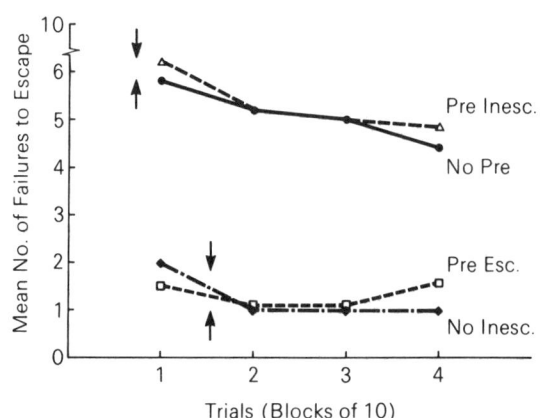

Figure 1
Mean number of failures to escape shock. The position of the arrow denotes whether the harness treatment occurred 24 hours before the first or second block of trials. (Figure 2 of Seligman and Maier, 1967. Copyright 1967 by the American Psychological Association and reproduced by permission.)

Clearly, the dogs with Pre-inescapable or No Pre-escapable histories performed most poorly, while those with Pre-escapable or No Inescapable histories fared pretty well, all things considered. From a clinical standpoint, the research would seem to have demonstrated that the ability to adjust does not necessarily have as a prerequisite a life in which no trauma has been experienced. Trauma *per se* need not be disabling, provided the person undergoing it has learned he can have some control over it when it occurs (as had the dogs in the Pre-escapable condition).

The reader is, however, cautioned against drawing oversimplified conclusions. As Seligman, Maier, and Geer (1968) point out, the contingencies are somewhat more complex:

> Overmier and Seligman (1967) found that if 48 hours elapsed between the inescapable shock in the harness and escape/avoidance training in the shuttlebox, dogs did not show the interference effect. Thus, although experience with inescapable trauma might be a necessary precondition for such maladaptive behavior, it was not a sufficient condition. However, Seligman and Maier (1967) found that the interference effect could be prolonged, perhaps indefinitely. If 24 hours after inescapable shock in the harness the dog passively accepted shock in the shuttlebox, the dog again failed to escape after further rest of 168 hours or longer. Thus, chronic failure to escape occurred when an additional experience with non-escaped shock followed the first experience (p. 258).

While Seligman and his colleagues do not have clinical interests as their primary concern, the concept of "learned helplessness," as they termed it, leads them to allude repeatedly to clinical analogues, as in the following illustrative material from Seligman, Maier, and Geer (1968, p. 258):

> The maladaptive failure of dogs to escape shock resembles some human behavior disorders in which individuals passively accept aversive events without attempting to resist or escape. Bettelheim (1960, pp. 151–152) described the reaction of certain prisoners to the Nazi concentration camps:
>
> "Prisoners who came to believe the repeated statements of the guards— that there was no hope for them, that they would never leave the camp except as a corpse—who came to feel that their environment was one over which they could exercise no influence whatsoever, these prisoners were, in a literal sense, walking corpses. In the camps they were called 'moslems' (*Muselmänner*) because of what was erroneously viewed as a fatalistic surrender to the environment, as Mohammedans are supposed to blandly accept their fate."
>
> ... Bleuler (1950, p. 40) described the passive behavior of some of his patients:

"The sense of self-preservation is often reduced to zero. The patients do not bother any more about whether they starve or not, whether they lie on a snow bank, or on a red-hot oven. During a fire in the hospital, a number of patients had to be led out of the threatened area; they themselves would never have moved from their places; they would have allowed themselves to be burned or suffocated without showing an affective response."

Indeed, while they do not call it such, Seligman, Maier, and Geer (1968) have done some research on "therapy" for dogs suffering from "learned helplessness," pointing out that "such retroactive treatment resembles the traditional treatment of human psychopathology more than does the preventive procedure" (p. 259). Some interesting results followed, as the next section shows.

Treatment

The philosophy of the movement called "community mental health" is that prevention is to be preferred to cure. Needless to say, however, preventive measures on a large scale are, at this stage, still far from a reality. A large share of the work of clinicians still consists of attempts to undo what was not prevented. As reported above, Seligman and Maier (1967) had earlier approached the problem from the preventive end, finding that it did seem possible to "immunize" dogs against later breakdown (in the shuttlebox) by giving them prior experience with *escapable* shock (in the harness). Now Seligman, Maier, and Geer (1968) were interested in approaching the problem from the other end, attempting to "cure" dogs in whom maladaptive behavior had developed. Treatment consisted of two phases. If Phase 1 worked, the dog entered the recovery period; if it did not, Phase 2 was instituted. The procedure was as follows.

Four mongrel dogs were exposed to inescapable shock in the Pavlovian harness, receiving 64 trials of unsignaled shock for a total of 226 seconds. Twenty-four hours later each dog received 10 trials (although one dog avoided shock on one trial). Each dog took 500 seconds of shock in the shuttlebox, where it could readily have escaped simply by jumping over the barrier during the ten-second *CS-UCS* interval — that is, the time between presentation of the conditioned and the unconditioned stimulus (see Walker, 1967). Clearly, then, the investigators had four subjects in need of treatment. (Further confirmation lay in the fact that, when retested in the shuttlebox seven days later, the dogs again failed on every trial to escape shock.)

Phase 1 of the treatment plan was therefore instituted. Here the intent was to make the escape/avoidance response as simple as possible while at the same time encouraging the subject in the attempt. The barrier (which had been shoulder-high) was removed so that in order to escape or avoid shock the dog only had to step over a five-inch divider. In addition, during the *CS-UCS* interval and during shock, an experimenter opened the observation window in the compartment opposite the dog and called "Here, boy." The intent in Phase 1 was thus to get the dog to make the appropriate response *of its own accord.* The treatment succeeded with only one of the four dogs. This dog therefore entered the recovery period, while its mates were given Phase 2 of the treatment program.

Since the three dogs had not exposed themselves to the response-reinforcement contingency—that is, since they had not on their own made the response of stepping into the other compartment where shock would have been terminated—the experimenters instituted "directive" therapy. They forced the dog to make the appropriate response by putting two leashes around its neck, one leading to one end of the shuttlebox, the other to the opposite end. It was thus possible for experimenters standing at each end to drag the dog from one compartment to the other as necessary, in order to have it escape or avoid shock. A maximum of 25 such trials was given per day, and the treatment continued until each dog made the appropriate response on its own.

During the "recovery" period the barrier was gradually raised over 15 trials until it reached shoulder height. Five escape/avoidance trials were given at that point and another five a week later in order to test for the persistence of the new behavior. The results (pre- and post-treatment) are shown in Figure 2.

Without being either called or forced, each subject now escaped or avoided shock on every trial. The dog that had recovered with Phase 1 treatment alone had needed only 20 treatment trials; the dogs that had required Phase 2 recovered with an additional 20, 35, and 50 treatment trials respectively. Accordingly, the experimenters concluded that physically compelling the dogs to make the escape or avoidance response had, indeed, effected recovery. They summarize the results as follows:

> That the dogs escaped and avoided at all after being forcibly exposed to the response-relief contingency confirmed the suggestion that they had initially learned that their responses were independent of shock termination and that this learning was contravened by forcible exposure to the contingency. The finding that so many forced exposures to the contingency were required before they responded on their own (before they "caught on") confirmed the suggestion that the initial learning inhibited the formation of a response-relief association when the dog made a relief-producing response (p. 261).

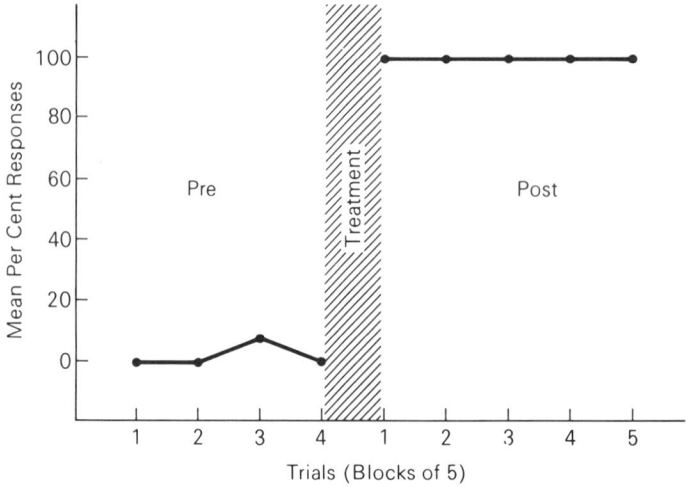

Figure 2
Mean percentage of escape plus avoidance responses before treatment and during post-treatment recovery trials. (Figure 1 of Seligman, Maier, and Geer, 1968. Copyright 1968 by the American Psychological Association and reproduced by permission.)

The dogs used by Solomon, Kamin, and Wynne (1953) needed to learn that no dire consequences would ensue if they remained in a situation that was traumatic originally but had ceased to be. They had learned to make avoidance responses that actually were no longer serviceable. The dogs of Seligman, Maier, and Geer (1968) needed to learn that they were not helpless, that they could do something about their situation. They had learned *not* to make escape responses that would have been serviceable.

Clinical parallels to this situation are not hard to find. The man of 35 who is a confirmed bachelor not because it allows him to "play the field" but because he is avoiding contact with women wherever possible is not unlike Solomon's dogs: he has yet to learn that staying around to interact with women need not be dangerous. And the patients described above by Bleuler (1950) who would not move from a burning building are not unlike Seligman's dogs: they have yet to learn that there *is* something they can do about their situation.

"Learned Helplessness": Human and Animal

Experimenting with different modes of treatment is not always feasible, nor is it always ethical in the case of human subjects; with animals, more freedom is possible. At any rate, other investigators have shed further light on the clinically meaningful concept of helplessness, among them Cannon on the behavior of primitive people and Richter in his experiments with animals.

In his article on "voodoo" death, which antedated by some time the "learned helplessness" concept of Seligman, Cannon (1942) offered some dramatic instances of the potent psychological effects that feelings of helplessness and hopelessness can express in physical terms. A typical account, which he quotes from an observer of the behavior of Nigerian tribesmen, reads as follows:

> "I have seen more than one hardened old Haussa soldier dying steadily and by inches because he believed himself to be bewitched; no nourishment or medicines that were given to him had the slightest effect either to check the mischief or to improve his condition in any way, and nothing was able to divert him from a fate which he considered inevitable. In the same way, and under very similar conditions, I have seen Kru-men and others die in spite of every effort that was made to save them, simply because they had made up their minds, not (as we thought at the time) to die, but that being in the clutch of malignant demons they were bound to die" (p. 169).

Although Cannon, famous for his contributions to neurophysiology, would prefer firsthand physiological data to support the many similar accounts available, he is nevertheless impressed by the phenomenon, remarking: "The suggestion which I offer, therefore, is that voodoo death may be real, and that it may be explained as due to shocking emotional stress—to obvious or repressed terror" (p. 189).

Richter (1957), however, does have firsthand data, having experimented with rats on the phenomenon of "sudden death." Impressed by Cannon's earlier writings on the subject, Richter had made some significant observations of his own. Placing domestic rats in a specially designed water jar, where they had to swim or drown, he found that, on the average, the length of swimming time varied as a function of the water, being shortest at the coldest (65° F.) and warmest (120° F.) temperatures.

Richter was interested, however, in individual differences within the normal group and in a comparison between these tame rats and wild rats in the same situation. In a previous experiment on metabolism he had shaved the rats' whiskers, so that food accidentally carried on them would not confound the results, whereupon, to his surprise, he noticed peculiar behavior on the part of the shaved rats. It occurred to him, therefore, that it would be interesting to note how whiskerless rats might behave in the water jars. The results, in some cases, were dramatic. As he describes the situation: "The first rat swam around excitedly on the surface for a very short time, then dove to the bottom, where it began to swim around, nosing its way along the glass wall. Without coming to the surface a single time, it died two minutes after entering the tank" (p. 194).

But the findings were not clear-cut. Of twelve domesticated rats tested, two more died in a similar way. Yet the other nine swam for as long as 40 to 60 hours. When, however, hybrid rats were tested—that is, rats that were a cross between tame and wild rats—five out of six died within a very brief time. More significantly, in the case of a group of wild rats placed in the water jar after having had their whiskers shaved, the results were especially striking. Richter describes them as follows: "We then tested 34 clipped wild rats, all recently trapped. These animals are characteristically fierce, aggressive, and suspicious; they are constantly on the alert for any avenue of escape and react very strongly to any form of restraint in captivity. All 34 died in 1–15 minutes after immersion in the jars" (p. 194).

It would have been easy to conclude that clipping the rats' whiskers had deprived them of their accustomed means of relating to their environment and consequently led to their apparent resignation. Richter and his team felt a need to look at the picture more completely, however, and analyzed the step-by-step procedure by which such wild rats are caught and handled. Significantly, several of the steps in the process involved situations that could signify hopelessness of escape. It was apparently a *combination* of circumstances—being trapped in a dark bag, being held firmly in the experimenter's hand, being placed in an upright position—all signifying the fate of having been inescapably caught, that resulted in the capitulation of these previously aggressive creatures.

The "clinical" aspects of such behavior become even more interesting as one thinks of how to "treat" such rats, for, several years before Seligman's work, Richter too had made some pertinent observations. He found that the behavior of the rats changed significantly if they were given some chance to experience hope of escaping a traumatic situation. Richter described his efforts thus:

> This is achieved by repeatedly holding the rats briefly and then freeing them, and by immersing them in water for a few minutes on several occasions. In this way the rats quickly learn that the situation is not actually hopeless; thereafter they again become aggressive, try to escape, and show no signs of giving up. Wild rats so conditioned swim just as long as domestic rats or longer (p. 196).

Evidently there are significant implications here for some aspects of human behavior. And apparently, too, recovery of rats in the latter situation and the behavior of natives in the voodoo situation have relevance for the study of response to stress in general and the understanding of certain forms of psychopathology in particular. At any rate, Richter further observed:

> Like the wild rat, primitive man, when freed from voodoo is said to recover almost spontaneously, even though he had recently seemed more dead than alive . . . in human beings as well as in rats we see the possibility that hopelessness and death may result from the effects of a combination of reactions, all of which may operate in the same direction . . . there is the further suggestion that the incidence of this response varies inversely as the degree of civilization, or domestication, of the individual, since it occurs more frequently in wild than in domesticated rats and so far certainly has been described chiefly in primitive man, that is to say, in creatures living in precarious situations (p. 197).

Perhaps at this point, then, it may be well to intermingle research involving human subjects with clinically relevant research in the animal realm. For the purpose of this discussion, let us look at some illustrative studies in the area of aggression.

The Study of Aggression

The theme of aggression figures prominently in a good deal of clinical theory. The psychoanalytic school, for example, dwells heavily on its nature and etiology, looking into such factors as the amount of aggression a person is believed to harbor, the part it plays in his "psychic economy," and how he handles it. Since the concept has such a central role in human adjustment, it becomes important to clarify its characteristics by whatever means are at the disposal of the researcher, theorist, and practitioner. Let us turn to some recent work in animal behavior that offers profitable new sidelights.

Earlier work by Dollard and his colleagues (1939) had provided interesting but oversimplified notions concerning the relation between frustration and aggression; they alleged that frustration invariably led to aggression of some sort, while aggression, in turn, always betrayed the existence of prior frustration. Miller (1941), one of the investigators, soon came to question the inevitability of such relationships, suggesting instead that aggression was only one response among several to which frustration might lead. On the other hand, Buss (1961) points out that psychologists, with few exceptions (Maslow, 1941; Rosenzweig, 1944), tended until recently to assume that the other half of the original theory was correct—namely, that the appearance of aggression attested to prior frustration. In his comprehensive review, Buss (1961) offered an amended theory that frustration *may* lead to aggression but also to other responses and, conversely, that aggression *may* be caused by frustration but stem also from other sources.

Prominent as it is, aggression has struck the fancy of many researchers as an interesting focus of investigation. Thus, in 1945 McClelland and Apicella were attempting to study the consequences of frustration by experimentally inducing failure in laboratory situations by presenting subjects with an ostensibly solvable, although actually insoluble, task. To make matters worse, the subjects were roundly "bawled out" in the course of their efforts for their apparent ineptitude. (It should be added that in a subsequent debriefing session the design of the experiment was explained to the subjects; their general reaction, as the experimenters describe it, was ". . . to swear a little in relief . . . and then to become very interested in the experiment" [p. 378]). Although there was some correlation between the degree of the experimenter's (feigned) hostility and the counteraggressiveness of subjects, aggression was only one of several responses to the frustration induced by the experimental situation.

Berkowitz and Geen (1966), whose work will be discussed in a later section, have devised their own ingenious methods for creating laboratory situations in which to study how aggression is elicited and discharged against others. Nor has the "treatment" of aggression gotten short shrift from clinical psychologists and psychiatrists conducting exploratory studies. Thus, Kidd and Walton (1966) investigated the efficacy of dart-throwing by aggressive youngsters as a means of reducing aggression, with pictures of familiar persons as targets (perhaps akin to the older practice of sticking pins in one's enemy). While the treatment period consisted of only four weekly half-hour sessions, aggression toward peers and authority figures declined appreciably, although the experimental group did not improve significantly more than a control group in aggression directed toward parents and siblings. (The results were confounded, however, by the disproportionate amount of time spent in throwing darts at the respective targets.)

Gittelman (1965) developed a novel procedure for the treatment of aggressive youngsters, using "behavior rehearsal" as his technique. The method consisted of helping the youngsters learn to control themselves by having them actually *practice* restraint in contrived situations that would normally provoke their aggression. With the help of the youngster concerned, Gittelman proceeded first to analyze what types of situations made the latter "mad," then created a hierarchy of such situations (from those described as least aggression-provoking to those designated most aggression-provoking). In a quasinatural setting, the particular youngster then served as the target, while his fellow subjects acted as instigators in a variety of situations designed to provoke him to aggression.

The resultant behavior of the one being provoked was subsequently rated by his peers and the therapist on a scale running from −2 (striking out overtly) through zero (neutral response) to +2 (making a verbal, rather than physical, response designed to mollify the instigator). Every boy was willing to take his turn as the target, knowing he too would have the chance to play instigator for someone else, thereby indulging his own aggression in a socially acceptable context. This approach proved successful in reducing the aggressive behavior of boys who had failed to respond to earlier efforts by persons using more orthodox techniques.

The above constitute a small sample of the efforts of those using human subjects in an effort to clarify the dynamics of aggression. Let us return, however, to the contributions animal research can make to the understanding of human behavior.

Animal Research on Aggression

As often happens in research, Azrin's research in animal aggression yielded an unexpected discovery that proved more interesting than the object of his original quest. Originally he was interested in teaching rats to interact with each other. The easy way would have been positive reinforcement, such as rewarding two rats with food whenever they made an approach movement toward each other. However, Azrin was interested in achieving the same result by negative reinforcement. If the rats were subjected to electric shock (a noxious stimulus), which was terminated as soon as they made any approach responses, approach behavior should increase in frequency.

The results (Azrin, 1967) were unanticipated—and more interesting than those sought. Instantaneously upon presentation of brief shock, the rats made what looked like attack responses, rearing up on their hind legs, baring their teeth, and slashing at each other with their paws. Such attacks, which lasted about one second, did not seem mere startle reactions; they occurred each time shock was turned on, showing no tendency to adaptation. Also, they had a reflexlike quality, occurring in many other species (raccoons, roosters, alligators, and snakes, among others), and found even in rats raised in isolation (so that learning did not seem to be a factor). Further, they seemed to occur with "push-button" effect, each species attacking instantaneously and in its own style.

The universality of the reaction (the attacks were made on any conveniently available object—an animal of the same or different species, a stuffed animal, even a tennis ball) and its clearly observable and definable character suggested that theorists and researchers interested in the area of aggression had a golden opportunity here to study the phenomenon. Indeed, by shaving a monkey's tail, attaching an electrode, harnessing the animal so that it could not escape, and providing a rubber tube as its only object of aggression, Azrin was able to establish objectively the relationship between pain (electric shock) and "aggression" (biting on the rubber tube), as his "bitometer" automatically recorded the behavior of the animals.

There are several clinically relevant issues here. For example, what outcomes might be expected when two subjects under conditions of periodic shock had options of attacking one another or of leaving the field (that is, escaping from the painful situation)? It was to questions of this sort that Azrin and his co-workers next addressed themselves. Escape conditioning, as in the study of Solomon, Kamin, and Wynne (1953) described earlier, is usually carried out with a single animal. In Azrin's study, there were two animals present in every case, but there was no opportunity for escape. Azrin, Hutchinson, and Hake (1967) put the situations together in a sense—aversive stimuli were administered with two animals present, but this time one of the animals had a possibility for escape. Figure 3 shows a schematic drawing of the arrangement.

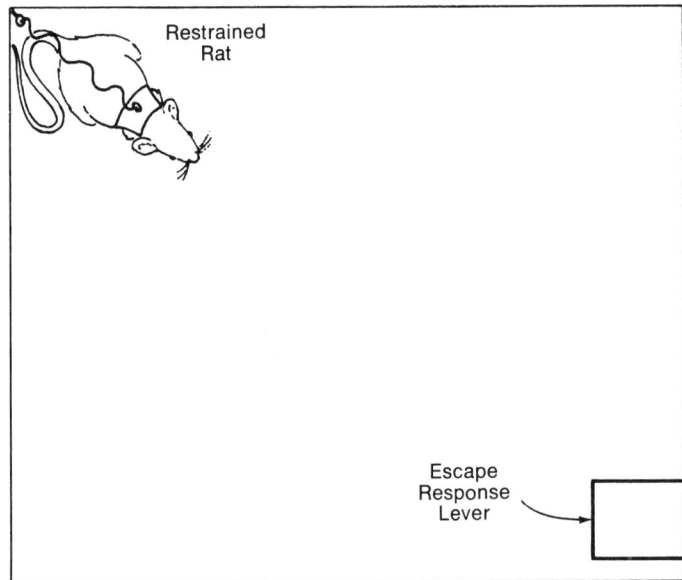

Figure 3
Schematic drawing of chamber used in studying escape and attack behavior. (Figure 1 of Azrin, Hutchinson, & Hake, 1967. Copyright 1967 by the Society for the Experimental Analysis of Behavior, Inc., and reproduced by permission.)

The target rat was placed on a plastic plate, so that it would be insulated from whatever shock was to be administered through the floor grid; by the same token, since it was restrained, it had no chance to escape from the chamber. The other rat would experience shock when it was applied, although, since it was not restrained like its partner, it could escape if it learned to press the escape lever shown in the drawing. Shock, when administered, was on for one second at a time. It could not be avoided, but it could be terminated by a lever press; that is, escape, but not avoidance, was possible. Azrin et al. were interested in several aspects of the experimental situation that could influence an attack reaction to the shock experience. Would rats conditioned individually learn the escape response more quickly than animals conditioned in the social situation (that is, in the presence of a restrained rat)? Once the escape response was learned, would it continue to predominate, or would it yield to the attack reaction? If the escape response became the more dominant of the two, would making it more demanding (for example, requiring several lever presses rather than one for shock termination) affect its frequency of occurrence in relation to the alternative attack response?

Although animals are the subjects here, the reader may wish to extrapolate from such questions to analogous situations in human relationships. For, as will be shown in a later section, investigators in other areas have been directly interested in the conditions that foster or inhibit, trigger or curtail, human aggression. Since an appreciable amount of clinical theory involves the dynamics of aggression, the parameters of such behavior constitute a critical domain of inquiry.

The questions posed by Azrin and his colleagues are of clinical interest. Let us look at their series of findings. First was the matter of whether animals exposed to the unavoidable but terminable shock in an individual situation would learn the escape response (that is, the lever press that terminated shock) more, less, or equally as quickly as those in the social situation (that is, in the presence of the restrained rat). Figure 4 tells the story.

As shown, the individually trained rats showed the escape response appreciably more frequently from the beginning than did the other group which, even after its probability of using the escape response had increased, still alternated between escape and attack after 500 trials. Since the various data points represent an average of the responses of groups of ten rats, the line showing the responses of the rats in the social situation includes the record of four rats in the social group which did not learn to escape. This failure to learn may have been an artifact, since, as the experimenters note: "These four rats spent the major portion of the session near the target rat and facing away from the response lever, a position that appeared to preclude the

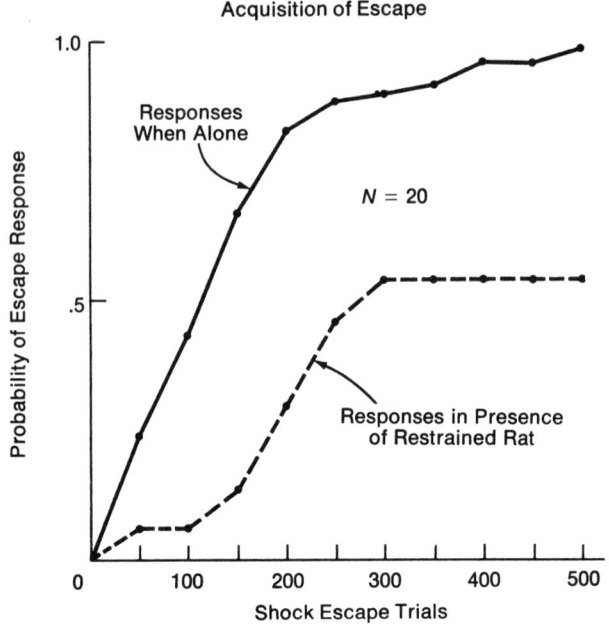

Figure 4
Acquisition of the escape response (lever press). The probability of escape was calculated by dividing the number of shocks that the rat terminated by the number of shocks delivered. This probability of escape was calculated for successive groups of 100 shock deliveries or trials. Each data point is the averaged performance of 10 rats. The solid curve is for the rats that were alone in the experimental chamber; the dotted curve is for the rats that were paired with a restrained target rat. (Figure 2 of Azrin, Hutchinson, & Hake, 1967. Copyright 1967 by the Society for the Experimental Analysis of Behavior, Inc., and reproduced by permission.)

opportunity to learn to escape the shock [although they did at times 'accidentally' achieve the response by brushing up against it with their tails or bodies]" (p. 133).

Would the nonlearners have behaved otherwise, had they learned the escape response, so that it was available to them as an alternative to the attack reaction? To investigate the question, the experimenters trained one of the four nonlearners in an individual situation, where, like the other individually trained rats, it learned the escape reaction. At the point where it was escaping 97% of the shocks, it was reintroduced into the social situation—that is, the chamber containing a restrained rat. The result: ". . . the escape response predominated, and the attack reaction was reduced to near zero" (p. 134).

The findings suggest that aggression is an inevitable response under the circumstances in which Azrin et al. induced it *only when* an alternative response is not available. In this connection it is interesting to note the progressive behavior of the rats who did learn the escape response during the series of 500 trials. The course of the attack and the escape responses for the six learners in the social situation is shown in Figure 5.

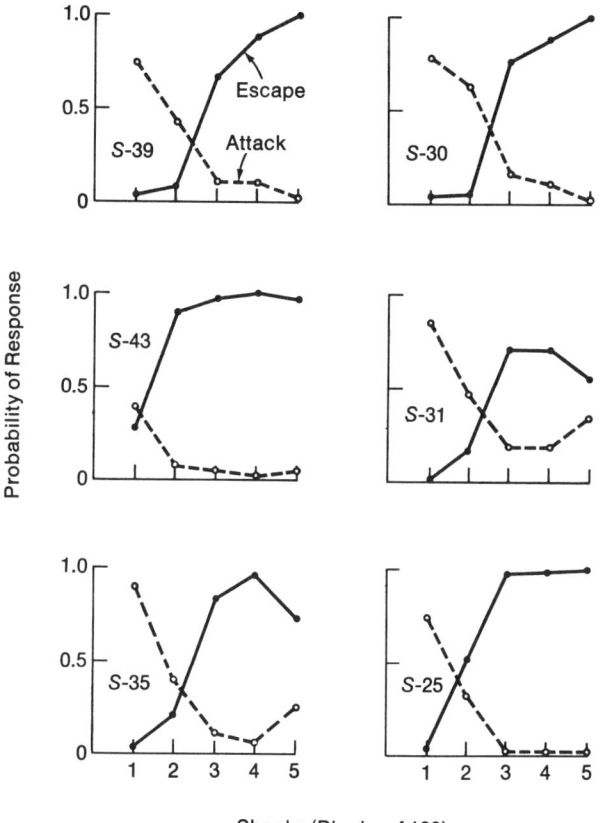

Figure 5
Probability of escape (solid line) and of attack (dashed line) for each of six rats that were given escape conditioning in the presence of a restrained target rat. Each data point represents the proportion of shocks that resulted in attack or escape. (Figure 3 of Azrin, Hutchinson, & Hake, 1967. Copyright 1967 by the Society for the Experimental Analysis of Behavior, Inc., and reproduced by permission.)

Here the inverse relationship between attack and escape is apparent; the former declines, the latter becomes predominant. But in order to be able to say something more definitive about the relationship, the experimenters felt it necessary to manipulate another variable—namely, the complexity of the escape response. Granted that the latter becomes dominant over the attack reaction when escape involves a simple, single lever press, what would the situation be if escape required greater effort, say three lever presses, or five, or even seven? (Since each shock lasted only 1 second, the number of lever presses to be required for escape could, of course, not be raised beyond the point where that number could not realistically be made within the course of 1 second). The fixed ratio for successful escape was raised after every 100 trials, so that two lever presses were required after 200 trials, three after 300 trials, and so on. The results under this arrangement, in which escape required progressively more effort, are shown in Figure 5.

In the case of each of four rats run under these conditions, it is evident that the more demanding the requirements become for the escape response, the less frequently does the escape response occur. In the individual situation it declines progressively as the required lever presses are stepped up, while in the social situation it gives way to the attack reaction in the inverse relationship previously noted in Figure 6.

One may well speculate about the clinical implications for human behavior on the basis of three points that stand out in the animal experimentation:
1. given no alternative in a pain-shock situation, attack against another object (even an inanimate one) seems inevitable;
2. given the alternative of escape, attack predominates until the escape reaction has been learned, from which point on escape becomes the predominant response;
3. in a situation with such alternatives, escape remains dominant up to the point at which it requires excessive effort, whereupon it gives way to the attack reaction.

As Azrin (1967) reports elsewhere, it seems that "pain-evoked aggression can be controlled or eliminated by establishing effective, peaceful means for avoiding the pain" (p. 32).

Granted, clinicians are not directly concerned with animal behavior; furthermore, one cannot always extrapolate with impunity from the findings of animal research to human behavior. At the same time, one can subject animals to the kind of experimental manipulations not possible with people (choosing primates like the monkey if one feels the usual white rat too low an order of species) in order to find fresh leads relevant to the continuing study of human behavior. If this leaves one still feeling that the animal findings are too many steps removed from man, and if one maintains his

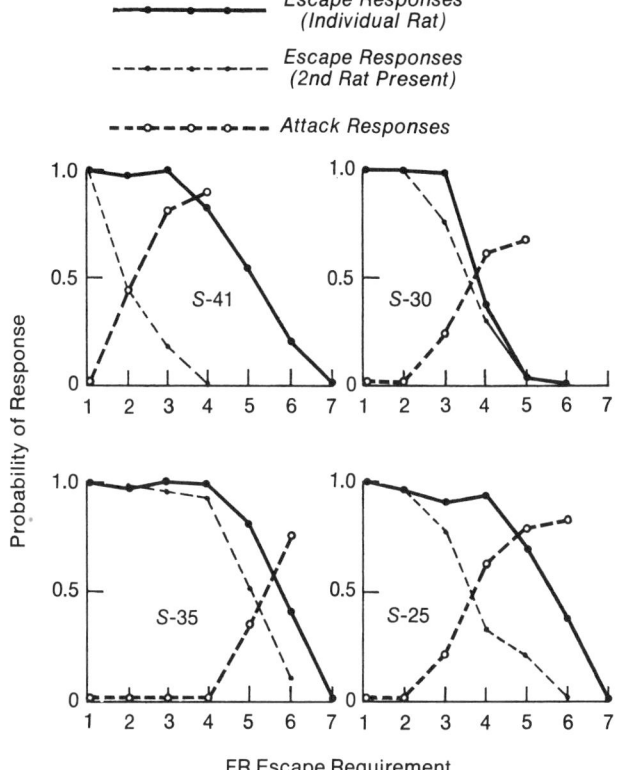

Figure 6
Probability of escape and attack during escape conditioning under different fixed-ratio (FR) escape requirements for each of four rats. The "FR escape requirement" designates the number of lever presses required to terminate a shock. The solid curve shows the escape responses of the rat when it was alone in the experimental chamber. The broken curves are for the escape (dotted curve) and attack (dashed curve) responses of the same rat when a restrained target rat was present in the chamber. Each data point is the average of two sessions. Probability is calculated as the proportion of shocks on which an escape (or attack) response occurred. (Figure 4 of Azrin, Hutchinson, & Hake, 1967. Copyright 1967 by the Society of the Experimental Analysis of Behavior, Inc., and reproduced by permission.)

interest in staying informed about the work of nonclinical psychologists whose contributions might shed further light on matters of direct clinical concern, one might profitably look at the research of those social psychologists who use human subjects exclusively, concerned with such areas as aggression. Berkowitz has been a leading figure in such investigation, and his continuing program of research in the area merits serious attention. Because the construct of aggression plays such a central role in much of clinical theory, it is worthwhile to look at some typical studies by Berkowitz and his colleagues.

Aggression Involving Human Subjects

As indicated in Chapter 3, laboratory experimentation does have some aura of artificiality about it. Therefore, when one studies a phenomenon like aggression in the laboratory, the emotion elicited and expressed may not have quite the texture of the raw brand of aggression one sees, for example, when two street gangs lock horns. But such natural, unrestrained emotions can seldom be caught by the experimenter's shutter—the cameraman is not always around, and, even if he were, the aggressors might hardly be in a mood to "watch the birdie." Furthermore, even if it were possible to catch aggression in the raw (as in these days of predictable confrontation), it would be difficult, in such a fast-moving situation, to objectify and measure the reactions in any but the grossest ways. While laboratory-produced aggression is, then, perhaps somewhat less full-blown than its real counterpart, the latter proves relatively intractable to direct study.

In a creative series of experiments, Berkowitz and his colleagues have contrived laboratory situations designed to study the dynamics of aggression at close range by eliciting it under controlled conditions where it can be assessed objectively in relation to its immediate antecedents. With the help of a confederate, regarded as a fellow subject by the real, unsuspecting subject, Berkowitz and Geen (1966) devised an elaborate procedure allegedly dealing with "problem-solving under stress" but actually designed to measure the course of aggression objectively. The experimental subject was given a written task to perform (such as proposing techniques by which a gas-station owner might attract new customers), and his product was then presumably evaluated by his fellow subject. From a separate room the latter would administer an electric shock or shocks to the real subject (who was strapped to an apparatus) to reflect his evaluation of the written product, the number of shocks ranging from 1 (satisfactory) to 10 (very poor). Other things being equal, a subject who received seven shocks for an essay he thought was pretty good was thereby presumed to be more angry than one who had received only a single shock (an assumption borne out by questionnaires completed by the subjects after they had been shocked). The experimenters intended to achieve two conditions in otherwise comparable groups—anger (in the group that received seven shocks) and nonanger (in the group that received only one shock). The number of shocks to be administered by the bogus subject had actually been decided in advance for each group and bore no relation to the actual quality of the written productions.

Of interest to the investigators was how the subjects in the two groups—angry and nonangry—would compare when given a chance to reciprocate—that is, to evaluate the product of their fellow subject, dispensing shocks to him in turn. (Each of the subjects was to receive the identical essay for evaluation, one decided upon in advance of the experiment.) But, to add another dimension, Berkowitz and Geen interpolated an additional experience between receipt of shock by the real subjects and their administration of shock to their partners. Subjects in the two conditions, angry and nonangry, were further divided into two subgroups. Each viewed arousing movie films. One film dealt with the theme of aggression (a seven-minute sequence from *Champion,* in which Kirk Douglas takes a severe beating in the boxing ring); the other was exciting but nonaggressive (a seven-minute sequence showing the first man to run the mile in the record time of four minutes). As part of the total procedure the groups had been subdivided from the start, subjects in one case having the peer introduced to them as Bob Anderson and in the other as *Kirk* Anderson, a variable to be analyzed in relation to whether the film viewed had or had not involved *Kirk* Douglas. (In checking on the authenticity of the results, the investigators found, at the conclusion of the experiment, that all 88 University of Wisconsin undergraduates who had served as subjects recalled correctly the name of their respective partners as well as the number of shocks they had received.)

Here then was a 2 × 2 × 2 design—two emotional conditions (angry or not angry), two arousal conditions (the aggression-laden fight film or the nonaggressive race film), and two different target persons (Kirk, associated with the aggressive Kirk Douglas film, and Bob, unrelated to aggression). The experimenters were concerned with the extent to which the two groups would differ in the amount of aggression they expressed (as measured by the number of shocks they administered to their respective peers). The results are shown in Table 4.

Table 4
Mean number of shocks delivered by actual subjects to presumed fellow subjects.

Accomplice's Name	Aggressive Film		Track Film	
	Angered	Nonangered	Angered	Nonangered
Kirk	6.09_a	1.73_c	4.18_b	1.54_c
Bob	4.55_b	1.45_c	4.00_b	1.64_c

Note: Cells having a subscript in common are not significantly different from each other. (Table 2 of Berkowitz & Geen, 1966. Copyright 1966 by the American Psychological Association and reproduced by permission.)

It would seem that aggression can, indeed, be aroused and controlled in a laboratory situation. The subscripts in Table 4 identify significant differences among the various experimental conditions; where subscripts are the same, there is no significant difference between figures shown; where they differ, a statistically significant difference exists. In the nonangered condition, for example, where all four cells carry the subscript c, there is no significant difference among any of them; whether subjects are aroused by the aggressive or nonaggressive film and whether their peer is called Kirk or Bob does not influence the number of shocks nonangered subjects administer to their fellow subjects. When one looks at the angered groups, however, some interesting results are found. First, all four of the subgroups differed significantly from the nonangered groups, in that the angered groups administered significantly more shocks than the nonangered. And, second, the identity of the peer does not affect the amount of aggression (number of shocks directed toward him) when arousal is achieved through nonaggressive means (via the track film), but when arousal has been produced by a situation connoting aggression (the fight film), it does matter whether the peer has an identification (his name) with aggression. Kirk, who is identifiable with the central figure in the fight film received significantly more shocks from the angered group that had viewed the Kirk Douglas film.

One might wonder whether the peer would have received more shocks as well if his name had been associated with the nonaggressive film; that is, it might be that association with *any* arousing scene, whether aggressive or nonaggressive, would make the target person vulnerable. A subsequent experiment of this sort in which the peer's name was associated with the nonaggressive film did not, however, result in his receiving significantly more shocks than the peer not so associated. What conclusions might one then draw about the expression of aggression in general? Berkowitz and Geen summarize their findings thus: "Observed aggression . . . does not necessarily lead to open aggression against anyone. Particular targets are most likely to be attacked and these are objects having appropriate, aggression-eliciting cue properties" (p. 529).

Such controlled experimentation can contribute to a clearer understanding of the factors influencing aggression. And the findings are of more than academic interest to the clinical psychologist who, along with psychologists in other areas, may well find himself asked to serve as an expert witness on the subject. Clinical psychologists are increasingly called to testify in court cases where the issue is whether the defendant in a murder trial committed his act as a consequence of "mental disease or defect." (The reader may remember newspaper accounts of such trials, involving the assassination of some prominent political figures, in which the testimony of the psychologists received considerable adverse publicity.) Further, clinicians are increasingly being sought as consultants in matters of public policy involving the problem of aggression in various forms. What factors lead to the eruption of violence on campus? What are the determinants of conflict between the races in the Marine Corps, where open conflict had previously been absent? Should stricter gun-control legislation be passed?

The answers to such questions are seldom simple; in fact, in some cases they are not yet available. The questions are nonetheless legitimate and pressing, and as consultant on social problems it is up to the clinician to keep abreast of the contributions of his colleagues in other areas of psychology, in order to be able to integrate relevant findings with his own knowledge. In this connection, the work of Berkowitz and LePage (1967) not only speaks to particular issues (for example, gun-control legislation) but also contributes to the understanding of aggression in general.

The clinician feels a need to help a troubled person distinguish between thoughts and acts. It is one thing to be angry at one's father, another to strike him; it is one thing to be sexually aroused by someone else's wife, another to attempt to seduce her. Berkowitz and LePage were interested in the expression of aggression but particularly in the degree to which stimuli associated with aggression might increase the probability of its actual occurrence in people predisposed to act aggressively. While congressmen and lobbyists debated the merits and demerits of gun-control laws, these investigators attempted controlled research on the psychological factors at issue.

One hundred male undergraduates taking an introductory psychology course at the University of Wisconsin volunteered to serve as subjects in the experiment, with no prior knowledge of its nature. The general design was patterned after that of Berkowitz and Geen, with the real subjects of each pair again being treated in a way intended to make them angry (seven shocks) or nonangry (one shock). The partner, a confederate of the experimenter, was again presented as a legitimate subject, in this case being described either as an undergraduate who had wanted to sign up for another experiment or as a student running a separate experiment. Two additional differences entered this design. First, in some conditions subjects found certain objects lying on the table near the shock key as they prepared to administer shocks to their partners—weapons in one case and neutral objects (a badminton racquet and shuttlecocks) in the other; no objects except the shock key were present in the control group. A second difference lay in the identification of the alleged owner of the weapons. In one case they were said to belong "to someone else" who "must have been doing an experiment in here" (unassociated weapons condition). In the other they were said to belong to the subject's partner, previously referred to as a student doing research in some other study (associated weapons condition).

The thrust of the experiment by Berkowitz and LePage, then, was to study the influence of the presence of weapons on the instigation to aggression (measured by number of shocks delivered to one's partner) as well as the possible effect of an association between the weapons and a person toward whom one felt angry. The results are shown in Table 5.

Table 5
Mean number of shocks delivered by actual subjects to presumed fellow subjects.

Condition	Shocks Received	
	1	7
Associated weapons	2.60_a	6.07_d
Unassociated weapons	2.20_a	5.67_{cd}
No object	3.07_a	4.67_{bc}
Badminton racquets	—	4.60_b

Note: Cells having a subscript in common are not significantly different from each other. (Table 2 of Berkowitz & LePage, 1967. Copyright 1967 by the American Psychological Association and reproduced by permission.)

There is little doubt that being angry made a difference. The angered (7-shocks) subjects in each condition delivered significantly more shocks to their offending partners than did the subjects in any of the nonangered (1-shock) conditions. Further, within the angry condition, subjects administered significantly more shocks in the presence of weapons than did those in the neutral (badminton racquet) settings. Finally, although the difference is not statistically significant, the angered subjects who associated weapons with their offending partner delivered more shocks as a group than did those who associated the weapons with someone else.

Berkowitz (1968) elsewhere sums up the implications of such results for gun-control legislation in his reminder that ". . . guns not only permit violence, they can stimulate it as well. The finger pulls the trigger, but the trigger may also be pulling the finger" (p. 22). The more clinical implications of his program of research are hinted at by Berkowitz elsewhere in the same article:

> Both common sense and personality theory tend to neglect the weapons effect. . . . Instead, they stress motives . . . what is often overlooked, perhaps because it is a frightening idea, is that much violence is *impulsive*. It is not primarily planned, purposeful activity; neither is it the inevitable result of internal drives or maladjustment. These things set the stage and help carry the action forward but in many cases it is also important that there be a stimulus or immediate cue to trigger aggression.

It is quite conceivable that many hostile acts which supposedly stem from unconscious motivation really arise because of the operation of aggressive cues. The aggression can even be thought of as a conditioned response to the stimulus (p. 19).

In clinical work it is common to view the feelings of others as coming from the wellsprings of their being, and indeed they do. By the same token, however, it is possible to underestimate, or even overlook, the cue properties of a person's external environment, particularly with regard to interpersonal perception, that may serve as powerful determinants of his thoughts, feelings, and actions. If the work of social psychologists like Berkowitz, or even animal experimenters like Azrin, helps the clinical psychologist put the various factors in clearer perspective, clinical efforts become the better for it.

Indeed, it is worth our while to look yet further, for, in the hands of imaginative investigators, present technology yields still other promising leads.

Technological Inventiveness

In our increasingly electronic age, it is not surprising that one should find technological aids employed in research on animal and human behavior. The electronic pacemaker worn by cardiac patients has received its share of attention, as have the electronic devices that aid people with paralyzed limbs. Less widely known, however, is research on the application of electronics to the control of psychological behavior, both with "normal" people who, for example, have trouble controlling assaultive rages, and with patients with disorders serious enough to require institutionalization.

Again, the origins of such applications lie in prior research with animals, and here one of the foremost researchers is José Delgado, who has been carrying on an extensive series of studies with monkeys in his laboratory at the Yale University School of Medicine. His research on aggression, as triggered by stimulation of certain portions of the brain, is of particular clinical interest. Let us therefore look at some typical studies and their findings.

Others, working with rats (for example, Olds and Milner, 1954), have experimented with the implantation of electrodes in animals' brains in order to map such areas as a "pleasure center" or a "pain center." The behavioral correlates would typically consist of a rat's performance at such tasks as lever-pressing to obtain electrical stimulation through electrodes implanted in certain areas or to avoid noxious stimulation from electrodes implanted in others.

As a rule, rats were studied individually. However, although the wire to which they were attached did not appreciably hamper their movement, it did limit the possibilities for having a number of rats roam about together. Using the techniques of electrode implantation, Delgado has introduced features in his studies of monkey behavior that overcome these limitations. He implants subcutaneous leads connecting the terminal socket of the electrodes to a radio pack carried on the monkey's back, which makes it possible to provide brain stimulation by telemetry, obviating the need for loose-hanging wires that could get entangled. In addition, he studies the monkeys not in individual cages but in colonies—that is, in the context of the social situation provided by the presence of a group of monkeys. Such a combination of features makes the arousal and expression of aggression accessible to study in more natural social settings.

Aggressive behavior is, indeed, easy to produce by radio telemetry, as Delgado (1967) has shown. A film, *Radio Stimulation of the Brain in Monkey Colonies,* provides graphic evidence that, at the touch of the experimenter's button, monkeys display a predictable series of behaviors, depending on which area of the brain is stimulated. Thus, in literally push-button fashion, they can be made to bare their teeth, crouch, emit vocalizations, and so on, all in stereotyped fashion according to which area of the brain receives radio stimulation. Of greater interest to Delgado, however—and to clinicians interested in the implications of his work for their own field—are less stereotyped and more complex phenomena such as the elicitation and execution of aggressive behavior. Given a monkey equipped with radio stimulator and free to roam about in a colony of monkeys in a sizeable laboratory cage, how does he behave—not only motorically, but especially socially—as he receives stimulation to areas of the brain associated with the display of aggressive behavior?

Delgado cites some examples of the interesting behaviors elicited:[2]

> Aggression between friendly animals: in monkeys, the aggressiveness evoked by stimulation of the nucleus ventralis posterolateralis of the thalamus, or of the central gray, was very seldom or never directed against animals with whom relations were peaceful. In cats, however, as soon as one animal was stimulated in the tectal area, ferocious fights occurred between previously friendly animals; after a few repetitions of the experiment a state of distrust developed, and the cats snarled and hissed at each other even without provocation (p. 183). [Delgado cautions against drawing parallels between such aggressive behavior in cats, which are by nature predatory animals, and nonpredatory monkeys and men].

[2] From Delgado, 1967. Originally published by the University of California Press. Reprinted by permission of the author and the Regents of the University of California.

> Aggression of the boss monkey against the group: electrical stimulation of areas involved in antagonistic behavior evoked well-organized attacks in boss monkeys directed against specific animals, but affecting the entire colony, except for the bosses' special friend, second in rank, who usually escaped attack . . . (p. 183).
>
> Increase in aggression resulting in superior rank: stimulation of the central gray in two monkeys who each ranked second in its colony of five evoked running around the cage and sometimes smashing against other animals, including the boss, who did not retaliate but retired to the swing or to a corner, leaving a greater amount of territory for the stimulated monkey (p. 183).

Like the clinician concerned with interpersonal relations, Delgado is interested not in the phenomenon of aggression in isolation but in the manner in which it is displayed in inter-monkey relationships. And evidently, while stimulation of certain areas of the brain will instigate aggressive behavior as such, the form it takes is largely a function of the social context in which the aggression plays itself out. For that matter, stimulation of other areas of the brain has an inhibitory function on the expression of aggression. Delgado cites the following examples:

> Inhibition of aggression resulting in loss of rank: caudate nucleus stimulation is known to produce inhibitory effects . . . , including a decrease in offensive-defensive reaction. . . . Within the colony, telestimulation of the caudate nucleus did not modify nestling, balling, lying down or being groomed, but inhibited aggression so effectively during the period of excitation that the boss could safely be touched with bare hands and easily caught inside the cage. These stimulations produced a marked change in the social structure of the colony. Territoriality of the boss diminished, and the other monkeys circled freely, approaching him without signs of submissiveness (p. 183).
>
> Inhibition of aggression by heterostimulation: a subordinate monkey learned to press a lever located inside the cage which activated radio stimulation of the caudate nucleus in the boss, inhibiting its aggressiveness, and even stopping it while chasing another animal (p. 183).

At the conference at which Delgado presented these findings, some of the participants had their own explanation of the phenomena reported. Interestingly, one of them sees a connection with the research of Schachter and Singer (1962), to be described in Chapter 15. Thus, Scott (1967) remarks:

> It seems to me that they [the results of the radio stimulation] can be interpreted fairly easily: what is happening to the animal, in all probability, is simply that it is getting some sort of internal sensation from the electrical stimulation, which may be similar to sensations it normally receives, or perhaps sensations which normally are never active at the same time.

However, what the animal actually does in this situation is to look around in an apparently puzzled fashion, as if to try to discover what in the world has happened to it. Then it proceeds to interpret its internal sensations in terms of the outside stimuli and other features of the situation, and acts accordingly. The results do not require a very complicated interpretation, but simply that the experimenter has hit some center in the brain which produces a sensation similar to a normally experienced emotional sensation (p. 188).

Such findings cannot help but suggest some applications in the area of human behavior that are at once intriguing and awesome. In fact, Delgado himself has already been experimenting with its use in helping people given to periodic assaultive rages to control their behavior by receiving telemetered radio stimulation to implanted electrodes. Although such control sounds like somewhat gruesome science fiction, it is now within the realm of possibility to monitor the behavior of people at a distance and to telemeter to them radio stimulation that will help control behavior that has been causing them difficulty. A recent account of some experimental work by Schwitzgebel (1968) describes his monitoring of the location of parolees who were willing to carry a small radio pack on their person for the purpose. In this way the investigator was able to plot their whereabouts within a restricted section of the community, much as the air-traffic controller plots the positions of incoming and outgoing planes on his radar grid.

If some of this experimentation smacks of Orwell's *1984,* it may be well to point out that control of human behavior by electrophysiological means is still far from accomplished. Perhaps the investigator who has most directly studied the possibilities with humans is Heath (Heath & Mickle, 1960), who worked with psychiatric patients in an effort to establish measures to which they might respond in a way that would ameliorate their condition. Having implanted electrodes in various portions of the brain of his subjects, he proceeded over several years to study the effects of systematic application of electrostimulation. The dramatic consequences in some instances may be noted in such excerpts as the following (1954), which describes the case of a 27-year-old male with the diagnosis of schizophrenic reaction, hebephrenic type, who on readmission to the hospital was described as ". . . silly, . . . apathetic, uninterested in his surroundings . . ." (p. 549):

> During the stimulation to the rostral part of the septal region the patient perceptibly brightened, smiled, recognized a number of the doctors about him, and became more productive. When the same area was stimulated again, his voice seemed much louder as he said, "I'm starting to wake up." During the third stimulation the patient again showed progressive brightening and alertness as the current was increased. During the fourth

stimulation the results were more equivocal; the patient was seemingly more productive and described a dream that indicated some of his anal preoccupation and hostility (Heath & Monroe, pp. 550–551).

Suggestive as such findings were, Heath and Mickle (1960) felt obliged some time later to review systematically the work of the previous decade. That they were far from convinced they had found an overall solution is evident from the following:

> We have reviewed our experiences with depth electrode studies over the past 7 years. We believe that data we have gathered have been useful in extending our studies in schizophrenia. . . . Results with the therapeutic procedures recently used have not been sufficiently good to warrant our recommending stimulation through depth electrodes as a therapy for schizophrenia (p. 240).

It should be clear to the reader by now that, while the problem of human behavior has been studied from what looks like every conceivable angle—in animals as well as humans, biologically, psychologically, electrophysiologically, socially, among others—the behavioral scientist is hardly about to run out of unanswered questions. Increments of knowledge seem to raise new questions as often as answer old ones. The clinician hoping for new challenges will not have far to look, as the following chapter on stress and conflict will attest.

6
The Analysis of Conflict

Like death and taxes, stress and conflict seem inevitable. As has been pointed out, even the task of choosing between two equally attractive alternatives (two luscious desserts, for example) represents a conflict—an "approach-approach conflict." In contrast, the "avoidance-avoidance conflict," a situation in which the choice is between two undesirable alternatives (going to the dentist versus tolerating a toothache), presents more of a problem. And, as Miller (1959) has shown, the "approach-avoidance conflict," where the same object or situation contains both positive and negative features (being in love with a divorced woman whom one, as a good Catholic, is not supposed to marry), is even more troublesome.

Yet the inevitable is not always undesirable, and stress, while temporarily unpleasant, may serve a purpose. Levine (1960) found, to his surprise, that rats subjected daily to mildly stressful electric shock turned out to be healthier—both psychologically and biologically—than a comparable group of rats that were never handled by the experimenter. Yet, as Selye (1956) has pointed out in a book entitled *The Stress of Life,* prolonged stress that an organism cannot cope with effectively may have devastating consequences.

Assuming, then, that stress is inevitable and that a person's methods for coping with it are central to the understanding of his behavior, it becomes a highly pertinent area for clinical research and theory. Three methods of exploration suggest themselves: (1) clinical data-gathering (for example, via personality tests); (2) systematic study of natural events (for example, analysis of suicide notes); (3) experimental manipulation (for example, the induction of stress under controlled laboratory conditions). Let us look at each in turn.

Clinical Data-Gathering

Psychological tests used in the study of personality cover a wide range. In contrast to the personality inventories, which ask pointed questions (for example, "Do you often cross the street to avoid meeting people?"), the projective tests present material that is purposely vague, ambiguous, and unstructured. The set of inkblots originally devised by Rorschach (1921) is a good example. These meaningless blots elicit all kinds of responses that clinical psychologists regard as clues to personality structure. It seems intuitively reasonable to assume, for example, that a person who sees in the blots such things as "bullets piercing flesh," "splattered blood," "a tornado," "an atomic cloud," and percepts of a similar character may well be experiencing more stress than one who typically sees "fields of ripe hay in the sunshine," "pretty orchids," "a lagoon," "cows grazing in a pasture."

If such assumptions are well founded, one can go on to investigate how a person seems to handle the degree of stress he experiences. For this purpose the Thematic Appercention Test (TAT) is a useful projective technique. Again the stimulus materials are quite vague—this time a set of pictures around which the person is to build stories—and the clinician looks for clues in the stories told. Does the person tend to take a Polyanna-like attitude that everything will come out all right? Does he, ostrichlike, deny that conflict exists? Is he given to rationalization as a method of coping with stress? Does he typically resign himself to events, passing easily into depression?

While much has been written on the subject of analyzing such clinical data in the interest of a fuller understanding of stress, conflict, and coping mechanisms (see Rapaport et al., 1968, for an extensive exposition), this approach is by no means the only one available to the clinician. Let us, therefore, turn to some other avenues along which exploration may fruitfully proceed.

Study of Natural Events

If it is true that stress is a natural part of life, then one ought to be able to study it more directly than by tests and less artificially than in the laboratory. Naturally occurring events are there for the asking. Few would question the fact that suicide, for example, is surrounded by stress. Similarly, those who have undergone major surgery will remember the stressful nature of the experience. Different in character, although stressful even for those who have experienced it many times, is the act of parachuting from a plane. The following sections present some efforts at collecting such data.

Suicide

In their comprehensive research on suicide, Shneidman and Farberow have drawn on many sources, suicide notes among them. Such notes, they point out, may almost be regarded as projective devices which yield products somewhat akin to those of the Thematic Apperception Test. Consequently, they have been interested in comparing the notes left by suicidal persons with others written by nonsuicidal subjects, in the belief that the differences, when highlighted, might provide clues to the cognitive, affective, and general psychodynamic processes characterizing persons who take their lives.

Pairs of such notes, one genuine, the other simulated (by nonsuicidal persons from such sources as labor unions, fraternal groups, and others) yield some interesting comparisons. In order to get a firsthand appreciation of the problem, the reader may wish to try his hand at deciding which of the following members of each pair, reported in Shneidman and Farberow (1957), is the genuine suicide note and which the simulated version.[1]

>
> **7-A** Dear Mary. I don't know why I am doing this unless my reasoning has gone all to pot. Something must have slipped.
>
> Bill
>
> **7-B** My Dearest Wife: I cannot endure this situation any longer. I cannot believe I have been so bad a husband as to merit this. Something is certainly wrong. I honestly don't know what it is.
>
> Whatever you may be searching for I hope with all my heart you find. Please be good to little Betty, our daughter, I love her so.
>
> I am talking over this Cyanide deal to myself. God knows what I'll do. I have it here. Possibly 20 grains — 5 more than is necessary. I still love you. Be good to Betty Please (p. 203).
>
> **14-A** Mary Darling. It's all my fault. I've thought this over a million times and this seems to be the only way I can settle all the trouble I have caused you and others. This is only a sample of how sorry I am. This should cancel all.
>
> Bill
>
> **14-B** Dear Mary. I can go on no longer so will take the easy way out. I've taken care of everything. Sorry
>
> Bill (p. 206).

[1] Copyright 1957 by McGraw-Hill Book Company. Reprinted by permission of the authors and publisher.

17-A Dear Wife; I am sorry to cause you this embarrassment but I can't seem to stand life this way. This is the easy way for me. You will get over it in time too.

17-B Dearest Mary—I just can't go on without Tom, John and you. I hope some day you can forgive me. I know you will find someone better for you and the boys. God bless you all.

Love, Bill (p. 207).

30-A Dear Wife. My health has broken and I no longer feel that I can be of help in the Support of the family therefore becoming a burden—So Im ending it all. Sorry to leave in this manner but feel that it is best for all concerned—Love.

30-B Honey. I am sorry this is the only way I know. I am all wrong. I love you very much.

Bill (p. 213).[2]

That such comparison need not remain purely qualitative or intuitive was shown by Osgood and Walker (1959) in a careful study of how language habits may be affected by the heightened state of motivation presumably characteristic of persons on the verge of suicide. They compared genuine suicide notes, furnished them by Shneidman, with ordinary letters of people to friends and relatives on the one hand and with simulated suicide notes on the other. The first comparison yielded a number of interesting differences. Suicide notes were more stereotyped; they contained shorter, simpler words, showed less diversity, were more repetitious, used more action terms (nouns and verbs) and fewer qualifying terms (adjectives and adverbs). In the second comparison (where writers of the simulated notes were attempting to intuit how a suicidal person would express himself), the differences were smaller, but a number of quantitative indices distinguished the pairs nonetheless. In any event, here is a good illustration of how a psychologist in another area of study, psycholinguistics in this case, can contribute special knowledge and methods to a fuller understanding of clinical phenomena.

Shneidman and Mandelkorn (1967) remind us of the need to distinguish between "fact and fable" in this area. To this end, Shneidman and Farberow have pioneered the Suicide Prevention Center, which serves, among other things, as a data-gathering center and clearing house for social scientists studying the problem of suicide. The reader interested in more specialized study is referred to their writings on the subject (1957) as well as the research sponsored by the National Institute of Mental Health (Shneidman, 1967).

[2] The reader may wish to know that the genuine notes are the following: *7-B; 14-A; 17-B; 30-B.*

Surgery

Less drastic, but no less relevant clinically, is the stress surrounding an event like major surgery. Like suicide, these occasions present researchers with an opportunity to collect data that can contribute to understanding the methods used in coping with stress. Let us cite a typical study.

Granting that personality factors loom large in the characteristic response of a person to stress, Tsushima (1968) was interested in exploring the role of ethnic differences (for example, Irish subjects compared with Italian subjects) and social-class differences (for example, lower-class compared with lower–middle-class subjects). He located 100 suitable male patients on the surgical wards of two hospitals and obtained permission to study the preoperative stress reaction of each by administration of suitable tests—a Tension-Hostility Questionnaire (constructed specifically for this research), the Thematic Apperception Test, and the Marlowe–Crowne Social Desirability Scale. Two hypotheses were tested: (a) that more signs of emotional tension and hostility would be found in one ethnic group than in the other, and (b) that more of the same evidence would be found in one social class than in the other.

Tsushima hypothesized that the Italian patients would show more overt signs of tension and hostility preoperatively than would the Irish patients, and that lower-class patients in either group would show more signs of these traits than would the lower–middle-class patients of either group. Table 1 presents the findings.

Table 1
Mean emotional tension and hostility scores derived from subjects' questionnaires.

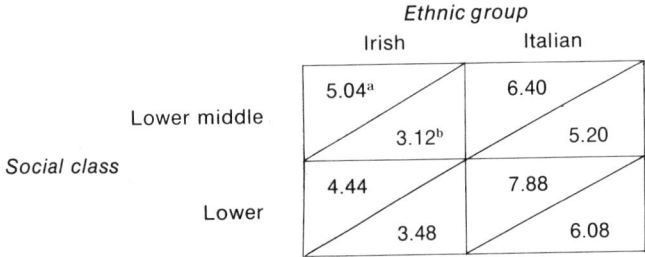

[a] Emotional tension scores in upper part of each cell.
[b] Hostility scores in lower part of each cell.
(Adapted from Tables 1 and 3 of Tsushima, 1968. Copyright 1968 by the American Psychological Association and reproduced by permission.)

When analyzed statistically, ethnicity did yield a significant difference; social class did not. While this is only a single study, it serves to remind psychologists of the necessity of taking into account the body of research which suggests that we study social and cultural factors as well as psychodynamic determinants of reactions to stress. Singer and Opler (1956) sparked interest in such research, and Hollingshead and Redlich (1958) found interesting relationships between social class and mental illness.

Let us, however, turn to a further area in which naturally occurring stress may be studied with a respectable degree of control and to good advantage.

Parachuting

In Chapter 15 we will see how Schachter and Singer (1962) attempted to study emotion through its on-the-spot arousal by giving subjects injections of epinephrine. As will be pointed out, however, the injection itself not only confounded the results somewhat but also gave rise to the question of how "real" such arousal was. In fact, the authors stressed the desirability of accomplishing arousal by methods that would circumvent these shortcomings.

Epstein (1962) has found a convenient way around the problem. Rather than be criticized for manipulating subjects (and possibly even harming them unintentionally), why not study subjects who have voluntarily placed themselves in admittedly stressful situations? And what better one than parachute jumping? Even veteran parachutists will admit that each new jump holds a measure of unmistakable stress. Availing himself of the opportunity, Epstein compiled some interesting findings. With parachutists as his subjects, he arranged to have them make self-ratings of the strength of their approach and avoidance tendencies at various specified stages of the jump situation, from the period preceding it to the time of landing. Some representative findings are shown in Figure 1.

Interestingly, the point of maximum stress is reached not at the moment the subject actually jumps from the plane but rather at the time the "Ready!" signal is given. From this point on his anxiety actually begins to abate, being less as he waits to be tapped to jump, still less as he actually exits from the plane, and, strangely enough, fairly minimal by the time the chute actually opens (if we are to believe the self-ratings).

We are not interested in parachute jumping per se but rather in the light it may throw on the stress that is part of so many clinical situations. It has often been suggested,

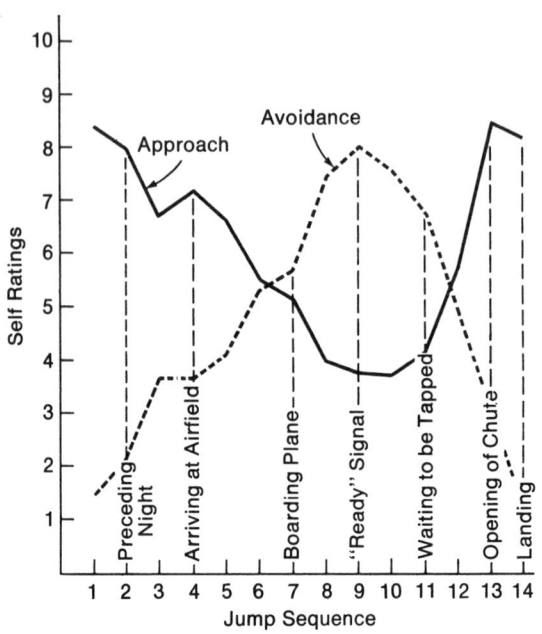

Figure 1
Self-ratings of approach and avoidance as a function of the sequence of events leading to and following a jump. [Figure 31 of Epstein in M. R. Jones (Ed.), *Nebraska Symposium on Motivation 1962*. Copyright 1962 by the University of Nebraska Press and reproduced by permission.]

for example, that once the suicidal person has made the definitive decision to end his life, his anxiety between that point and the commission of the act may actually lessen. Indeed, it has been noted that some suicidal persons become less depressed, even somewhat cheerful, just prior to their suicide. Is there an analogue here to the parachutist's abatement of stress after the "Ready" signal?

Epstein sees some interesting implications:[3]

> It is immediately apparent that approach is much greater than avoidance to begin with, but as the time to the jump diminishes, there is a rapid falling off in approach and an increase in avoidance, so that by the time the

[3]Copyright 1962 by the University of Nebraska Press. Reprinted by permission of the author and publisher.

aircraft is boarded, avoidance is greater than approach. This is a somewhat peculiar finding as the parachutists, after all, do jump. Apparently, they are jumping on psychological momentum rather than because of their immediate desire. The momentum consists of commitment and the difficulty in reversing the decision once in the aircraft. Avoidance continues to become increasingly greater than approach, reaching a peak when the signal is given to get ready to jump. It is noteworthy that the greatest avoidance reaction is not associated with the moment of jumping, but with a point that involves a final commitment to jump. When the parachutist is standing out on the wheel waiting to be tapped, where jumping is a foregone conclusion, there is actually a decrease in avoidance. At point 12 in the sequence, where the subject is freefalling, approach once again exceeds avoidance. Actually, the freefall precedes the most critical moment of all, the opening of the chute, and might be expected to be highly anxiety inducing. However, here again, the point of decision and commitment rather than that of objective danger produces the strongest fear reaction. It is as if the parachutist were to reason that there is nothing more that he can do, and so he might as well relax and enjoy the scenery, although we doubt if it goes quite that far. In this respect, it is important to consider that the novice parachutist does not pull his own ripcord, but relies on the jumpmaster, and so the last meaningful voluntary action when he still has control over his fate is when he gets ready to jump (pp. 179–180).

But such research, while natural in character and interesting in conception, is not without its price. It can be costly in terms of man-hours; it often depends on the willingness of other agencies to cooperate and must therefore defer to their schedules and wishes; and, despite some built-in controls, it still lacks the rigor and precision that are possible in more conveniently arranged and tightly managed laboratory situations.

Hence, let us turn to our third avenue of approach to the study of stress and conflict—laboratory research.

Experimental Manipulation

Like clinical psychologists, social psychologists too have been interested in the study of stress, although with more interest in how it is experienced in group situations. Mintz (1951), for example, was among the first to carry out some simple but ingenious laboratory research intended to simulate the behavior of groups of people in panic situations. Compared with Feldman's study of parachutists, Mintz's stress situations were decidedly more artificial. They nonetheless made possible objective observation, recording, and analysis of behavior under various conditions in a safe, but paniclike, setting.

In brief, Mintz set up a laboratory situation in which a number of subjects shared a common problem—pulling pieces of paper (on strings) through the neck of a large bottle before the papers got wet from water entering the bottle through a valve at the bottom (as shown in Figure 2).

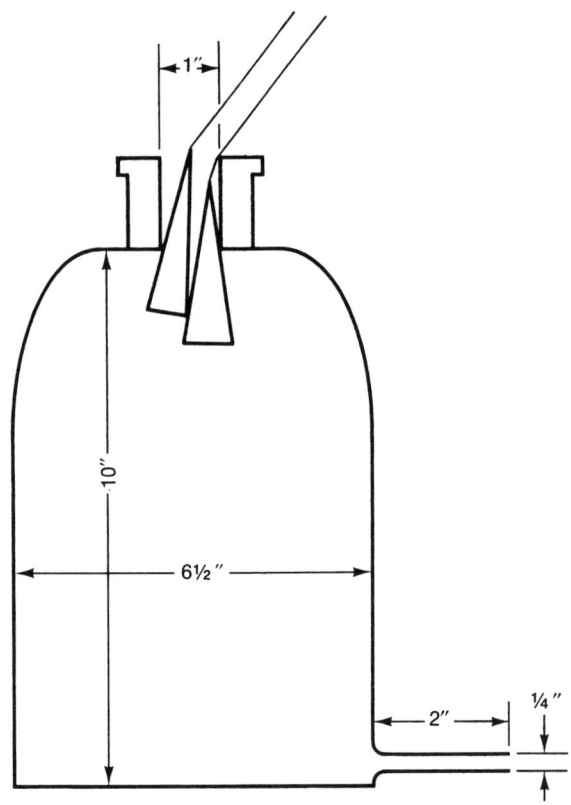

Figure 2
Illustration of apparatus used in the study of nonadaptive group behavior. *Note:* Water entered through opening at bottom right, its level steadily rising in the jar. (Figure 1 of Mintz, 1951. Copyright 1951 by the American Psychological Association and reproduced by permission.)

Subjects striving to pull out their tabs before getting them wet (lest they suffer a penalty) experienced a kind of panic at the literal bottleneck as the water level rose relentlessly. Some years later, Kelley and his colleagues (1965) used electronic equipment in place of Mintz's more horse-and-buggy apparatus to study the same type of problem—namely, under what conditions stress is most likely to be disabling and under what conditions it is most constructively handled by a group. He was interested in the variables of threat, size of the group, and effect of communication.

While the work of such researchers as Mintz, Kelley, and others adds a meaningful third dimension to the understanding of the phenomenon of stress—namely, its sociopsychological aspects—let us return to some more directly clinical features. Again in a laboratory setting, Lazarus (1964) was interested in studying as rigorously as possible how an inherently stressful situation is handled as a function of the context in which it is experienced. With this in mind, he had subjects view a film depicting the initiation rites of a primitive tribe, including the incisions suffered by a young tribesman in the course of the ceremonies. Wishing as exact an index of stress as he could get, he took skin-conductance measures of the subjects during the course of their film viewing. As expected, and shown in Figure 3, they were apparently experiencing significantly more stress during the incision scenes than during a neutral hair-dressing scene that was part of the ceremony.

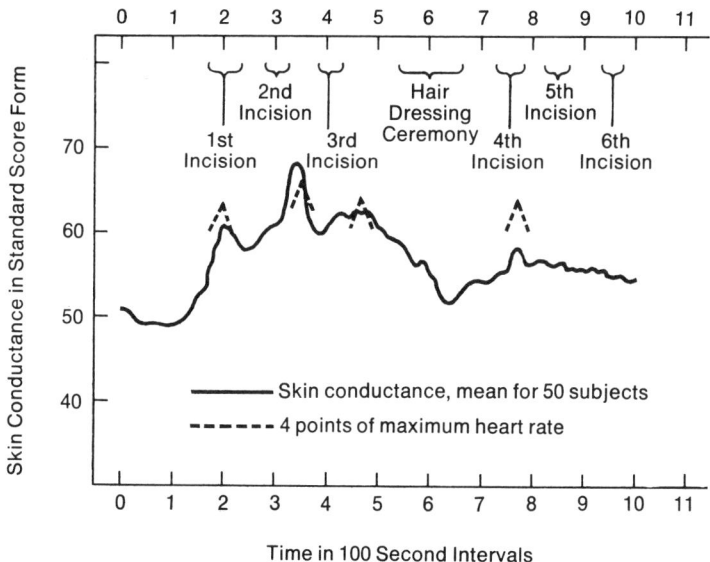

Figure 3
Variation in skin conductance (of 50 subjects) during viewing of film. (Figure 1 of Lazarus, 1964. Copyright 1964 by the American Psychological Association and reproduced by permission.)

However, Lazarus reasoned, in real life we do not take stress lying down; it is in the nature of man to defend himself against it as best he can. Hence, if one could simulate typical defenses in the film-viewing situation, one might then observe from the skin-conductance measures how well or poorly the stress was being handled. Accordingly, Lazarus designed his study so that four comparable groups of subjects would be exposed to four different types of sound tracks as they viewed the film. Each sound track was to provide a defense (or lack of defense) against stress.

In the "trauma" sound track the commentator left no doubt that the young tribesman was experiencing pain, even if for a good cause. In contrast, the group with the "denial" sound track was led to believe that while he *appeared* to be suffering pain, he actually was not. The "intellectualization" sound track glossed over the physical aspect of the situation to focus on the sociological significance of the initiation rites. And, finally, one group had a "silent" sound track. The results are shown in Figure 4.

Clearly, "defenses" help. As reflected in the skin-conductance measures, subjects exposed to any of the nontraumatic sound tracks (intellectualization, denial, or silence) apparently experienced the film as significantly less stressful than did the group exposed to the traumatic sound track. But is *any* defense effective? Or do some of us resort to certain defenses while others use different ones? To attempt to answer these questions, Lazarus (1964) devised an ingenious spin-off experiment.

Students and airline executives, he conjectured, seem like two fairly different groups in terms of personality structure. Students, given to intellectualization, can probably "talk themselves out of" situations experienced as traumatic. On the other hand, airline executives (of middle level) are probably more interested in "getting places," more concerned with status, less given to philosophizing, and more apt to handle anxiety by overlooking it (via the mechanism of "denial"). These were admittedly stereotypes, but it was hoped that they were sufficiently valid to be used in testing the hypothesis that certain defenses serve certain people better than they do others. In short, how would a group of students using intellectualization (that is, exposed to an intellectualization sound track while viewing the film) experience the incision rites (according to their skin-conductance measures) as compared with a group of students using denial (that is, exposed to the denial sound track)? And how would these two groups compare with two groups of airline executives exposed to the same denial and intellectualization sound tracks? The results, shown in Figure 5, have implications for clinical theory.

Interestingly, with intellectualization as a defense, students seemed to find the experience much less stressful than did other students with denial as their defense.

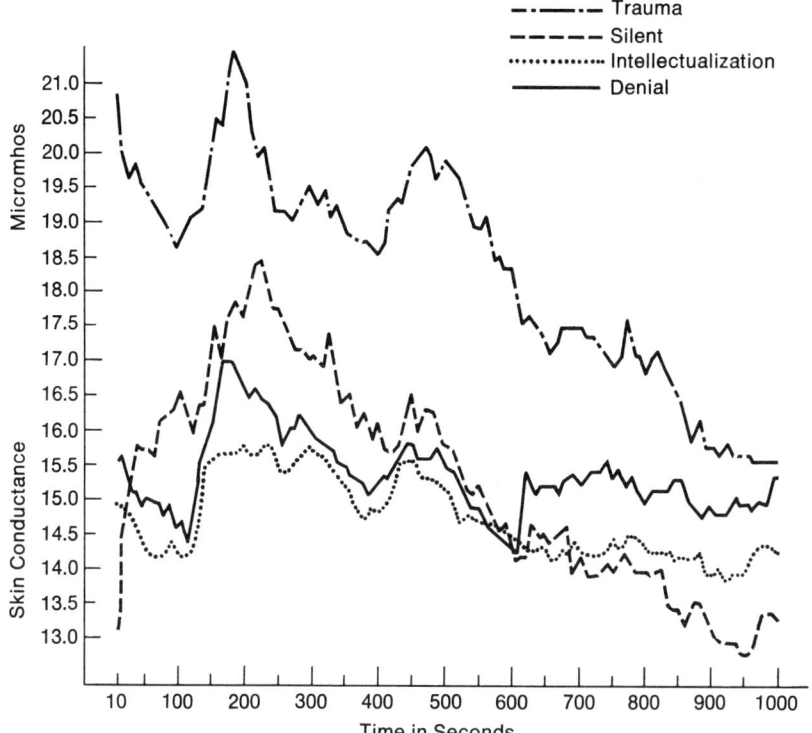

Figure 4
Skin-conductance patterns of subjects viewing the same film under various sound-track conditions. (Figure 2 of Lazarus, 1964. Copyright 1964 by the American Psychological Association and reproduced by permission.)

However, with the airline executives the situation was just the reverse—denial served them much better as a defense than did intellectualization. In other words, one cannot speak simply of how much more effective one defense is than another—its serviceability is a function of who is using it. That is, there is an "interaction effect" between the effectiveness of a defense mechanism and the personality structure of the person using it.

Lazarus is not one to oversimplify matters. He offers some qualifying interpretations of the results and suggests additional factors to be taken into account. Nevertheless, on the basis of the above and some related further studies he concludes that ". . . the

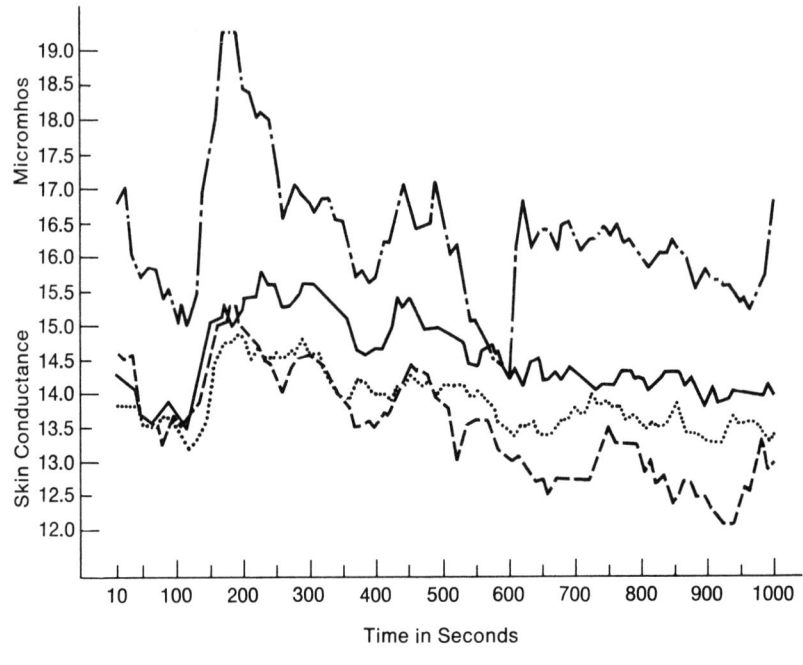

Figure 5
Interaction effects on skin-conductance patterns of groups of subjects under different defensive sound-track conditions. (Figure 3 of Lazarus, 1964. Copyright 1964 by the American Psychological Association and reproduced by permission.)

findings on the general success of the defensive sound tracks in reducing the threat normally conveyed by the subincision movie are not in doubt" (p. 408). His theoretical explanation, however, is presented with characteristic care:

> It should be made absolutely clear that, although the discussion has referred to ego-defense theory and employs the terms *intellectualization* and *denial and reaction formation,* in describing the sound tracks, the experiments are analogues of cognitive appraisal and not ego defense. We have merely borrowed from defense theory in constructing our appraisal statements. Defense is usually considered to involve first the arousal of threat, and then, by principles that are still not clear to us, the

activation of certain self-induced modes of thought which reduce the threat that has once been aroused. In these experiments, the modes of thought that short-circuit threat are encouraged by manipulation of the situation; they do not follow the generation of threat in the subject, nor are they self-induced by the subject. We cannot consider our findings as resulting from defensive processes, although we can learn something about the threat-reducing effectiveness of various defensive modes of thought from systematic manipulation of the kinds of statements we give orienting the subjects. Thus, indirectly they contribute to the theory of ego defense (p. 409).

The construct of "defense mechanisms" is a complex one. To think, for example, that "a good laugh" could be anything more than that would seem to be stretching a point. Yet psychoanalytic theory has some provocative things to say on the subject of humor, not always funny ones, and the research of the following section attempts to test some of the hypotheses.

Humor as a Mechanism of Defense

Animal behavior can be rather stereotyped—in both peace and war. The ring dove goes through an elaborate, yet highly inflexible, sequence of behavior as it courts its mate; and, as we have seen in Azrin's work, animals of all species can be made to execute aggressive attacks in a very mechanical way, literally at the push of a button. For all their foibles, people are at least more creative in the way they make love or fight. Even when their adjustment is less than adequate, versatility and ingenuity characterize their efforts.

It is not surprising, then, to find people expressing something as prevalent as aggression in unique ways. Freud (1905), in fact, had some original thoughts on the subject, and his thesis, as usual, had considerable face validity. Whether it would stand empirical test, however, was something Gollob and Levine (1967) deemed worth investigating.

Freud's hypothesis was that humor, in certain forms at least, could serve as a socially acceptable outlet for the expression of aggression. To pass hostile remarks is considered at best gauche, at worst unpardonable; yet to laugh at the plight of the central figure in a joke is quite acceptable, if not praiseworthy. As the leading character in one of the most successful pieces of his repertoire, "The Poor Soul," TV performer Jackie Gleason invariably suffers the most embarrassing and unfortunate of experiences to the sheer delight of his audience. One might well hypothesize, then, as Freud did, that laughing uproariously at the misfortune of a convenient target figure in a socially approved context might serve to drain off, in the form of "sublimation," some of the aggression of those who "appreciate" the joke.

Freud proposed that an important aspect of "tendentious humor," humor having sexual or aggressive functions, was that the person laughing at the joke be *distracted* from the character of the unacceptable impulses involved. That is, to fulfill psychodynamic functions, aggressive humor must serve as a disguised, symbolic attack with which the listener can innocently empathize. To confront him directly with the baldly aggressive character of the joke would be to mobilize in him inhibitions that would reduce or eliminate the cathartic effect of the aggressive humor.

It was this aspect of Freud's thesis that Gollob and Levine (1967) were primarily interested in testing. With the aid of a set of cartoons, some of which constituted aggressive humor, the rest being only mildly or not at all aggressive, one might first allow people to enjoy the jokes in their own way, later confront them with the point of the jokes, and subsequently note whether the aggressive humor was now more, less, or equally appreciated than originally. Taking pains to distinguish among high-aggression, low-aggression, and nonsense (minimal aggression) cartoons in a pool of 40 jokes (with graduate students serving as judges), the experimenters arrived at a set of 12 to be used as the stimulus materials. The reader can form his own estimate of the aggressiveness of the humor involved (although at this point inhibitions may already have been sufficiently aroused, so that it will not seem as funny as it might have without the preceding introduction). In any case, a couple of the high-aggression cartoons were the following:

> A rifle is rigged to shoot anyone who enters the room. A woman, looking toward the door, calmly and seductively calls out, "It's not locked, honey" (p. 370).

In contrast, a low-aggression and a nonsense (minimal aggression) cartoon were the following:

> A service-station attendant says, "Oil's dirty," as he casually wipes the oil dipstick on his customer's tie (p. 370).
>
> While his surprised wife watches, a man paints his living room by holding a paint roller against the wall as he rides back and forth on a bicycle (p. 370).

In the experiment, a set of 24 cartoons was presented to 14 female undergraduates enrolled in an introductory psychology course, to be rated for funniness on an 8-point scale, ranging from "very funny" to "not funny at all." Subjects received the cartoons in booklet form, each of the booklets arranged in a different sequence, and they performed the task anonymously. Ten days later each subject was given 12 of the original set of cartoons—4 of each category—each set arranged in a different random order. This time the subjects were asked to ". . . state what about the cartoon you think is funny, or is supposed to be funny. Describe as vividly as you can the intended point of the joke . . ." (p. 369). Once this step was completed for a given cartoon, the subject immediately rated it on the 8-point scale of funniness, then proceeded in the same way with the next cartoon in her set. At the end of this second session, each subject was asked to rate each cartoon according to the degree of "interpersonal aggression" it involved. The experimenters found, to their satisfaction, that the ratings "overwhelmingly supported" their own *a priori* judgment as to the high, low, or minimal aggression character of the respective cartoons.

A second study, three months later, involving 14 other female students, was essentially a replication of the first, so that the experimenters felt it reasonable to average the results of the two studies. The findings, presented graphically, are shown in Figure 6.

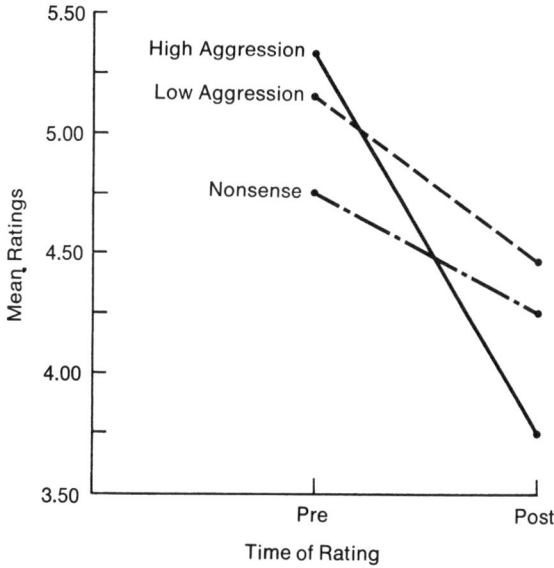

Figure 6
Cartoon humor as rated by subjects prior to and following their description of the point of the joke. (Figure 1 of Gollob & Levine, 1967. Copyright 1967 by the American Psychological Association and reproduced by permission.)

Pointing to some possible alternative explanations and ruling out each in turn, Gollob and Levine were led to increased "... confidence in the heuristic and predictive usefulness of Freud's hypotheses concerning distraction as an important factor in the enjoyment of aggressive humor" (p. 372). They would hardly argue that the last word has been spoken on the subject and, in fact, one of their earlier collaborators has subsequently (Singer, 1968) carried out a more real-life piece of research on "Aggression Arousal, Hostile Humor, Catharsis" showing the complex nature of humor as represented in such socially involving situations as feelings between the races. Nonetheless, Gollob and Levine typify the social scientist who not only finds theoretical concepts interesting but feels a concomitant responsibility and displays the necessary ingenuity for testing them empirically. Raush and his colleagues have shown similar inventiveness and methodological sophistication in their program of research on conflict in marriage to be discussed in the next section.

Interpersonal Conflict and Conflict Resolution

One might think the best way to deal with conflicts among people is to see to it that they do not occur. Some, however, would argue against this preventive philosophy. Some psychologists, at least (Bach & Wyden, 1969), advocate an occasional good clean verbal fight as a vital ingredient in a happy marriage. Whatever one's position in the matter, there is probably agreement that the more we know about the dynamics of conflict, the better it can be resolved when it occurs, whether it is international wrangling among countries or a domestic quarrel between husband and wife.

In any case, a program of research on marital interaction, begun some years ago under government sponsorship at the National Institute of Mental Health (NIMH) in Bethesda, Maryland, has contributed materially to our understanding. At the University of Michigan a series of related doctoral dissertations has emerged under the chairmanship of Raush, one of the original NIMH investigators.

Goodrich and Boomer (1963) had found that one could readily set up laboratory situations that would result in differences of opinion, if not actual conflict, between two people—newlywed couples in this case. Their contrived Color Matching Test soon led to an alternative form—the Stereognosis Test of Flint and Ryder (1963)—which was used in following the newlyweds through later phases of marriage. This test was an object-matching test that consisted of a simple apparatus into which the experimenter could insert stimulus materials. Husband and wife, sitting on opposite sides of the apparatus, would successively reach in to feel the particular object (without being able to look at it), whereupon each would record separately which of six objects (sitting on top of the apparatus) it resembled. Thereafter they would disclose their respective choices, and, if they differed, would try to resolve the disagreement through discussion. The procedure consisted of 21 such mutual choices for various objects.

As the reader may suspect, the experimenter was having husband and wife feel different objects, although each assumed the other was feeling the identical object on any given trial. It is obvious that here were the roots of conflict, major or minor, depending upon the personalities of the particular spouses and the nature of their relationship. What interested the investigators was the characteristic way in which the various couples would resolve the inevitable disagreements.

As part of the program of research on the interaction of newlywed couples, Blank, Flint, and Goodrich (1962) had proceeded to develop a set of more lifelike situations that could readily breed conflict between two people, while providing at the same time a medium through which such conflict might be resolved or, for that matter, escalated. There follow four such "Improvisations," as the scenes to be enacted by husband and wife in the laboratory were called.

> *Scene 1.* The husband and wife are jointly informed that it is their first wedding anniversary. Each is then taken to a separate office by his (her) instructor. The husband is told that he wishes to make this a very special celebration and that he has planned to take his wife to dinner that evening at a favorite restaurant. He is asked which restaurant he would choose. He is told that he has made arrangements for the meal. The instructor asks him to specify what he would order for himself and his wife; he tries thus to involve the subject in the process. After the meal has been planned, the husband is told that he has made reservations and has paid in advance. The wife is also told that she wishes to make this a very special occasion. She has taken a half-day off work (all wives in the sample were working at this stage of marriage) to prepare a very special dinner at home. She is asked to plan the meal and to imagine the setting (candles, china, wine, etc.), the instructor gauging his remarks to the orientation of the couple. The dinner is cooking and almost ready as her husband comes from work. The husband and wife enter the "living room" from different doors, she from the "kitchen" and he from the "front door." They begin interacting at a signal.
>
> *Scene 2.* Both are told that the wife is pregnant and will soon (in a couple of months) deliver. Separately the husband is told that there is a special T.V. program that evening at 9 o'clock, and he is asked what such a program might be, i.e., one that he would especially want to watch. If the husband refers to a program that is part of a weekly series, it is suggested that this is much more special. Choices range from special sports programs such as the World Series to Presidential news conferences. The

wife is told that there is a special panel show on at 9 o'clock which will discuss the naming of babies and the implications of various names, that Dr. Spock and other psychological and psychiatric authorities are on the panel, and that she especially wants both to watch this program because they have not settled on names for the baby. Subjects are brought back into the "living room" and are seated on the couch in front of an imaginary T.V. set. They are told that it is a few minutes before 9 o'clock and then signalled to begin.

Scenes 3 and 4. These scenes are reciprocals of one another and are designed to be more emotionally involving. For scene 3 the husband is asked by his instructor whether he has ever felt toward anyone that he wanted to have nothing to do with this person, that he could not bear the sight or presence of the person, etc. The attempt is to get him to feel the mood or at least to imagine it. Then he is asked whether he has ever felt this way toward his wife. Most newlyweds denied having had such feelings toward their wives. The husband is then encouraged to imagine something about his wife or some behavior of hers which might cause him to feel that he could not stand having her near him. As in the other scenes, efforts are made to involve the imagination of the subject and to induce a mood. . . . The wife is told that her husband has been cold and distant for the last few days, that this behavior is very disturbing to her and disruptive of their relationship. Again attempts are made to get her involved and concerned. Tonight she is resolved to break down the barrier between them, find out what is disturbing him, and get close to him. The husband is placed in the "living room" setting looking out a window. The wife enters the room, and they begin. Scene 4 is the reciprocal of scene 3. The wife's position is that of maintaining distance, the husband's that of achieving closeness (Barry, 1968, pp. 30–32).[4]

Raush and his colleagues saw here an excellent opportunity for an intensive study of the dynamics of interaction, which they had previously explored (Raush, Dittmann, & Taylor, 1959) in the interaction patterns of emotionally disturbed, as compared with normal, children. From some pilot work with the above set of improvisations (Raush, Goodrich, & Campbell, 1963), it was evident that they produced a rich store of data. Couples could constructively handle and actually settle their disagreement or they could let it get completely out of hand and remain unresolved. In some cases the area of disagreement was readily contained; in others it spread quickly to further areas of contention. Some couples were sensitive to each other's needs; others engaged in wily manipulation. In short, there seemed to be all manner of possibilities for better describing the nature of conflict, for predicting the course of conflictual interaction, and perhaps even for eventually developing methods for the control of conflict and its subsequent resolution—all matters of basic interest to clinicians.

[4] From an unpublished doctoral dissertation. Reproduced by permission of the author.

While the material was undoubtedly a storehouse of clinical information, it was obvious that it could not be handled with any amount of rigor in its raw, narrative form, which lent itself to impressionistic hunches but hardly to the systematic testing of clinically relevant hypotheses. What was needed was a system of "coding" the various elements of the script typed from the tape recordings of the couples' interaction. After much collaborative effort, the NIMH investigators developed the necessary manual—a Coding Scheme for Interpersonal Conflict—by means of which the elements of recorded interaction could be systematically labeled for subsequent analysis. Some representative categories, with illustrative remarks, are listed in Table 2.

Table 2
Representative categories of the coding scheme for interpersonal conflict.

Category Number	Category Description	Illustrative Remarks
0	Conventional remarks	"Hello, dear."
5	Suggesting a course of action	"How about going out to dinner?"
15	Using humor	"I'm going to trade you in."*
20	Accepting the blame or responsibility	"I admit I'm wrong."
24	Seeking reassurance	"I've been pretty stupid, haven't I?"
31	Appealing to fairness	"What would you do if *I* behaved that way?"
43	Recognizing the other's strategy or calling the other's bluff	"You can't win that way."
51	Inducing guilt or attacking the other's motives	"You know you have just ruined my whole day."
53	Disparaging the other	"Oh, now you're a doctor as well as a psychiatrist."

*While coding the typescript, coders would listen simultaneously to the tape recording. The inflection and context characterizing this remark would need to be such as to convince the coders that humor, and not something else, was intended. (From the *Coding Manual,* as reported in Barry, 1968, pp. 127–143.)

Altogether the investigators came up with 36 of these action categories. (The category numbers run through 55, but some of the original categories were dropped or combined with others, leaving only 36.) The reader may have noted that the examples in Table 2 fall into groups of different character. For this reason, the investigators found it helpful, for certain purposes, to "lump" the 36 discrete categories into three large clusters, namely *cognitive, affiliative,* and *coercive* behaviors. Categories 0 and 5 of Table 2, for example, are of a cognitive nature; that is, they amount to a simple intellectual exchange. In contrast, categories 15, 20, 24, and 31 may be called affiliative; their intent is to "make up" rather than to continue or even escalate the disagreement. Categories 43, 51, and 53 have a coercive thrust.

Just as the action categories can be grossly differentiated in this way, so can the various phases of the conflict situation. The investigators found it useful to think of the interaction that preceded introduction of the conflict in each scene as the *Introductory phase.* As soon as the conflict issue had been introduced, the *Conflict phase* began, which lasted until some strategy developed. From that point on it was convenient to classify the action as belonging to either the *Resolution* or *Post-Resolution phase.*

Raush and his colleagues took pains to check the adequacy of both the judges, who were given between 60 and 100 hours of training, and the coding procedure, which included both independent and consensus coding. With such a system in hand, the investigators could afford to take on the job of systematically classifying the large pool of data that had resulted from having 49 couples enact the four improvisation scenes described above. The subjects were paid volunteers, largely of middle-class background, white, and in their first marriage. The husbands ranged in age from 20 to 27, the wives from 18 to 25. All had completed high school; none had advanced degrees. Since they were to be seen on several evenings, both at home and at the laboratory, they were required to be living within a half-hour of the National Institute of Mental Health, where the data were gathered.

Should the reader imagine that little more than artificial role-playing would take place with such an experimental design, he would be quickly disabused of the notion by listening to a few sample tapes. Improvised though the scenes were, couples participated vigorously, and the action grew pretty hot on occasion. Although the spouses could wind up kissing and making up after a stormy session, the preceding interaction did not lack authenticity.

It would be most useful to be able to predict at a given point in such a situation what turn the discussion will have taken five exchanges hence. That is, had the husband made an affiliative rather than a coercive remark at point X, what would be going on between the couple at point Y as a result? Hertel (1968), one of Raush's students, has, in fact, explored the possibilities, using sophisticated techniques from the field of probability theory to explore how well a mathematical model—the so-called Markov chain—might predict the course of such exchanges.

Some couples in the study were remarkably effective in resolving the improvised conflicts, while others not only were less successful but actually aggravated the situation in the experimental setting. For various technical reasons the model was not as successful as one might have hoped. However, Hertel offers helpful suggestions for further research of this type, so that in the future it may be possible to get some useful insights into how successful couples differ from unsuccessful ones, to wit:

> ... whether or not the increased length of the unsuccessful couples' conflict could be attributed to a greater amount of "tit-for-tat" behavior, rigidity on the part of one or both spouses, lack of responsiveness on the part of one or both spouses, earlier escalation of the conflict, or lack of flexibility in "handling" or responding to the other's coercion (p. 96).

Others of Raush's students have moved the research effort in different directions. Looking more generally at the quality of the interaction between spouses, Barry (1968) was interested in comparing couples who differed on various factors that had been identified earlier. As he reports the findings elsewhere (Barry, 1970),

> ... those couples whose marriages are in trouble are characterized by the husbands being far more coercive and punitive and less conciliatory than the rest of the husbands in the sample, while the wives in these marriages do not differ much from the rest of the wives. The "happiest" marriages in this sample were characterized by husbands being very conciliatory and supportive (p. 52).

Swain (1969), on the other hand, was particularly interested in how the interaction patterns of husband and wife might change over time. And, indeed, as couples moved through different stages of the marriage cycle—from newlywed, through pregnancy, to being confronted with a newborn—their modes of interacting with one another changed significantly. For example, when their wives were pregnant, husbands were more reconciling (conciliatory) than at either of the other two stages.

As investigators record such typical human interaction, so that they—and, indeed, the participants themselves—can take a closer look at what is going on, we may well wonder to what extent people are conscious of how they characteristically behave in the rapid-fire sequence of interpersonal transactions. Awareness of one's typical interaction patterns could be a necessary precondition for altering them.

Indeed, "awareness" in one form or another has been the focus of a variety of psychological research. The next section addresses itself to the problem on several fronts, illustrating among other things the interrelation between psychological and biological processes, as well as the possibilities for bringing under control behavior that has heretofore been regarded as relatively autonomous.

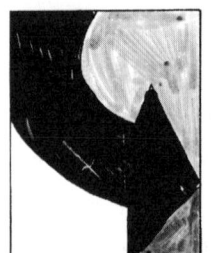

7 Research on Levels of Awareness

In science, problems are sometimes best attacked indirectly rather than head-on. Clinical research is no exception. To speak of unconscious processes, for example, is almost by definition to imply that there are phenomena that must be studied in a roundabout way. Thus, there is considerable room in clinical psychology for research tools and techniques that get at psychological processes not amenable to direct confrontation. The following sections will illustrate some possibilities for bringing into focus behavior not immediately available to awareness.

Pupillometrics

The clinical investigator is interested in finding a dependent (outcome) variable that can reliably index the effect of the independent (experimental) variable(s) under study. Unfortunately, satisfactory dependent variables are harder to come by in the behavioral sciences than in the physical sciences; clinical psychology in particular is often hard put to assess, as neatly as it would like, the outcome of procedures in which considerable skill and effort have been invested.

There is no prohibition, however, against borrowing serviceable dependent variables from other areas of psychology in order to study clinical problems more rigorously. The skin conductance measure is one such variable, as is the EEG record (described in Chapter 2). While both continue to serve useful functions in clinical research (helping measure anxiety levels and monitoring dreams, for example), there has recently emerged in the area of perception, a different kind of dependent variable that might have great usefulness in clinical investigations, if research clinicians prove sufficiently creative to harness its potential. This new variable is simply the degree to which the pupil of the eye dilates (or contracts) under varying conditions. Appropriately enough, the pioneers in this area have dubbed its study accordingly — "pupillometrics."

It has long been known that pupil dilation varies with circumstances that go far beyond the simple fact of amount of light available. Oriental merchants, for example, are said to watch the size of a customer's pupils when determining what to ask for a piece of jade as they haggle over prices. It was not until recently, however, that Hess (1965), among others, began rigorous laboratory investigation of the phenomenon. Having chanced upon the possibilities for exploring psychological processes that could be indexed by this measure (pupil dilation), he began a series of studies that suggest considerable payoff for clinicians in quest of an easily measured, readily quantifiable, dependent variable. Let us, therefore, cite briefly some typical research, so that the reader may speculate about uses to which this versatile measure might be put in clinical research.

With fairly simple, relatively inexpensive laboratory equipment, it is possible to photograph the changes in the pupil size of persons looking at or reacting to stimuli presented to them. Thus, by first taking a baseline measure (that is, the average size of a person's pupil when looking at a standard experimental slide), it was possible for Hess (1965) to present subjects with a succession of slides, photographing the changes in pupil size throughout the series. (The slides must, of course, be comparable in the amount of light they reflect, lest changes in pupil size represent simply the available light rather than the psychological impact of the stimuli, but this is a technical detail that can readily be handled.) Running simple experiments at first, Hess was intrigued by the findings. For example, there seemed notable sex differences — men and women reacted quite differently — as shown in Figure 1.

But beyond revealing such gross perceptual differences, pupil size proved also a sensitive measure of cognitive functioning, reflecting almost instantaneously the

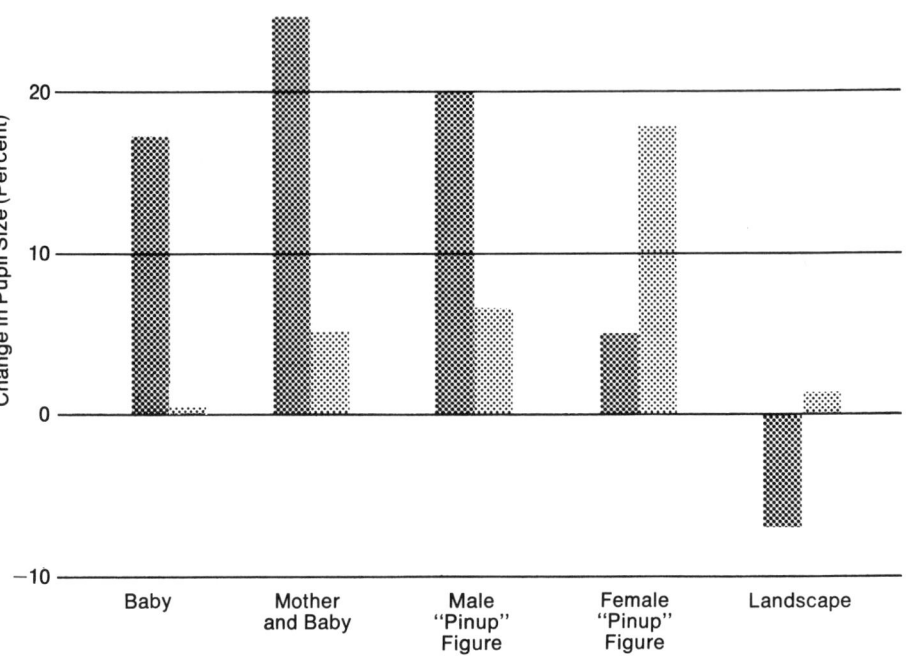

Figure 1
Change in pupil size of male (light bars) and female (dark bars) subjects as a function of stimulus material viewed. (From "Attitude and pupil size" by Eckhard Hess. Copyright© 1965 by Scientific American, Inc. All rights reserved. Reproduced by permission of the author and publisher.)

momentary experiences during such processes as mental arithmetic. Figure 2, for example, shows the results Hess obtained when subjects were asked to do progressively more difficult multiplications (8 × 13; 13 × 14; 16 × 23).

P represents the point in time at which the problem was presented to the subject, *A* the moment at which he gave his answer. Note the pupil dilation during the period in which the mental operation was being performed and the rapid diminution in

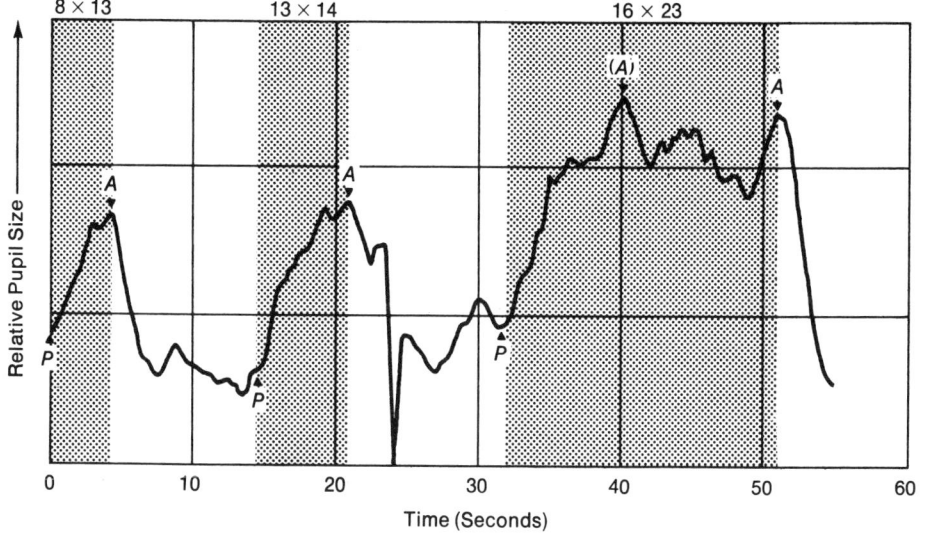

Figure 2
Changes in the pupil size of a subject engaged in mental arithmetic of varying orders of difficulty. *Note:* P denotes the point at which the problem is presented, A the point at which the answer is given. In the case of the third solution (16 × 23), the subject checked his answer mentally at (A) before giving it at A. (From Hess, 1965. Copyright © 1965 by Scientific American, Inc. All rights reserved. Reproduced by permission of the author and publisher.)

pupil size immediately following the giving of the answer. The 16 × 23 problem in particular illustrates the fidelity with which fluctuation in pupil size mirrors the mental process going on. In this case the subject was about to give his answer at point (A) but decided to double-check it mentally before he actually gave it at point A. Again, note the rapid shrinkage in pupil size immediately following the giving of the answer.

Spurred on by related findings, researchers in the area of perception (for example, Kahneman & Beatty, 1966) have begun a series of sophisticated experiments on such complex problems as information-processing and short-term memory. Illustrative of the research more directly relevant to clinical matters is the recent study by Nunnally et al. (1967) of pupillary response in relation to anticipation of emotion-provoking events. Aware of the importance of equating the amount of light reflected by visual displays, these investigators circumvented this technical problem by measuring pupil size in response to *anticipation* of a slide intended to precipitate an emotional response. Using as control stimuli two slides that contained an asterisk in their center, the experimenters informed subjects they would see in sequence slides bearing individual numbers from 1 to 5, the series to be repeated several times. Subjects were also told that a gun might be fired during any series but if the gunshot occurred, it would be when the slide bearing the number 3 appeared on the screen and never during the appearance of other numbers. Actually the gun was never fired. Yet note in Figure 3 the dramatic changes in pupil size as subjects anticipated number 3 and a possible gunshot, although the gunshot failed to materialize.

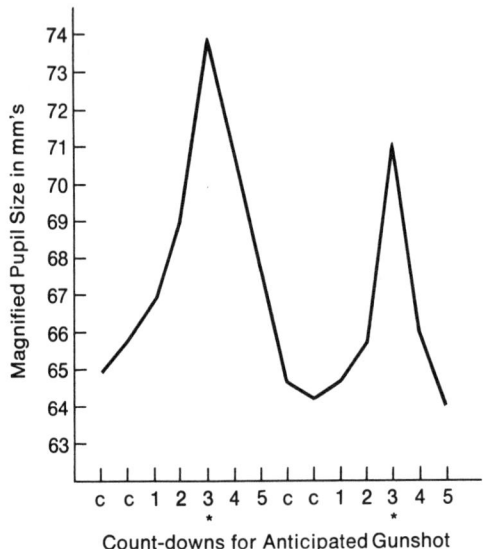

Figure 3
Pupil size as a function of an anticipated gunshot. (Figure 3 of Nunnally et al., 1967. Copyright 1967 by Psychonomic Press and reproduced by permission.)

Such dramatic evidence of the sensitivity of this dependent variable (pupil size) to psychological experiences should whet the interest of clinicians in exploring fully the usefulness of such a measure—objective, quantifiable, and sensitive as these preliminary studies make it out to be. As Hess pointed out, imaginative researchers in almost any area should be able to see numerous possibilities—assessing consumer preferences for products, judging the public's response to various kinds of art or music, studying the effects of various arguments or brands of propaganda on the listener or reader.

It is not wise to oversimplify the situation by declaring pupillometrics to be the millennium in scientific research. Many features require considerable further study (as in the cases where a dramatic stimulus—for example, the picture of a shark or of a murdered gangster—may result in sudden dilation of the pupil followed quickly by constriction). Nonetheless the research to date suggests it may well be that the eye is indeed "the window of the soul." Pupil size seems related in striking degree to the nature of the psychological experience being undergone.

Creative clinicians are speculating on the research possibilities in their field. Could this simple dependent variable serve to track down "repressed memories," unearthing them perhaps more effectively than does the process of free association? Could we acquire useful knowledge of the psychotherapeutic process by arranging experimental apparatus so that client and therapist talk to each other while hooked up to a camera that photographs momentary pupil size? Could the responses of examinees filling out a personality inventory be more adequately evaluated if pupil-size changes were recorded in synchrony with their answers?

We leave the reader to his own brand of speculation, turning meanwhile to another avenue of approach to levels of awareness that also captures the imagination and has brewed more than its share of controversy.

Hypnosis: Another Royal Road to the Unconscious?

The notion of an "unconscious" is a convenient abstraction. For the layman, who often sees it as a compartment lodged somewhere in the psyche, it serves as a prefabricated explanation for anything from a slip of the tongue to the reason his children forgot Father's Day. For the psychologist, it does yeoman's service as well. Fortunately, the psychologist is aware of the hypothetical nature of the construct and feels a continuing need to carry out empirical studies on the nature of unconscious determinants of behavior. In Chapter 2 we saw the study of dreams as ideal for the purpose. Let us now look at another research tool—the use of hypnosis.

Consider for a moment the interesting clinical speculations one can make on the basis of such observations as the following by Wolberg (1947), a psychiatrist who has been a pioneering investigator in the area of hypnosis:[1]

---

[1] Copyright 1947 by the American Psychosomatic Society, Inc. Reprinted by permission of the author and publisher.

The first case demonstrates how a conflict between an irrepressible impulse and a moral prohibition reflects itself in a generalized state of tension, with muscular tremors and neurocirculatory collapse. The subject was an individual who claimed he had no disturbing neurotic difficulties and had volunteered to act as a subject out of interest. An experimental conflict was induced in a deep trance by giving the subject the following posthypnotic suggestion. "When you awaken you will find next to you a bar of chocolate. You will have a desire to eat the chocolate that will be so intense that it will be impossible to resist the craving. At the same time you will feel that the chocolate does not belong to you and that to eat it would be very wrong and very bad. You will have no memory of these suggestions when you awaken, but you will, nevertheless, react to them."

When the subject was aroused, he looked casually about the room, yet avoided the table near him on which I had placed a bar of chocolate. He complained of a feeling of dizziness and of faintness. He asked for a glass of water and then decided to get it himself. He stood up from the chair, took two or three steps, then fell backward remarking that he felt so faint that he could hardly walk. His face was blanched and when his pulse was taken it was found to be rapid and thready. His forehead was covered with cold perspiration. He complained of feeling chilly. He then began to shiver and shortly after exhibited generalized muscular tremors. Almost compulsively his head moved sideways as he glanced furtively at the table. The moment he caught sight of the bar of chocolate his tremors became much more violent. He breathed deeply and seemed to go into a faint, leaning backward in the chair with his eyes closed. He remarked that he had no idea why he felt so bad and when questioned he had a complete amnesia for suggestions given him. When he was asked whether he would like a piece of candy, he shook his head emphatically and stated that he disliked chocolate bars. When I attempted to hand him the candy he became agitated and complained of such great physical distress that I found it necessary to rehypnotize him and remove the conflict (p. 337).

For the subject this was clearly not an artificial exercise. The clinical observations one can make about him are significant. It turns out, in fact, that to others he had appeared to be a pillar of the community, something which makes his behavior under hypnosis all the more noteworthy.

But, more interestingly, the same experience can produce radically different results. Note how a second subject reacted when placed in the identical situation:

Another subject, also without expressed neurotic problems responded to the same induced conflict with a generalized autonomic disturbance as well as with gastrointestinal symptoms.

Similar suggestions to produce an experimental conflict were given to the subject in the trance state. When he awoke, he appeared to manifest some tension and trembling. There was complete amnesia for the trance events. He talked spontaneously and loquaciously about foods and eating, and then he skillfully introduced the subject of how in a visit to a mutual friend he had politely refused to eat candy that had been offered to him. However, he insisted, visitors were usually expected to partake of food offered to them. Saying this he reached over, quickly unwrapped the chocolate and ate it with smacking satisfaction. When he had gotten through three-quarters of the bar, he looked up with a puzzled expression on his face and asked if there were something wrong with the chocolate. He remarked that it tasted bitter. He returned the remains of the chocolate to the table, wiped his mouth, and then talked about foods, eating, the virtues of dietary abstemiousness. In the middle of his discourse he began to complain of nausea and stomach pains. He then excused himself and went to the bathroom where he disgorged the candy he had eaten. When he returned to the room he remarked that he felt a great deal better. He kept avoiding commenting about the incident; however, when pressed, he hazarded a guess that the candy was probably spoiled (p. 338).

The same conflict situation—but two very different "solutions." Unlike his partner, Subject 2 is hardly one to take the situation lying down. Psychologically he wants to have his cake (candy) and eat it too. He indulges his appetite (eating the forbidden fruit), makes restitution (disgorges it), then rationalizes the whole business away (as so much spoiled candy). One would expect that if Subjects 3 through 10 were enlisted, one might see yet other styles of handling the same conflict situation. We are for the moment not interested in the repertoire of "solutions" that might be observed but rather in the dramatic way in which hypnosis and posthypnotic suggestion seem to highlight behavior in conflict situations that are, one might say, unconsciously determined.

In order to systematize our terms a bit, let us think not of some conscious/unconscious split but rather of different levels of awareness. One can be vividly aware, for example, of one's discomfiture (pounding heart, rapid breathing, sweating) as one waits to be introduced as "the next speaker on the program." On the other hand, one may be minimally (or not at all) aware of the fact that one invariably makes somewhat sarcastic remarks to a certain person, although, when this is pointed out and one reflects on the observation, it proves to be embarrassingly correct. If, then, it should be the case that one can turn the level of awareness up or down through the medium of hypnosis, it would serve as a useful tool for the study of the unconscious determinants of behavior. Typical phenomena reported in the literature raise one's hopes, as in the following example cited by Hilgard (1965):

> The dental surgeon gives the details of the operation, which included incision of the gums, then the bone over the third molar was removed with a bone chisel, exposing the roots of the tooth near the apices, after which the tooth was removed by forceps. His patient, who is in fact normally

sensitive to pain, showed no signs of pain or discomfort whatever, and in preparing the report for publication he asked the patient to write down his subjective impressions. Meares (the patient) has published widely on therapy, has been president of the International Society for Clinical and Experimental Hypnosis, and his integrity is beyond question. He writes, in part:

". . . When I sat in the dental chair I explained that when I let my arm fall in my lap I would be ready; and I explained that if I raised my arm during the procedure it would be a signal to stop dental work and allow me to regain my relaxation. In retrospect I realize that the thought of raising my arm to halt the dental work never once occurred to me. I was aware all the time as to what was going on; but the awareness was rather vague. When I realized that the bone was being chiselled and that I was not experiencing any pain, for the moment I felt myself becoming angry, as I thought that I must have been given an injection without my knowing it. I then realized that I would not be deceived in this way, and my momentary anger passed off. During the actual extraction I was aware of what was happening and experienced some sensation in that area. This sensation might possibly be described as pain without the hurt of it. There was practically no bleeding. There was not a spot of blood on my handkerchief when I returned home. After the extraction I was surprised at the completeness of the anesthesia, and the thought came to me that I might experience some after-effects. However, I had no after-pain at all. When I arrived home I remember trying to assess my mood, and I decided that I was neither elated nor depressed, but quite normal in my mood and comfortable in myself; and in fact I took my family to dinner at a restaurant and spent the evening at the theatre with no discomfort in my mouth whatsoever" (pp. 126–127).

What interests the clinician is how such possibilities can be turned to legitimate advantage as checks on his theories and as aids in his practice. If hypnosis can be used to induce analogues to unconscious processes *à la carte,* what a ready-made opportunity to subject them to rigorous scrutiny under closely controllable conditions! The possibilities would equal or exceed those presented by dream analysis. Indeed, it is even possible to induce dreams on the spot as part of the hypnotic procedure (see Moss, 1967, for an extensive treatment of this aspect of hypnosis).

But in psychology, as in politics, the parties do not always agree. Perhaps Sarbin (1965) has best described the state of scientific opinion on the subject, suggesting a dimension that runs from complete conviction (the credulous) to frank disbelief (the skeptical). The believers, like Erickson (1944) are convinced of the authenticity of hypnotic phenomena; others, like Sarbin, are very dubious.

What bothers the "nonbelievers" is that hypnotic subjects may not really be demonstrating some exotic behavior but rather they may simply be responding to the "perceived demand characteristics" of the experimental situation, as defined by Orne (1962) and described earlier in Chapter 4. It is argued that under the conditions of heightened suggestibility induced by the hypnotist (the experimenter), the subject behaves the way he has been led to believe subjects are *supposed* to behave in such circumstances. If so, one would need to interpret his behavior, interesting as it is, with considerable reservation. However, like other arguments, this one is best settled on the basis of evidence.

Barber and Hahn (1962), who would place themselves at the skeptical end of the continuum, asked themselves this question: could some of the admittedly unusual behaviors exhibited by hypnotized subjects be produced in subjects not under hypnosis? For the purpose they chose to study the phenomenon of "analgesia" — the ability often demonstrated by hypnotic subjects to bear pain as though anesthetized (as in the example cited by Hilgard above). As a convincing trial, they chose the experience of keeping one's hand immersed in ice water (of 2° C.) for 3 minutes (an ordeal the reader will probably agree he would not welcome).

Choosing subjects susceptible to hypnosis, Barber and Hahn were interested in what would happen if such subjects were given varying types of instructions. For example, members of one group were hypnotized and told that they would feel no discomfort during the experience. In contrast to this "Hypnotic Suggestibility" group, a second group—the "Waking-Imagined"—was subjected to the same trial without hypnosis, although with instructions intended to make the experience a comfortable one. Subjects of a third group—the "Uninstructed"—were simply asked to immerse their hands in the ice water for 3 minutes, while a fourth group—the "Controls"—were asked to do the same, although in their case the supposed "ice water" was actually at room temperature. The experimenters were particularly interested in how the "Waking-Imagined" group would perform, since its members might demonstrate behavior representing response to demand characteristics, as induced by the following instructions:

> In the next part of the experiment I want you to place your left hand in cold water. If you think about how cold the water is you may find it uncomfortable. However, if you try to imagine that the water is pleasant and try to think of it as not uncomfortable, you will be able to keep your hand in the water without being bothered by it at all. Everyone who tried to imagine that the water was pleasant and refused to think of it as uncomfortable was able to do well on this test. You see, this test all depends on your willingness to imagine and to try to think in a certain way. If you do not try to the best of your ability to carry out the instructions you will fail the test and ruin this part of the experiment. What I ask then is your cooperation in helping this experiment by carrying out the following in-

structions: When your hand is in the water, try to imagine that it is a very hot day, that the water feels pleasantly cool, and that your hand is relaxed and comfortable. I'm sure that you'll be able to continue imagining this and that you will not fail this test (p. 412).

Out of 192 female college students who had volunteered as subjects, the experimenters had screened 48 highly hypnotizable subjects (as determined by suitable tests of susceptibility) and assigned 12 at random to each of the four groups. As measures of the effects of the experience, they had both a psychological scale (subjective ratings of comfort/discomfort) and physiological indicators (muscle potential, heart rate, respiration, and skin conductance).

Did all subjects "pass"—that is, hold their hands in the water for 3 minutes? Five did not—the reader may wish to guess from which group(s) they came. Two were from the Uninstructed group, two from the Hypnotic Suggestibility group—only one was from the Waking-Imagined group! To Barber and Hahn the results tell an interesting story. On the Subjective Rating Scale, subjects had indicated, after the experience, whether the ice water had felt cool (a rating of 1 on the scale), uncomfortable (rating of 2), painful (3), or very painful (4). Table 1 shows the results.

Table 1
Subjective impression scores of groups under different treatment conditions with reference to the nature of the experience.

Estimated Stimulus Minute	Experimental Conditions			
	Hypnotically-Suggested Analgesia	Waking-Imagined Analgesia	Uninstructed	Control
First minute	1.6_{ab}	1.8_b	2.8_c	1.1_a
Second minute	2.2_b	1.8_{ab}	3.1_c	1.1_a
Third minute	2.2_b	2.4_b	3.0_b	1.0_a

Note: The lettered subscripts indicate where significant differences occur within and among treatment conditions. Where the subscripts differ, the differences between group means are significant; where subscripts are similar, no significant difference between means exists. (Adapted from Table 1 of Barber & Hahn, 1962. Copyright 1962 by the American Psychological Association and reproduced by permission.)

According to Barber and Hahn, the moral is clear—hypnosis is not as unique a phenomenon as one has been led to believe. Given the same experience without benefit of hypnosis, the Waking-Imagined subjects endured it as well as the hypnotic subjects. Both groups found it less uncomfortable than did the Uninstructed group.

The Control group yields another important finding—namely, that its subjects bore the (admittedly easier) situation better than did the hypnotic subjects who, according to protagonists of hypnosis, are anesthetized. In other words, the hypnotic subjects, while able to bear the experience, were nevertheless still feeling some discomfort, and the Waking-Imagined group, although unhypnotized, suffered no greater discomfort.

The physiological measures tell essentially a similar story, as shown in Table 2.

Table 2
Autonomic lability scores of groups under different treatment conditions.

Physiological Measures	Experimental Conditions			
	Hypnotically-Suggested Analgesia	Waking-Imagined Analgesia	Uninstructed	Control
Forehead muscle potentials	48$_b$	47$_b$	58$_a$	47$_b$
Respiratory irregularity	51$_b$	51$_b$	56$_a$	42$_c$
Heart rate	53$_a$	53$_a$	52$_a$	42$_b$
Skin resistance	48$_b$	47$_b$	48$_b$	57$_a$

Note: To allow for comparisons across measures, the Autonomic Lability Scores were converted to standard scores (with a mean of 50 and a standard deviation of 10). The lettered subscripts indicate where significant differences occur within and among treatment conditions. Where the subscripts differ, the differences between group means are significant; where subscripts are similar, no significant difference between means exists. (Adapted from Table 2 of Barber & Hahn, 1962. Copyright 1962 by the American Psychological Association and reproduced by permission.)

Here Barber and Hahn point out the additional consideration that, whereas the hypnotic subjects showed some significant reductions in muscle potential and respiration (compared with the uninstructed group), such was not the case in heart rate and GSR. These latter two variables, it is noted, are not subject to voluntary control; the first two are, suggesting again that something other than a "trance" may be involved—namely, demand characteristics.

Thus, suggest Barber and Hahn, they have laid to rest the notion of "trance" as responsible for such effects. Not so, argues Hilgard (1965), pointing out that the experimental design of studies such as that of Barber and Hahn leaves much to be desired. Bowers (1966), in a recent doctoral dissertation, tries ingeniously to resolve some of the issues experimentally, and to disentangle the various considerations so that each might be viewed on its merits.

If demand characteristics enter into the behavior of subjects in hypnosis experiments, as well they might, one could wonder whether there is not still such a phenomenon as the "trance state." The problem, Bowers felt, was to design a study in such a way that the demand characteristics variable and the trance variable could be separated in order to determine whether both were contributing in some measure to the overall effect.

Using "simulators"—people who would *pretend* to be hypnotized—and genuinely hypnotized subjects, Bowers planned to compare the groups in two respects. After the experiment was over, would members of one group be better able to recall (that is, verbalize) what they had done during the period of hypnosis (either feigned or real) than would the other? And, once having their behavior under hypnosis described (by themselves or by the experimenter), would one group be able more readily to justify the behavior (that is, to say it had acted voluntarily) than would the other? To help answer these questions, Bowers designed a four-part experiment:

1. Both groups would be instructed to behave in a similar way—one receiving its instructions in the presumed trance state, the other while feigning trance.
2. The instructions would be carried out by each.
3. Both groups would subsequently be made to feel the experiment was over (when actually it was not).
4. Subjects would be examined to see how well they could remember what they had done under hypnosis (or simulation) and how readily they could justify the behavior (that is, term it voluntary).

The somewhat intricate four-phase operation involved three experimenters and proceeded as follows. A pool of 450 undergraduate women students, mostly from the introductory psychology course at the University of Illinois, who had volunteered for an experiment, were given the Harvard Group Scale of Hypnotic Susceptibility. Subjects who passed eight items out of twelve were subsequently seen in one or two individual sessions, where they were given items from the Stanford Hypnotic Susceptibility Scale, and on the basis of the two screening procedures 37 suitable subjects remained. Eight were used in preliminary pilot work, the other 29 were assigned randomly to either the hypnosis group or the simulator group. Data from 27 of the 29 subjects figured in the final results.

In order that the behavior of the two groups might subsequently be compared objectively, simple tasks in which language behavior could be analyzed were chosen.

In one—a so-called Taffel-type task (Taffel, 1955)—the subject was given a series of 3 × 5 index cards, each of which bore a verb and the pronouns *I, he, she, you, we,* and *they* (in different order on the various cards). In each case, the task was to construct a sentence beginning with one of the pronouns and using the particular verb shown. The second task introduced the Make-a-Picture-Story (MAPS) test, in which the subject was asked to make up five sentences for each of two pictures.

Before subjects were given their instructions under hypnosis or simulated hypnosis (at the beginning of the third or fourth individual session), Experimenter I conspicuously turned on a tape recorder which was in full view, a necessary feature of the experimental design. Each subject in the hypnotic group was then hypnotized by Experimenter I by a standard technique which suggested that by the time her arm touched her face, she would be more deeply asleep than she had ever been before. At that point instructions were read to the sleeping subject to the effect that (a) on a task to be presented she would always begin sentences with the "correct" response—namely, "they" or "he," (b) she would be unaware that she was so doing, and (c) on awakening, she would have no memory for these suggestions. The subjects were then awakened and introduced to Experimenter II, who was to administer the Taffel-type task and the MAPS pictures; Experimenter I absented himself during this period.

Subjects in the simulator group underwent the same procedure, except that they *were awakened prior to* the above instructions and told:[2]

> In a moment . . . I am going to read you exactly the same instructions hypnotized subjects are read . . . and later on I want you to pretend as though you had been hypnotized when you were read the instructions, and act just like you think the subjects who had been hypnotized would act under the circumstances. Do you understand? Fine. Here are the instructions (Bowers, 1966, p. 44).

After Experimenter II had administered the experimental task to the subject, Experimenter I reentered the room, seated himself at the desk, and conspicuously switched off the tape recorder. At the same time, by means of a foot pedal, he inconspicuously switched on a second tape recorder hidden in the desk drawer. Turning off the first machine was accompanied by the experimenter's comment: "Well, the experiment is over. Do you have any questions about it?" Hence—and this was a central feature of the design—whatever demand characteristics might have been operating up to

[2] Copyright 1966 by the American Psychological Association. Reprinted by permission of the author and publisher.

that point should no longer be continuing to exercise an influence. That is, the need of any subject in either group to "perform successfully" from that point on should have vanished, since ostensibly the experiment was over (although actually it was not).

Experimenter I subsequently made the remark:

> The purpose of the experiment was to see if the way subjects make up sentences to the index (Taffel) cards has an influence on the way they make them up to (MAPS) pictures. And the reason I had a third person administer the task is because theoretically at least I could have unwittingly biased the responses in the way I wanted them to come out (p. 45).

After any final comments by the subject, Experimenter I asked, just as the subject was preparing to leave, whether she would be willing to talk for a moment to another person (Experimenter III), who was doing a pilot project of his own and had asked whether he might talk briefly to the subjects of Experimenter I before they left. After the subject had agreed, Experimenter I added: "And listen, since we are all finished here, *I want you to be completely honest with him, regardless of what I've said before.*"

Bowers emphasizes the importance of this last statement as follows:

> The purpose of the italicized portion of Experimenter I's "closing speech" was to convince the subject that experimenter I wanted her to tell everything to Experimenter III she could remember, *despite* any suspicions she might have had about whether the experiment was in fact over. Thus, two factors were operating to promote the subject's "confession" concerning her use of "he" and "they." First, the experiment was declared to be over, thereby removing an experimental subject's normal tendency to perform successfully from that point on. Secondly, a new and different demand was established to the effect that the subject was to be honest despite any previous instructions (p. 45).

Experimenter III, like Experimenter II, had no knowledge of whether a given subject belonged to the hypnotic or to the simulator group. With each subject he engaged in a conversational exchange imbedded with a series of standardized questions asked in a given order. These questions were arranged to begin with quite general, unstructured items, leading progressively to more specific, structured questions. Thus, Questions (a), (b), and (c) were as follows:

> (a) Tell me, how did you go about making up sentences to the pictures? (pause) For example, was there any regularity or consistency about the kind of sentences you made up to either of the two pictures?

(b) Was there any similarity in the way you made up sentences to the pictures and the way you made them up to words on the index cards?

(c) Was there any regularity or consistency in the way you made up sentences to the index cards? (p. 45).

In contrast, later questions were as follows:

(f) *At the time* you were actually doing the task did you realize that you were starting all your sentences with "he" and "they"? [If "yes," Experimenter III went on to Question g; if "no," then f_1 was asked.]

(f_1) When you said "no" . . . one possibility is that even though you knew you were using "he" and "they" it was really very natural . . . therefore you simply didn't have to think much about it . . . the second possibility is that you really didn't have the slightest idea that you were starting your sentences with "he" and "they." . . . which of these possibilities seem closer to the truth . . . ?

(g) If you were aware of using "he" and "they," did you realize *at the time* why you were using the words? (p. 46)

With Experimenter III having completed phase 4 of the design, the experiment was *really* over. Bowers and his collaborators had made a noteworthy attempt to separate out the demand characteristics of the situation, in order to ascertain whether there was indeed a trance-state variable over and above methodological artifacts. What did the results show?

In actuality, the two groups did not differ significantly in the extent to which they began sentences with "he" and "they." However, with respect to the ability to recall how they had behaved, all 13 of the simulator subjects verbalized their use of "he" and "they," while only 8 of the 14 hypnotic subjects did so—a statistically significant difference.

In the matter of "justifying" their behavior—that is, asserting they had used "he" and "they" voluntarily—the difference was even more striking. Again, all 13 of the simulator subjects asserted they had behaved voluntarily; only 2 of the 14 hypnotic subjects made such a claim.

Statistically, these differences are highly significant, but as Bowers pointed out, certain objections can still be raised. For example, Experimenter I, who knew to which group a subject belonged, might have unintentionally given a more convincing "closing speech" (that is announcement that the experiment was over) to the simulators than to the hypnotized subjects. To check on this possibility, the 27 tape-recorded closing speeches were given to four independent judges, who were to try to determine for each recording whether it had been given to a simulator or to a hypnotic subject. Three of the four judges did no better than chance; one, however, made significant discriminations. When asked how he had achieved his results, he replied that "... Experimenter I seemed more convincing and persuasive with the hypnotic subjects."!

Feeling he had excluded other possible alternative explanations, Bowers concluded:

> Neither the hypnotic subjects nor the simulating subjects received any specific information about how to behave after the announced conclusion of the experiment... the subsequent termination of the experiment, together with a directive to be honest despite previous suggestions altered the situation for simulating subjects so that it became all right for them to "confess." The fact that an identical alteration in the demand characteristics did not similarly affect the hypnotic subjects is, of course, the critical finding of this investigation. The effects of receiving suggestions under hypnosis evidently take precedence over subsequent, countermanding alterations in the demand characteristics. It is reasonable to conclude that hypnotic behavior is not wholly reducible to acting in accordance with demand characteristics, and that hypnosis seems in part to be an altered state within which suggestions have a peculiarly potent effect (p. 50).

Despite Bowers' methodological ingenuity, there may still be some who would question whether his subjects were "completely honest" with the experimenter when they were implored to tell all. Also, some might doubt that subjects really believed that there was no connection between Experimenter I and Experimenter III. Some theorists (Festinger, 1957) would have further ideas on how subjects could reduce "dissonance" by continued insistence on having been hypnotized, once they had taken that position.

One observer (Gordon, 1970) states the general argument in broader terms as follows:

> The logic of the debate goes like this: if "trance" exists, then so does "unconsciousness." If "trance" behaviours can be ascribed to social psychological variables (demand characteristics, role structuring, etc.), then they cannot be ascribed to "unconsciousness." The flaw in the logic is the first premise; it assumes that "unconsciousness" cannot be related to or ascribed to social psychological variables in the same manner as "trance" behaviours can be. That seems to me to be a patently false assumption. Indeed, if "unconsciousness" — repressions, dissociations, etc. — were not responsive to the individual's position occupations and the role expectancies and prescriptions for those positions, then one

could not defend the notion of unconsciousness. In other words, the concept of unconsciousness *requires* the potency of social stimuli, rather than being inconsistent with the idea that demand characteristics influence behaviour.

Looked at this way, the debate over the existence of "trance" strikes me as irrelevant, the result of a failure to conceptualize adequately. It is not strictly an empirical question. . . . It is a logical problem which stems from asking the wrong question (trance vs. demand characteristics) (Personal communication, 1970).

Apparently the above controversy is not yet resolved, and whether hypnosis is indeed a royal road to the unconscious remains a moot question. Meanwhile other interesting routes to a fuller understanding of human behavior are being followed by still other investigators. The territory they are exploring is virtually uncharted, as will be evident in the following discussion.

Conscious–Unconscious Control of Behavior

Even a person whose knowledge of psychology comes from *Reader's Digest* has learned that psychological conflicts, of which one may be quite unaware, can manifest themselves in disorders affecting any organ system of the body. These conflicts can appear in such varied forms as ulcers, hypertension, asthma, tachycardia, spastic colitis, and others.

Until recently it has seemed that such disorders could be treated only by a combination of medication and psychotherapy. Attempts to bring the malfunctioning organ system more directly under control would have seemed foolish. But interesting signs have now appeared on the horizon. The recent work of Kamiya on the control of brain waves and of Miller on the conditioning of autonomic processes holds real promise for clinicians. Let us, therefore, look at some typical research being conducted by these two experimental psychologists.

The Conscious Control of Brain Waves

Interest ran high when it was first demonstrated that a variety of electrical wave patterns are emitted by various parts of the brain in several states of the organism. Here was objective evidence that brain waves in one condition (for example, resting with one's eyes closed) differed from those in another condition (for example, concentrating on an arithmetic problem with one's eyes open). It was easily demonstrated that the EEG patterns could be altered by having the person assume various states.

(The reader will recall that, in the discussion of dream research in Chapter 2, sleep was characterized by several alternating EEG patterns, with the Stage 1–REM condition signaling the event of dreaming.)

These findings are interesting in their own right. Until recently, however, it was assumed that such brain-wave activity, while possibly a valuable key to the understanding of behavior in general, was outside the individual's control, except as he might alter it in such gross ways as opening or closing his eyes. This proves, however, not to be the case. With proper practice one can gain control over the electrophysiological processes going on inside one's "black box" (the skull), as Kamiya (1968) reports in his work on "conscious control of brain waves," which makes collateral use of the techniques of experimental psychology, computer technology, and electrophysiology.

Kamiya, who became interested in EEG patterns during his dream research at the University of Chicago, centered his attention on the alpha rhythm in particular. This wave pattern, the most prominent in the activity of the brain, appears when a person is resting with his eyes closed and disappears when his eyes are open. The possibility that one might actually gain control over such a process (that is, learn to recognize whether it or some other pattern was operating or, stranger yet, learn to turn it on or off at will) seemed as unlikely as gaining control over the activity of one's stomach or heart. To Kamiya, however, the effort was worth a try. If other behavior can be conditioned, why not this?

Pilot projects using single subjects showed that with some practice and feedback they could, indeed, guess, at better than chance levels, at what times during a given period they were emitting alpha or non-alpha waves. There seemed every reason to pursue the possibilities, and further research at the Langley Porter Neuropsychiatric Institute in San Francisco produced equally promising results. Here the goal was not to have subjects learn to discriminate between patterns, but rather to see whether they could be trained to emit alpha waves at will. Prior discrimination training was therefore omitted. Instead, subjects in a darkened, sound-deadened room were told that a tone would sound and continue as long as their EEG tracing, which would be monitored in another room, showed alpha waves. When the alpha waves disappeared, the tone would cease; when they returned, it would begin to sound again. The task of the subjects was simple—to try to keep the tone sounding as long as they could—that is, to try to gain control over the emission of alpha waves.

Again the findings were encouraging, not only to Kamiya but to others who, he reports, have succeeded in training subjects with a light rather than a sound and with their eyes open rather than closed. Kamiya and his group showed, furthermore, that individual subjects could be trained to increase the length of their average alpha cycles (which differ from person to person). Using a high-pitched click to signal to the subject that a cycle had exceeded his average cycle length and a low-pitched click to signal that a cycle had been shorter than his average, the experimenters assigned the task of increasing the length of alpha cycles.

The ability to produce alpha waves was apparently a rewarding experience for the subjects. Kamiya (1968) reported that people described themselves as "tranquil, calm, and alert" when they were in the alpha state. About half of Kamiya's subjects reported that the alpha state was very pleasant, and some of them asked to repeat the test so they could experience it again.

These reports were reminiscent of descriptions of Zen and Yoga meditation, and practitioners of the latter were subsequently tried as subjects. As predicted, they achieved alpha control much more readily than the average subject. Viewing the overall results of his investigations, Kamiya speculated that it might be possible to train people to reproduce certain mental states. Thus, for example, instead of taking a tranquilizer a person might simply reproduce the state of tranquility by using techniques which he had learned.

The Unconscious Control of Autonomic Processes

Thanks to the recent work of Neal Miller and his associates, what began as basic research on physiological processes in animals may prove to have significant clinical applications in the area of human adjustment. And, in some measure, these exciting findings stem from the willingness of enterprising researchers to question some assumptions previously taken for granted. Specifically, it had been assumed (even with a feeling of appreciation) that the autonomic nervous system was, as its name implies, pretty autonomous. Supposedly, in its own way, it regulated many vital functions—such as respiration, heart rate, blood pressure, and glandular secretion—usually to good advantage, although sometimes it seemed to misfire. The ulcer patient got more than his share of stomach acid, and the person suffering from tachycardia (rapid heart beat) could have done with less vigorous heart action. Pharmacological and psychological approaches to treatment made sense, but this implied a willingness to grant the automatic or autonomous nature of the autonomic nervous system. Could the latter be brought under control directly rather than indirectly? Miller and his group had the courage to ask the question and the ingenuity to find some answers.

The reader is undoubtedly familiar with the oft-cited work of Pavlov and a long line of successors who have shown that, by the process of classical conditioning, such autonomic nervous system functions as salivation can be manipulated. A hungry dog who consistently hears a bell shortly before a puff of meat powder is blown into its mouth gradually comes to salivate at the mere sound of a bell (unaccompanied by food powder), a response which the autonomic nervous system had not previously shown. But while classical conditioning procedures had revealed such contingencies, Miller and his colleagues were more interested in pursuing the possibilities that would arise if autonomic processes were found to be susceptible to control by the techniques of operant conditioning or instrumental learning. (See Walker, 1967, for a full account.) Miller (1969) describes the distinction thus:

> In classical conditioning, the reinforcement must be by an unconditioned stimulus that already elicits the specific response to be learned; therefore, the possibilities are quite limited. In instrumental learning, the reinforcement, called a reward, has the property of strengthening any immediately preceding response. Therefore, the possibilities for reinforcement are much greater; a given reward may reinforce any one of a number of different responses, and a given response may be reinforced by any one of a number of different rewards (p. 435).

Results speak louder than words, however, and Miller and Carmona (1967) set themselves the task of using operant conditioning procedures to manipulate the salivation of thirsty dogs. Using bursts of spontaneous salivation as the unconditioned response and presentation of water as the reinforcing stimulus, the investigators attempted to influence the autonomic process of salivation. In order to be certain that instrumental learning was responsible, they divided the dogs into two groups, one of which would be reinforced for increasing bursts of spontaneous salivation and the other for long intervals between spontaneous bursts. The former group should, then, show increased salivation, the latter decreased salivation. The results of training, carried out over 40 days of a single 45-minute session per day, are shown in Figure 4.

While the investigators considered some possible artifacts that might be responsible (noting, for example, that the dogs who increased salivation were more active), the results were sufficiently impressive to invite further and more complex experiments. Thus, they wondered about the specificity of such conditioning—that is, whether certain visceral responses could be learned independently of one another. This time the animals were rats, and the reinforcement was electrical stimulation of the brain via electrodes implanted in the "pleasure center." (See Butter, 1968, for a discussion of Olds' original work in this area.) In order to rule out the possibility that the rats were simply learning a skeletal rather than a visceral response (so that, for example,

Figure 4
Mean curves of instrumental learning by three thirsty dogs rewarded with water for increases or decreases in spontaneous salivation. (Figure 1 of Miller and Carmona, 1967. Copyright 1967 by the American Psychological Association and reproduced by permission.)

tensing the abdominal muscles directly might affect intestinal contractions indirectly), Miller and Banuazizi (1968) designed an experiment to test the *specificity* of conditioned autonomic responses.

The rats were divided into two groups; in one group conditioning was to be directed to intestinal responses, in the other group it was to be directed to heart rate. The two groups were further subdivided so that in the intestinal group one subgroup was to be reinforced for intestinal contraction and the other for intestinal relaxation, while in the heart rate group one subgroup was to be reinforced for increase in heart rate, the other for decrease.

With the rats paralyzed by injections of curare and maintained on artificial respiration, electrostimulation of the brain was to serve as the reinforcement. If autonomic responses could indeed be instrumentally conditioned, they should show properties similar to those of skeletal conditioned responses, among them the characteristic of specificity. And if this were so, then not only should the rats in the intestinal group show the differential effects of being reinforced for increased or decreased intestinal responses, but also such conditioning should not have affected their heart rate — that is, the effects of conditioning should be specific to the intestinal function. The other group, reinforced for either increase or decrease of heart rate (but not for intestinal responses) should show differential effects in heart rate but not in intestinal reactions. Figures 5 and 6 detail the results.

As predicted, and as shown in Figure 5 the heart rate subgroups did not differ significantly from each other with respect to intestinal responses, while the intestinal subgroups did. When heart rate was measured (see Figure 6), on the other hand, the expected reversal occurred. The heart rate subgroups reflected the effects of differential reinforcement (one showing increase of heart rate, the other decrease), while the intestinal subgroups did not differ significantly from each other with respect to heart rate.

The results seemed convincing, and Miller and his fellow investigators have extended their research into such areas as kidney function, gastric changes, vasomotor responses, and other aspects of visceral functioning, all of which are of vital interest

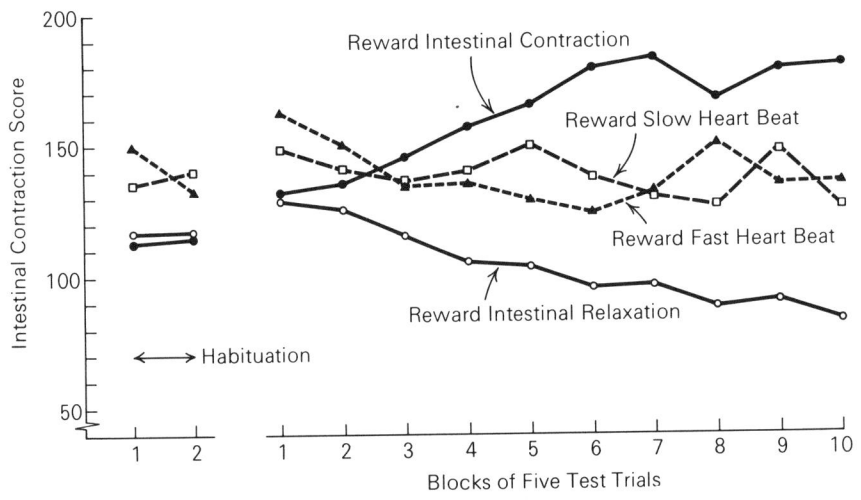

Figure 5

Intestinal contraction scores of four subgroups of rats, two of which were rewarded for increase or decrease of intestinal motility (but not heart rate), the other two for increase or decrease of heart rate (but not intestinal motility). (Figure 3 of Miller and Banuazizi, 1968. Copyright 1968 by the American Psychological Association and reproduced by permission.)

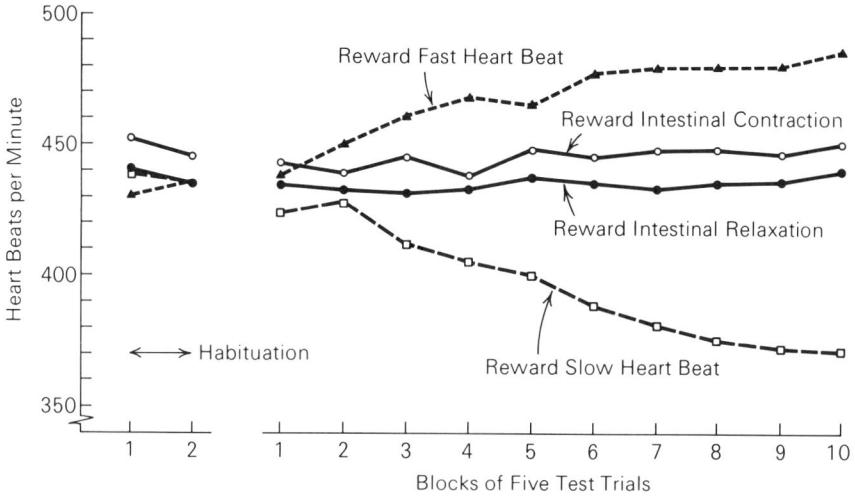

Figure 6
Heart rate scores of the same four subgroups specified in Figure 5, rewarded as noted in Figure 5. (Figure 4 of Miller and Banuazizi, 1968. Copyright 1968 by the American Psychological Association and reproduced by permission.)

to the clinician. Miller (1969) is mindful of the implications, and some of his examples are most apt, as, for instance, the following:

> ... suppose a child is terror-stricken at the thought of going to school in the morning because he is completely unprepared for an important examination. The strong fear elicits a variety of fluctuating autonomic symptoms, such as a queasy stomach at one time and pallor and faintness at another; at this point his mother, who is particularly concerned about cardiovascular symptoms, says, "You are sick and must stay home." The child feels a great relief from fear, and this reward should reinforce the cardiovascular responses producing pallor and faintness. If such experiences are repeated frequently enough, the child, theoretically, should learn to respond with that kind of symptom. Similarly, another child whose mother ignored the vasomotor responses but was particularly concerned by signs of gastric distress would learn the latter type of symptom. I want to emphasize, however, that we need careful clinical research to determine how frequently, if at all, the social conditions sufficient for such theoretically possible learning of visceral symptoms actually occur. Since a given instrumental response can be reinforced by a considerable variety of rewards, and by one reward on one occasion and a different reward on

Research on Levels of Awareness

another, the fact that glandular and visceral responses can be instrumentally learned opens up many new theoretical possibilities for the reinforcement of psychosomatic symptoms (p. 444).[3]

In the same article, Miller (1969) states the clinical significance of some of the findings of his research team. As he puts it:

> If the patient who is highly motivated to get rid of a symptom understands that a signal, such as a tone, indicates a change in the desired direction, that tone could serve as a powerful reward. Instructions to try to turn the tone on as often as possible and praise for success should increase the reward. As patients find that they can secure some control of the symptom, their motivation should be strengthened. Such a procedure should be well worth trying on any symptom, functional or organic, that is under neural control, that can be continuously monitored by modern instrumentation, and for which a given direction change is clearly indicated medically, for example, cardiac arhythmias, spastic colitis, asthma, and those cases of high blood pressure that are not essential compensation for kidney damage.... The obvious cases to begin with are those in which drugs are ineffective or contraindicated. In the light of the fact that our animals learned so much better when under the influence of curare and transferred their training so well to the normal, nondrugged state, it should be worth while to try to use hypnotic suggestion to achieve similar results by enhancing the reward effect of the signal indicating a change in the desired direction, by producing relaxation and regular breathing, and by removing interference from skeletal responses and distraction by irrelevant cues (p. 444).

Although his subjects are animals, Miller is clearly willing to speculate about the implications of his research for humans, a predilection that is to be admired, since it attests to a desire to consider the broader significance of one's findings. If, however, one feels safer in using human subjects as a basis for talking about human behavior, there is certainly ample opportunity. Indeed, one of the areas clinicians are interested in is the behavior of clinicians themselves; the following section presents some possibilities for carrying out such exploration.

[3] Copyright 1969 by the American Association for the Advancement of Science. Reprinted by permission of the author and publisher.

8
Research in Clinical Assessment

One cannot help being impressed by the way in which young student nurses are able to describe their patients. Without benefit of technical terminology, they have a knack for observing behavior keenly and describing it vividly. In a typical instance, the high-fidelity portrayals of incoming patients by one such beginner consistently outshone the more stereotyped write-ups of the professional staff. Six months later, alas, after she had learned her full share of diagnostic terms, she dispatched new patients summarily with such phrases as "paranoid schiz." Undoubtedly the fledgling nurse now felt herself an old hand at the game. Unfortunately, she had sold her priceless gift of first-rate description for a mess of technical jargon.

This is not to say that diagnostic nomenclature serves no purpose; it does. But too often the neophyte acts as if learning this new language automatically makes him a professional. It is as if he feels that the ordinary language of description serves no further purpose. Actually the great taxonomers in this field doubtless ranked high in the ability to make the finest of descriptive discriminations. The psychiatrist Kraepelin (1915) proposed a system of classification which, with some variations, still forms the basis of the diagnostic scheme used in clinical settings today. When some outstanding clinicians, like Menninger et al. (1963), now advocate return to a more global approach, they do so in large measure out of dissatisfaction with the slavish way in which Kraepelin's system is often misused. The mechanical application of technical labels is a poor substitute for the dual process of careful observation and painstaking description.

The situation reminds one of the unfortunate bastardization of some of Freud's seminal concepts. An interested party reads a work of Freud—or more likely "a book on Freud"—and soon begins tossing off terms like superego, cathexis, and castration anxiety with abandon in describing the character in a novel, a hospital patient, or perhaps his own brother-in-law. What began as the creative speculation of a great thinker and theorist like Freud thereby becomes psychological jargon that obscures rather than delineates psychodynamics.

The Rorschach inkblots are another case in point. Early in the century, the psychiatrist Hermann Rorschach had the interesting notion that if one presented people with a situation that was completely unstructured—for example, a stimulus such as a meaningless inkblot—one might find interesting differences in the way it is perceived. This proved to be the case when Rorschach presented a set of such blots to a large number of patients. Encouraged, he took the next step of devising a systematic procedure whereby responses could be catalogued and "scored." Thus, one person may see an inkblot as a single thing (for example, "a butterfly") while someone else regards various parts of it as separate percepts. Still another may see things in only the very tiniest details of the blot, ignoring the rest of it. Again, different aspects of the card seem important "determinants" for different people. Thus, one can see a blot, or parts of it, as "a peach" because of its color, another because of its shape, a third because of both its color and shape. The differences are no less striking in content interpretation. One person might not see a single human element in any of the ten blots, but would identify many animals. Another person's set of responses might be characterized by vehemence—"Looks like a tornado tearing up a town"; "This could be a surgeon's scalpel cutting through a stomach"; "Here is a sharp bayonet that seems to be jabbing this man in the back."

Development of a schema for coding and scoring responses required originality, sensitivity, and perceptiveness. The clinical student who feels it his duty to memorize Rorschach's scoring system, only to write test reports that are at best stereotyped and at worst superficial, is like the psychiatric intern who mechanically assigns diagnostic labels. For these reasons, the reader (who has undoubtedly already learned his share of diagnostic terms, if only from reading newspaper accounts of murder trials) would do well to imagine himself living in the pre-Kraepelinian era before a formal diagnostic nomenclature had been developed. How might the inmates of a mental hospital then be classified?

Clearly there is a need to bring some kind of conceptual order out of the chaos that exists as 100 disturbed people wander around a ward behaving in their different ways. As an observer, one might decide to begin with a simple, quite observable, objectively describable aspect of behavior—the act of talking. Does a patient talk at all? The simple yes-no distinction may yield a number of patients who do not talk at all and who, according to their attendants, have not uttered a word for a year or more. Having identified a group of patients who do talk, how do they differ from one another? We note that some speak in monosyllables, others in paragraphs; some talk only when spoken to, others spontaneously, still others incessantly; some speak almost inaudibly, while some characteristically shout.

Assuming that, as observer, we have recorded such aspects of talking as frequency, amplitude, and other dimensions, we might choose next to assess the *content* of the patient's speech. Again it would not be difficult to obtain reasonably good agreement among observers as to such a quality as coherence. The exchange: "How are you today?" "I'm feeling a little better" differs from "How are you today?" "There was a rose and its name I cannot tell." Or we might examine content for its congruence with reality. "They don't give us enough to eat in this hospital" differs from "When they find out I'm an astronaut, they'll move me from this radar station to Cape Kennedy."

The reader is left to think about the many other aspects of the relatively straightforward act of talking that an observer could note and attempt to classify. Equally simple and still fairly objectifiable behaviors—mode of dress, movement and activity, posture, facial expression, mannerisms, to name only a few—will occur to one as he visualizes how he would go about developing a classification scheme. If, having pondered the problem at some length, the reader is still not discouraged, he may wish to turn his attention to somewhat more complex and not as easily observable aspects of behavior—such as thought processes, mood and feeling tone, or motivational strength. And if, instead of becoming frustrated and confused by that time, he finds himself challenged by the complexity of categorizing behavior (let alone explaining it) and captivated by the diversity of possible approaches, he may well be a budding taxonomer.

Meanwhile clinicians continue to wrestle with man-sized problems in the areas of assessment and prediction, making continuing efforts to review their progress.

Clinical Prediction

Clinicians seem to get twitted about their efforts more than most. It seems easier for a psychologist to predict whether a rat will turn right or left after several trials in a T-maze than to predict how an alcoholic will behave at a party. Indeed, clinicians are not above rubbing salt into their own wounds when research studies point up typical frailties of some of their techniques.

In what follows we shall try to give the flavor of some representative research on clinical prediction, beginning with a paper by Kadushin (1963) that good-naturedly reminds the mental health professions (in this case social workers) of some of their foibles. Next, Weiss (1963) and Soskin (1954, 1959) deal with the predictive ability of psychologists as compared with nonpsychologists and of psychologists as compared with each other. Finally, we shall turn to some studies that point up typical artifacts in research of the type done by Weiss and Soskin, while suggesting the kinds of investigation needed at this point. After seeing both sides of the coin, the reader can better estimate its value.

"Diagnosis and Evaluation for (Almost) All Occasions"

That is how Kadushin (1963) entitled his article. In it he cites an early study by Forer (1949) in which 39 introductory psychology students were asked to complete the Forer Diagnostic Interest Blank, after which each was to be given a personality sketch based on his set of responses. Unknown to the subjects, Forer had prepared a single sketch in advance, one which was to be given to each of the subjects (as though it were intended for him personally). It contained statements like the following:[1]

> "You have a tendency to be critical of yourself."
>
> "At times you are extroverted, affable, sociable, while at other times you are introverted, wary, reserved."
>
> "Disciplined and self-controlled on the outside, you tend to be worrisome and insecure inside."
>
> "Your sexual adjustment has presented problems for you" (p. 12).

Upon completion of the Forer Diagnostic Interest Blank, every subject was given the personality sketch that was presumably (although not really) based on his responses. Each was asked to rate it on a 5-point scale in terms of how well it applied to him (0 = poor to 5 = perfect). The mean rating for the group as a whole proved to be 4.26! That is, although the sketch was neither based on the responses of the subjects nor tailored to any individual, most students evidently thought it fit them almost perfectly.

The hooker, of course, was that the sketch was mainly composed of what Kadushin calls "Aunt Fanny" statements—statements that could be as true of one's Aunt Fanny as of oneself. Paterson had earlier mentioned the "Barnum effect," referring to the penchant of circus impresario Phineas T. Barnum for making much ado about nothing. On the assumption that many social work reports contain their measure of such

---

[1]Copyright 1963 by The National Association of Social Workers. Reprinted by permission of the author and publisher.

Aunt Fanny statements, Kadushin was interested in how experienced social workers (in contrast to Forer's beginning psychology students) might overcome, or fall victim to, the influence of the same phenomenon. Accordingly, he designed the following study.

Subjects were 60 student supervisors who were attending an institute on supervision in social work. All had master's degrees from schools of social work, and all but one had experience in supervision. They came from a variety of social work settings, including child guidance clinics, hospitals, family service agencies, and parole units. Prior to the study, Kadushin had gone to various sources for case summaries, selecting three widely different examples—one describing a boy of 5, another a girl of 15, and a third a woman in her late 30's. Dividing the group of 60 social work supervisors into three groups of 20 subjects each, Kadushin presented the case summary of the boy to one, that of the girl to another, and that of the woman to the third group. Along with her particular case summary, each subject received a diagnostic statement she thought was related to it. Actually a *single* diagnostic report had been prepared by the experimenter, so that all 60 subjects received the same statement, which had been prepared *before* the case summaries had been selected. As the reader may suspect, the diagnostic statement was composed essentially of Aunt Fanny descriptions —as the author puts it, it ". . . was designed to have near universal validity."

An introductory excerpt from each of the case summaries should convince the reader that they were actually very different from one another. The respective opening paragraphs read as follows:

> *Case 1:* Larry was a 5-year-old boy who was referred to a child guidance clinic for casework. He had recurrent bloody diarrhea of one-and-a-half-years' duration, diagnosed as ulcerative colitis. The mother thought that episodes of diarrhea often occurred at times of emotional stress . . . (p. 14).
>
> *Case 2:* Sylvia's problem was brought to the attention of a family service agency by the group worker in the recreational agency to which she belonged. The other youngsters in the group had made it plain that they disliked her. Sylvia, at 15 years of age, was bright and able, but tried to win recognition by aggressive, intellectual behavior that antagonized the group into frank hostility. On several occasions Sylvia had expressed to the group leader her deep feelings of rejection and isolation, and eventually she accepted the suggestion that she needed individual help. She also suffered from frequent headaches . . . (p. 15).
>
> *Case 3:* Early in June, Mrs. L. was referred to the family service agency by a psychiatric clinic in which she had been interviewed once. When she first came to the office Mrs. L. was extremely tense and frightened. She

was an attractive woman in her late 30's, neatly dressed but very thin and pale. Her symptoms were a feeling of tension and panic which became particularly acute at times, a fear that she was "going to crack up," and phobic reactions when she was away from the house, particularly on public transportations. When she had the nervous spells—which she could describe only as a terrible feeling—she became very frightened that something awful was going to happen to her and that she could not continue to carry on . . . (p. 16).

The reader will probably agree that the respective cases are, indeed, different from one another. He will probably also agree that the prefabricated diagnostic summary (of which each subject received the identical copy, regardless of what group she was in) contains its share of Aunt Fanny statements. A brief portion of the diagnosis reads as follows:

> Larry [or Sylvia, for Group 2; or Mrs. L., for Group 3] is reacting to a difficult life situation. The situational problem is, however, superimposed on the trauma of emotional deprivation during earlier, crucial periods in the client's developmental history. There is ambivalence toward parental figures and while the client shows some capacity to develop healthy object relationships, potentialities in this regard show some impairment. There is a tendency to convert emotional difficulties into physical symptoms as a mechanism of defense. The client's tendency toward anxiety is evident in relation to dependency needs and in the area of sexual identification . . . (p. 17).

The subjects had a clear-cut assignment. They were to study both the case summary and the accompanying diagnostic statement, then simply to rate the quality of the statement on a 7-point scale ranging from "Definitely inadequate" to "Definitely superior." The results are shown in Table 1.

Table 1
Distribution of ratings for standard case description.

Rating Level	Cases		
	Larry	Sylvia	Mrs. L.
7 – Definitely superior	0	3	1
6 – Excellent	8	4	5
5 – Slightly above average	6	4	8
4 – Average	2	5	2
3 – Slightly below average	4	2	2
2 – Poor	0	2	2
1 – Definitely inadequate	0	0	0
Totals	20	20	20

(Table 1 of Kadushin, 1963. Copyright 1963 by *Social Work* and reproduced by permission.)

Without quoting some of his less charitable concluding sentiments, we shall let the case rest with the following remarks by Kadushin on Table 1:

> The mean rating for all three cases is almost identical—4.9 in the case of Larry, 4.75 for Sylvia, 4.75 for Mrs. L. A mean of 5 is the equivalent of a "slightly above average" rating. This implies that a student who had submitted this same diagnosis on any of the three cases, even before he saw the client, would have been given a rating close to "slightly above average" for his diagnostic ability (p. 18).

Our intent here is not to cast stones at another profession; Kadushin, himself a member of the profession of social work, has amiably enough taken himself and his colleagues to task. Let us therefore look more squarely at how psychologists themselves fare in some of their own efforts at assessment.

Prediction in the Form of Postdiction

In his concern with the problem of prediction, Soskin (1954, 1959) utilized the interesting notion of "postdiction" as a device for evaluating ability to assess others' behavior, given some information about them. Rather than attempt to predict what someone will do in the future, one might try to postdict—that is, to guess how a person had actually behaved in given situations in the past.

Postdiction has advantages. If someone *predicts* about John Smith that he will always have difficulty in relating to women, (a) it will take some time to find out whether the prediction is true, (b) someone will have to keep track of Smith over the years, (c) the terms of the prediction—"difficulty in relating to women"—will have to be more clearly defined, and so on. On the other hand, given some information about Smith, and given an actual situation that we know has taken place, someone can be asked to *postdict*—that is, to judge how Smith must have behaved in the situation.

Soskin's "Criterion Test" (1954) was devised for the purpose. In the following case, "Linda," along with her husband and several close friends designated by her, provided the actual information about her previous behavior in various real-life situations. The task of the experimental subjects, being tested for their ability to "postdict," was to judge which of four multiple-choice statements was correct in the various instances. Some typical items follow:

> 4. In the immediate neighborhood she (a) has a wide circle of casual friends who frequently "drop in"; (b) is the confidant of several young mothers; (c) has one intimate friend and has only fleeting contacts with others; (d) is considered a gossip, hence not too popular.

5. As a housekeeper she is (a) meticulous and tidy, rather intolerant of toys, clothes, etc. not in their proper places; (b) rather untidy — doing about as much as needs to be done; (c) spends a considerable amount of time adding new feminine touches to the interior; (d) so incompetent that on two occasions neighbors have complained to the Board of Health.

8. Last summer the family went on a long trip to visit Linda's parents-in-law. Linda (a) was rather excited about the trip since she likes her husband's parents better than her own parents; (b) privately felt a little bitter about spending the money this way, when it would be no vacation for her to have to take care of the children as usual; (c) was opposed to taking the trip because the money would have to be taken out of savings they were accumulating to buy a house; (d) induced her husband to fly instead of driving — to get the maximum thrill out of the trip (p. 69).

When given the test, subjects were provided with some basic information about Linda — that she was a 26-year-old white married mother of two children, who had some college education and was the daughter of a moderately successful businessman, etc. Without dwelling on the details of the study, it is sufficient to say that Soskin was interested in how novices (beginning graduate students in clinical psychology) compared with more experienced clinicians and in how helpful it is to judges to have additional information about the subject in the form of personality-test responses — Rorschach and Thematic Apperception Test (TAT) in this case.

The findings were instructive. Novices tended early in their training (before taking a course in the TAT) to see Linda as the relatively well-adjusted person she was, whereas the experienced clinicians saw her as more disordered. With further training, and with benefit of such additional information as Linda's TAT stories, the novices came to regard Linda as more maladjusted, as had the experienced clinicians from the start. Too, the accuracy scores of the experienced clinicians and those of the novices at the end of their TAT course, did not differ significantly.

A series of related studies has raised similar questions about the degree to which students do or do not improve with clinical training and the degree to which they do more poorly, as well as, or better than experienced clinicians from the start. The research to be discussed in a later section will deal with some of the methodological artifacts that lend perspective to such findings. For the moment, Soskin's (1954) own interpretation of his results provides some comfort. He states:

> As the foregoing implies, these results cannot be taken to indicate that there is no difference between novices and more experienced persons in their ability to use projective devices accurately. It seems sounder to assume that which is most in accord with observation, viz., that some peo-

ple learn with experience while others do not, and that among more experienced users of these instruments there will be both "good" and "poor" predictors (p. 74).

**Effect of Background Training
and Fund of Information
on Prediction**

Like Soskin, Weiss (1963) found herself drawn to research on clinical prediction yet puzzled by some unexpected and sometimes contradictory findings reported by various investigators. Certain studies, for example, suggested that prediction becomes more accurate, the more information judges possess; others indicated that accuracy does not necessarily increase with amount of information and, in fact, may in some cases actually decrease. Some studies showed experienced clinicians as more accurate in their prediction than relatively inexperienced ones, yet in other studies graduate students turned out to be as good predictors as Ph.D. psychologists.

Weiss felt, understandably, that further aspects of the general problem warranted attention. If, for example, one matched age, intellectual status, and educational level, how would a group of trained clinical psychologists compare with another profession in ability to predict the behavior of a person? Further, how would subgroups compare when one group was given little prior information on the person whose behavior was to be predicted, while another was given substantially more information? Finally, how would a group given correct information about the mental status of the person whose behavior was to be predicted compare with a group given incorrect information?

Weiss started with some commonsense expectations: (a) clinical psychologists should prove better predictors than members of a nonclinical profession; (b) judges with more information about a person should be able to predict his behavior better than judges with less information; and (c) judges with correct information about a person's status should be able to predict more accurately than judges with incorrect information.

Taking advantage of Soskin's earlier work, she adapted his Criterion Test to her ends, framing 28 multiple-choice questions such as the following:

> There was a lot of talk at the restaurant where Ruth works about something she had done. The incident involved:
>   a. Ruth's necking with a black employee at a party.

b. Ruth's organizing a strike for higher wages.
c. Ruth's reporting to work one night drunk.
d. Ruth's keeping tips left for other waitresses (pp. 258–259).

So that the stem (introductory part) of a question would not give away the correct answer, a larger pool of items had been pretested with the help of undergraduate volunteers (80 students taking the first draft of the test and 50 the second). The 28 items adopted were those which would not, by their wording alone, enhance anyone's predictive ability. Doctoral-level clinical psychologists were to be asked to postdict the correct answer in each case; their accuracy was to be compared with that of members of a nonclinical profession—physical scientists, with a degree in either physics, chemistry, or engineering. Of a larger pool of subjects, 60 in each group were chosen for the task, psychologists having been selected from the directory of the American Psychological Association and physical scientists from the tenth edition of *American Men of Science*. All were males, born after 1900, who had received both their undergraduate and graduate degrees in the United States.

The people whose behavior was to be predicted (that is, postdicted on the Criterion Test) were three undergraduate students—Ray, Ron, and Ruth—volunteers from an undergraduate psychology course, naive as to the object of the experiment. Each was taken individually to a room and asked to talk spontaneously about himself (herself) into a tape recorder for not more than 30 minutes, using as a guide ten such general topics as ". . . educational and vocational goals, family experiences, emotional relationships, ethical and religious views, and so on." With this information in hand, Weiss set up a factorial design for her study. That is, she divided the 60 judges of each group randomly into 5 subgroups of 12 subjects each, so that each subgroup represented a different combination of the variables of professional background, amount of information available, and correctness of the information supplied. Amount of information could be minimal (that the subject was a [age]-year-old [sex] college student) or maximal (similar information plus a typescript of the subject's previously tape-recorded self-interview). So that subgroups of judges would differ in terms of set, half were given accurate information about the subject's status (that the subject was a student who had been hired to participate), the other half inaccurate information (that the subject was a student being seen in the University Counseling Service for help with personal problems).

The results, interesting in their implications, are shown in Table 2. Some significant differences are worth noting. In terms of predictive efficiency, there is, for example, an interesting interaction between the profession of the judge and the amount of information available. Whether a judge did better with more information than with less depended on his profession; physical scientists did better than clinical psychologists when more information was available, while clinical psychologists did better than physical scientists when less information was available. Analyzing the performance of the two professions separately again reveals some interesting contrasts. Within the clinical psychologist group there was a trend (although not statistically

Table 2
Accuracy scores on multiple-choice, four-foil, 28-item test for all treatment combinations.

| | | Self-Interview ||||||
| | | Correct Minimal ||| Incorrect Minimal |||
		Ruth	Ray	Ron	Ruth	Ray	Ron
Psychologist	M	6.80	7.20	6.80	6.60	5.40	7.60
	SD	1.72	0.75	1.94	1.50	1.02	1.62
Physical scientist	M	9.00	9.20	9.40	6.40	7.60	9.60
	SD	2.68	2.79	1.74	1.20	1.36	2.15

| | | No-Self-Interview ||||||
| | | Correct Minimal ||| Incorrect Minimal |||
		Ruth	Ray	Ron	Ruth	Ray	Ron
Psychologist	M	6.00	7.80	8.00	8.80	7.00	8.20
	SD	1.79	1.17	2.45	3.54	2.28	2.14
Physical scientist	M	6.40	6.80	6.80	5.40	5.60	7.40
	SD	1.50	0.98	0.75	2.06	0.80	2.24

(Table 1 of Weiss, 1963. Copyright 1963 by the American Psychological Association and reproduced by permission.)

significant) toward doing more poorly when given more information; that is, subgroups of psychologists without the self-interview data tended to do better than those psychologists having the additional self-interview data. In contrast, within the physical scientist profession there was a significant positive relationship between amount of information and predictive efficiency; that is, subgroups of physical scientists who had more information—the additional data contained in the self-interview—did better than the physical scientists in subgroups that were without such self-interview material.

At first glance, the findings may seem rather unflattering, if not embarrassing, to the clinician. Weiss, however, adds some consoling explanations. In the earlier study of Soskin (1954), it was suggested that part of the explanation might lie in the apparent proclivity of clinicians to read into data more pathology than is actually there. Weiss suggests that such a factor may have been operating in her experiment also. Fifty-four of the physical scientists worked in industrial settings; 56 of the 60 clinical psychologists were from academic settings. It is possible, then, she suggests, that the psychologists do better with minimal information because of their greater familiarity with the behavioral base rate of college students. Given fuller information, however, they may yield to their tendencies to see more pathology in the material than is really there, thus doing more poorly with college students as objects of prediction.

Whatever the proper explanation may be, in the last analysis Weiss' study raises interesting questions for further research. Is it possible, for example, that additional information in a case may serve to lower rather than increase diagnostic accuracy? Although clinicians think they are using all of the data at hand, might they really be basing their predictions on such fairly limited, although perhaps decisive, information as age, sex, and occupation of the person being assessed?

While similar questions interest other investigators, Weiss expresses some pertinent reservations about whether such research provides adequate opportunity for the clinician to display his special skills. Perhaps her comment on the central instrument in her study will help comfort any reader whose faith in clinical expertise may have been somewhat shaken at this point, as well as provide a fitting transition to the views of others, discussed in the following sections, who would not take the results of studies like Weiss' too seriously. As Weiss comments:

> Perhaps the finding of major importance in terms of the criterion tests is that although improvement in scores is possible, the tests are quite difficult and all the means hover around the expected chance mean. Though there is some evidence from an undergraduate population that on retest judges tend to respond to the items in a manner consistent with their original responses (Thorson, 1962) and may not be responding on a random basis, the reader still may question whether the criterion tests afford an adequate or meaningful opportunity for the psychologist to test his predictive abilities (p. 261).

The Other Side of the Coin

In trying to give the clinician a fairer hearing, Lewinsohn et al. (1963) remind one of criticisms that have been leveled at past studies of predictive skill. Some of them, for example, had asked the clinician to make predictions of a kind with which he was relatively unfamiliar (for example, the attitude of someone toward social drinking) and/or required him to use a rating scale with which he was equally unfamiliar. Given the tools of his trade and situations with which he was used to dealing, would he not do better? Lewinsohn and his colleagues set out to examine the question with a design intended to study the clinician in his more natural surroundings.

If earlier studies had forced prefabricated instruments upon them, why not meet this objection by having the clinicians participate in the development of the rating scale to be used in the research? Further, rather than require them to make assessments or predictions in unfamiliar situations, why not allow them to do so in the case of patients, a population with which they were familiar? If one asked clinicians to make judgments under these circumstances, after they had been given substantial prior opportunity to use the special rating scale in their daily work, one should have a much fairer basis on which to evaluate their hit-and-miss ratios.

Lewinsohn et al. proceeded in just this way. After the foregoing had been accomplished, five Ph.D.-level clinical psychologists were asked to use the special rating scale to record their judgments about unidentified patients whose test protocols they were given, having been told only each patient's age and sex. One hundred such test records were selected at random from among those patients whose files contained complete and adequate test protocols. Each judge was assigned 40, so that there would be two judges rating each record. The task, then, was to do a "blind analysis" of the test records (that is, without knowing who the patients were), recording judgments by means of the various items of the rating scale — 23 items such as intellectual impairment, thought processes, motor speed, mood, sexual identification, amount of pathology, and other items of clinical interest.

The validity of the blind ratings was assessed in two ways. Four other psychologists used the same scale, but based their ratings on a review of the information in the patients' hospital folders (from which all test reports and protocols had been removed). Additionally, a psychologist unaware of the results interviewed the patients and recorded their behavior on the Multidimensional Scale for Rating Psychiatric Patients (MSRPP) devised by Lorr (1953). By appropriate statistical techniques, the ratings made by the judges using only the test materials of the patients could be evaluated against (a) ratings made by those judges who used patients' hospital charts and (b) ratings made by the psychologist who used interview behavior as his basis. The results, as interpreted by Lewinsohn and his group, show clinicians in a much better light than do studies that omit essential methodological features. The investigators summarize the findings and their implications thus:

> It appears that in the context of this study, ratings based upon tests of such variables as intellectual functioning, bizarreness of fantasies, disturbances of thinking, reality testing, depression, anti-social tendencies,

schizophrenicity, neuroticism, psychoticism, and anxiety, are sufficiently valid to be of clinical usefulness in the study of an individual case.... We interpret these findings as support for the impression held by clinicians that they can make some valid judgments on the basis of psychological tests. Why, then, one may ask, does this study show positive results when so many others have found little validity for individual interpretation of psychological tests? The major differences in methodology between this and previous studies appear to be as follows: (a) The judges in this study were working with a rating scale which they had helped to develop. ... (b) The ratings were made on a population which was well-known to the judges. (c) The judges were predicting criteria with which they were familiar. These three considerations seem to us to be crucial prerequisites in attempting to gain any accurate picture of the reliability and validity of clinical inferences made from tests (pp. 72–73).

Lest one now conclude that justice has been done, clinicians exonerated, and the problem of prediction laid to rest, let us turn to a more recent and carefully sequenced series of experiments by Chapman and Chapman (1967). They remind us that only by continuing research on the nature of their operations will clinicians be able to avoid the pitfalls of prediction while at the same time progressively improving their techniques. The reader who wonders what the shouting is all about has only to put himself in the position of a clinician asked to make some typical predictions.

Imagine yourself a clinical psychologist on the staff of a psychiatric hospital. John Smith is an applicant for a job as attendant. Should he be hired? You are free to interview him and/or administer a test or tests in the brief time available. You have in front of you Mr. Smith and the application he has filled out. Any number of questions are at issue. Is Smith dependable? How well motivated is he for this type of work? Is he qualified (whatever the qualifications may be)? Does he drink to excess? (He would doubtless say no, even if he does, since he evidently wants the job.) As a 35-year-old man, who has never married, does he have any sexual difficulties that may get in the way of his relationship with patients (or with other attendants or nurses, for that matter)? With a master's degree in education, why has he left teaching to seek a job as attendant, which he describes as "noble work"? True, if hired, Smith will be on probationary appointment for 90 days, so that he can be released during that period if he proves unsatisfactory. But the time and money used to train him will have been wasted under the circumstances and the job will again be vacant.

Posed in these terms, the problem may begin to seem real rather than academic to the reader. Perhaps he will better understand, too, why clinicians are continually seeking assessment devices that will help in the many kinds of situations in which they are called upon to make predictions. Thus, when one of their number proposed the notion that analysis of drawings made by people could provide useful clinical insights, they were understandably quick to look into the possibility. Indeed, the Draw-a-Person Test (DAP) of Machover (1948) gained considerable popularity in clinical work. Peoples' drawings reveal a wide range of individual differences—some draw a man, some a woman; some draw a large figure, some a small one; some figures are nude, others clothed, some menacing, some docile. These are but a few of the distinctions readily apparent as one examines the productions drawn by a dozen people in response to the identical request: draw a person.

Partly because of the rich store of distinctive responses elicited by the DAP, the clinical literature abounds in articles describing the many ways in which the test has been used. Clinicians seem able to agree among themselves about the way characteristics, whether of disordered or of normal individuals, are revealed by various aspects of the drawings people produce. However, the reports of research studies have frequently called some of these assumptions into question. That is, "signs" said to be indicative of a particular trait or condition have frequently failed to hold up under empirical test.

The instances were widespread enough to lead Chapman and Chapman (1967) to design a series of interlocking studies whose aim was to help explain the discrepancies. They chose as subjects naive users of the test, whose performance was to be compared with that of experienced clinicians. The fact that the clinicians could agree with each other so well—although the results of research frequently did not substantiate assumptions made about various test "signs"—suggested the presence of some systematic error. That is, while the research results could lead one to doubt the *validity* of statements made on the basis of the DAP, the *reliability* of the statements was impressive—as a group, clinicians consistently showed high agreement among themselves. What interested Chapman and Chapman was whether the "reliable inaccuracy," the systematic error, could be ". . . produced by variables inherent in the stimuli observed, and are of such a nature that entirely naive observers who view psychodiagnostic materials would report the same erroneous correlates of patients' symptoms" (pp. 193–194). After all, they point out, normal people looking at some of the well-known illusions, for example the Müller-Lyer illusion, where the direction of arrowheads makes two equal lines look unequal, are ready prey and systematically err in agreeing that one line is longer than the other.

The investigators began by collecting signs in the DAP used by experienced clinicians to delineate traits or conditions of those making the drawings. A group of clinicians was given a questionnaire composed of items like the following:

He is worried about how manly he is.
The pictures drawn by such men would more often be characterized by:
1. _____
2. _____ (p. 195).

The replies of 44 psychodiagnosticians, all of whom used the DAP regularly, and almost all of whom were doctoral psychologists, served as a basis for the experiment. The investigators used all the categories of drawing characteristics that had been listed by at least 15 percent of the respondents as associated with at least one of the following symptom statements to be paired with drawings to be used in the experiment:[2]

1. He is worried about how manly he is.
2. He is suspicious of other people.
3. He is worried about how intelligent he is.
4. He is concerned with being fed and taken care of by other people.
5. He has had problems of sexual impotence.
6. He is very worried that people are saying bad things about him (p. 195).

As their naive subjects, the experimenters used a total of 108 students from undergraduate psychology classes, mainly the introductory courses. Drawings were collected from state-hospital patients and from graduate students in clinical psychology. Of the 45 drawings used in the experiment, 35 were from psychotic patients, 10 from nonpsychotics. Three sets of 15 drawings each—Forms A, B, and C—were constructed. Each drawing was accompanied by two of the above six statements, allegedly the symptoms of the persons who had drawn it. Actually the symptom statements were assigned systematically to the 45 drawings so that ". . . each drawing characteristic occurred as often with one symptom statement as another" (p. 196). The experimenters took pains to avoid any differential relationship. "For example," they report, "the symptom statement, 'He is worried about how intelligent he is' was paired as often with drawings having small heads as with large or medium-sized heads" (p. 197).

In other words, the alleged relationship between any drawing and the symptom statements accompanying it was a contrived one. With the naive subjects led to believe it was the actual relationship, the investigators were interested in how these subjects would characterize the DAP productions of people with various symptoms. That is, once the students themselves had become "experienced," how would the test signs they associated with various symptoms compare with those associated with these symptoms by truly experienced clinical psychologists?

[2] Copyright 1967 by the American Psychological Association. Reprinted by permission of the authors and publisher.

The process of giving the subjects the chance to gain "clinical experience" with the DAP, after which they would be asked to render judgments themselves, consisted of the following steps:

> Each S was handed one drawing, face down. At prearranged signals, Ss looked at the drawings and then passed them in a pattern such that each S saw each of the 45 drawings only once. The signals were timed so that each S had 30 seconds to examine each drawing together with the two symptom statements that accompanied it.
> After all of the Ss had seen all 45 pictures, they were given questionnaires which contained items of the following format:
> Some of the pictures were drawn by men with the following problem:
> He is worried about how manly he is.
> The pictures drawn by these men were more often characterized by
> 1. _____
> 2. _____
> 3. _____
> Five additional items of a format identical to the above were built around the other five symptoms statements (p. 197).

Before presenting the results of this first experiment in a series of six, let us recapitulate the design briefly. Naive subjects were to be compared with experienced clinical psychologists with respect to which drawing characteristics they associated with various symptom statements (for example, "He is worried about how intelligent he is."). The data were obtained from the experienced clinicians by questionnaire. The naive subjects were given a chance to acquire some information about the DAP by having an opportunity to look at 45 drawings, each of which was accompanied by two statements allegedly characterizing the person who drew it. Actually these symptom statements were contrived, in that they had simply been assigned systematically to the various pictures so that no statement appeared with any more regularity with one type of drawing than with another. On the basis of what they had presumably learned from the experience, the subjects were then asked to indicate what kinds of drawing characteristics they associated with the respective symptom statements. The results of comparisons are shown in Table 3.

In view of the fact that the experience gained by the subjects was actually bogus, it is noteworthy how closely their final judgments match those of the experienced clinicians. In half of the six symptom statements, the drawing characteristic (from the set of 15) appearing with the highest frequency is the same in both groups. More impressive is the fact that when one looks across the rows for the highest drawing-characteristic frequency and notes the symptoms for which it is reported as a correlate, the students are in agreement with the experienced clinicians in every instance.

Table 3
Percentage of clinicians and naive observers reporting various drawing characteristics as accompanying six symptom statements.

Drawing	Manliness		Suspicious		Intelligence		Fed and Cared for		Impotence		Say Bad Things	
	Clinician	Observer	Clinician	Observer	Clinician	Observer	Clinician	Observer	Clinician	Observer	Clinician	Observer
Characteristic												
1. Broad shoulders, muscular, manly	80	76	0	6	0	8	0	12	25	31	0	6
2. Feminine, childlike	23	22	7	12	2	11	32	39	23	25	11	13
3. Hair distinctive	23	13	2	2	2	8	0	1	11	6	0	3
4. Eyes atypical	0	0	91	58	0	6	0	3	2	2	43	26
5. Ears atypical	0	0	55	6	0	3	0	0	2	0	64	7
6. Facial expression atypical	0	17	18	44	2	21	2	21	2	14	18	52
7. Head large or emphasized	0	5	0	13	82	55	2	7	0	3	9	10
8. Detailed drawing	20	8	2	6	34	13	0	3	7	3	2	6
9. Mouth emphasis	0	0	7	5	0	1	68	8	2	1	5	5
10. Passive posture, outstretched arms	5	4	2	8	0	2	36	21	2	2	0	8
11. Buttons	0	0	0	0	0	0	23	1	0	0	0	0
12. Sexual area elaborated	14	5	0	0	0	0	0	0	55	8	0	0
13. Sexual area deemphasized	0	0	0	0	0	0	0	0	18	27	0	0
14. Phallic nose, limbs	9	0	0	0	0	0	0	0	23	2	0	0
15. Fat	0	2	0	1	0	0	7	16	0	4	0	1

(Table 1 of Chapman & Chapman, 1967. Copyright 1967 by the American Psychological Association and reproduced by permission.)

As the investigators summarize it: ". . . these results show that Ss see each drawing characteristic as systematically occurring with one symptom more than others and that different Ss agreed on which symptom occurred with each drawing characteristic" [although no drawing characteristic had occurred more frequently with one symptom statement than with any other in the actual drawings viewed] (p. 198).

Chapman and Chapman conclude: "It is clear that the experimental Ss showed massive illusory correlation and that the illusory correlates that they reported showed a remarkable similarity to the correlates that clinicians reported from their clinical practice" (p. 198).

As good experimenters, Chapman and Chapman felt the need to rule out some possible alternative explanations, and the subsequent five experiments were designed with this intent.

Experiment II gave subjects a greater opportunity to view the drawings on the chance that the subjects might not show the same errors with repeated exposure. The results were similar to those of Experiment I.

Experiment III checked whether subjects might not simply be confirming the prior expectations they may have had about relationships between symptoms and drawing characteristics. The experimenters summarize the results as follows: "The similarity of the guesses to the reports of illusory correlates in the first two studies indicates that the illusory correlates corresponded to the observers' expectations. This also leads one to suspect that the similar observations by practicing psychodiagnosticians may also be based on the same prior expectations" (p. 201).

In Experiment IV the investigators for the first time introduced actual relationships between certain symptom statements and drawing characteristics—but in a negative direction! That is, the relationship shown was actually opposite to that usually described by clinicians. In part, this study was intended to handle the objection that in the preceding studies subjects might not really have been attending to the pictures. Although the results were not as striking as in Experiments I-III, the investigators report that ". . . the illusory correlates show surprisingly strong survival in the face of negative evidence"—that is, the negative relationships between drawing characteristics and symptom statements (p. 202). In other words, the subjects continued to behave to a surprising degree as they had before.

Experiments V and VI made further efforts to map the extent to which the illusory-correlate phenomenon would continue to manifest itself. Experiment V tried to insure high motivation by offering a $20 prize to the subject who proved most accurate, while Experiment VI not only offered the monetary prize but also gave subjects every opportunity to examine the drawings at length, even to the extent of furnishing scratch paper, ruler, and pencil while allowing subjects to sort out the drawings by categories and to make whatever notations they wished. Although the illusory correlates dropped under these conditions, they did not disappear, leading the investigators to remark on ". . . the resistance of error to the influence of reality" (p. 203).

When findings call long-standing assumptions into question, the true scientist neither becomes cynical nor adopts an I-told-you-so attitude but, instead, proposes constructive next steps. Chapman and Chapman do just this. If their series of studies is sound—and at least they worked painstakingly at trying to make it so—the findings should prove helpful rather than demoralizing. Thus, they present first the moral of the story, then a constructive solution.

The moral?

> The present findings indicate that illusory correlates reported by clinicians do not reflect personal defects as much as difficulties inherent in the clinician's task. The errors are ones to which most, or perhaps all, people are prone. Even the most open-minded person is likely to believe what he sees rather than what someone else reports, unless he has some good reason to believe that his own observations are faulty. By analogy, if the members of some profession had as their task the estimation of the length of lines, would the practitioners be regarded as inferior if one should discover that most members of the profession were subject to the Müller-Lyer illusion? Surely not (p. 204).

The solution?

> One partial solution might be to attempt to reduce the tendency toward forming illusory correlations by special training. Each graduate student in clinical psychology could be asked to serve, during his training, as an observer in a task like those used in the present studies, and he could be shown the source of the illusory correlates which he reports. He would then probably have a keener awareness of the difficulties of making such observations, and he would be better able to guard against them in his future clinical practice. Hopefully, he would also be more receptive to relevant research evidence as a result of such training, and would be less inclined to rely solely on his own clinical observations. He would also be aware that "consensual validation" may reflect shared systematic error rather than shared accuracy.
>
> Such training, however, would not solve the more basic problem that the clinician's cognitive task often apparently exceeds the capacity of the

human intellect. The ultimate solution, as suggested by Meehl (1960), may lie in at least partial replacement of clinical psychodiagnostic methods by actuarial prediction (p. 204).

That this is not a simple solution will be evident from discussion of the broader issues in Part Four. But while clinicians conscientiously pursue the possibilities here, they can look at the same time at how the contributions of their colleagues in other areas might be used to good advantage in resolving still other problems. The following section offers some representative illustrations.

9
The Hospital as a Social System

Communication Processes

As a rule, the social psychologist deals with normal subjects, in a natural setting or in a laboratory, rather than with mentally disturbed people in a hospital. Nevertheless, it is instructive to see whether the findings of sociopsychological research have clinical analogues. Let us turn, for example, to the area of communication, first noting the efforts of some clinicians, then looking in turn at the work of social psychologists whose research and theorizing hold rich promise for the clearer understanding of clinical problems.

Some investigators have been interested in how the communication process figures in psychopathology in general. Some representative studies are those of Ruesch (1961) on the process of communication itself, Silverman (1964a) on how schizophrenics process information, and Kasanin (1946) on schizophrenic language and thought. Others have made intensive investigations of communication processes in clinical settings. Stanton and Schwartz (1954), for example, undertook a systematic 3-year study of the interaction among patients and staff at Chestnut Lodge with a view to understanding a psychiatric hospital as a social system rather than as a collection of patients with assorted pathology.

The results of the longitudinal study by Stanton and Schwartz were revealing. In the area of communication, for example, it became clear that the character of the communication that goes on among hospital personnel affects not only the administrative and clinical efficiency of the staff but the psychological status of the patients as well. When links in the communication chain are skipped, when information is blocked at one level and prevented from reaching a source that needs it, when disagreement is not voiced but remains covert, not only is the general effectiveness of the staff reduced, but the general recovery of the patients is also impeded. This situation is summarized well by the investigators:

> All patients who were the center of attention for the ward for several days or longer during the period of study were the subjects of such a covert disagreement. The most striking finding was that pathologically excited patients were quite regularly the subjects of secret, affectively important staff disagreement; and, equally regularly, their excitement terminated, usually abruptly, when the staff members were brought to discuss seriously their points of disagreement with each other (p. 345).

Given such indications, it makes sense to conceive of a hospital as the large social system it is. As an expert in the analysis of social processes, the social psychologist might therefore have significant contributions to offer, if not directly as a consultant in a hospital setting, then certainly indirectly by the character of the research in which he is engaged. Such is the case with Milgram, who has recently given the study of communication a new twist with his "small world problem." Let us describe briefly what is involved, then consider how some of the procedures and analyses might be applicable to clinical settings.

If two people who know each other discover that they both have nephews studying at a Turkish university, who, in fact, live in the same boardinghouse in Ankara, they may well remark "It's a small world!" So, too, two people may suddenly discover that they know the same Baptist minister, who is now in Portland, Oregon, but who has served as pastor for one person in Minneapolis and for the other some years later in Nashville. The laws of chance, of course, give coincidence plenty of room to operate, but experiences of this sort led Milgram to wonder whether the world was really all that big. Perhaps communication links put more people in touch with one another than one might imagine.

Milgram (1967) hit on a simple, objective procedure for testing relevant hypotheses. He spelled out the rules of a game in which the object is to see how many (or how few) links in a communication chain are needed to get a given message from Person A (the "starting person") to Person Z (the "target person"), the two being unacquainted with each other and each person in the chain being allowed to pass the message along only via someone he knows by first name, that is, personally. Thus, Milgram had a simple experimental procedure and a readily measurable dependent variable — the number of persons constituting the chain. The independent variables might be any that one found interesting and psychologically relevant — such as the race of the communicators, their social class, or the nature of the message.

Under the rule that the message could be passed from one person to the next only if they knew each other on a first-name basis, how many persons would you guess it would take to move a message from a Kansas wheat farmer to the wife of a divinity-school student in Cambridge, Massachusetts? This was an actual situation used by Milgram, who got subjects who volunteered to serve as "starting" persons via newspaper ads and gave them the simple instructions involved, together with the name of the "target" person and some information about him. By means of a simple postcard method Milgram could subsequently trace the route of the message through the intermediate links, as the starting person sent the message on its way toward its target.

The findings are surprising. The message from the Kansas wheat farmer got to the wife of the Cambridge divinity-school student with the use of only two intermediaries! The farmer gave it to his Episcopalian minister, who sent it to an instructor at the Episcopal Theological Seminary in Cambridge, who, in turn, handed it to the target person. Other chains of this sort—for example, from a widowed clerk in Omaha, Nebraska to a Boston stockbroker who lived in Sharon, Massachusetts—proved equally surprising in that many fewer links were needed than one would have guessed. In fact, in the study using starting persons in Omaha, the median number of links in 44 chains was five, the modal number being six. Although the average number of links in broken chains might have been higher, had they been completed, Milgram's results nevertheless shed new light on the processes by which communication is facilitated or broken down. Thus, in more recent work (Korte & Milgram, 1970) he has sought to apply the small-world methodology to the study of acquaintance networks between racial groups; for example, he found, with 540 white subjects recruited as starting persons, that the number of completed chains was two and one-half times greater for white target persons than for black target persons.

It could prove instructive, then, for the clinical psychologist to borrow such methodologies from the social psychologist, adapt them to the clinical situation, and reflect on the findings. Milgram has reminded us that "a chain of 1,000 miles may die one hundred feet from the door." One might wonder, in turn, whether a chain of 100 feet might not seem like one of 1,000 miles to the delusional patient trying vainly to see the doctor so that he can protest his incarceration.

As central as communication is to the effective treatment of people requiring psychological help, the channels existing in a large hospital are labyrinthine. True, the relationships among a hospital staff can conveniently be laid out in an organizational chart, with the chain of command (presumably) forged tight—the manager at the apex, several chiefs of service reporting to him, their staff in turn reporting to them, and so on down the line to the attendant who reports to the nurse. The patient may be shown at the bottom of the chart, or, more democratically, at the top, since all services are supposedly in his behalf.

Such organizational charts are at best dull affairs and at worst unrepresentative of the way the hospital really runs. For, while Nurse X theoretically reports to Dr. Y, she may often be circumventing him and going directly to Dr. Z, who is over Dr. Y organizationally and has little respect for him professionally. As a result of such human factors, the organizational chart often misrepresents the actual ebb and flow of interaction. What is more, it fails to reflect many of the interpersonal transactions that are at the very core of the social system in which patients live while institutionalized.

In searching for models that may more accurately capture the spirit of what actually goes on in the hospital, one might profitably look to some of the work of social psychologists on "person perception." For the way in which people interact proves to be more a function of how they perceive one another than of how an organizational chart tells them to behave. Let us, therefore, look at the hospital with the aid of some theoretical models that will help illustrate what the social psychologist can contribute to clinical psychology.

Theoretical Models of Social Interaction

Newcomb (1953), in his *A-B-X* system, has neatly conceptualized the set of forces at work as two people (*A* and *B*) perceive each other in relation to some idea, object, or other person (*X*). Newcomb represents the system in its simplest form thus:[1]

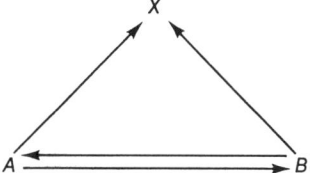

That is, *A* has a certain orientation toward *B* as well as toward *X; B,* in turn, has his own orientation toward *A* and *X*. The hospital patient (*A*), let us say, has a particular orientation toward his psychiatrist (*B*) as well as toward the prospect of discharge (*X*). The psychiatrist, for his part, has his own orientation toward the patient and his discharge.

Actually the situation is more complicated, for not only does each person have his characteristic orientation, but his behavior is influenced as well by what he perceives

[1] Schematic illustration of the minimal *A-B-X* system. Figure 1 of Newcomb, 1953. Copyright 1953 by the American Psychological Association and reproduced by permission.

the orientation of the other person to be. That is, the patient not only perceives the situation in a certain way but also has notions about how the psychiatrist perceives it, and vice versa. Thus, McGrath (1964) pictures the "subjective system" of Newcomb's model as shown in Figure 1.

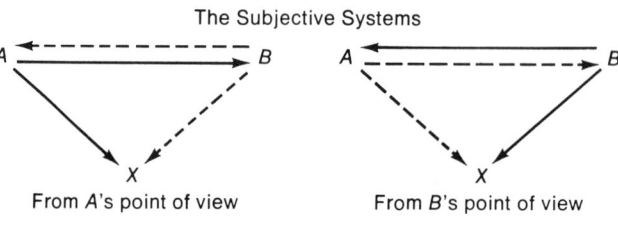

The Subjective Systems

From *A*'s point of view

A's attitudes toward *B* and *X* and *A*'s perceptions (estimates) of *B*'s attitudes toward *A* and *X*

From *B*'s point of view

B's attitudes toward *A* and *X* and *B*'s perceptions (estimates) of *A*'s attitudes toward *B* and *X*

Figure 1
Representation of an aspect of Newcomb's *A-B-X* Model of Systems of Interpersonal Relationships. *Note:* Solid arrows represent the actual orientations of persons *A* and *B* toward each other and toward some object, idea, or other person. Dashed arrows represent the presumed orientations of each person as perceived by the other. (Figure 1 of McGrath, 1964. Copyright 1964 by Holt, Rinehart and Winston and reproduced by permission.)

Newcomb's system is a dynamic one; its elements are interdependent, and a change in any part of the system (for example, in *B*'s attitude toward *X*) affects the system as a whole. As Newcomb describes it: "The implications of this model are: (a) that while at any given moment the system may be conceived of as being 'at rest,' it is characterized not by the absence but by the balance of forces; and (b) that a change in any part of the system . . . [that is, in any of the four relationships pictured in Figure 1 above] may lead to changes in any of the others" (p. 395).

Social psychologists have been busily developing a series of such models, each making its distinctive contribution in the general area of what has come to be called person perception or attitude theory. Some (for example, Harary et al., 1965) have presented detailed methods for quantifying interpersonal interaction to enable us to talk about the degree of imbalance in a social situation.

The reader may feel that such a course unduly mechanizes social interaction, or he may feel it helps clarify important aspects of human relationships that might otherwise remain unnecessarily mysterious. In any case, social psychology has put at our disposal a variety of models, theories, and methodological strategies that clinical psychology may find useful in understanding more clearly the psychological processes that operate as patients and staff interact in the special social system of the hospital. Transplanted to the clinical area, such models provide new lenses through which to view old problems.

In a delightful piece, Brown (1962) has presented the diversity of "models of attitude change" that have been proposed by various theorists. We will draw on his analysis to illustrate how serviceable such models could be in clarifying the manifold relationships that determine what goes on in a particular system—in this case a hypothetical mental hospital and its staff.

Let us assume that, as sometimes happens, the chief of service (A) and one of his psychiatrists (B) differ on a number of issues relating to the treatment of patients as a result of B's seeing A as one of the conservative old guard and A's viewing B as a brash young man who still has a lot to learn. One of the models presented by Brown would picture the relationship between the two as follows:

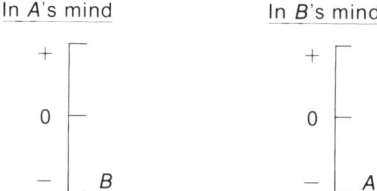

In simple graphic terms, the figure shows B low (that is, at the minus end of the scale) in A's estimation and A low in B's. Although unfortunate in one sense, the relationship is nevertheless "balanced"—it is one of mutual dislike.

Let us assume, however, that both A and B suddenly discover that, while they dislike one another, each favors the intensive use of tranquilizing drugs for patients. The model would now represent this additional fact:

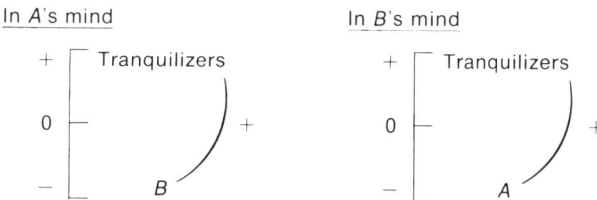

A and B have little respect for each other, but the tranquilizing drugs are viewed positively by both. The (+) signs to the right of each figure, connecting tranquilizers and

B in one case and tranquilizers and *A* in the other, represent the associative bond each is seen as having with the drugs. Parts of the attitudinal scale that should be *dissociated* (the positive level at the top and negative level at the bottom) are here positively associated. Hence the (+) to the right of each one's attitude scale signifies the presence of *disequilibrium* in the relationship.

What was formerly a situation in equilibrium (mutual dislike) is now temporarily in disequilibrium when, as panelists in a symposium at the AMA Convention, *A* and *B* learn that each hails the tranquilizing drugs, whereas both had expected to debate opposing positions hotly.

In such a situation something would have to give. One way of restoring equilibrium could be represented as follows:

```
        In A's mind                    In B's mind
    +  ┌ Tranquilizers             +  ┌ Tranquilizers
       │     ⎞                        │     ⎞
    0  ├     ⎟  −                  0  ├     ⎟  −
       │     ⎠                        │     ⎠
    −  └  B                       −  └  A
```

What restored the equilibrium, as represented above, was that, on their return from the medical convention, *A* and *B* happened to discover (each in his own way) the "real" reason the other favored the tranquilizing drugs. As *A* now saw it, all *B* wanted to do was to accumulate a large number of discharged patients as a means of establishing a reputation; presumably he cared little about the therapeutic benefits that might be credited to the tranquilizing drugs and more about self-serving statistics. Meanwhile, as *B* now saw it, all *A* wanted was a quiet, prim hospital, in which semi-drugged patients "behaved themselves" rather than one in which these patients began to show the more spirited behavior that would signal their readiness to return to the community. In view of the way each sees the other having spurious respect for the drugs, the model indicates that elements at the favorable (top) and unfavorable (bottom) ends of the scale are now dissociated (having a minus bond in each case). Hence, equilibrium has been restored.

Under other circumstances, *A* and *B* could have returned from the medical convention with newfound respect for each other, both surprised to note the other's "progressive" attitude toward chemotherapy. If so, the model would have represented that situation as follows:

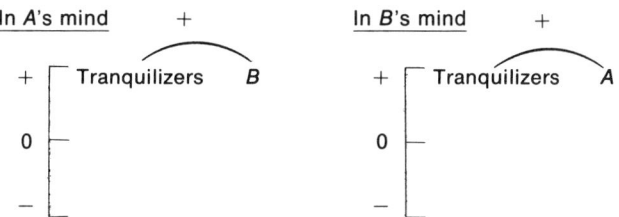

Each person now views the other favorably (at the top end of the scale), as he does the tranquilizers, which he also sees his colleague as genuinely favoring. Thus, a condition of equilibrium has been restored.

One should not assume that psychologists can try on theoretical models like a glove and that they invariably fit as snugly. However, such models are useful means of focusing the clinician's attention away from the distracting pull of interpersonal considerations to the larger context of the hospital as a social system. The role of "systems analyst" is an important one, for unless the larger context in which treatment of patients takes place is itself examined, one might end up perpetuating a system as much in need of treatment as are the patients within it.

The progressive hospital administrator would do well to include in his staff someone experienced in social-systems analysis—be he a sociologist, a social psychologist, or a social psychiatrist. Where such a specialist is not available, however—and most often a hospital will be without his services—a broad-gauged clinician, conversant with advances in areas outside his own, may need to fill this need.

Perhaps the possibilities are again best discussed with some hypothetical illustrations. Let us assume that our enterprising clinician has kept abreast of various models of attitude change being proposed and is particularly interested in how one of them—the congruity model of Osgood and Tannenbaum (1955)—might serve to represent the relationships among key personnel of the hospital. For the purpose he may select the members of the psychiatric staff, inasmuch as they wield significant power in determining how the system will operate, based on the particular philosophy of treatment to which each subscribes.

For the reader unfamiliar with the Osgood–Tannenbaum model, the following hypothetical situations will help illustrate its nature. Let us suppose, for example, that the clinical psychologists of this hospital are able to achieve consensus in ranking the psychiatrists on a scale from "progressive" to "reactionary" with respect to therapeutic philosophy (in the psychologists' value system). The resultant ranking might look like that shown in Figure 2, where the letters opposite the scale positions denote the individual psychiatrists and their respective attitudes from "progressive" (+3) to "reactionary" (−3).

+3 — L Open hospital (viewing hospital stay as very temporary, emphasizing speedy return to community)
+2 — M Patient government (involving patients in decision making)
+1 — N Total push (keeping patients busy at various activities all day)
 0 — O Status quo
−1 — P Chemotherapy (using new drugs as they are discovered)
−2 — Q Benevolent firmness (treating patients humanely but with little hope for their recovery)
−3 — R Closed hospital (believing most patients will need confinement most of their lives)

Figure 2

The Osgood–Tannenbaum model makes several working assumptions:

(a) *Associative* ties between elements on the same scale level (that is, between Dr. M and patient government, or between Dr. R and the notion of a closed hospital) cause no problem. When the clinical psychology staff hears that Dr. M is urging that patients be represented on hospital committees, or that Dr. R is arguing for more repressive measures, this is just what is expected.

(b) Likewise, where *dissociative* bonds exist between elements on mirror-image scale positions (for example, +3 and −3), the ranking need undergo no change. Thus, when Dr. R denounces Dr. L for allowing patients to go into town whenever they please, each retains his original scale position from a given observer's point of view. This, again, is a situation which that observer can readily visualize.

(c) In all other cases, however, the model predicts that a shift in attitude will occur on the part of the observer. That is, elements will move from one scale position to another as a function of other events. And here the model posits certain rules, to wit:

(1) the elements involved will move *toward* one another, meeting jointly at a new scale position somewhere between their old ones;

(2) the more polarized element (that is, the one closer to +3 or −3) will move less, the less polarized element will move more;

(3) the distance between the two elements involved in the attitudinal shift will be shared in inverse proportion to their polarization; that is, if elements at positions +2 and −3 are involved, the more polarized of the two (−3) will move two units while the less polarized element (+2) will move three units, thus dividing the five units between them as they meet at a common −1 scale position. (The interested reader is referred to the aforementioned analysis by Brown for further illustrations of how the model works.) If now the ordering of psychiatrists in Figure 2 represents the attitudinal structure shared by the psychologists vis-à-vis the psychiatric staff, the occurrence of certain events should cause some attitudinal shifts in the psychologists' frame of reference. Let us suppose, for example, that Dr. M and Dr. Q submit a joint letter to the hospital manager. In it they urge him to provide a hospital bus so that patients can be taken to a carnival being held 15 miles away. The letter goes on to assure the manager that, once the patients get there, they will be kept inside the bus, being allowed to watch the goings-on through the bus windows.

What would the model predict? Since Dr. M and Dr. Q, normally of different persuasions, are apparently of one mind here, both would undergo a shift in the attitudinal frame of reference of the psychologists. M would move toward Q, and Q toward M. Since they are equally polarized (both at +2 positions), they would share the four units separating them, thus meeting at scale position zero, as shown in Figure 3.

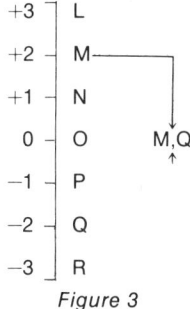

Figure 3

On the other hand, suppose during the following week Dr. N is overheard remarking to Dr. R, "I think you're rubbing off on me," implying that Dr. N is becoming progressively more disenchanted with patients. Here the model would predict a significant attitudinal shift as the psychological staff reacts to the distasteful news, and, according to the rules of the model specified above under (c), the consequent realignment of elements would look like Figure 4.

On the surface, such models seem plausible. The real test, however, must be an empirical one. Depending on how well its predictions are confirmed by actual outcomes, such a model will either be adopted as is (although this would be a truly ideal case), refined on the basis of the findings, or possibly even scrapped in favor of a new and better one.

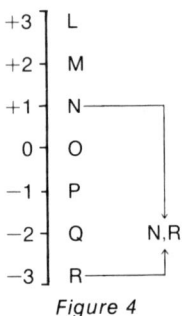

Figure 4

For the moment we are less concerned with the effectiveness of such models than with their intent, for it is these kinds of conceptual habits that distinguish the clinician as behavioral scientist from the clinician as simple practitioner. The second type of clinician, in his more immediate concern with application, may not take time to look at the larger picture; the first, interested in the theoretical third dimension that rounds out his efforts, is as much concerned with the accumulation of new knowledge as with the application of the old.

As we move to a discussion of aspects of psychopathology (using schizophrenia for illustrative purposes), we will deal with the contributions of psychologists who exemplify this spirit of enterprising inquisitiveness.

10
Psychopathology: Real and Experimental

People are not as easily sorted as eggs nor as readily classified as flowers. The mental hospital patient who habitually sits in a corner, seemingly oblivious of his surroundings, may suddenly make a statement that startles those who had casually labeled him "schizophrenic" since, in line with the diagnostic manual, he exhibited "characteristic disturbances of thinking, mood and behavior."[1]

It is with respect for the complexity of behavior that Shakow and his collaborators have carried on, for the past several decades, a program of research into the performance of schizophrenics. Shakow has been interested not so much in the grosser aspects of their behavior as in the nuances of their performance. Without such refinements we might otherwise underestimate the potential of the schizophrenic, in the way that a teacher might mistake a shy, hard-of-hearing child for one who is mentally retarded.

But before looking in detail at the efforts of Shakow and his colleagues, we ought to note for a moment some autobiographical accounts of patients themselves. Peters (1949), for example, describes in retrospect the period during which he was living in "the world next door"—the world of psychosis. The first passage of Peters' book dramatizes the differences in perspective that doctor and patient may have during a

---

[1]Committee on Nomenclature and Statistics of the American Psychiatric Association. *DSM-II Diagnostic and Statistical Manual of Mental Disorders*, 2nd ed. (1968). p. 33.

clinical interview. As Peters viewed his session with one of the psychiatrists, it went as follows:

> "Well, son, how do you feel?"
>
> I knew that he could not be addressing me since he was not my father. I looked around the room and finally turned to look in back of me. No one in back. No one next to me. Where was the Chief of Police? He had vanished, the other man had vanished, even the handcuffs were gone! I shook my free wrists, pleased. But what about the man's son? . . . I smiled, regretting my inability to find his son for him. He drummed his fingers on the table top and then fixed my eyes with his again.
>
> "Come on, son, you can talk to me. How do you feel?" He must be talking to me. Perhaps it was a form of kindness, calling me "son," like an old man calls any young man "son." But he was a person with absolutely no kindness, and not much older than I. . . .
>
> I leaned towards him. "Are you by any chance talking to me?" He smiled and looked away and then looked back at me again, straightening his face with effort. "Yes, my boy. I'm talking to you."
>
> "My boy?" Was he laboring under some delusion? Or was he really my father? I thought for a moment, remembered the face of my own father clearly, and then smiled at him again. No, . . . But if he thought so, then I should be gentle with him.
>
> "I don't see how I can help you. I'm not your son. But, of course, all men are brothers."
>
> I hoped this was all right. It would have been unfair to him to allow him to believe that he was really my father (pp. 13–14).[2]

Clearly, unless one is unaware of the frame of reference, the patient's external behavior will seem bizarre, although it actually makes sense from a phenomenological point of view. The elaborate thought processes frequently at the heart of behavior that looks "crazy" to an outside observer are even more apparent in the following excerpt in which Peters describes in retrospect what was passing through his mind during an unpleasant period in which he was restrained in cuffs.

> The conversation in the room had begun again and I was no longer the center of attention. My only real problem was to get out of the handcuffs. By bending my head over my hands and raising them as much as the belt would permit, I managed to extract the cigarette from my lips and hold it between the thumb and index finger of my left hand. It seemed to me that since there was no way to get the handcuffs off, the only solution was to burn my hands off. I applied the burning end to the back of my right hand and held it there. I could smell the burning flesh and hair but I could not

[2] Copyright 1949 by Arthur A. Peters. Reprinted by permission.

feel anything, so I pressed down harder. After some time, I lifted the cigarette and found that I had made almost no progress. I shifted the cigarette to my right hand and performed the same operation on my left. When I had burned a small hole in the back of each, I put the cigarette, hardly more than a butt now, back between my lips and surveyed my hands. I was struck by a sudden memory of the nails that had been driven through Christ's hands on the cross, and realized at once that it was the disbelief of this man in white that had forced him, through his own fear, to put me in handcuffs. When he saw the scars he would of course realize who I was and deliver me from the handcuffs. I spit the cigarette end out of the window and turned away from it. There he was. I walked over to him and stopped in front of him with my hands spread out in front of me.

"Jesus Christ!" he exclaimed and called out to someone. I was very pleased. "That's right! Will you please take these off now? I can't burn them off" (pp. 21–22).

The Study of Schizophrenia

In his long-term study of schizophrenia, Shakow (1963) reports, he and his colleagues were bent on looking as closely as possible at factors influencing the performance of schizophrenics as measured in laboratory tasks. As he puts it, "... such perceptive clinicians as Kraepelin and Bleuler [two illustrious pioneers in the study of pathology] saw things that we might also see if we look carefully" (p. 276).

To Shakow the problem was far from simple, as is evident in the following comments:

> Absolute constancy and consistency, whether within an individual or within a group of schizophrenics is, of course, illusory. Schizophrenia, particularly in its less chronic phases, is a fairly continuous succession of action and reaction, of regression and restitution—processes which sometimes appear at an overt, easily discernible level, but most frequently at a more cryptic level. Should the patient come for study during a reaction phase, one may be led to place him in the opposite part of the dichotomy from that in which he characteristically belongs. For this reason several readings on a patient need to be taken (p. 276).

For several decades, Shakow and his collaborators have tested the performance of a large number of schizophrenics in a wide variety of situations, studying responses that range from the latent time for simple reflexes all the way to group behavior involving competition and cooperation. In some of these (for example, various sensory and psychophysical comparisons), the investigators found few differences between schizophrenics and normals, when they controlled for the relevant factors. In other areas (for example, reaction time and autonomic responses), there were consistent differences between the two groups. An area of particular interest, however, comprised those tasks on which original differences between schizophrenics and normals disappeared as a function of various factors—that is, tasks in which "normalizing trends," as Shakow calls them, could be observed. A few typical studies will illustrate this phenomenon.

One such task, involving a kind of pursuitmeter, required subjects to follow a target on a moving turntable with a pointer. The turntable stopped every time the pointer was off target, and the score was the number of seconds required to complete ten trials of ten revolutions each. Hence, the lower the score, the better the performance. The times taken by nine schizophrenics and two normal subjects (the latter highly intelligent and very adept at motor tasks) are shown in Table 1.

Table 1
Scores of individual schizophrenic patients and normal controls on 33-day prodmeter experiments.

		Co-operation*	Mean Score** First Day	Mean Score Lowest Day	Lowest Trial Score	Day Lowest Trial Score Reached
Patients	1	A	37	12	11	22
	2	B	38	13	11	24
	3	B	39	15	12	30
	4	B	34	16	13	17
	5	B	36	16	14	30
	6	C	39	17	13	27
	7	C	64	17	15	33
	8	C	43	18	16	18
	9	C	39	19	16	28
Normals	1	A	24	12	11	26
	2	A	30	13	11	24

*Cooperation of subjects was rated by experimenters as A, maximum effort; B, moderate cooperation; or C, perfunctory effort.
**Time in seconds required; hence lower figures represent better scores.
(Table 2 of Shakow, 1963. Copyright 1963 by James G. Miller and reproduced by permission of the author and publisher.)

Each of the schizophrenics did notably poorer than the normal subjects on the first day. Had the experimenters stopped at that point, this would have been regarded as one more task on which schizophrenics seem to do less well than normal subjects (assuming that replication of the study with a larger number of subjects in both groups would have yielded the same initial results). Shakow and his group, however, ran trials on 33 consecutive days, excluding Sundays; and a look at the rest of the data alters the picture appreciably. When we consider the mean score obtained by a subject on the best of his 33 days, we see that two of the schizophrenics match the scores of the normals, while the remaining schizophrenics show results significantly better than their original scores. Similarly, when we examine the best time made by each subject during the series (the column labeled "Lowest Trial Score"), two schizophrenics again match the scores of the normal subjects. Had the investigators stopped gathering data after the first day's trials, very misleading conclusions might have been drawn.

In the above study, it is important to note that the gap between schizophrenic and normal performance was closed despite the fact that only one of the schizophrenic subjects was rated as cooperative as the normals. In a series of other experiments in which the cooperation level was rated, many of the assumed differences between normals and schizophrenics were washed out when this variable was controlled. That is, some differences that might otherwise be ascribed to inability of schizophrenics to perform could more properly be attributed to the subjects' level of motivation.

Another factor underlying the so-called normalizing trends impressed Shakow and his co-workers—the importance to the schizophrenic of time for preparation. In the typical reaction-time experiment the subject is forced to respond without delay, a situation in which schizophrenics consistently do more poorly than normals. How would performance be affected if the schizophrenic had sufficient time to prepare himself for a task? If, for example, one were to count how many taps he could make in five seconds, letting him start when he felt ready—that is, letting him set his own pace—how might his performance compare with that of normal subjects? Again the results were enlightening. Whereas the schizophrenics as a group showed a poorer tapping rate than the normals, those rated high on cooperation did notably better than their fellow patients, with a subgroup of cooperative paranoid schizophrenics actually approaching normal performance on the task. Evidently, schizophrenics who put forth maximum effort on a task that allows them to set their own pace do virtually as well as normals.

Like the rest of us, the schizophrenic has assets as well as liabilities. Of particular interest to the clinician, though, should be those studies in the Shakow series that involve performance under conditions of interpersonal involvement. These studies are aimed at analyzing variations in schizophrenic performance as a function of such social variables as cooperation and competition.

Suppose, for example, that one had obtained a baseline of performance for each individual in a group of schizophrenics on a simple task and then put matched pairs in competition with each other on the same task, interspersing such matched competitive trials with trials on which the individual worked alone. Would performance in the competitive situation be different from that when performing the task alone? Or suppose that, instead of having subjects compete in pairs, one was interested in how they would do as members of a group—that is, to what extent "team spirit" might affect their performance as compared with their scores in individual situations. Shakow and his group looked into this matter.

The task selected was simple. Subjects were given a pack of cards, each bearing a five-digit number, of which one digit was either 1, 2, or 3. The job was simply to place each card in one of three compartments labeled correspondingly 1, 2, or 3. The score was the number of seconds required to sort 60 such cards. Fifteen schizophrenics served as a control group, Group *A*, learning to perform the task individually. Their scores were recorded for eight such individual consecutive trials. Group *B* consisted of six schizophrenics whose initial scores closely matched those of Group *A*. They were given four individual trials on the same task and were then brought together in subgroups of three subjects each on trials 5 and 6, with individual competition among them emphasized by the experimenter, after which they retired to their respective rooms for individual trials 7 through 10. Group *C*, in which group competition rather than individual competition was to play a role, was composed of twelve schizophrenics whose initial scores also closely matched those of control Group *A*. They were first given eight individual trials, then brought together in two groups of three patients each to compete against each other as *teams*, rather than individuals, during trials 9 through 12. The average scores of the groups under the three conditions are shown in Figure 1.

The control group (solitary performance) shows some degree of improvement as the trials proceed. So do the subjects in Group *B* (competition between individuals) during individual trials 1 through 4. Note, however, the dramatic speedup in the performance of Group *B* on trials 5 and 6, when they are in competition with each other. Of their performance and that of Group *C* (team competition), Shakow remarks:

> It is to be noted that there was a drop in score (a low score, of course, being a good score) for trials 5 and 6 when compared with trial 4, and a rising, more or less flattened, curve thereafter. The patients appeared generally to retain most of what they had gained during the period of competition (p. 282).

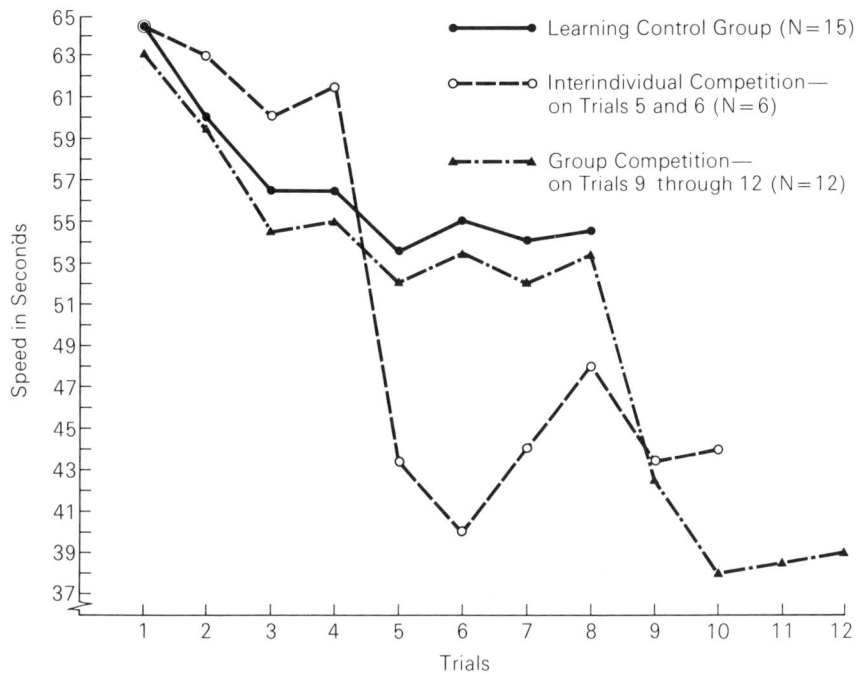

Figure 1
Card-sorting performance of schizophrenic subjects under conditions of solitary performance, cooperation, and competition. (Adapted from Table 6 of Shakow, 1963, whose data are here converted to graphic form. Copyright 1963 by James G. Miller; adapted by permission of the author and publisher.)

Here again was a striking change of behavior under competitive conditions as compared with individual performance.

On trials 1 through 8, the scores of Group C resemble the trend in Group A. Trial 9, however, the first of the team-competition trials, shows a significant increase in speed (that is, decrease in time required for the task), an improvement that is maintained in the remaining team-competition trials 10 through 12.

Shakow's long-term research has a clear moral. To speak simply of "impaired performance" in schizophrenics is to omit some significant qualifications. Schizophrenic performance is a variable affair. To evaluate it properly, one needs to give the patient a fair chance to show what he can do. Allowed time to prepare himself, tested when his level of cooperation is high, and provided with some incentive (competition or cooperation, for example), the schizophrenic shows to much better advantage than he is usually given credit for.

It is small wonder, then, that theorists of many minds have set themselves the problem of elucidating what must be involved in the many-faceted disorder known as schizophrenia. The following section illustrates how varied the approaches can be.

Models, Research, Proof, and Disproof

Someone seeking a working definition of schizophrenia would find one ready-made in the guide to classification most widely used in psychiatric hospitals—the *Diagnostic and Statistical Manual of Mental Disorders* (1968), prepared under the auspices of the American Psychiatric Association. There the message is straightforward:

> This large category [schizophrenia] includes a group of disorders manifested by characteristic disturbances of thinking, mood and behavior. Disturbances of thinking are marked by alteration of concept formation which may lead to misinterpretation of reality and sometimes to delusions and hallucinations, which frequently appear psychologically self-protective. Corollary mood changes include ambivalent, constricted and inappropriate emotional responsiveness and loss of empathy with others. Behavior may be withdrawn, regressive and bizarre (p. 33).[3]

While such a definition may help identify and label the disorder where it is present, it does not purport to do much to improve one's *understanding* of schizophrenia. There are, however, many theoretical models that attempt to do this. Each model sounds plausible—each has "face validity." While some would caution against taking any model seriously until it receives empirical confirmation, others would argue that their daily professional experience is an ongoing informal experiment that provides data in the form of repeated clinical instances testing their model. But before engaging in such an argument, we should look at some representative models of the schizophrenic process.

Lest we oversimplify, it should be pointed out at the beginning that the problem of definition is a real one. The term "schizophrenia" is very broad, applied to schizophrenics who are in the acute phase of the disorder as well as to those who are chronic patients. It includes several diagnostic subcategories, among them one class

---

[3]Committee on Nomenclature and Statistics of the American Psychiatric Association, *DSM-II Diagnostic and Statistical Manual of Mental Disorders,* 2nd ed., 1968.

of patients (paranoid) who differ significantly in tests of performance and other measures from other schizophrenics. In what follows, the reader should bear in mind, then, that schizophrenia is a collective term for a group of disorders having something in common.

"What is schizophrenia?" is perhaps not the best way to ask about the disorder. "How might schizophrenia be viewed?" seems a better way to phrase the question, for there are at least half a dozen perspectives on the disorder, each of which makes intuitive sense. Buss (1966) has outlined the situation effectively, and the following presentation makes use of his format.

The psychoanalytic formulation could be called the regression model of schizophrenia. It has been discussed at length in many sources (for example, Fenichel, 1945; Cameron, 1963; see also Blum, 1966, for an overall presentation of "unconscious mental forces"). We shall therefore not dwell on it here, except to note that a very plausible and clinically serviceable model can be built around the notion that in schizophrenia the course of personality development has been reversed, the person having regressed to a very early stage of development.

Others (for example, Sullivan, 1947) have stressed the interpersonal factors in the etiology of the disorder; some (for example, Lidz and Fleck, 1960) have specifically emphasized the nature of family interaction. As these conceptions have also received considerable attention, we shall bypass lengthy discussion and turn to the next sections, which are intended to demonstrate that psychological theory in general provides many focal points around which to organize yet other, perhaps more clinically useful, models as the basis for both theory and practice. Better yet, these types of models lend themselves quite readily to empirical test—a situation which, as we shall see, is a mixed blessing, for research findings often prove equivocal and sometimes contradictory.

What, for example, is to stop one from constructing a model of the schizophrenic process around the general psychological principle of *motivation?* The apathetic schizophrenic looks grossly undermotivated, to say the least. Or, on the other hand, since his speech is sometimes incoherent to the point of unintelligibility, why could one not try to build a model around the notion that *cognition* has gone awry? For that matter, the more one observes schizophrenics as a group, the more one might be tempted to construct a model on the premise that each of these individuals must have acquired his characteristic mode of functioning to cope with otherwise intolerable life experiences; that is, a *learning* model might well be defended. We shall not extend the possibilities, except to mention that others have taken to genetic, physiological, and biochemical models as well. Let us, then, take motivational, cognitive, and learning models as cases in point. On the one hand, they illustrate the feasibility of grounding clinical research, theory, and practice in principles of general psychology. Further, they lead to an appreciable amount of investigation that reveals how the complexity of a disorder like schizophrenia can belie the apparent simplicity of its definition.

Motivational Model

Creative as theorists are, a concept such as motivation can lead them down a number of roads. As Buss (1966) points out, one might speculate that the schizophrenic who is mute, sits by himself in a corner of the ward, and looks lifeless is *under*motivated; one could conclude that he needs increased motivation, so that he can come out of his retreat, relate to others, and look alive. Someone else, however, equally sold on the concept of motivation, might arrive at just the opposite conclusion. The schizophrenic, he would argue, must have resorted to such a drastic retreat from reality for a reason. He may be so sensitive to what goes on about him and so much more fearful of criticism and rebuff than the average person that his only defense is to shield himself from others, of whose presence he is all too aware. He is, in fact, not apathetic at all but actually so hypersensitive that he needs to guard himself constantly against involvement of any kind. In short, he is, if anything, *over*motivated rather than undermotivated. Who is right? Data should tell—but sometimes they too leave one less than sure. Let us look at some typical results.[4]

If the schizophrenic is *under*motivated, attempts to increase his motivation should improve his behavior. One might, then, select tasks that schizophrenics are able to do and compare their performance with that of normals under various conditions designed to increase motivation. Extensive research of this type has been undertaken, and, as Buss suggests, one might look at the results in terms of the methods used to increase motivation in the various experiments. When one does so, it turns out that under the mildest condition—verbal reward—normals as a rule do better than schizophrenics. However, in experiments using more insistent attempts to increase motivation—active urging or even verbal punishment—schizophrenics tend to do about as well as normals on the laboratory tasks involved. None of the foregoing results has helped substantiate the thesis that schizophrenics are particularly undermotivated, since if this were so they should have been differentially affected in contrast to normals. Where, however, motivational efforts take a more extreme form—for example, when they involve electric shock that can be terminated by correct responses—the

---

[4] In what follows, the reader may find it appropriate to think of overmotivated and undermotivated as overaroused and underaroused or as overstimulated and understimulated.

performance of schizophrenics improves more than that of normals, as demonstrated in a number of experiments using noxious stimuli to increase motivation. As Buss suggests, the undermotivation theory would therefore still seem tenable if amended to read that strong biological stimulation represents the mode and degree of motivation required to improve schizophrenic behavior.

As it turns out, though, the matter is not that simple. From the above, one might conclude that the schizophrenic is typically in such a state of lethargy that only the strongest jolt, literally, can stir him. Such speculation is plausible, except that it does not square with some of the evidence. Thus, Venables and Wing (1962) were interested in the extent to which level of arousal (as measured by skin potential) covaried with the degree of withdrawal shown by the patients. One might well suspect—and the foregoing hunches are in line with such an expectation—that the more withdrawn a patient is, the lower will be his level of arousal. The facts, as shown in Figure 2, bring one up short.

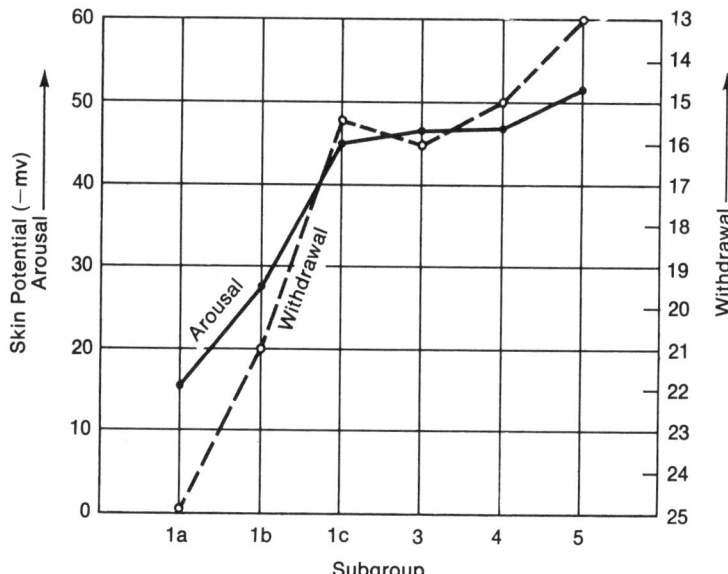

Figure 2
Skin potential and withdrawal measures of clinical subgroups of schizophrenics. (From Venables, P. H. & Wing, J. K. Level of arousal and the subclassification of schizophrenia. *Archives of General Psychiatry,* 1962, **7**, 114–119. Copyright 1962 by the American Medical Association and reproduced by permission.)

If anything, the situation is the opposite to what one might have anticipated. The more withdrawn a patient is, the higher is his arousal level as measured by skin potential; the less withdrawn he is, the lower is his arousal level. The correlation between the variables is positive, not negative, as one might have expected.

Similar evidence comes from other than physiological sources. The behavior of schizophrenics has repeatedly been shown to be disturbed by affective (emotional) stimuli. What bothered Deering (1963) was that it was not always clear whether the disturbance was due to affective (in contrast to neutral) stimuli, or whether the difficulty level of the affective material (in complex cognitive tasks, for example) was responsible, since it was not of the same order as the neutral material. In other words, the schizophrenic behavior may have been as much (or primarily) a function of level of complexity of the stimulus material as of its affective character.

Deering sought to clarify the situation. Word associations constituted the dependent variable; a list of affective and a list of neutral words would serve as the stimulus materials. Judges were employed initially to sort 80 adjectives into categories of pleasant, unpleasant, or neutral. Representative of those judged were words like loving, metric, brutal, freckled, stupid, lanky, bloody, graphic, lonesome, yearly, and so on. The patient group was made up of 40 schizophrenics who were in a mental hospital for the first time, had been hospitalized for fewer than 11 months, had no organic impairment, and had received no shock treatment during the previous 6 months. The normals were 40 subjects who were apparently functioning well in their occupations and not receiving any kind of psychological treatment. The two groups were closely comparable in age and educational level. Thus, one of the aims of the study was to note how they might differ in the number of associations elicited to affective vs. neutral stimulus words. The total of 80 subjects was formed into four subgroups of 20 each, in order to compare schizophrenics and normals at both high school and college levels of education. Table 2 reports the mean number of associations given by each subgroup under the several conditions.

"The mean idiosyncratic association score," as defined by Deering, "refers to the mean number of different associations given to the 40 affective and 40 neutral words by the subjects in the schizophrenic and normal groups. High idiosyncratic association scores for a group indicate an abundance of different associations" (p. 340).

As is evident from the data, no noteworthy differences between the two groups appear with respect to neutral words. In the case of the affective stimuli, however, the schizophrenic groups show a statistically significant increase in the number of different associations given to the stimulus words, while the normals do not. Educational

Table 2
Means and standard deviations of idiosyncratic association scores for affective and neutral stimulus words, with 40 words in each category and 20 subjects in each group.

Group and Education	Affective Words M	SD	Neutral Words M	SD
Schizophrenic High School	13.42	3.10	10.98	3.54
Normal High School	10.78	3.30	10.42	3.30
Schizophrenic College	13.82	2.88	10.90	3.20
Normal College	11.85	2.48	10.32	2.92

(Table 1 of Deering, 1963. Copyright 1963 by the American Psychological Association and reproduced by permission.)

level exerts no influence, the two groups behaving in their characteristic ways whether they have only a high school education or have had some college experience.

In view of further findings reported in both spheres, physiological (as in the case of Venables and Wing) and symbolic (as in the case of Deering), it comes as no surprise that some theorists have constructed their models of schizophrenia at the other end of the motivational dimension. That is, if data at hand warrant the conclusion that schizophrenics are characteristically in a state of high arousal, although outward appearance suggests the opposite, one might try to account for their behavior on the basis of characteristic *over*motivation. In light of the findings cited above, Venables (1964), for example, has theorized that the withdrawal of the highly aroused schizophrenic makes sense when viewed as an attempt to cut down on incoming stimulation, since the patient already has proved unable to handle the situation up to that point.

Again, such a model makes sense intuitively. And, indeed, there is suggestive evidence that this line of thought might help illuminate many features of the schizophrenic process that are now unclear. If, for example, one assumes that the schizophrenic is overmotivated in the sense of operating characteristically at a high level of arousal, then drugs such as amobarbital, which are depressants in that they lower arousal level, should produce improved behavior. In administering the drug to chronic schizophrenics, Fulcher et al. (1957) found just such an increase in lucid intervals — that is, periods during which the patients were relatively coherent and in touch with reality.

Perhaps the above will suffice to show that plausible theoretical cases can be made on both sides of the question. In the last analysis, the issues are decided when all of the facts are in — a state that has hardly been reached — and/or when some more comprehensive model encompasses what had previously looked like antithetical positions and reconciles them within the framework of a larger conceptualization.

Let us, therefore, leave the area of motivation at this point to illustrate the possibilities for theory formulation and model construction in quite another sphere — cognition. In order to bridge the gap, we shall describe in some detail the model advanced by McReynolds (1960), since it ultimately rests on how the schizophrenic handles a high state of arousal, although this time in the form of anxiety generated from perceptual and cognitive rather than motivational origins.

Perceptual/Cognitive Models

There are psychologists and psychologists. Some love the "smell of the lab"; others choose neither to run white rats nor even to take GSRs of human subjects. Doubtless one could make some interesting clinical speculations about the preferences on either side, but that is not our concern at the moment.

In any case, there are also laboratories and laboratories. Freud felt the consulting room was his; many a research-oriented clinician feels the same. He wears a business suit rather than a lab coat, his laboratory is the clinic, and his data are the transactions that take place between him and his client-subjects. There are few, if any, gadgets in the situation, although it would readily be possible to "hook up" the person with whom one is interacting, gathering physiological as well as other measures in the course of clinical interaction. But even without such procedures, the fact remains that in the clinical situation information is constantly accumulating. Like the data of the laboratory, it is there for the processing. Whether the focus is to be on its practical application or its theoretical contribution rests with the particular psychologist and his purposes. Either aim is legitimate, but we shall for the moment concern ourselves with the formulation of theory on the basis of clinical experience.

As is evident from the foregoing account of Shakow's efforts, one can take the schizophrenic into the laboratory and deal with him as one might deal with a normal subject, testing his reaction time, studying his ability to learn and recall, recording his behavior on perceptual tasks, or investigating countless other performances. On the other hand, having talked with and listened to many schizophrenics, one might retire to the armchair to speculate about their behavior. What makes a person feel people are putting poison in his food? How does it serve another person to imagine he is Jesus Christ? Why would a third man talk in a gibberish others cannot understand?

McReynolds (1960) has some interesting theoretical views on the general subject, and we shall take a few liberties in the way we present them. One could begin, he suggests, with a general notion that all of us—whether normal or disordered—cannot escape a universal chore: the processing of the information that constantly floods us. Events occur, and we try to make sense out of them; just as food must be digested, so the data of experience must be "perceptualized," as McReynolds puts it. Fortunately this is usually not very difficult, for many of the events of daily life are quite predictable. My friend will greet (rather than ignore) me when I pass him later today; the college newspaper will say some uncomplimentary things about the administration in tomorrow's editorial; my cousin will soon send his customary airmail letter apologizing for having forgotten my birthday (again), and so on.

Conceptually, suggests McReynolds, one might imagine each of us as having a set of mental rubrics under which he can file classes of events. For example, in the case of a particular college student, a small sample of such "schemata," as McReynolds terms them, might look as follows:

| By and large, most people are well-meaning. | Universities are not perfect, but you still get a lot out of college. | I am intelligent. |

Having evolved such schemata over time, so that they encompass the general range of life experiences, we find it possible to accommodate most of the events of daily life in such cognitive file cases. To be sure, the fit is not always perfect. In most cases, however, the events perceived fit conveniently into our set of available schemata. Where they do not, they can be "assimilated" into one of the existing rubrics in somewhat Procrustean fashion.

Not always, though. Thus, certain events may not fit readily into our college student's rubric of "I am intelligent." Let us assume, for example, he has just received a letter stating that his application to graduate school has been rejected by Stanford University. That hard fact can still be assimilated under his schemata of "I am intelligent," since Stanford is considered one of the two or three leading universities in the country. When, however, a letter of the following day informs him that a school of lesser stature has rejected him, assimilation of the event becomes more difficult. And when, a week later, a school generally regarded as less than second-rate follows suit, the event is not readily assimilated. It is then that "incongruency," as McReynolds calls it, results.

While into each life some incongruencies must fall, McReynolds suggests that, in one way or another, we manage to tolerate a certain measure of them. With the schizophrenic, however, such incongruencies abound, the argument runs. The defenses of the normal person do not serve the schizophrenic well enough; either he lacks skill at assimilation, or else a life history filled with inconsistent contingencies has left him without a serviceable set of schemata by which to catalog and store his perceptions of events. As a consequence, he is left with a large share of *unassimilated* percepts, a situation that spells a chronically high level of anxiety, cognitive confusion, and characteristic schizophrenic behavior.

Although such theorizing proceeds from the armchair rather than the laboratory, it rests on extensive experience in a special kind of laboratory—the clinical situation. In any case, it leads McReynolds to further interesting conjecture. Assuming that the foregoing theoretical notions have some basis in fact, what courses are then open to the schizophrenic? Two choices are available to him: (a) he can shut himself off from further inputs (since he already has difficulty handling those he has experienced), and/or (b) he can drastically reinterpret the events of experience, resorting to explanations that most people would find implausible.

Interestingly, we find in schizophrenia the very phenomena one might expect if the above were the case—hallucinations, if course (a) is chosen; delusions, if alternative (b). That is to say, if perceptual input cannot be handled, one understandable reaction is to "unplug" oneself from life—like the patient who spends days in a corner, his shirt pulled over his head, lest any further interaction with the world occur. Anyone who has visited the wards of an understaffed state hospital has witnessed such a scene. To McReynolds it is all too reminiscent of experiments in sensory deprivation. Like the normal laboratory subject, resting on a bed in isolation, eyes taped, ears muffled, with a minimum of sensory input, the schizophrenic patient seems to be engaging in a self-imposed experiment in sensory deprivation. It is not surprising then that he may experience hallucinations, much like his normal counterpart in the formal laboratory experiment.

But suppose another patient takes the other course. If experience is unassimilable, he can restructure his perception of events (much as Humpty Dumpty in *Alice in Wonderland* made words mean what he wanted them to mean). Where previously he seemed to have been shunned by others, presumably because he was "queer," he may suddenly perceive the "real" reason—he is actually Christlike. Such "sudden clarification," as McReynolds calls it, makes all of the events immediately assimilable. One does not take liberties with Christ; one keeps a respectful distance. He is Christ; people behave accordingly. The patient has a newfound explanation. Unfortunately, he now also has a delusion.

Unlike the empirical approach of some other investigators, McReynolds' contribution is frankly theoretical, intended as a helpful explanatory set of constructs. Admittedly cut from whole cloth, it grows out of long and conscientious observation of subjects labeled schizophrenic, and it makes use of notions embedded in research on perception. It awaits confirmation or disconfirmation, in whole or in part, by empirical means. Whatever its fate, it represents the kind of creative theoretical speculation open to the observant, imaginative, and experienced clinician intent on advancing psychological knowledge in basic areas of interest.

Meanwhile, many other investigators are offering their own perceptual/cognitive models, which also constitute interesting explanations of the anomalies seen in schizophrenic behavior. Thus, in reviewing the results of the long-range research program discussed earlier, Shakow (1963) has characterized the schizophrenic's performance as follows:

> ... he has two major difficulties: first, he reacts to old situations as if they were new ones (he fails to habituate), and to new situations as if they were recently past ones (he perseverates); and second, he overresponds when the stimulus is relatively small, and he does not respond enough when the stimulus is great (p. 303).

Their distinctive ways of paying or not-paying attention have struck other investigators as a further way to differentiate schizophrenics from normals and from each other. Some (for example, McGhie and Chapman, 1961) have attributed the schizophrenic's difficulty in processing information from his environment to an inability to distinguish between relevant and irrelevant inputs; the latter, when present in too large number, overtax the person's information-processing capacity. Along the same line, Buss (1966) remarks:

> ... schizophrenics lack an efficient 'filter mechanism' (Broadbent, 1958) and fail to shift readily to the changing environment about them. In contrast, normals filter out trivial aspects of the environment, focus properly on crucial aspects, and are able to shift their attention with changing requirements of the situation. The normal person is thus an efficient information-processing machine capable of adapting to his environment through attention to relevant stimuli and owing to a relative absence of 'noise' in the system (p. 288).

But, as we have noted, attempts have been made to differentiate not only schizophrenics from normals, but also one schizophrenic from another. Thus, Silverman (1964b) makes a distinction between the attentional habits of "process" schizophrenics (those with a poor premorbid history, who have shown a gradual breakdown and have a relatively poor prognosis) and "reactive" schizophrenics (those with a relatively good premorbid history, whose breakdown developed in acute form and whose prognosis is generally more favorable). The former, he suggests, still respond to sensory input from the environment but tend to "gate out" ideational inputs that are disturbing, while the reactive schizophrenics are still responsive to both sensory and ideational inputs, although the latter may be "gated out" under stress in the reactive schizophrenics as well.

A study by Draguns (1963) is relevant in this connection. Given blurred carbon copies of stimulus materials, subjects were asked to begin with the worst carbon and work their way up through progressively clearer ones until they felt they could make sense out of a series of stimulus materials so presented. Normals required relatively clear copy before they felt confident they could distinguish the images, reactive schizophrenics were willing to describe them on the basis of a more blurred representation, while process schizophrenics responded on the basis of even the most blurred copies. The results have been offered in support of the proposition that process schizophrenics are so intent on protecting themselves from any outside input that they quickly attempt to reduce the uncertainty present by excluding any possibly threatening connotations. Such attentional habits provide perhaps a degree of "safety," but only at the expense of adequate reality testing.

In computer terms, one might ask whether the schizophrenic's information-processing capability is deficient in its "hardware" (that is, in the sensory, perceptual, and cognitive apparatus of the person), or in its "software" (that is, the "programs" used in processing, storing, and retrieving information), or in both. Heredity presumably plays a significant role in the former case, life experience in the latter. In this connection, Buss (1966) remarks:

> Interference theory . . . attempts to specify the essential element in schizophrenia—an inability to inhibit or filter out irrelevant stimuli—but it does not state the cause of this cognitive difficulty. . . . Perhaps schizophrenics are 'built that way,' and the explanatory variables reside in heredity or early development. Cognitive theories can remain neutral about etiology because their concern is with the *essence* of schizophrenia, not its cause . . . interference theory is more consistent with a biological orientation toward etiology than with a personal-social or dynamic orientation. Nevertheless, interference theory can be squared with theories of early development . . . (pp. 307–308).

From a somewhat different direction, Maher (1966) comes upon related alternatives. The attentional difficulties of the schizophrenic, he suggests, may be looked at from at least four different points of view:

1. Taking a biological approach, one might reason that there is something inherently defective in the schizophrenic's attentional apparatus—his reticular activating system, for example (see Butter, 1968, as well as Meehl, 1962). As a result, he may be less easily arousable and/or he may have difficulty "damping out" the irrelevant aspects of external stimulation.

2. Or, one might assume that there is nothing innately wrong with the schizophrenic's capacity for attention; the problem may simply be that he attends closely to internal stimulation (as in listening to hallucinatory voices, for example) rather than to external events.

3. Taking a nonbiological approach, one might begin with the premise that attending appropriately to events in the outside world is something that is learned through a history of reinforcement. According to this psychological point of view the schizophrenic must not have been reinforced for attending during his developmental period, or else the reinforcement received from his interpersonal environment must have been delivered on a fairly random basis. Thus, he has learned *not* to attend.

4. Again, staying with a psychological approach, one might hypothesize that the developmental experiences of the schizophrenic have been primarily punitive; hence, the problem is not that he has difficulty in attending to the external environment, but rather that he has learned to react to it with a repertoire of predominantly avoidant responses.

The latter two possibilities lay great stress on the influence of the individual's learning experiences during his developmental period. And, just as models of schizophrenia have been built in the areas of motivation, perception, and cognition, so too, others have explored the area of learning for some conceptual bedrock on which to found their own models. Mednick is one who has approached schizophrenia in this way; his work is discussed in the following section.

A Learning Model

To Mednick it seemed natural that one could *learn* a schizophrenic pattern of adjustment much as one learns so many other things in life. Consequently, in his early work (1958) he attempted to integrate the principal features in such a learning process, citing representative studies in support of the following sequence of propositions:

a. the schizophrenic characteristically operates at a higher level of anxiety than does the normal person;

b. like the normal, he reacts to stress, but much more acutely;
c. after each stressful experience, it takes him longer to return to his physiological baseline than the normal takes to recover his;
d. as a result, the schizophrenic, whose environment is filled with stress, is likely to experience a new stress before he has even recovered from the preceding one;
e. the combination of high drive level and slow recovery rate finds him easily conditionable;
f. further, the high drive leaves him especially prone to stimulus generalization (see Walker, 1967), and as a result of the "reciprocal augmentation" between anxiety and generalized fear responses ". . . stimulus events that are in some way similar to the stimulus situations he has learned to fear will also elicit anxiety responses" (pp. 320–321).

Mednick argues that just as the young boy (described in Chapter 2) whom Watson and Rayner (1920) conditioned to respond fearfully to a rabbit generalized his fearful reaction to his mother's fur piece, a ball of cotton, and so on, so does the schizophrenic generalize his fear reactions to people and situations more than does the normal: ". . . some of the stimuli which were once safe and comfortable for him now fill him with uneasiness. While he once felt comfortable in the presence of his superior, the incremented gradient of fear stemming from learned reactions to his father now cause him to experience discomfort" (p. 321).

Some (for example, Buss, 1966) question several of the assumptions Mednick makes —the presumed tendency of the schizophrenic to overgeneralize, for one—but let us for the moment grant Mednick his points in order to follow the course of his theory. What happens as an acute breakdown progresses, Mednick suggests, is that, as generalization proceeds, the schizophrenic responds to stimuli more and more remote from the original stimulus to which his response was attached. That is, his reaction to a certain situation triggers off a whole string of associations, which become more and more unlike the original situation from which the conditioned fear generalized. By this process, he argues, the schizophrenic's attention is diverted from anxiety-provoking stimuli—especially as more and more remote associations become involved—until the stimuli, because they are so different from the original life crisis that constituted the "precipitating event," are accompanied by progressively less anxiety and hence are drive-reducing in nature. In line with this function of reducing anxiety, chronicity is gradually learned, much as an avoidant response is learned.

This kind of learning exacts its price, however. Take a young man who is conflicted about his sexual identity, for example. Let us assume he is handsome almost to the point of being pretty, is ill at ease among members of the opposite sex, has had no heterosexual experiences to date, and feels embarrassed about such of his hobbies as flower arrangement. He has for a long time been wondering whether he is homosexual and, although he has had no sexual encounters with men, he feels more and more that they are making disguised overtures toward him. A real-life incident has almost thrown him into a panic, as he felt himself about to put his arms around a male co-worker while in the office lavatory, although he resisted the impulse at the last moment.

As he continues to struggle privately with his conflicts, he may gradually begin to misinterpret various sensory inputs, perhaps at times confusing his own ruminations with external events, so that what were at first recognized as his own thoughts are now at times interpreted as the voices of others; he might hear those others uttering words that have a sexual, if not homosexual, connotation. As the "anxiety-generalization spiral" continues, remote, tangential associations can be assumed to compete increasingly with the more differentiated, reality-bound reactions. In the process, Mednick suggests, such a ". . . remote associate will be accompanied by drive reduction which will reinforce it as a response. . . . This will increase the probability of its occurring again in the context of the antecedent anxiety provoking thought or similar thoughts" (p. 324).

This assumed progression of events helps Mednick explain the transition from the acute to the chronic phase of the disorder. Thus, he describes the schizophrenic's fate as follows:

> . . . eventually (perhaps after several acute breaks) his thinking will present a varied though disorganized picture. At this point, if the patient, perceiving the disorganization, responds with the anxiety provoking thought, "I am going crazy," he can defend against it by making an immediate associative transition to an irrelevant, tangential thought or making use of a well-learned rationale such as "the radiators are broadcasting to me." This disorganized thinking will be continually self-reinforcing since it will enable him to evade anxiety provoking stimuli (p. 324).

As mentioned earlier, other investigators are not prepared to accept the details of Mednick's model without question. In their comprehensive analysis of psychological deficit in schizophrenia, Lang and Buss (1965) cite the results of research that fail to substantiate, and in some cases actually contradict, some of the assumptions on which Mednick's thesis rests. And, in their opinion, if there is no such experimental verification, the theory is correspondingly weakened. In fairness to Mednick, however, they take account of his own recognition of possible objections. Their assessment of his learning model is as follows:

The theory places all its eggs in one basket in that it accounts for schizophrenia solely in terms of anxiety. The difficulty is that, with anxiety so prevalent, it is necessary to explain why schizophrenia is still relatively rare in the population. Mednick was aware of this issue of "over-explanation":

> "Why doesn't everybody proceed to schizophrenia after an extremely anxiety provoking event? The answer lies in three factors: the individual's original drive level, his rate of recovery from anxiety states, and the number of stimuli that elicit anxiety responses from the individual . . . high drive, slow recovery rate, and the number of fear arousing stimuli are highly correlated factors [p. 323]" (p. 87).

Lang and Buss continue:

> Only those with all three factors tend to become schizophrenic, but Mednick himself admitted that the three factors are all highly correlated. Thus an extremely anxious individual, being high on all three factors, should become schizophrenic. Clearly, Mednick has not answered his own question. We may guess that he cannot answer it because he identifies anxiety as the sole cause of the thinking disorder in schizophrenia. This explanation will not be acceptable to the majority of psychologists. It is evident that many individuals with extremely high levels of anxiety never become schizophrenic, whereas Mednick's drive theory clearly implies that they should (pp. 87–88).

I will not try to referee that argument, except to add that it has been said that the only good theory is one that can be disproved. Whether or not Mednick's theory, in its original form, has been disproved is perhaps a moot question, but, to its credit, it has been stated with sufficient clarity to allow experimental results to confirm or disconfirm it in whole or in part. It will probably be helpful to the reader at this point to learn how Mednick's penchant for theorizing has led him down newer paths of interest stemming at least indirectly from his learning model and leading to the actual development of his Remote Associates Test (Mednick & Halpern, 1959).

Like most popular adages, the expression "genius is just a step away from insanity" is at best an overstatement, at worst a falsehood. Nonetheless the genius, in his sometimes uncanny flight of ideas, baffles the normal mind, which has trouble fathoming his bursts of creativity. Consequently, it is probably as hard to grasp the methods by which his creative processes blossom as it is to understand the "word salad" of the incoherent schizophrenic. If it can be said that both have a tendency toward remote associations, one can note that the genius uses them in a way we can appreciate, if not imitate, while the schizophrenic seems at their mercy. In any case, the interest Mednick developed in the concept of remote associations has carried him into the analysis of possible relationships between creativity and mental illness. Let us note the byways into which the work of this imaginative investigator led him.

A Research Spin-off

If the reader were asked what word he might associate with all three of the following — rat, blue, cottage — he might shortly hit upon "cheese" (rat cheese, blue cheese, cottage cheese). To call such an association a "remote associate," as Mednick does, is not a bad choice of terms. And if that item of his Remote Associates Test (RAT) seems too simple, the reader may wish to test his capacity for conjuring up remote associates on such other test items as:

wheel	electric	high
surprise	line	birthday

Because the RAT has turned out to yield impressive individual differences, Mednick has found it a serviceable instrument for investigating creative potential in a number of populations, both well-adjusted and maladjusted. Before examining the interesting results, we should illustrate the manner in which associations operate to produce differences. One could first contrast the capacity of two stimulus words to elicit associations. The words "table" and "comfort," for example, show the interesting contrast pictured in Figure 3.

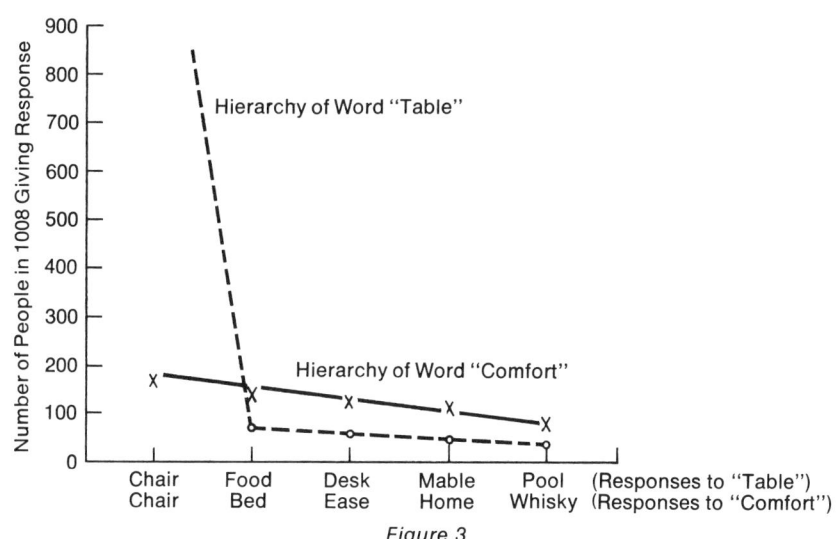

Figure 3
Associative hierarchies for "table" and "comfort." (Figure 1 from Mednick & Mednick in C. W. Taylor & F. Barron (Eds.) *Widening Horizons in Creativity,* 1964. Copyright 1964 by John Wiley & Sons, Inc., and reproduced by permission.)

It is evident that while "table" tends predominantly to elicit the association "chair," the word "comfort" has a much flatter gradient—that is, it elicits a variety of associations without any one of them being especially prominent (as was "chair" with "table"). But we are less interested in differences among words than in differences among people, which we find to be equally striking. Figure 4 represents the contrast between two persons, A and B.

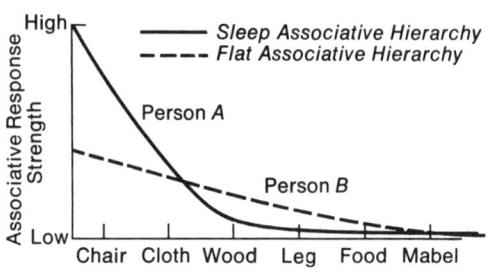

Figure 4
Associative hierarchies around the word "table." (Adapted from Figure 1 of Mednick, 1962. Copyright 1962 by the American Psychological Association and reproduced by permission.)

The associative processes of Person A and Person B seem impressively different, if their response to the stimulus word "table" is representative of their associative processes in general. Person A responds quickly with the dominant response but, having done so, seems to have shot his bolt; for him, a response with high associative strength takes over, leaving him to struggle for further associations. His associative strength gradient is a steep one. Person B's is flatter. While he too may give a popular association as his first response, he has many less conventional ones waiting in the wings, and they appear promptly in succession. This phenomenon of individual differences in associative processes coupled with his Remote Associates Test has led Mednick and his collaborators into some interesting fields that yield various hypotheses about creativity in both normal and disordered people. To look briefly at a few will show how a model designed for study of a specific behavior like schizophrenia can spawn hypotheses of interest for the study of behavior in general.

In a study by Houston and Mednick (1963) it was assumed that the creative person is "driven by a *need* for associative novelty" much in the way people in general are driven by such basic needs as the satisfaction of hunger and thirst. If such an assumption is correct, then providing associative novelty should prove reinforcing for the creative person, although not necessarily for the noncreative. To test this proposition, the investigators selected two groups of subjects—a high-creative and a low-creative group—and presented them with a situation in which one response would be reinforced in a trite way, another in a novel way. If high-creative people do indeed have a drive for associative novelty, they should show an increase in the type of response that leads to the novel reinforcement, while such an effect may be absent in the low-creative group. Specifically, Houston and Mednick presented subjects with cards, each bearing two words, a noun and a non-noun. In each case, the subject was instructed to read aloud which of the two words he preferred. If he chose the non-noun (for example, "black"), the experimenter responded with a trite association (for example, "black-white"), while if the subject chose the noun (for example, "father"), the experimenter responded with a novel association (for example, "father-eggbeater"). If it were true that highly creative people were driven to seek associative novelty, this second type of experimenter response should prove positively reinforcing for them, with the result that the high-creative individuals should have chosen more nouns during the experiment than the low-creative group (assuming the groups showed low initial noun–non-noun preferences).

Mednick and Mednick (1965) summarize the results in another report:

> ... such a relationship was observed. It was also of great interest that the low-creative tended to increase their choice of non-nouns as if they were avoiding the (noxious?) novel associations or as if they were being rewarded by the trite associations. The results suggest that a need for associative novelty may be one of the important motives influencing, if not instigating, creative behavior. Perhaps the satisfaction of this need is in part responsible for the strong feelings of satisfaction (aha! experience) which have often been reported to accompany the attainment of creative solutions ... (p. 161).

Findings of this sort have encouraged Mednick and his co-workers to pursue leads down still other paths. Thus, McNeil (1969), one of Mednick's students, focused his doctoral dissertation on the relationship between mental disorder and creativity. He conducted his research in Denmark, one of the few countries that have efficient record-keeping systems whereby mental health data can be accurately checked and the adjustment patterns of patients effectively traced. The reader who is interested will find in McNeil's dissertation ample references to continuing work in this general area. We will be returning to additional efforts by Mednick and McNeil in the following section.

The Interpersonal Model

Probably no one would argue with the assumption that, other things being equal, it is better to be reared in a family where one's parents are psychologically healthy than in a family where one's parents are psychologically maladjusted. But to what extent maladjusted parents increase the likelihood that their children will be maladjusted is a moot question, despite a plethora of studies on the subject, especially in connection with the etiology of schizophrenia.

The somewhat tongue-twisting term "schizophrenogenic mother" bears testimony to the notoriety the distaff side of the family has achieved. The characteristics of such mothers have been described repeatedly, although often in contradictory terms. In reporting the findings from several sources, Buss (1966) points out: "Mothers were found to be both overprotective and rejecting, both overtly and subtly hostile, both neglectful of the child and intrusive into his activities, and both unduly and insufficiently restrictive" (p. 355).

For Buss, many of the studies have raised issues rather than settled them. As he puts it:

> The only unequivocal finding to emerge from these investigations is that schizophrenics' mothers tend to be more controlling than mothers of normals. This fact may be interpreted in two ways. First, this over-restrictiveness may make it more difficult for the child to mature, to initiate new activities, to socialize, and in general to make his way in the world in a normal fashion. Consequently, the child has tendencies that may lead to schizophrenia.
>
> The second interpretation assumes that the preschizophrenic child is *initially* deviant, and the mother's overcontrol is a *response* to the child's abnormal tendencies. The mother's response is presumably the kind of reaction we would expect to *any* deviance or illness in her child. For example, if the child had a chronic heart ailment, the mother would be forced to be restrictive and overcontrolling (p. 356).

More belatedly, the role of the father has also received attention, and the trend is to study the presumed relation between family constellation in general and the development of schizophrenia in particular. Despite some intriguing hypotheses, the problem has not yielded to any simple solution, however. Rodnick and Garmezy (1957), for example, early suggested the plausible notion that schizophrenics are unduly sensitive to social censure, as reflected in their performance under criticism. Unfortunately, experimental evidence did not always bear out the social-censure theory; in some experimental studies schizophrenics did more poorly when censured, while other investigators obtained contradictory results. As amended more recently by Garmezy (1965), the theory spells out the conditions under which, and the direction in which, censure will affect the performance of schizophrenics. When the censure is irrelevant to the task, so that the schizophrenic's behavior has no effect on dispelling the criticism, schizophrenic performance is said to worsen. When, however, the schizophrenic can, by his performance, cause censure to cease, his performance is said to improve. Unfortunately, the amended theory, though an improvement over the original, does not square with all of the experimental evidence either in this complicated area of the nature and etiology of schizophrenic behavior.

Other investigators have tried a different route — one with characteristic detours — namely, the study of twins. It has been suggested that if one gathers data on the relative incidence of a disorder such as schizophrenia in persons of different degrees of blood relationship, one may be able to differentiate the relative contributions of hereditary and environmental factors to the occurrence of the disorder. Unfortunately, again, there are more obstacles than anticipated. Identical twins, for example, conveniently have the same genetic makeup; it happens too, however, that they are often treated similarly by parents and others. How to sort out hereditary and environmental influences under the circumstances is a problem. In his sophisticated analysis of the contributions of twin research to psychology, Vandenberg (1966) points up some of the difficulties and offers recommendations for future research.

Those who have made the study of the broader family their business have not had an easy time of it either. Like Rodnick and Garmezy, Bateson and his collaborators (1956) proposed an interesting thesis — the "double-bind." Relations in the family of the schizophrenic are so conflicting, they suggested, that the child is damned if he does, damned if he doesn't. The mother may make overtures to him that seem affectionate. If he responds in kind, she withdraws; if he does not, she feels resentful. The conflicting messages leave the child in an essentially insoluble situation — in a double-bind. Where, as is often the case among parents of schizophrenics, the father is weak and ineffectual, he serves to complicate the communication process even further.

Again, the hypothesis is an intriguing one, and, as in the case of the social-censure hypothesis of Rodnick and Garmezy, it has undergone revisions, elaborations, and extensions over the years. Reviewing the literature, Schuham (1967) points out, however, that while "The birth of the double-bind hypothesis was greeted by enthusiastic predictions that one of the elements in the individual's life experience producing schizophrenic behavior had finally been isolated . . ." (p. 413), little empirical evidence has been mustered to date. After reviewing the work of a decade in this area, he is forced to conclude: "It is apparent that not until tenets of the theory have been further limited, clarified, and operationalized will it become a reliable phenomenon capable of empirical validation. . . . Those who believe in the validity of the double-bind hypothesis cannot expect others to accept it on the basis of clinical evidence alone" (p. 415).

To date, the whole area of the relationship between family constellation and incidence of schizophrenia in offspring remains an interesting but foggy domain of exploration. Despite the efforts of such capable and indefatigable investigators as Mishler (1963), Lidz and Fleck (1960), and Farina (1960), definitive answers to many questions remain to be offered. As one of the major contributors, Fontana (1966), in reviewing studies on familial etiology to help answer the question "Is a scientific methodology possible?," comes to some sobering conclusions:

> Four general findings are consistently supported by the few methodologically adequate research studies reviewed here: (a) there is no evidence for the proposed "schizophrenogenic" pattern of dominant mother–passive father, (b) there is little support for the proposed interaction between parental dominance pattern and premorbid adjustment of patients, (c) there is more conflict between the parents of normals, and (d) communication between parents of schizophrenics (or a schizophrenic subgroup) is less clear than it is between the parents of normals (p. 225).

Lest the reader himself despair at this point, let us turn to one of the more optimistic researchers, who feels that the Gordian knot *can* be cut if only we do a 90-degree turn in our approach to schizophrenia. There is little that cannot be resolved by an appropriate methodological strategy, Mednick would argue, even in such a complex area of investigation as the etiology of schizophrenia. His strategy is the "high-risk-group method." Whether this is indeed the answer remains to be seen, but, in order to instill some optimism in the reader, let us look at what Mednick proposes.

The High-Risk-Group Method

Mednick is not so much disposed to question the particular theories advanced in connection with schizophrenia (although he had proposed one of his own, as noted earlier). Instead he is primarily concerned with the research methodologies that have gained currency. In his view, each has serious shortcomings, and he and McNeil (1968) point them out in their critique but also offer an interesting alternative. For example, a primary source of data consists of the observation of persons labeled schizophrenic, but it is not easy to tell which aspects of behavior characterize the disorder *per se* and which reflect the effects of a period of institutionalization. The study of Silverman et al. (1965), mentioned earlier, showed, for example, that "normal" San Quentin prisoners jailed for long periods of time resemble schizophrenic patients in some significant respects. Along the same line, a study comparing schizophrenics with evening college students found the two to be quite dissimilar. When, however, the schizophrenic patients were compared with normal medical and surgical patients hospitalized for long periods, the performance of the two groups showed many similarities, presumably as a function of the length of institutionalization. Again, the research of Goffman and Braginsky (reported in Part Four) suggests that schizophrenics retain both the need and the capacity to present to others the impressions they wish to convey.

The newer methods of observing the families of schizophrenics likewise have serious deficiencies, according to Mednick and McNeil (1968). Assuming that investigators can agree on interpersonal-relationship patterns observed, are these patterns the *cause* of schizophrenia or its *effect*? Further, even if the efforts of family researchers help delineate unequivocally some crucial aspects of the family constellation, can these be said to be basic to the disorder? After all, Mednick and McNeil point out, schizophrenics differ from control group subjects on more than this dimension — they have less sexual experience, marry less frequently, do not enjoy the same degree of occupational success, suffer educational disadvantages, and endure the loneliness of institutionalization, none of which are to be dismissed lightly. The same question, then, arises again — are these factors causes of schizophrenia or its consequences?

There is yet another common research strategy — examination of childhood histories of those who have developed schizophrenia. This method has its own shortcomings, as Mednick and McNeil view it. For one thing, it often depends on retrospective recall by parents, teachers, and others having knowledge of the schizophrenic. As such, the information yielded is often incomplete. More seriously, it may include a good deal of bias, both intentional and unintentional. Thus, it is because of these serious technical shortcomings that Mednick and McNeil suggested the adoption of a new approach. Why not study individuals who are *likely to* become schizophrenic, gathering data on them consistently *before* they develop schizophrenia, if indeed they do? Many advantages presumably accrue to such a procedure. For one, the element of possible bias should be reduced considerably, information having being gathered before rather than after the fact. For another, such information would be current rather than retrospective, complete rather than spotty, and uniform rather than unsystematic. It is these ends that the "high-risk-group method" is intended to achieve.

Who constitute the high-risk-group subjects? In the terms of Mednick and his research team they are "children who have chronically and severely schizophrenic mothers." On the basis of their extensive research in Denmark, a country whose records are uniquely adapted to such study, Mednick and Schulsinger (1965) identified 207 such children, who have already been examined extensively, along with 104 individually matched control subjects. The investigators have plans to follow the subjects closely for the next 15 to 20 years, expecting, on the basis of previous investigations, that from 23 to 32 of the 207 children will be hospitalized for schizophrenia, while about half of the 207 will become seriously "deviant." The longitudinal research plan, as described by Mednick and McNeil is as follows:

We intend to follow these children closely for the next 15 to 20 years. When some appreciable number become seriously deviant (including schizophrenic), we will be able to look back at the 1962 examination and determine early premorbid characteristics which distinguish those that succumb, investigate the interaction of these premorbid characteristics with life circumstances, and plot these factors as they change from the time of the first examination to breakdown (p. 687).[5]

The longitudinal strategy, starting with subjects who are not yet schizophrenic but have a good likelihood of becoming so (or otherwise deviant), on the basis of having severely disordered schizophrenic mothers, provides some interesting comparisons. First, the course of children so identified can be compared with that of children of normal mothers, each of the low-risk-group subjects being matched individually with a child of the high-risk group. Secondly, high-risk children who eventually become schizophrenic can be compared with high-risk children who do not. And, thirdly, high-risk children who become schizophrenic can be compared with those high-risk children who become otherwise deviant.

Graphically, the design of the longitudinal study is depicted in Figure 5.

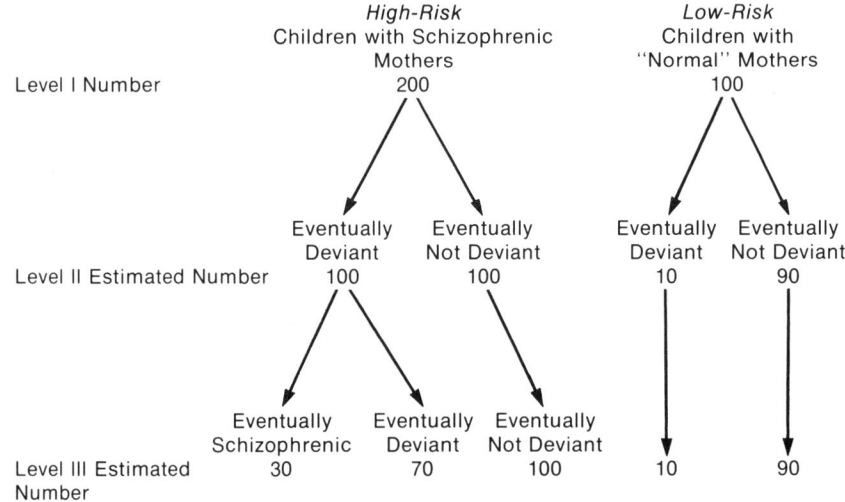

Figure 5
Design for a study using high-risk samples of 200 children with schizophrenic mothers and 100 low-risk control subjects. (Figure 1 of Mednick & McNeil, 1968. Copyright 1968 by the American Psychological Association and reproduced by permission.)

[5]Copyright 1968 by the American Psychological Association. Reprinted by permission of the authors and publisher.

As Mednick and McNeil point out, such a design has its built-in replications. For example, at Level II the estimated 100 subjects who become deviant may be viewed as suffering breakdown in five waves of 20 each (if they do not differ appreciably in age at time of breakdown or in diagnosis). Similarly, at Level III, the estimated 30 subjects who eventually become schizophrenic may be considered as having broken down in two waves of 15 each (assuming that age at breakdown does not differ significantly). Since others may not wish to try to repeat a similar long-term study, such built-in replication, the authors point out, would be all the more valuable.

The authors maintain that the proposed design eliminates the alleged disadvantages of the more common methodologies. Since the subjects are not yet schizophrenic, their test performance would probably not introduce artifacts such as the effects of institutionalization and other "epiphenomena" of mental disorder. Similarly, since no one, including the person himself, knows that a given subject will become schizophrenic, the introduction of bias in the information gained from parents, relatives, and others is reduced considerably, if not eliminated. The information is also current rather than retroactive, and the data can be collected uniformly and systematically. Above all, the matter of control groups is neatly handled; both high-risk subjects who do not become schizophrenic and those who become otherwise deviant serve as controls for high-risk subjects who become schizophrenic.

Although they eschew the methodologies in current use in favor of their own, Mednick and his group do not scoff at the data that have been painstakingly amassed in studies of subjects who are already schizophrenic. They suggest, in fact, that existing information about etiology can provide valuable leads in connection with the premorbid characteristics of their own subjects. What they do regret is that their design, as it stands, would yield primarily correlative data—that is, information showing how one thing (for example, intelligence) covaries with another (for example, seriousness of breakdown). Such data do not, however, get at *causes;* they simply point up the fact that two things tend to go together. The determination of *causal* relationships demands the experimental procedure of manipulating one or more variables while controlling others.

The authors describe the situation thus:

> We can point to maternal, physiological, and associative variables that markedly distinguish the premorbid state of a group that later suffered breakdown, but we cannot be sure that any of these variables are, or are closely related to, primary causal agents. They certainly help define areas which should be further studied. *But correcting all or any of these deviancies in our breakdown subjects back in 1962 may not have circum-*

> vented their eventual breakdown if the breakdown sprang from inherited or acquired biochemical anomalies, early behavioral experiences, life experiences since 1962, or an interaction of all or some of these factors (p. 691).

Clearly, the ethics of research would prohibit the kind of manipulation that might be thought to induce schizophrenia; society is not willing to pay the price of contributing to the breakdown of even one person in order to learn the cause of any disorder. But what about "interfering" in the lives of subjects in a way believed likely to *prevent* potential disorder—experimental manipulation in a constructive sense? The authors talk of such a proposal as follows:

> Mednick and Schulsinger are currently planning research which will combine the preventive and high-risk models in a single study. Several all-day nursery schools are planned which will care for 3-year-old children with schizophrenic mothers as well as matched control children. The nursery schools will provide an ideal framework for highly intensive and extensive study of young high-risk children. The result of this study will be compared to the results already obtained on older high-risk samples. The nursery schools will also supply the framework for the highly systematic and controlled study of the efficacy of preventive techniques. The techniques to be applied will be suggested by earlier high-risk-sample results which are supported by the study of the 3-year-old sample. It is perhaps necessary to add that the interventions will be administered in a tightly controlled, factorial design which should make possible the assessment of interaction effects. The research will, of course, be longitudinal (p. 691).

Whether the work of Mednick and his associates will prove to hold the key to clearer understanding of the etiology, nature, and course of schizophrenia remains to be seen. But the dedication of this team of researchers is evident from the arrangements made to insure that the study reaches completion during their lifetime. Without intending it as an obituary, it seems appropriate to end this description of their efforts with their own words in this connection: "To maximize the probability that the principal investigators would survive the study, the subjects' mean age was set at 15 (range 9–20); the subjects will have been through the major risk period for schizophrenia when the principal investigators should reach 60 years of age" (p. 689).

One cannot deny the fact that much is to be learned by studying psychopathology at first hand. However, there may be advantages to stepping back from the problem a bit, perhaps even studying a more synthetic version of it, if such research tactics permit greater control over the investigation. Whatever the merits of the respective strategies, some creative investigators have chosen to create laboratory analogues to processes that are presumably involved in psychopathology proper. Their innovative approaches are stimulating, and some representative efforts, reported in the following section, may help spark the reader's own imagination.

Experimental Clinical Diagnosis

Do some of us pay more attention to internal cues than others? If so, might not such differences have interesting implications for the study of personality? Valins (1967) hypothesized that "individuals who are psychometrically classified as relatively unemotional will make less use of information concerning their internal reactions when evaluating emotional stimuli than will individuals who are classified as emotional" (p. 458). To test his hypothesis, Valins devised an ingenious study in which subjects were led to believe they were hearing the beat of their own hearts when actually they heard a recording in which the beats had been purposely arranged to be faster at some points, slower at others. This audible, synthetic heartbeat was heard as the subjects performed the experimental task.

In order to classify subjects on the basis of emotionality, Valins had used two questionnaires, one developed previously by Lykken (1957) and one devised by himself (Valins, 1963). Lykken's questionnaire consisted of forced choices between two distasteful situations (for example, having an accident with a borrowed car vs. cleaning out a cesspool; or knocking over a glass in a restaurant vs. cleaning up a bottle of spilled syrup). The second alternatives in the pairs—that is, the tedious choices—would presumably be less distasteful to emotional subjects than the first, which represent embarrassing or anxiety-provoking situations. Administering the Lykken questionnaire to 1800 male undergraduates at a freshman orientation meeting, Valins selected those who scored either very high or very low in the extent to which they chose the anxiety-provoking alternatives; these two groups were presumably low emotional and high emotional subjects respectively. The two extreme groups were subsequently given Valins' own questionnaire, and the subjects chosen for the experiment were those who fell in the same extremes on *both* questionnaires. A further check of the two groups, using the Minnesota Multiphasic Personality Inventory, showed them to differ significantly on the anxiety factor. Valins could, therefore, feel certain that he had a high emotional and a low emotional group.

Told that the experiment dealt with the study of heart rate reactions to sexual stimuli, the subject was to have his heartbeats measured through a microphone taped to his chest, with an amplifier and signal tracer recording the results. As a necessary part of the experiment, the subjects were misinformed that, owing to a defect in instrumentation, they would be hearing their heartbeats but that they should ignore the sounds while performing the task. The task consisted of rating a series of ten color slides of nude women, taken from *Playboy* magazine, each projected for 15 seconds at 1-minute intervals. The experimenters described the procedure thus:

> The slide presentation was coordinated with the tape recording and began with the third minute. Using this procedure, the subjects heard a marked change in the bogus heart rate to five of the slides but not to the other five. After the tenth slide, the subjects heard their "heart" beating normally for 3 minutes. The slides were then repeated in the same manner with subjects hearing the identical reactions. To control for variations in the attractiveness of the nudes, the slide order was systematically rotated within conditions (Valins, 1967, p. 459).[6]

Prior to the performance of the experimental task, 20 subjects were assigned to each of four conditions:

1. High emotional—heart rate increase. That is, subjects who scored as emotional on the questionnaires and who would be hearing their "hearts" beating normally on five of the slides and beating faster on the other five.
2. High emotional—heart rate decrease. Emotional subjects who would hear a normal heartbeat on five slides and a slower heartbeat on the other five.
3. Low emotional—heart rate increase. Subjects who scored as unemotional on the questionnaires and who would be hearing their "hearts" beating normally on five of the slides and beating faster on the other five.
4. Low emotional—heart rate decrease.

As described by Valins (1967), the necessary data were obtained as follows:

> *Slide ratings.* On the pretext that the experimenter wished to reduce the number of slides to the most attractive ones, the slides were shown a third time (with no heartbeat feedback), and subjects rated the attractiveness of each girl, using a 100-point scale.
>
> *Photograph choices.* As an additional reward for participation (the subjects were paid $3.00 for this experimental session and another to be discussed below) the subject was told he could take five of the 10 photographs from which the slides had been made. Copies of his choices, presumably donated by the publisher, would be given to him with his paycheck (pp. 459–460).

In order to gather further information on how the heart rate feedback might have affected the rating of specific details of the pictures, the subject was asked, after he

---

[6]Copyright 1967 by the American Psychological Association. Reprinted by permission of the author and publisher.

had chosen his five photos, to rate "what about those photographs is good or bad." He subsequently rated all 10 photographs with respect to how "nice" the breasts, face, hair, and general pose were.

As part of the original plan, the subjects had agreed to participate in a second session, to which they were invited by letter about six weeks later. At this time another experimenter had the subject fill out a questionnaire which was actually irrelevant to the experiment. The subject was then given his paycheck before the second part of the experiment was presumably to begin and was also told by the experimenter, who handed him the original 10 photographs: "Rather than looking over my records to see which photographs you wanted, take the 5 that you want and I'll get some copies" (Valins, 1967, p. 460). Thereupon the experimenter left the room, presumably to get copies, and, upon his return, explained that the experiment was over and obtained the subject's reaction.

It turned out that all but two of the subjects—a high emotional subject and a low emotional subject, both in the heart-rate-increase condition—had accepted the fake heartbeats as their own. In order to keep the number of subjects equal in all conditions, the data of these two were retained in the analysis. Had they been dropped, the major conclusions would, however, have been even more strongly confirmed.

Table 3 shows some interesting findings with respect to the attractiveness ratings and photograph choices.

Table 3
Mean ratings of slide attractiveness and mean number of reinforced photographs chosen. Each subject chose 5 of the 10 photographs; the figures in parentheses indicate how many of the 5 reinforced slides were among the 5 photographs chosen.

Slides	Conditions			
	High Emotional		Low Emotional	
	Increase	Decrease	Increase	Decrease
Reinforced	79.99 (3.70)	66.50 (3.25)	69.77 (3.20)	66.39 (2.75)
Nonreinforced	56.65 (1.30)	51.78 (1.75)	56.01 (1.80)	60.75 (2.25)
Difference	+23.34 (+2.40)	+14.72 (+1.50)	+13.76 (+1.40)	+5.64 (+.50)

(Table 1 of Valins, 1967. Copyright 1967 by the American Psychological Association and reproduced by permission.)

It is clear that the "internal" cues—the bogus heartbeats—did have an effect, whether the subjects were high emotional or low emotional. The reinforced slides (whether of the heart increase or heart decrease variety) were rated as significantly more attractive than the nonreinforced slides (that is, those on which the subjects heard a normal heartbeat), although the slides reinforced by heart rate increase were rated as more attractive than those reinforced by heart rate decrease. More important, however, is the fact that high emotional subjects responded significantly more strongly to inner cues (their "heart"), whether in the form of heart rate increase or decrease, than did low emotional subjects.

Attractiveness ratings of specific details of the pictures showed equally impressive results. As with the overall ratings and photograph choices, the specific details of the reinforced photos were, virtually in every instance, rated as more attractive than the corresponding details of the nonreinforced photos. This effect obtains whether reinforcement consisted of heartbeat increase or decrease, although, as before, it is more evident with the heartbeat increase condition. And again (as shown in Table 3), while both high emotional and low emotional subjects responded more to the reinforcement condition than to the nonreinforcement condition, the former did so significantly more than the latter. That is, high emotional subjects seemed more responsive to inner cues than low emotional subjects.

As a careful investigator, Valins felt it necessary, however, to rule out an alternative explanation. Could it perhaps be that just the change in rate of *any* sound might have achieved the same results—that is, that the subjects might have reacted similarly even if they had not construed the sounds as internal feedback from their own heart? To test this possibility, two additional groups of high emotional and low emotional subjects (9 in each group) were formed and exposed to the identical first-session procedure, except that, instead of being told the sounds represented heartbeats, they were told that they were simply "extraneous sounds." No significant differences were found between these two groups of control subjects on any of the measures. Thus, concluded Valins (1967):

> ... the [original] differences are due to the sounds functioning as information about internal reactions.... Individuals do utilize information concerning their internal reactions, and the degree to which this is done can be predicted by knowing whether an individual is more emotional or less emotional. These individual differences highlight the importance of cognitive processes in mediating emotional response. Although physiological reactions may indeed be important determinants, perhaps more important is whether an individual feels it necessary to have a label or explanation for his internal state (p. 462).

Interesting as these conclusions are, Valins recognized further possible relationships with clinical implications. As he put it:

> It is conceivable, for example, that an individual who is characterized by marked physiological reactivity could be relatively unemotional, whereas someone who is less reactive could be relatively emotional. The former might ignore his internal reactions, and the latter might experience much pressure to label and evaluate them (p. 462).

These possibilities are the very ones that led Schachter and Latané (1964) to investigate the theme of "crime, cognition, and the autonomic nervous system." It is well at this point, therefore, to take a look at their research.

Physiology and Sociopathy

As is frequently the case, it was the white rat that first led Latané and Schachter (1962) to speculate about whether some interesting observations made on this animal might also hold for human subjects. It had turned out, for example, that in an avoidance learning task (that is, one in which the job is to learn a behavior that will avoid a noxious stimulus), rats injected with epinephrine (adrenalin) did significantly better than a control group injected with a placebo (neutral solution). The experimenters saw interesting possibilities for applying these findings to human subjects.

Earlier, Lykken had speculated about the characteristics of so-called sociopaths in these terms. A person so labeled by clinicians typically displays a number of features. He usually has a long history of social transgression, beginning with minor acts like petty stealing and progressing to such serious offenses as forgery. Somehow he never seems to profit from experience, getting in and out of trouble over the years. In many cases he is quite likeable, an attribute that abets his penchant for getting into trouble, since superficial charm often aids him in getting out of it. He usually shows little anxiety, being in this respect quite unlike most people who, in similar circumstances, would be anxious both about what they had done and about its consequences. Cleckley (1955) devoted a book to the subject (although some of the persons he described would in some clinical settings be regarded as psychotic). Perhaps the most convenient description for our purposes is a definition from the *Diagnostic and Statistical Manual of Mental Disorders* (1968) of the American Psychiatric Association,[7] describing a category of "antisocial personality":

> This term is reserved for individuals who are basically unsocialized and whose behavior pattern brings them repeatedly into conflict with society. They are incapable of significant loyalty to individuals, groups, or social values. They are grossly selfish, callous, irresponsible, impulsive, and un-

---

[7] Committee on Nomenclature and Statistics of the American Psychiatric Association, *DSM-II Diagnostic and Statistical Manual of Mental Disorders*, 2nd ed., 1968.

able to feel guilt or to learn from experience and punishment. Frustration tolerance is low. They tend to blame others or offer plausible rationalizations for their behavior . . . (p. 43).

Interested in the anxiety-free character of the sociopath, Lykken (1957) speculated that (a) since anxiety reduction is a central feature in avoidance learning, and (b) the sociopath seems relatively anxiety-free, (c) he should have particular difficulty with avoidance learning tasks. Schachter and Latané were intrigued by the possibilities for research here, particularly since in an earlier study they had found that with the injection of a sympatholytic agent (one that depresses autonomic nervous system functioning), chlorpromazine in this case, subjects seemed to behave less "normally"; specifically, they were more inclined to cheat in an experimental situation. How might this be explained? Were subjects under the influence of the drug less inclined to label and more inclined to ignore their physiological state? In any case, were there clues here that might clarify the behavior of the sociopath?

Schachter and Latané (1964) stayed on the trail, this time going to prisons (Stillwater State Prison in Minnesota and Bordentown Reformatory in New Jersey) for their subjects. The criteria sought were emotional flatness (as described by Cleckley and as determined from the Lykken questionnaire) and incorrigibility (as measured by the number of offenses and time in prison). Prisoners high on these counts were regarded as sociopaths, those low on them as "normal" prisoners. The experimenters were interested in two questions. How "unemotional" are such sociopaths when emotionality is defined in terms of autonomic reactivity as indicated by physiological measures (rather than simply assessed clinically)? And how would such sociopaths compare with "normal" prisoners on both positive learning and avoidance learning tasks?

Paying the prisoners for their services as subjects, Schachter and Latané presented the experiment as one in which they were studying the effects of a hormone (fictitiously named "Suproxin") on learning ability. Actually some subjects were to be injected with adrenalin, others with a placebo. Maze learning was chosen as the measure of performance, the task was explained, and the subjects were given a fixed number of trials.

In order to measure both positive learning and avoidance learning, the experimenters devised an ingenious combination in which positive learning was the manifest task while a measure of avoidance learning was surreptitiously built into the procedure. The task was to learn to negotiate without error a maze that had 20 choice points. At each of these points there were four switches, one of which was the correct one.

Pulling the correct switch allowed the subject to proceed to the next choice point, while each of the other three constituted an error. The positive learning task was therefore obvious—learn to use the correct switch at each choice point in order to negotiate the entire maze without a mistake.

A measure of avoidance learning was, however, hidden in the procedure. Of the three wrong switches at each choice point, one delivered an electric shock if used. Thus, in learning the maze, subjects could make their mistakes by using any one of the three wrong switches, but in only one of the three cases would they be shocked for their error. To what extent they would, or would not, learn to avoid the electrified mistakes sooner than the nonelectrified mistakes was the question that interested the investigators. In other words, how good or poor were they at avoidance learning?

The findings were revealing. Using two conditions—adrenalin and placebo—Schachter and Latané were interested first in positive learning performance. Here they found no significant difference between sociopaths and normal prisoners under the two conditions. But what about avoidance learning? There, without the drug and injected only with a placebo, normal prisoners apparently do better than sociopaths, as shown in Figure 6.

Is it true, then, that the presumably anxiety-free sociopath is indeed poor at avoidance learning, thus accounting for his inability to profit from experience in real life? Looking at both groups under the adrenalin condition, Schachter and Latané had some quick second thoughts, as suggested by the data in Figure 7.

The reader will note that under the drug condition the respective performances shifted dramatically. Here the sociopath by far exceeds the normal prisoner in avoidance learning ability! The situation is not as simple, then, as had been thought. An "interaction effect" is involved. Without the arousal-producing drug adrenalin, normals do better than sociopaths at avoidance learning; with the drug, sociopaths do better than normals.

It is understandable that the investigators were tempted to take some direct measures of autonomic reactivity. Again they found results that seriously undermined some of the assumptions that had been made, as shown in Figure 8.

Apparently the presumed "unemotional" sociopath is not nearly as unemotional as external appearance might suggest. In both the placebo and adrenalin conditions, the sociopaths as a group were, in fact, more "emotional"—that is, they registered greater autonomic reactivity than normals, as measured by pulse rate.

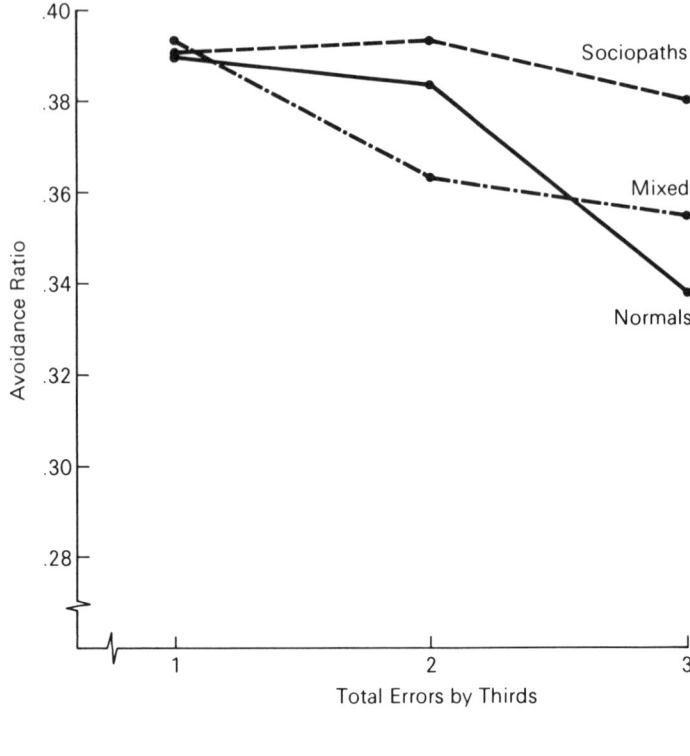

Figure 6
Mean avoidance ratio scores under placebo. The avoidance ratio is the proportion of shocked errors to total errors; hence the lower the ratio, the better the performance. The total errors of the subjects are shown by thirds rather than by blocks of trials, since some subjects learned the maze in fewer than the standard 21 trials. [Adapted from Figure 2A of Schachter and Latané from D. Levine (Ed.), *Nebraska Symposium on Motivation, 1964.* Copyright 1964 by the University of Nebraska Press and reproduced by permission.]

What now? Schachter and Latané (1964) saw some interesting implications, perhaps best expressed in their own words:

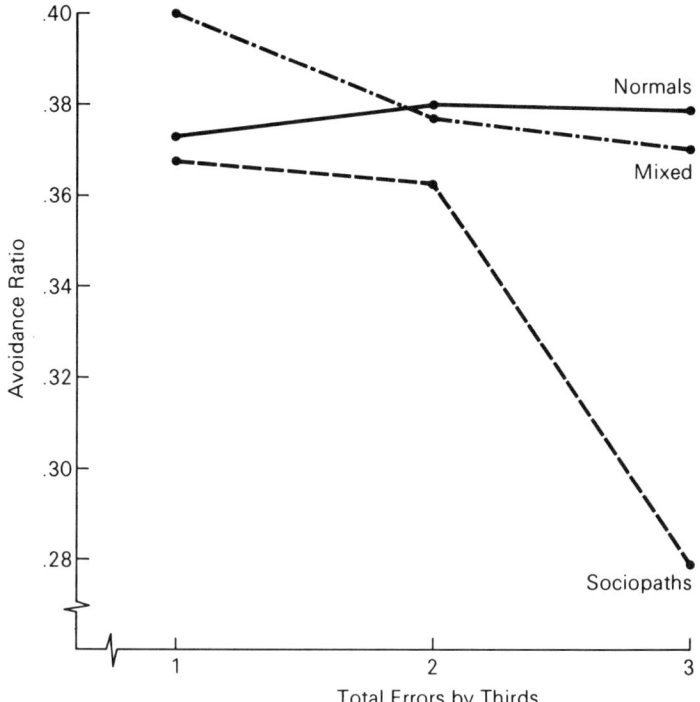

Figure 7
Mean avoidance ratio scores under adrenalin. [Figure 2B of Schachter and Latané from D. Levine (Ed.), *Nebraska Symposium on Motivation, 1964*. Copyright 1964 by the University of Nebraska Press and reproduced by permission.]

The crucial problem, then, appears to be one of labeling. How does the sociopath label his bodily feelings? . . . Such generalized, relatively indiscriminate reactivity is, we would suggest, almost the equivalent of no reactivity at all. If almost every event provokes strong autonomic discharge then, in terms of internal autonomic cues, the subject feels no differently during times of danger than during relatively tranquil times. Bodily conditions which for others are associated with emotionality are, for the sociopath, his "normal" state. It would appear from the data on the effects of adrenalin on avoidance learning that only intense states of autonomic reaction, presumably stronger than, and differentiable from, his normal reactions, acquire emotional attributes for the sociopathic subject. Given a chronic history of autonomic reactivity only a marked

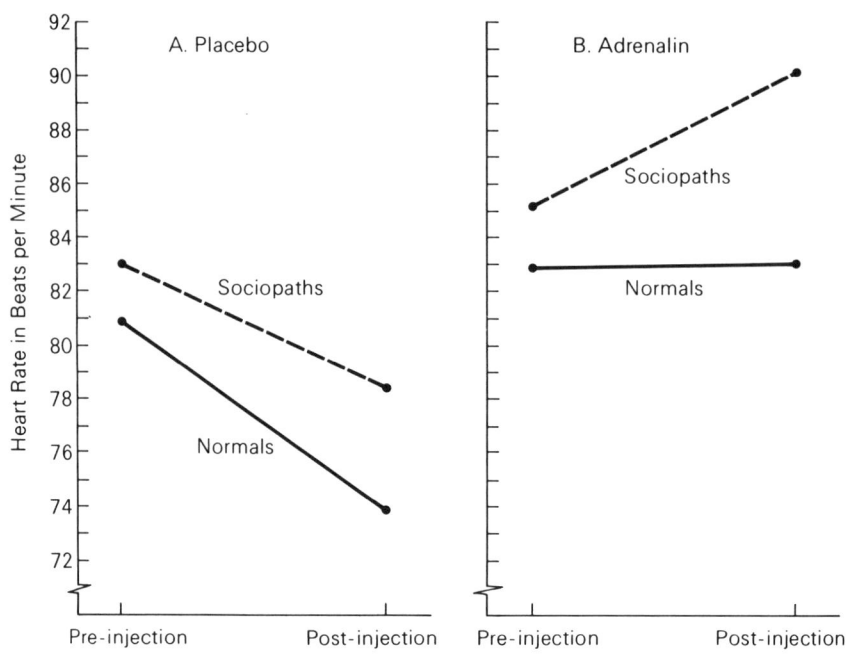

Figure 8
Mean pulse rate under placebo and under adrenalin. [Figure 4 of Schachter and Latané from D. Levine (Ed.), *Nebraska Symposium on Motivation, 1964*. Copyright 1964 by the University of Nebraska Press and reproduced by permission.]

increase in activation will be labeled as an emotional state, and perhaps even noticed (pp. 266–267).[8]

Pursuing the issue, Schachter and Latané saw some interesting contrasts between the sociopath and the psychoneurotic with an anxiety reaction:

> ... the autonomic hyper-reactivity of the anxiety neurotic and of the sociopath arise from entirely different causes. Where the autonomic reactivity of the sociopath is caused by an innate sensitivity to adrenalin, the reactivity of the anxiety neurotic is cognitively determined and unrelated to adrenalin sensitivity. ... Fanciful though it may seem, it is just conceivable that these two conditions may both be derived from a common state of adrenalin sensitivity. If an individual can learn not to apply

[8]Copyright 1964 by the University of Nebraska Press. Reprinted by permission of the authors and publisher.

> emotional labels to his bodily feelings in situations that customary social usage defines as emotional [as in the case of the sociopath], it seems equally possible that the opposite will hold, that is, that an autonomically hyper-reactive individual can learn to apply emotional labels to his bodily feelings in situations that would customarily be defined as non-emotional [as in the case of the anxiety neurotic].... If this general line of thought is correct, it should be anticipated that anxiety neurotics will prove as sensitive to adrenalin as are sociopaths (pp. 269-270).

Schachter and Latané do not indulge their penchant for creative speculation with impunity. Throughout their thought-provoking article they constantly reiterate the need for further research. As they put it: "Ad hoc explanations do have the feel of eating Puffed Rice. Alternative explanations of this unexpected pattern of findings are, at this stage, so numerous that, short of direct experimental attack, any attempt to fortify this particular interpretation seems gratuitous" (p. 267).

Such an injunction makes it all the more important to take note of more recent research on "Psychopathy, Autonomic Functioning, and the Orienting Response" by Hare (1968), who has risen to the challenge, undertaking with care the "direct experimental attack" that Schachter and Latané suggested. To him, interesting as their analysis sounded, it was still largely speculative. Feeling there was more to the problem, he not only took a considered look at other investigations to date but also designed a research program of his own.

Hare's review disclosed a number of points deserving closer attention. For one, the results of previous investigators were often at odds. Schachter and Latané, for example, found the sociopath (or psychopath, as Hare calls him) hyperreactive, while some others have found his autonomic functioning normal, or even underreactive. Methodological differences might help explain some of the discrepancies, Hare felt, but a more significant explanation might be found in the criteria used to designate subjects as psychopathic. Several of the studies, for example, did not distinguish between the primary psychopath, the "true" anxiety-free person described by Cleckley (1955), and the secondary psychopath, actually described by Eysenck (1964) as an "extraverted neurotic."

Making such differentiations, Hare (1968) used 51 inmates of the British Columbia Penitentiary as his subjects, studying the performance of primary psychopaths, secondary psychopaths, and nonpsychopaths on a number of different aspects of autonomic functioning—heart rate, skin resistance, and digital vasoconstriction. Using several conditions—presentation of repetitive stimuli, novel stimuli, and a task requiring concentration—he was able to compare the three groups with respect to the *orienting response*—that is, the manner in which, having habituated to repeated presentation of the same stimulus (a tone in this case), they then responded to the presentation of a novel stimulus.

While there was some difference in autonomic functioning between Hare's psychopathic and nonpsychopathic subjects, in general the findings that psychopaths "... tended to exhibit very little autonomic variability during the resting period suggested that in the absence of specific stimulation psychopaths may be autonomically and cortically underaroused" (p. 13). Such findings led him to his own brand of speculation as follows:

> The finding in the present study that psychopaths generally gave smaller ORs [orienting responses] than did non-psychopaths suggests that the former would be less sensitive to novel environmental stimuli . . . also . . . that the psychopaths should be less receptive to external stimuli. There are several implications in this analysis. First, the psychopath may have a higher detection threshold for stimuli in general. . . . A second implication of the present reasoning is that psychopaths should be hyporesponsive to environmental stimuli in general, and particularly to those that are not relatively salient (pp. 14–15).

While Hare grants Schachter and Latané the right to speculate about the reasons the psychopath seems anxiety free and unable to profit from experience, he describes a number of reservations about their experimental procedure and the conclusions drawn. In turn, based on his own study, he offers the following alternative explanation to account for characteristic psychopathic behavior:

> Although based upon only electrodermal activity, the results of these [Hare's] studies suggest that psychopathy may be related to rapid homeostatic recovery from stress. One of the consequences of this short-lived autonomic activity is that the emotional components of a stressful situation would be largely confined to the temporal period in which the situation occurs. A related consequence is that the length of time during which autonomic responses can become conditioned to external and internal stimuli would be relatively short. . . . Taken together with the earlier discussion on the OR, sensitivity to stimulation, and awareness of the environment, this would mean that, compared with the normal person and the neurotic . . . there would be fewer cues with the capacity to elicit the autonomic components of fear and anxiety in the psychopath (pp. 20–21).

The reader may come away with the notion that psychologists find it more difficult to "prove" things than physicists do. That, by and large, is true—at least at present. But we would remind him that, in this fast-moving world with its knowledge explosion, even the physicist is no longer sure his theory of today will hold tomorrow. The electron microscope and the space satellite are boons to knowledge, but, in letting us take both smaller and larger looks at what we know, they continue to upset a number of conceptual applecarts. Yet it is gratifying to reassemble such concepts into their more accurate, and temporarily more stable, versions.

It is with such caveats in mind that the reader should approach the next chapter. Clinical theory makes no pretense of being any more than just that—it is theory, not gospel. And like all good theory, it changes as new evidence comes in. Meanwhile the world continues to turn, the theorist is asked to apply such knowledge as is available, and if the clinician does not yet have the wisdom of Solomon, he has at least the patience of Job. What matters most is that the appliers of knowledge remain in close touch with its discoverers.

Part Four
Theory and Practice

11
The Observation of Behavior

One would like to feel that theory and practice move like the hands of a skilled juggler, one feeding into the other in an endless, well-coordinated exchange. Actually, theory and practice move more like the feet of an unskilled skater, one shuffling ahead of the other, the two sometimes getting entangled and tripping over each other, and ultimately with the body of knowledge often winding up on its scholarly rump. But progress is not bought cheaply, as we will see when we review the lot of the clinician as he tries to combine theory and practice in order to understand human behavior.

Perhaps this review is best accomplished by examining the three major functions that clinicians share with their fellow behavioral scientists—*observation, prediction,* and *control*. They will be our broad problem areas, while some specific clinical concerns—such as problems of adjustment, techniques for coping with stress, methods of behavior change, and individual differences—will illustrate the variety of possible approaches. In this chapter we will focus on the domain of observation, examining the area of psychopathology from several frames of reference.

Psychological Constructs

Eric Berne's best seller, *Games People Play,* makes embarrassingly clear some of the typical strategies we adopt, consciously or unconsciously, in relating to one another. In a more restricted way, we use some of the same subterfuges on ourselves. Rather than face the actual reason he wants a new car every year (as a status symbol), a man gives himself a "good" reason (namely, that he wants to be sure his car is always "in running order"). Rather than admit to herself that a hypochondriacal, demanding mother is snuffing out her freedom, the unmarried daughter showers her with gifts and attention, proclaiming love for "one who means everything to me." It has proved useful to classify such "defense mechanisms," labeling the man's "rationalization" and the daughter's "reaction formation."[1]

Classification serves good theoretical and practical purposes, but one could be tempted to settle for these useful descriptive constructs without bothering to check whether they square with evidence. Of course, one cannot run an experiment every time he is about to make a statement about another's behavior, but the clinician is nevertheless in a position to constantly accumulate evidence for his statements, presumably validating his constructs as he goes. There are also several other ways in which to gain reassurance that one is on the right track: one can take a frankly empirical approach; one can chase down constructs theoretically; or one can even go to a computer to attempt to simulate a process. Granting each its due, let us look at some typical examples of these three approaches, as each tries in its own way to shed light on the nature of defense mechanisms.

An Empirical Approach

One of the defenses that has received special attention in the psychological literature is the mechanism of *projection,* typically defined as "the process of unwittingly attributing one's own traits, attitudes, or subjective processes to others" (English & English, 1958, p. 412). In an ingenious experiment—which is perhaps questionable on some grounds, however (see Part Two on the use of human subjects in research)—Bramel (1962) sought to study the mechanism of projection. Interested in noting how this clinical process might be explained in terms of dissonance reduction, he borrowed some serviceable concepts from social psychology, such as Festinger's theory of cognitive dissonance.[2]

In brief, Festinger (1957) holds that an organism has a fundamental need to reduce, or preferably eliminate, dissonance—dissonance being a state that exists when one notes a discrepancy between one's behavior and one's attitudes. For example, an honest man who finds himself cheating would experience dissonance and feel a need to resolve the inconsistency. Or suppose a man purchases one of two equally priced cars and then hears complimentary things said about the car he decided not

---

[1] For a comprehensive account of the many identifiable mechanisms, see Blum (1966).
[2] See Geiwitz (1969) for an extended account of dissonance theory as originally proposed by Festinger.

to buy. He too would experience dissonance. In his captivating theory, Festinger documents the versatility of people in achieving dissonance reduction. Bramel went on to speculate that resorting to the mechanism of projection is but another way of reducing dissonance, and he devised an experiment to test this hypothesis.

At the outset Bramel (1962) conjectured that if a person of high self-esteem suddenly discovered a very undesirable thing about himself, the discovery would create much dissonance for him, as it would represent a salient threat to his unimpeachability. On the other hand, a person of low self-esteem could take the situation in stride. One who already accepts himself as unscrupulous or immoral is likely to experience little dissonance when, let us say, he finds himself secretly longing for his neighbor's wife. If *projection* is one way of reducing dissonance, Bramel reasoned, then one should find the high self-esteem person engaging in considerable projection of an undesirable trait in himself; the person of low self-esteem, on the other hand, should have significantly less need for this mechanism. Experimentally, the problem was twofold: (1) to insure conditions of high and low self-esteem, and (2) to introduce a cognition so undesirable, yet undeniable, that one could feel sure that it was dissonance producing.

Bramel handled both problems. Subjects were informed at the start that the research had the dual purpose of discovering which people had insight into themselves and of measuring the ability of people to judge others' personalities on first impression. On the basis of their scores on several personality measures (Taylor Manifest Anxiety Scale, Minnesota Multiphasic Personality Inventory, Adjective Checklist), he paired subjects according to similarity of level of self-esteem and estimates of their own masculinity (all subjects were male). The two subjects of each pair were then introduced to each other. In the presence of both, the experimenter asked each one about himself and his attitudes toward certain current events.

Next, subjects in each pair were randomly assigned to one of two rooms in which each received, in private, a report of his performance on the personality measures. This phase of the experiment was intended to manipulate self-esteem, creating in one member of the pair a favorable impression of himself (by reporting complimentary things about his creativity, maturity, and so on) while giving the other member of the pair an unfavorable report designed to create low self-esteem. That the maneuver was successful is indicated in Table 1 where the ratings on self-esteem before the manipulation are comparable for the two members of the pairs, while, following the manipulation, the self-esteem of the subjects in the Favorable condition is significantly higher than that of their partners in the Unfavorable condition.

Table 1
Means and standard deviations of variables measured prior to introduction of the undesirable cognition.

Variable	Favorable ($n = 42$)	Unfavorable ($n = 42$)
Before self-esteem manipulation		
Initial self-esteem (checklist)		
M	14.5	15.1
SD	3.6	3.3
After self-esteem manipulation		
Self-esteem (seven-point scales)		
M	5.52	4.20
SD	.54	.86
Favorability of rating of partner		
M	4.79	4.90
SD	.69	.68
Rating of masculinity of partner		
M	5.39	5.30
SD	1.11	1.32
Rating of own masculinity		
M	5.87	5.56
SD	1.00	1.02

(Table 1 of Bramel, 1962. Copyright 1962 by the American Psychological Association and reproduced by permission.)

In order to check whether the two members of each pair saw one another in roughly similar ways at this point, the experimenter had requested that the partners rate each other, as well as judge their own and their partner's masculinity. As is apparent from Table 1, in general the feelings were mutual.

Now came the task of introducing a clearly undesirable cognition — that is, information about oneself calculated to produce dissonance. This information had to be introduced in such a way as to prove undeniable, lest the subjects simply ignore it. What more undesirable fact for most people in our culture to accept than their own homosexual inclinations? Thus, for the ostensible purpose of noting their reactions, the two members of each pair were seated side by side at a table, with a panel separating them, in order to view simultaneously a succession of fifteen photos of nude men. So that each would have information about his own reactions to the pictures, he was hooked up to some recording apparatus and provided with a dial on which a needle would register his "level of sexual arousal." In a notebook provided for the purpose, each subject was told to privately record his own dial reading in each case. He was also asked at the same time to estimate the dial reading of his partner (whom he could not see). The partner, in turn, would be engaged in similar recordings, as together they viewed one picture after another.

Actually the dial readings were controlled by the experimenter (without the subjects' knowledge) and bore no relationship to anyone's sexual arousal or homosexuality. To reassure the reader, we hasten to add that at the conclusion of the experiment the subjects were so informed—that is, "debriefed." What Bramel was interested in, however, was the measure of projection such a ruse could provide, since here was a situation in which one was manifestly attributing an undesirable trait (homosexuality) to another, in greater or lesser degree, as reflected in the dial readings assigned. As a Projection-score (P-score), he used a simple formula: P-score = assumed dial reading of partner minus own dial reading. Thus, the more positive the P-score, the more projection; the more negative the P-score, the less projection.

How did the members of the pairs behave? Table 2 shows the respective P-scores of members in the Favorable and Unfavorable conditions (that is, the high self-esteem and low self-esteem groups respectively) following the introduction of the undesirable cognition (dial readings of one's own presumed sexual arousal).

Table 2
Attribution scores measured after manipulation of self-esteem.

Attribution	Favorable ($n = 42$)	Unfavorable ($n = 42$)
Raw P score		
M	−2.95	−11.45
SD	25.52	27.96
P score adjusted for prethreat judgment of masculinity of partner		
M	+4.65	−4.76
SD	24.28	23.99

(Table 2 of Bramel, 1962. Copyright 1962 by the American Psychological Association and reproduced by permission.)

As hypothesized earlier, those members of the pair who had been exposed to the Favorable condition (high self-esteem) resorted significantly more to projection than did their partners in the Unfavorable condition (low self-esteem). The findings lent support to Bramel's notion that projection as a defense mechanism illustrated the process of dissonance reduction. Figure 1 shows in graphic form the relationship between tendency to project and level of one's self-esteem. Evaluating the latter on a scale of 1 (low) to 7 (high), it can be seen that the lower the self-esteem, the less the projection; the higher the self-esteem, the more the projection.

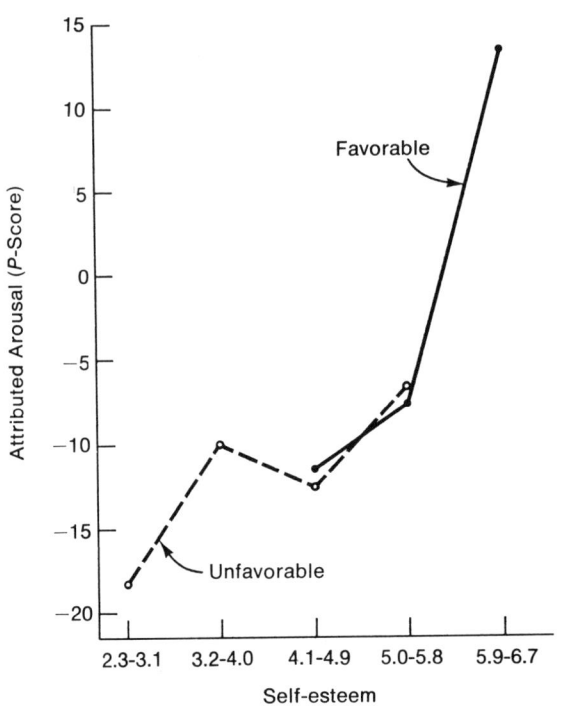

Figure 1
Mean attribution scores as a function of level of self-esteem. (Figure 1 of Bramel, 1962. Copyright 1962 by the American Psychological Association and reproduced by permission.)

But there was yet another interesting question. True, subjects who had experienced less dissonance—those in the Unfavorable condition—projected less than those in the Favorable condition. But was there any difference in the *nature* of their projection—that is, in the types of persons on whom they projected the undesirable cognition (of their possibly having homosexual traits)? It might be expected that usually one would project an undesirable trait more readily on those toward whom one was least favorably disposed. That is, one's projection pattern could be expected to reveal a halo effect—the more a person is disliked, the more we should project an unfavorable trait on him; the less a person is disliked, the less we should project an unfavorable trait on him. This is precisely what subjects in the Unfavorable condition did;

they showed little projection toward those they liked, but showed much projection toward those they disliked.

Subjects in the Favorable group, however, did not behave as simply. Having suffered considerable dissonance and consequently shown more projection than the Unfavorable group, they too projected considerably on partners who were least liked. With partners of whom subjects thought very well, however, the situation changed dramatically. Figure 2 illustrates the effect graphically.

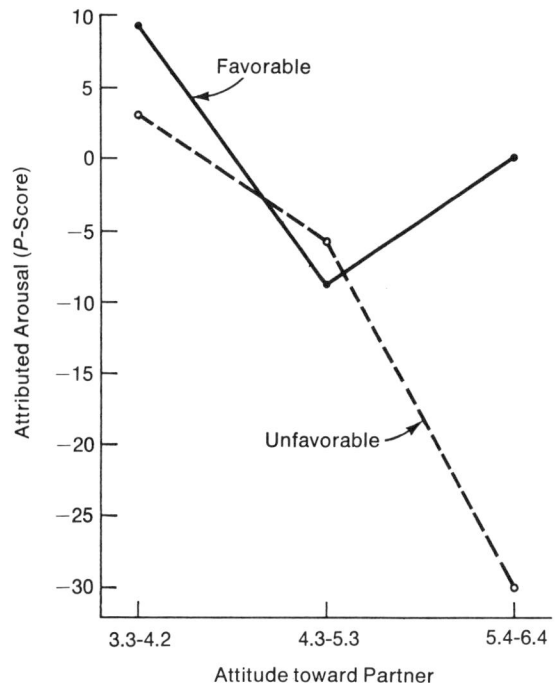

Figure 2
Mean attribution scores as a function of favorability of attitude toward partner. (Figure 2 of Bramel, 1962. Copyright 1962 by the American Psychological Association and reproduced by permission.)

The axis labeled Attitude Toward Partner refers to attitudes held *prior* to the introduction of the undesirable cognition—from Unfavorable (3.3–4.2) to Favorable (5.4–6.4). The axis labeled Attributed Arousal (p-score) represents the degree of arousal attributed to one's partner during the photo-observation phase. The amount of projection, measured in terms of the formula noted previously, could range from little projection (−30) to much projection (+10). Unlike subjects in the Unfavorable condition, those in the Favorable condition followed a halo pattern up to a point, then made a significant switch. There was much projection onto partners who were rated most unfavorably; there was less projection onto partners who were rated less unfavorably, that is, moderately. With partners rated very favorably, however, there was again much projection! Evidently, subjects in the Favorable condition had two ways of reducing dissonance: (1) projecting an undesirable trait on people they much disliked (in line with the halo effect), or (2) ascribing an undesirable trait to people they much respected (thus handling dissonance by getting the latter "into the same boat," as Bramel put it). The projection pattern of subjects in the Favorable condition would thus appear to be curvilinear—that is, high for those they greatly disliked and high for those they greatly liked (lower only for those toward whom they felt lukewarm).

Clearly, projection is not as simple an affair as the student reading his first book in psychopathology might like to believe. If Bramel's study helped point out some of the complications, Holmes' more recent review of the literature on projection adds even more dimensions. His review will also help illustrate the second of our three approaches, the attempt to theorize about defense mechanisms.

A Theoretical Approach

Holmes (1968) suggests that we look at two aspects of projection—*what* is projected (that is, whether the trait itself or its complement) and how *aware* the person is that he possesses the particular trait. Someone who is frightened, for example, may project his fright onto another, convincing himself that it is *he,* rather than I, who is frightened. On the other hand a person might project the *source* of his fright onto another—"I am frightened because he is frightening" (the *complement* of fright). Thus, what is projected may be either a trait or its complement—that is, something other than the trait as such.

One can distinguish also between levels of *awareness* involved in projection—a person may be aware of the trait in himself or unaware of it. Holmes represents the psychodynamic possibilities he sees in a 2 × 2 table like Table 3.

Within this framework Holmes reviewed the literature for studies that might illustrate and/or substantiate the several types of projection. He made some pertinent discoveries. "Similarity" projection, the kind most often assumed in the psychoanalytic literature, seemed to have little empirical support. Freud's plausible account of this mode of projection had made sense intuitively; for example, a person whom no one likes because he is unfriendly can feel it is others who are unfriendly. Thus, in his

Table 3
Types of projection in relation to subjects' awareness of the trait in themselves.

	Type of Projection	
S awareness	Same trait Projected	Different trait Projected
S not aware of the trait in self	Similarity	Panglossian-Cassandran
S aware of the trait in self	Attributive	Complementary

(Table 1 of Holmes, 1968. Copyright 1968 by the American Psychological Association and reproduced by permission.)

analysis of the famous Schreber case, Freud (1911) suggested that the patient's feeling of persecution (especially by homosexual pursuers) evolved as follows. Schreber, allegedly harboring homosexual impulses, "solved" the problem by perceiving others as having homosexual and persecutory designs on him. The process was assumed to consist of the following sequence:

(Denial): "I do not love him; I hate him."
(Projection): "He hates me."
(Rationalization): "I hate him, because he persecutes me."

Indeed, some of the early studies by Sears (1936) seemed to bear out such formulations empirically. As Holmes points out, however, others (for example, Campbell et al., 1964) have indicated some methodological flaws in the Sears investigations. The studies were ingeniously conceived, to be sure. Subjects rated themselves and others on certain traits, and if a given subject rated himself low on a certain trait while others rated him high on that trait, one could assume he was lacking in insight about himself in this respect. It was interesting to note, therefore, whether such people would tend to ascribe the trait they possessed (without realizing it) to other people more than did persons who knew they themselves possessed the trait. The results showed this hunch to be correct, convincing Sears that the case for "classical" projection (here called similarity projection) had been established experimentally.

Not so, argued Campbell et al., pointing to what they called a statistical artifact. Because of the manner in which ratings were made in the Sears study, if one rated oneself low on a certain trait relative to how one rated others, one was automatically rating the others higher. Thus, instead of verifying a psychodynamic construct (similarity projection) by empirical evidence, one was simply verifying the laws of arithmetic. Examining a number of other studies (for example, Page and Markowitz, 1955; Murstein, 1956) that purported to have found evidence in support of classical projection, Holmes attempts to point out that in these, too, methodological features of the design could by themselves account for the findings. He concludes that ". . . there is no methodologically acceptable evidence for the concept of similarity [classical] projection, that is, there is no evidence for the projection of an individual's traits of which he is not aware" (p. 263).

In examining the Panglossian-Cassandran projection—the upper right-hand cell of his 2×2 table—Holmes finds the evidence equally unconvincing, or actually missing, as in the situation in which a person projects onto someone a trait *opposite to* an undesirable one in himself of which he is unaware. Pangloss, a character in Voltaire's *Candide,* glossed over the horrible situations in which he managed to get involved by proclaiming this "the best of all possible worlds." In contrast, Cassandra, who was given to evil prophecies, could be said to be denying herself a basically optimistic philosophy. Holmes had coined these literary labels for the process of attributing to others a trait opposite to one's own of which one is unaware, but he finds no research evidence in the literature that would confirm either construct.

Holmes *does* find considerable evidence, however, supporting the processes denoted by the two lower cells of the table—that is, those cases in which people attribute to others a trait either similar to or different from one which they themselves are *conscious* of possessing. As suggested earlier, complementary projection would be present where the frightened person sees others as being frightening. Murray (1938) hit upon the notion of his Thematic Apperception Test when he noticed that the girls at his young daughter's birthday party, when asked to tell stories about photos of faces before and after playing a nerve-wracking game ("Murder"), saw the pictures as significantly more frightening following the game than before. Holmes finds similar confirmation in the studies of Feshbach and Singer (1957) and Hornberger (1960) in which subjects who had experienced electric shock perceived people in certain situations (either observed directly or on photos) as more menacing than did control subjects who had not received shocks.

In the case of "attributive projection" (the lower left-hand cell of Table 3), Holmes again finds considerable research evidence that the process exists in which an individual ascribes to others a trait similar to one he feels he possesses. In the Bramel study described earlier, for example, subjects in the Favorable condition were displaying this phenomenon when they attributed sexual arousal to partners whom they respected. In a similar study, in which Edlow and Kiesler (1966) provided college subjects an opportunity to attribute an undesirable trait they were made to feel they possessed to either people like themselves (fellow students) or people unlike themselves (criminals), it was found that the subjects tended to project the trait onto their own reference group (students).

By now it should be clear that while it is interesting and convenient to use certain constructs—for example, a defense mechanism like projection—to help explain various facets of human behavior, it is risky to go beyond available evidence. As is often the case in clinical psychology, the situation is more complicated than we might like. By the same token, it becomes more challenging.

One is tempted to look further, indeed even to countenance such exotic possibilities as turning to the computer for help. Some have done so, and their exploratory efforts are worthy of attention.

A Computer-Model Approach

There is a temptation these days to cry "Foul!" whenever the computer creeps into our lives, for it is repugnant to be punched into an IBM card in an age where most claim to be struggling for identity. It is not surprising, then, that some consternation should greet the rather overwhelming notion that the computer could be a helpful aid to understanding the human condition.

Undaunted, some pioneering investigators have nonetheless pursued such a course and have apparently even won some converts. Regardless of *a priori* feelings in the matter, it is worthwhile to take a look at some of their efforts, the better to decide whether such research is presumptuous, artificial, and demeaning, or imaginative, forward-looking, and inevitable.

Simulation of a Neurotic Process

For obvious reasons, it is neither feasible nor ethical to deliberately set out to make someone neurotic, even in the name of science. Much as such controlled experimentation might contribute to our understanding of how the process originates and develops, the prospect of abetting maladjustment is unpleasant. We owe most of what we know about neurosis to the sensitive observations of clinicians engaged in diagnostic and treatment activities. At this stage of our knowledge, however, even the practicing clinician would welcome whatever broadened perspective one might get on this complex disorder.

Colby (1963) accepted the challenge. Would it not be enlightening, he mused, if we could somehow *simulate* a neurotic process in order to experiment with it without harm to anyone. And what more convenient "patient" than the computer? After all, we use these electronic servants as everything from FBI agents detecting fraud on income-tax statements to guardian angels directing astronauts safely to the moon and back. Why not program one to act like a neurotic—that is, to print out messages that express thoughts, feelings, and conflicts one might typically hear from its neurotic human counterpart?

Having listened to a neurotic patient for a year or so, and having taped the sessions with the patient's consent, it would be possible to pick a random sample of statements from among the many made by the patient in the course of psychotherapy. The sample would presumably characterize his personality structure, including such factors as feelings about his parents, clues to his self-concept, representative fears, attitudes toward women, authority, and need for achievement. Statements expressed in simple syntax—"I hate father"; "Women avoid me"; "I fear failure"—could reside in the computer's memory.

Colby suggests going a step further toward making the computer more neurotic-like. For example, if the particular patient on whom the computer program is based were extremely anxious about his hatred of his father (feeling very guilty about it) while somewhat less anxious about failure, the computer programmer would then set a higher "charge" (that is, level of anxiety) on the statement "I hate father" than on the statement "I fear failure." All of the statements would thus be programmed according to the clinician's estimates of how intensely the actual patient had felt toward each one.

Along with such "belief propositions," appropriately weighted, the computer would be programmed with a set of rules for handling inputs. Thus, before the computerized neurotic could express its beliefs in the form of some output, it would need to check the belief seeking expression against others in the same set of beliefs—that is, in a "complex." If the particular belief conflicted with one or more of the other beliefs, "anxiety" would register (in some quantitative form). The belief having the higher charge would then be modified or transformed in the interest of "allaying anxiety," after which output would be possible.

In Colby's model, such computer "transforms" would be the analogue of the defense mechanisms used by the real-life neurotic. Some (for example, rationalization) would be sufficient to handle a low order of anxiety; others (for example, projection) would be resorted to only when a belief in its raw, undisguised form would cause a high level of anxiety to register. The neurotic computer would thus be programmed to search its list of available transforms until it found one to suit the specific occasion. While recourse to these computerized defense mechanisms would allow the computer to express its beliefs in relation to any input, the transforms involved would, however, exact a price: "The transforms are adjustive mechanisms, but they are maladaptive, since they result in loss of information, misrepresentations of beliefs, and insufficient discharge leading to increasing repetitive preoccupation with conflictual areas" (p. 173).

Colby's comment about the computer's inability to be "honest" with itself reminds one again of the neurotic in real life who maintains his adjustment at the expense of self-deception: "If the program attempts to interrogate itself about its own information, it cannot express directly some of its most highly charged beliefs and it receives as answers distorted derivatives of these beliefs" (p. 173).

Thus, one would have a computer-patient who, while less complicated than his live counterpart, would nevertheless resemble him in some essential details and therefore make possible some interesting manipulations. Just as the real patient had listened to and "handled" statements made to him by the live therapist (for example, "But you seem to respect your father's ability, even though you profess to hate him"), so now the investigator might deliver such inputs to the neurotic computer in order to see what responses it would print out.

This is a very artificial situation, to be sure, but one that would nonetheless allow one to try with impunity many things that might lead to significant payoff in both theory and practice. Note, for example, that the therapist in real life can never completely retrace his steps. Once having said something to his patient, the patient is changed by it, however slightly. The therapist can only guess what might have been the effect of his not having made the statement, or of his having made a different one.

With a computer the situation becomes very different. The investigator can program it, run his experiment, note the results, wipe its memory clean for the interaction, and start over. Once having said to a real patient, "You seem to react a bit effeminately, don't you think?" the therapist can never quite retract the remark. The experimenter with a computer-patient, however, can take some refreshing liberties. He can present the statement as an input and see how the computer reacts. He then can test its reaction to an alternative statement (for example, "It means a lot to you to be manly, doesn't it?") by erasing the first interaction from the computer's memory, presenting the new statement instead, and noting his computer-patient's output under the new circumstance.

This may sound visionary (even when we omit some of Colby's wilder speculations). Yet, in the computer era, attempts have been made to simulate everything from the workings of a large corporation to the efforts of nations to achieve international peace. Why not, Colby asks, simulate the neurotic process?

In a later section we will discuss the work of Starkweather (1965a, 1965b), who also sees the computer as an invaluable aid to the clinician, this time as a teacher of clinical skills. For the present, however, we turn to a second large domain of human behavior—psychopathology—to note in that area, too, the variety of approaches open to the clinician as he continues his quest for broader understanding.

Psychopathology

If the philosophy of the "flower children" prevailed, clinicians might be able to devote their energies to studying the anatomy of joy rather than the dynamics of mental illness. As it is, psychopathology still requires the lion's share of their attention, so it is helpful to get some perspective on the ways in which it can be approached.

Maladjustment can be viewed in at least three ways—from the frame of reference of the professional clinician, through the eyes of the patient himself, and, less psychodynamically, in frankly objective terms. The following discussion attempts, therefore, to exemplify a clinician-oriented, a client-oriented, and an actuarial approach to psychopathology.

A Clinician-Oriented Approach

Werner Mendel, one of a new breed of psychiatrists ready to question old ways and search for new, has carried out a series of studies aimed at critical analysis of some clinical procedures. Specifically, he focused on the procedure by which a prospective patient is, or is not, admitted into a psychiatric hospital.

Think for a moment how it must feel if, on countless forms (driver's license, college application, and the rest), one must each time answer "Yes" to the question "Have you ever been hospitalized for a nervous disorder?" and then have to obey the further instruction "If yes, explain." For the professional, who makes hundreds of decisions a year as to whether to admit a patient to a hospital, the decision loses its dramatic significance; for the patient, it does not. Thus, Mendel suggests that we take a closer look at how the mental health professional makes—or thinks he makes—these fateful decisions.

In their study, Mendel and Rapport (1969) reviewed 269 consecutive decisions (hospitalize versus don't hospitalize) made by 33 professionals (psychiatrists, psychologists, psychiatric social workers, and psychiatric residents) over an 8-day period on 269 persons to be evaluated for admission to the Los Angeles County–University of Southern California Medical Center. As the investigators describe it, the plan of the study was as follows:

> At the time the decision was made, a clinical data form ... was filled out by the decision maker describing his assessment of the patient applicant for hospitalization. This assessment included the severity of symptoms, the social resources available to the patient, the attitude of the family, etc. ...
>
> Four weeks after the eight-day period of observation, during which the 269 consecutive decisions were studied, the thirty-three decision makers were asked to fill out a questionnaire ... in which they were asked to summarize their attitudes about the decision for hospitalization and to describe what they thought the relevant determinants were in making the decision. Three months later, each decision maker was interviewed individually to ascertain his description of the experience of making decisions for hospitalization.... At the time of the study, each of the 33 decision makers had at least one month's experience making such decisions. Many of the decision makers had several years' experience in these clinical tasks (p. 322).

Some sobering facts emerged when the data were analyzed. As might have been expected, on the follow-up questionnaire the decision makers asserted that the severity of a person's symptoms weighed heavily in their decision to recommend hospitalization. The more severe his symptoms, they felt, the more likely they were to recommend hospitalization for him—a plausible rationale. What was the actual situation, however? Table 4 tells the story.

Table 4
Relationship between decision to hospitalize and severity of symptoms.

Decision	Severity of symptoms	
	Mild	Severe
Hospitalize	13%	87%
Don't hospitalize	11%	89%

(Adapted from Table 3 of Mendel and Rapport, 1969. Copyright 1969 by the American Medical Association and reproduced by permission.)

The figures hardly support the assumption that symptom severity influences the decision—those hospitalized and those not hospitalized are virtually indistinguishable in this respect. Could other factors, then, have unwittingly influenced the decision—

whether or not a patient had been hospitalized previously, for example? Hardly, according to the decision makers. But again the facts suggest otherwise. Table 5 is revealing.

Table 5
Relationship between decision to hospitalize and history of previous hospitalization.

	History	
Decision	Previous Hospitalization	No Previous Hospitalization
Hospitalize	77%	23%
Don't hospitalize	34%	66%

(Adapted from Mendel and Rapport, 1969. Copyright 1969 by the American Medical Association and reproduced by permission.)

The data provide good reason to believe that, although they did not so intend, the decision makers *were* being influenced by the fact of previous hospitalization. Nevertheless, the situation would still be understandable if there were a relationship between a history of previous hospitalization and severity of symptoms. Table 6 fails to find this relationship.

Table 6
Relationship between history of previous hospitalization and severity of present symptoms.

	Severity of present symptoms	
History	Mild	Severe
Previous hospitalization	17%	83%
No previous hospitalization	14%	86%

(Adapted from Mendel and Rapport, 1969. Copyright 1969 by the American Medical Association and reproduced by permission.)

Mendel and Rapport had no perverse interest in pointing to frailties of clinical judgment. They felt it important, however, to take a critical look at the nature of a decision that, as they put it, "changes the destiny of the individual forever after" (p. 328).

Mendel (1967) was also interested in pursuing empirically the question of where credit belongs for the improvement so often noted soon after a patient's admission to the hospital. In his words one problem is ". . . that both the general population and the physician have come to put faith in the pill as the major source of healing

(p. 16). . . . Medication is expected to provide happiness when we are depressed, zest when we are tired, tranquilization when we are excited, rest when we are wakeful and clear thinking when the mind is clouded" (p. 16).

The majority of psychiatric patients are put on drugs on admission and show clinical improvement within a short time, making it difficult to discern what other factors might be contributing to their improvement. Suppose one assumed that patients might improve rapidly after admission anyway and accordingly decreed that drugs would be prescribed only under exceptional conditions. As chief of service, Mendel was in a position to declare just such a moratorium on drugs in the 25-bed open psychiatric ward (on which all patients were diagnosed schizophrenic) through which third-year medical students rotated in their 3.6 week clerkship in psychiatry (where, under supervision, each carried full responsibility for particular patients). The moratorium stated that ". . . no patient admitted to the ward was to receive a tranquilizer during the first 12 hours of hospitalization. This rule was to be broken only if the responsible physician felt that immediate tranquilization was indicated for the patient upon entry into the hospital, and then the medication could be prescribed only if he had first discussed the case with the chief" (p. 18).

The result? Although Mendel does not cite specific data, he suggests that the clinical improvement usually noted under drugs was observable without drugs as well. More importantly, he points to facts that tell us even more about the behavior of the professional persons involved. For example, although drugs could still be given if the medical personnel made an appropriate case for them with the chief of service, the drug prescription pattern changed markedly, as is evident from Table 7.

Table 7
Distribution of prescription of tranquilizers before and after 12-hour drug moratorium.

		Before Moratorium (2-month period) ($N = 158$)	After Moratorium (3-month period) ($N = 205$)
Prescription	Tranquilizer	82%	27%
	No tranquilizer	18%	73%

(Adapted from Table 1 of Mendel, 1967. Copyright 1967 by the American Psychiatric Association and reproduced by permission.)

One might assume the change could be explained quite simply. Perhaps, under the new ground rules, physicians did not want to take the trouble to make the case that certain patients should be on drugs. But additional findings suggest other reasons. Mendel was interested, for one, in the possible relationship between the experience or inexperience of medical personnel and their pattern of prescribing drugs. As it turned out, whether they were medical students, interns, or first-year residents, each group in training showed a notable decline in rate of tranquilizer prescription as it gained experience (and presumably greater assurance) in managing disturbed patients.

Clearly, one was dealing not only with the psychodynamics of patients but just as much with those of the staff. The doctor–patient relationship is a two-way street. When spelling out the dynamics of Disorder A or Disorder B, the clinician should remember that part of what he attributed to the disorder per se may well be a function of his own stereotypes, treatment preferences, expectations, and general orientation.

If such a clinician-oriented approach has its merits, might there not be virtue in a client-oriented approach to psychopathology as well? After all, a disorder exists not in pure culture but rather in a patient who also has attitudes, perceptions, expectations, and, indeed—no matter how maladjusted—purposes and motivations. Let us, then, shift gears.

A Client-Oriented Approach

Has the mental patient—presumably ineffectual in dealing with life and people—simply "found a home" in the hospital, so that he comfortably accepts the role of a passive recipient of care? Some theorists would support such a view. Others, among them Goffman (1961), are not prepared to write the patient off as that passive; yet they too see him as a pretty helpless pawn in the hands of the Establishment, which by subtle or not-so-subtle means manages to control his destiny. The research of Braginsky and several colleagues, representing another point of view, suggests (and confirms) a further thesis. There is no need to assume, they contend, that in becoming a patient one necessarily relinquishes all motivations, aspirations, needs, and other attributes that characterize people in general.

In contrast to Mendel's stance, theirs is a client-oriented approach to psychopathology. Taking their lead from Goffman (1959), Braginsky and his co-workers were interested in the extent to which mental patients engaged in "impression management"—that is, to what extent they attempted, and were able, to convey to others the image they wanted to portray. If one could differentiate patients who had indeed "found a home" from those who felt incarcerated against their will, would the former attempt to give the impression they needed institutionalization and the latter present themselves as ready to resume their places in society?

To attempt to answer this question, Braginsky, Grosse, and Ring (1966) distinguished between "old-timers," a group with the lowest average discharge rate (17%), who were presumably motivated to stay hospitalized, and "short-timers," patients experiencing their first hospitalization and belonging to a group with the highest average discharge rate (83%). The "short-timers" were presumably motivated to get out as soon as possible. If, then, one presented a written "test" to each group, but under instructions intended to induce varying sets, one might get some informative results.

Using appropriate criteria for distinguishing between old-timers and short-timers, the investigators chose 40 subjects, 20 in each group, and assigned them randomly to one of two conditions. In one case their test was titled "Mental Illness Test"; in the other the *identical pool* of items was titled "Self-Insight Test." The corresponding instructions used to induce the respective sets were as follows:

> *Mental Test Induction.* Subjects assigned to this condition prior to taking the Mental Illness Test were told by the experimenter the following:
>
> "This test is designed to measure how severely mentally ill a patient is. We have found that the more items answered True by a patient the more severely ill a patient is and the greater are his chances of remaining in the hospital for a long period of time. Patients who answer many of the items as False are less severely mentally ill and will probably remain in the hospital for a short period of time. We would like to find out how ill you are."
>
> *Self-Insight Test Induction.* Subjects assigned to this condition were told by the experimenter the following:
>
> "This test is designed to measure how much knowledge a patient has about himself. We have found that the more items answered True by a patient the more he knows about himself, the less severely ill he is and the greater are his chances of remaining in the hospital for a short period of time. Patients who answer many of the items as False know less about themselves, are more mentally ill and will probably remain in the hospital for a long period of time. We would like to find out how much you know about yourself" (p. 297).[3]

The test consisted of 30 true-false items from the Minnesota Multiphasic Personality Inventory,[4] chosen on the basis of an average social desirability value—that is, most

---

[3] Copyright 1966 by the American Psychological Association. Reprinted by permission of the authors and publisher.

[4] See Kelly, *Assessment of Human Characteristics*, 1967.

people would respond true or false just because it was the more socially acceptable or desirable answer. Half of the 20 old-timers were to take the test under one induction, half under the other; the short-timers were similarly divided. Added also, as a control group, were 20 old-timers, half of whom took the test titled "Mental Illness Test," the other half the test titled "Self-Insight Test." However, none of the control group received the above inductions; they simply took one or the other test, answering its items "true" or "false." (A comparable short-timer control group was not included.) The results are shown in Table 8.

Table 8
Influence of the ostensible nature of a test on the extent to which patients of differing motivations endorse test items as true. A response marked "true" would characterize "mental illness" in one test and "self-insight" in the other. Each test contained 30 items. The table shows the mean number of items marked "true" by each group. $N =$ total of 20 for each group.

Patient Motivation	Presumed nature of test	
	Mental Illness Test	Self-Insight Test
Old-timers	18.80	9.70
Short-timers	13.00	18.80
Old-timers (Control)	14.60	14.30

(Adapted from Table 1 of Braginsky, Grosse, & Ring, 1966. Copyright 1966 by the American Psychological Association and reproduced by permission.)

The differences found, as a function of the way the test was described by the experimenters, would occur by chance less than one time in 100. Note that the control group of old-timers, in which no elaboration of the purpose of the test was presented, behaved almost identically in the two instances. What are we to conclude? Braginsky and his co-investigators suggest the following:

> ... both old-timers and short-timers appeared to engage in impression management on the test. Old-timers present the group profile of being "ill" with the implication of their performance perceived as leading to a greater chance of remaining hospitalized. Short-timers present the group profile of "healthy" with the implication of their performance perceived as allowing for only a short stay in the hospital (p. 298).

In the present study, and in a related later one on the behavior of schizophrenic patients in an interview situation (Braginsky & Braginsky, 1967), the investigators recognize other considerations that must be taken into account in interpreting the findings. They are nevertheless left with the impression that, looking at psychopathology from the patient's point of view, one sees a person with many, if not most, of the same needs as normal people. As Braginsky and Braginsky (1967) put it:

> It is quite plausible and simple to view these findings in terms of the assumptions held about people in general; that is, schizophrenics, like normal persons, are goal-oriented and are able to control the outcomes of their social encounters in a manner which satisfies their goals (p. 547).

Small wonder that some inquisitive clinicians have felt a need to take a second look at some customary assumptions, lest we continue to accept on faith practices that may have little but tradition on their side. The lore surrounding various aspects of institutionalization could be particularly susceptible to such preconceptions. Have some hospital practices, for example, developed largely out of intuition of what is best for the patients? Are customary procedures validated by data, or have they simply been adopted on faith? Might statistics, systematically gathered, force us to question, or at least reexamine, some assumptions on which current practices rest? For a closer look at some of these questions, we turn to a person for whom such answers become practical necessities.

An Actuarial Approach

Imagine yourself the director of a large metropolitan hospital through which thousands of patients pass over the years, being admitted, hospitalized for various lengths of time, and discharged (some probably to be rehospitalized later). Suppose that incoming patients were assigned to shorter-term or longer-term wards simply on the basis of where beds were available as a result of the departure of other patients. That is, an incoming patient might wind up on ward 1, from which patients were typically discharged after 1 to 7 days of hospitalization; or on ward 2, where they were usually kept from 8 to 30 days; or on ward 3, where the average length of stay was between 31 and 60 days; or on ward 4, where patients stayed 61 days or more.

Such was the situation set up at the Los Angeles County General Hospital Psychiatric Unit for which Mendel (1966) served as chief and where he had the opportunity to study the data on 2926 schizophrenics (18 years or older) admitted between 1961 and 1964, on whom he did a follow-up study of 443 patients who were discharged between January, 1961, and July, 1962. Mendel describes the procedure as follows:

> At the time the study was done, patients were assigned to wards in the hospital by the admitting physician *on the basis of bed vacancies* [italics added] on the wards. That is, if ward 4 had more vacancies than ward 3 (or if, as was usually the case, a ward was less overcrowded), then a

patient who was admitted was sent there. Thus, the assignment was random on the basis of available bed space. Discharge from the ward was based on the clinical judgment of the clinician in charge of the case and could have occurred at any time during the designated period. That is, 1–7 days, 8–30 days, 31–60 days and 61+ days. What this meant in practice was that a patient on ward 2, who at the end of 30 days was not sufficiently improved to be returned to the community, would be transferred to another ward in the hospital which accepted longer term patients or to a State hospital. These patients were counted as not having been returned to the community. If they were admitted to one of the other wards after having an immediate prior hospitalization on a ward in our unit, they were not counted again in this study... (Personal communication, 1969).

Mendel's main interest was the relationship between length of hospitalization and a number of other variables, among them the quality of adjustment following discharge. Interesting were the number of factors to which length of stay in the hospital was *not* significantly related. For example, the discharge rate did not differ significantly across wards. Nor did patients discharged from the several wards differ significantly in the extent to which they needed to be rehospitalized. And there was no significant relationship between the length of stay and the extent to which the patients received subsequent outpatient treatment.

Interestingly, length of stay in the hospital was significantly related to the quality of adjustment following discharge—but in a direction opposite to what we might have expected. Those who had been hospitalized for *shorter* periods (that is, assigned to shorter-term wards simply because beds were available there at the time) had, as a group, improved significantly more over their pre-hospital adjustment than had those who had been hospitalized for longer periods! Table 9 presents the findings.

Table 9
Relationship between length of stay in hospital and quality of adjustment following discharge, as determined in a follow-up study of 443 patients from the original discharge group.

Quality of Post-Discharge Functioning	Wards classified by typical length of stay (in days)			
	1–7	8–30	31–60	61+
Same or better	74.6	70.1	61.2	55.0
Worse	25.4	29.9	38.8	45.0

(Adapted from Table 4 of Mendel, 1966, whose data are here converted to percentages. Copyright 1966 by The Williams & Wilkins Company, Baltimore, Maryland, and reproduced by permission.)

Assuming that the several groups of patients did not differ on pertinent variables, we might conclude that the shorter the period of hospitalization, the higher the level of subsequent functioning in the community. Mendel (1966) urges some cautions, however, lest conclusions be drawn too hastily:[5]

> Since the decision for length of hospitalization was made independently by clinicians both at the time of admission and during treatment, it is possible that certain unrecorded factors distinguished our patient population groups. Thus, it is quite possible that our patient population groups varied in terms of relatives available to them, amount of alienation from society, dependency needs, ability to reconstitute, and the like. It is necessary that a controlled study be conducted which is not retrospective as was this one, and which is designed to place patients arbitrarily for varying lengths of hospitalization independent of the admitting physician's judgment. If we can demonstrate that, with matched patient samples arbitrarily assigned to hospitalization of differing lengths, the findings are the same as ours, then, indeed, we will be justified in questioning the value of hospitalization as a method of treatment for periods longer than the briefest one studied (p. 231).

What are the implications for the profession and for society? Mendel concludes as follows: "In brief hospitalization with brief rehospitalizations becoming the rule rather than the exception, many facilities could be converted to treatment centers which provide partial care (day care, night care, outpatient care, after care) thus preventing the iatrogenic total alienation of the patient from society by total hospitalization" (p. 232).

By now the reader may have concluded that the simple observation of behavior nets thought-provoking data. Psychologists would agree. The second large task of the behavioral scientist—prediction—presents, if anything, even more grist for the clinician's mill, as will become apparent in the following chapter.

[5] Reprinted by permission of the author and The Williams & Wilkins Company.

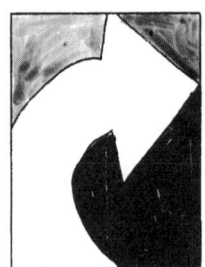

12
The Prediction of Behavior

However he may feel about it, the clinician finds the task of prediction essential to his work. The requests are manifold. How would college senior *A* fare scholastically in the graduate program of university *B*? Of 400 first-year students in clinical psychology training programs, which ones will have proved the best clinicians, and which the worst, as rated by their peers ten years hence? Of a pool of 400 men in top physical condition, which 25 would adjust best psychologically in a nuclear submarine that is required to stay under the polar ice cap for three months at a time?

Clinicians, among others, find themselves called upon to assist in making just such decisions. They have no special omniscience; they do, however, have methods and tools for making predictions. In large measure, much of psychological prediction involves the determination of assets and liabilities in two broad areas—general ability and personality structure. Cronbach (1960) describes the situation well as he classifies tests into two general categories: (1) "... those which seek to determine *maximal* performance of the subject ... how well the person can perform at his best ..." and (2) "... tests which seek to determine his *typical* performance, i.e., what he is likely to do in a given situation or in a broad class of situations" (p. 29). The first of these Cronbach calls *tests of ability,* while in the second category he includes *measures of "personality, habits, interests, and character."*

We might well expect tests of the second type to meet more than their share of technical difficulties. Personality is a somewhat comprehensive affair and character a rather fuzzy one. But testing something more "tangible," such as ability, should be a simpler proposition. Present a task that is clear-cut and objectively scorable—for example, the ability to substitute symbols for numbers—and it should be possible to obtain an unequivocal index of each person's performance. Standardizing the instructions and the procedures for administration should then allow us readily to compare one person with another on the task.

To expect performance on such a simple, straightforward digit-symbol test to be influenced by how the task is labeled would seem farfetched. It would seem equally as improbable that a person's score in such a standardized situation could be significantly affected by the identity of the person who administers this routine test. But, thanks to the contributions of colleagues in social psychology, clinical psychologists have come to realize the role of such variables in the measurement of ability, as will become apparent in the course of the following general discussion.

General Ability

The "Smart-Dumb" Dimension

To be thought poor does not seem to disturb people as much as being thought "dumb." Few of us are particularly apologetic about our financial status; most of us get somewhat defensive, however, if our intelligence is called into question. Possibly it is because there has been no moron-to-genius theme to parallel the rags-to-riches story.

Perhaps that is why psychological research of some types has become popular reading material. *Redbook* magazine has featured a story drawing the attention of the layman to the possibility that intellectual level, like socioeconomic status, is not nearly as fixed and immutable as might have been thought. The article deals with the research of Skodak and Skeels (1949), who have been interested in following the intellectual development of children in general and of adopted children in particular.

In a monograph reviewing the history of 30 years of interest in the developmental fate of children who had been wards of the state in an orphanage, Skeels (1966) presented the results of an extensive follow-up. The story had begun with two baby girls of mentally retarded mothers, who had been committed to the orphanage. On psychological examination the two youngsters, of 13 and 16 months, had shown developmental levels of 6 and 7 months respectively. They were, as Skeels describes them ". . . pitiful little creatures . . . tearful . . . emaciated . . . sad and inactive . . ." (p. 5), who spent most of their time rocking and whining. Subsequently the two children were transferred to a home for the mentally retarded, at ages 15 and 18 months respectively.

Six months later, when Skeels' duties happened to take him to this institution for the mentally retarded, he came upon ". . . two outstanding little girls. They were alert, smiling, running about, responding to the playful attention of adults . . ." (p. 6). They turned out to be the two children in question. When examined this time, their performance was markedly better, and when reexamined at 40 and 43 months of age respectively, they gave ". . . unmistakable evidence of mental development within the normal range" (p. 6).

Ironically, being "misplaced" in the home for the adult mentally retarded had proved the children's good fortune. For each had been "adopted" by one of the inmates and ministered unto by a whole series of "aunts." These older mentally retarded women, who showered the children with attention, affection, and even understanding, had managed in a very short time to produce two lively, gaily dressed, apparently healthy and happy youngsters. Presumably the two children were thus receiving from their elders the psychological nurturance responsible for their improved test performance.

This experiment of nature led to the setting up of a small-scale research project designed to determine whether this outcome had been merely a chance occurrence. Permission was granted to repeat such an experience with 11 additional children, who were to serve as the experimental group, while a dozen other children, comparable to the first group, would constitute the "contrast group" and remain in the orphanage until placement for adoption. So that no stigma would attach to the experimental group children as a result of commitment to a home for the retarded, they were officially classified as "house guests."

The results of the miniature experiment were as dramatic as the controversy raging around them was heated. Impressive gains were recorded for the experimental group on reexamination, while the children of the contrast group not only failed to achieve such gains but, indeed, suffered losses. Proponents of this type of investigation saw significant implications in the results; critics, on the other hand, pointed to the small size of the groups, questioned their comparability, and reasserted the weaknesses of tests at lower age levels.

The interest of the original investigators has persisted, however, and, by dint of painstaking search, all 25 subjects were located as adults, so that their adjustment, socially, vocationally, and otherwise, might be assessed. The findings proved impressive.

Of the 13 subjects who had been "house guests" in the home for the adult mentally retarded, all but two had been adopted. And the group did surprisingly well; all were self-supporting, the careers of the men including such jobs as staff sergeant, sales manager, and vocational counselor (the latter working toward a master's degree). Of the ten girls in the group, eight had married, and among the group's vocations were practical nurse, licensed beautician, and office clerk. Of the 25 children of the married group, the average IQ was 104, with a range from a low of 85 to a high of 125.

With one exception, the subjects of the contrast group showed almost the opposite picture. None had been adopted, and, of those who were employed, all but one held menial jobs. The one exception was employed as a linotyper, a skilled trade. To bear out the story, it turned out that, because of a severe ear condition, he had been transferred from the orphanage to a residential home for the deaf, where he received loving care from a solicitous house mother while enjoying the company of children who came from a variety of good homes rather than fellow orphans.

Although the study has a long history, during which it has met more than its share of controversy, it ties in with some current disputes over the nature of general ability, the relative contributions of heredity and environment, present-day techniques of measurement, and the implications that are drawn.

The questions are many — some theoretical, some practical. Is there a critical period in development when enriching experiences are most likely to reap their harvest and impoverishing experiences to take their toll? Is the relatively poor test performance of disadvantaged people — slum residents, for example — largely an artifact of how the tests are constructed and what they comprise? Are differences among groups on the tests a function of genetic stock, material and social advantages, or a combination of both?

A lively dialogue was begun when the *Harvard Educational Review* published an article by Jensen (1969a) which posed the question: "How Much Can We Boost IQ and Scholastic Achievement?" Its opening sentence read: "Compensatory education has been tried and it apparently has failed" (p. 2). Jensen's presentation is scholarly and bolstered by a variety of data, a fact that even his critics admit. But succeeding writers in the same journal have attempted to point out ways in which he has misinterpreted his data and drawn unwarranted inferences. Without trying to judge the merits of any particular position, we present the reader with the flavor of the argument and counterargument so as to make the point that the general area of ability and its measurement remains a complex and controversial one.

On the question of whether intelligence is "fixed," Jensen has some explicit notions:[1]

---

[1] Copyright 1969 by President and Fellows of Harvard College. Reproduced by permission of the author and publisher.

> The genetic factors are completely laid down when the parental sperm and ovum unite. Thus the individual's genotype, by definition, is "fixed" at the moment of conception. Of course, different potentials of the genotype may be expressed at different times in the course of the individual's development. But beyond conception, whatever we observe or measure of the organism is a phenotype, and this, by definition, is *not* "fixed." The phenotype is a result of the organism's internal genetic mechanisms established at conception and all the physical and social influences that impinge on the organism throughout the course of its development. Intelligence is a phenotype, not a genotype, so the argument about whether or not intelligence is "fixed" is seen to be spurious (p. 17).

It is in the course of developing his extensive general argument that Jensen makes some statements that have drawn the fire of many of his fellow social scientists. Thus, the following passage has been widely quoted:

> So all we are left with are various lines of evidence, no one of which is definitive alone, but which, viewed all together, make it a not unreasonable hypothesis that genetic factors are strongly implicated in the average Negro-white intelligence difference. The preponderance of the evidence is, in my opinion, less consistent with a strictly environmental hypothesis than with a genetic hypothesis, which, of course, does not exclude the influence of environment or its interaction with genetic factors (p. 82).

A later reply to his critics (Jensen, 1969b) expresses some of his points pictorially, as in Figures 1 and 2, with their accompanying captions.

The objections to Jensen's position rest on various grounds. Light and Smith (1969) take issue with some of his statistical analyses. For example, they point to conclusions Jensen has drawn from data on twins, where the size of the sample was small and the data from several studies were combined in ways they consider unwarranted. Further, they argue that differences between black and white mean IQs may be explained by nongenetic differences in the way the two races are distributed among different environments. As a result of a variety of such statistical artifacts, they conclude: "We have shown how a small amount of interaction between genetic endowment and environment can easily explain how two races with identical genetic endowments can have large differences in mean IQs" (p. 508).

The series of papers replying to and commenting on Jensen's initial article poses a variety of pertinent questions. Some raise further objections on methodological and statistical grounds (Kagan, 1969; Crow, 1969); others (Hunt, 1969) stress the importance of enriched environmental experience; still others (Elkind, 1969; Cronbach, 1969) raise basic questions about the concept of intelligence. That the general argu-

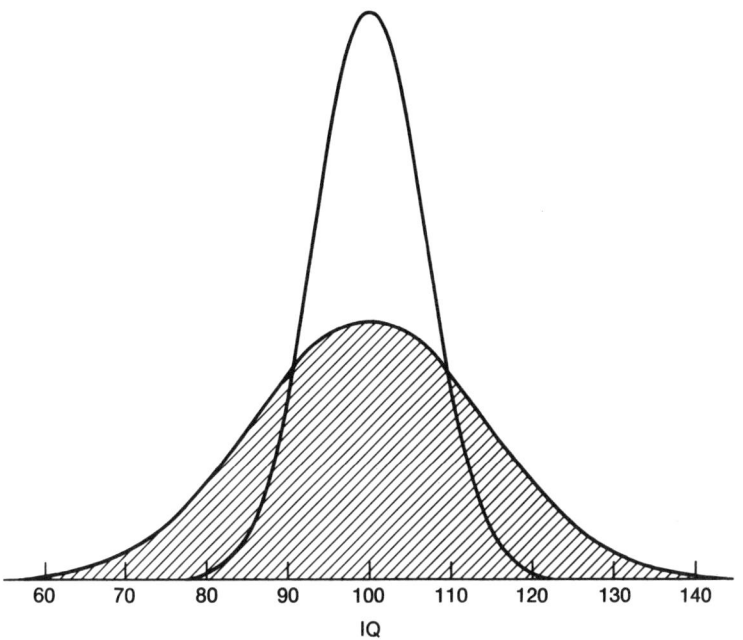

Figure 1
Comparison of what the distribution of IQs theoretically would be if all genotypes were identical (for IQ 100) in an "average" environment (assuming a normal distribution of environmental advantages) and all variance were due only to nongenetic (environmental) factors (heavy line). The shaded curve represents the normal distribution of IQs in the present population. (Figure 2 of Jensen, 1969b. Copyright 1969 by President and Fellows of Harvard College and reproduced by permission.)

ment did not seem a simple matter of cold logic to everyone is indicated in some of the reactions of Deutsch (1969): "I believe the impact of Jensen's article was destructive; that it has had negative implications for the struggle against racism and for improvement of the educational system. The conclusions he draws are, I believe, unwarranted by the existing data, and reflect a consistent bias toward a racist hypothesis" (p. 525).

In a somewhat more moderate later passage Deutsch has some nonetheless definite feelings about the whole testing enterprise. They are worth noting, particularly as

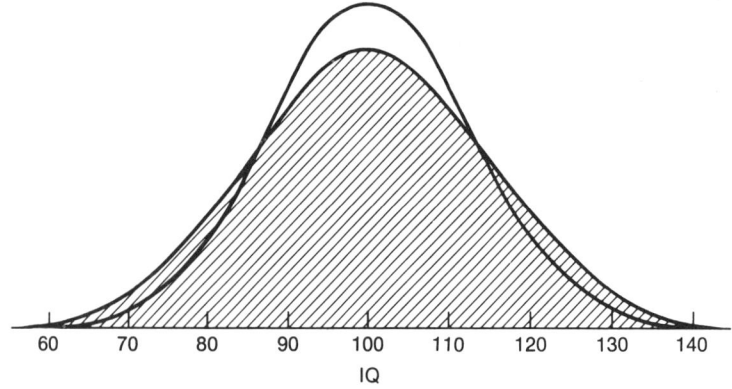

Figure 2
The theoretical distribution of IQs if all variance due to environmental factors were eliminated (with everyone having an "average" environment) and all the remaining variance were due only to genetic factors (heavy line). The shaded curve represents the normal distribution of IQs in the present population. (Figure 3 of Jensen, 1969b. Copyright 1969 by President and Fellows of Harvard College and reproduced by permission.)

they reflect some of the prevailing sentiments of today's youth, who have often found themselves in the role of examinee. Deutsch expresses it thus:

> Standard intelligence tests measure essentially what children have learned, not how well they might learn something new. Intelligence tests have been constructed within a certain kind of society and a certain kind of cultural milieu, basically white middle-class America. During a period of dynamic social change, tests have remained static and have become increasingly irrelevant for understanding the nature and evolution of an organism's intellectual behavior (p. 542).

As we shall show in a subsequent section, others have tried to study empirically the extent to which factors other than actual level of ability might affect a person's test performance. At this point, however, let us simply point out that the interaction of "ability factors and environmental influences," as Vernon (1965) titled an address on the subject, presents many more complications than had first been realized. Before moving on to the next section on the presumed structure of what is called intelligence, it is well to mark his words:

> The group of skills which we refer to as intelligence is a European and American middle-class invention: something which seems to be intimately bound up with puritanical values, with repression of instinctual

responses and emphasis on responsibility, initiative, persistence, and efficient workmanship. It is a kind of intelligence which is specially well adapted for scientific analysis, for control and exploitation of the physical world, for large-scale and long-term planning and carrying out of materialistic objectives. It has also led to the growth of complex social institutions such as nations, armies, industrial firms, school systems, and universities, though it has been notably less successful in working out solutions of group rivalries or providing harmonious personal adjustment than have the intelligences of some more primitive cultures. Other cultures have evolved intelligences which are better adapted than ours for coping with problems of agricultural and tribal living. The aboriginal in the Australian desert and the Eskimo in the Far North have many schemata far more efficient than our own. Again subcultures such as our lower working class, or rural groups, develop rather different intelligence (p. 727).

The "IQ"

Ask people what their Social Security number is, and they may well have to look it up. Ask them what their "IQ" is, and many of them may readily answer 120 or 114 or 132. Especially where test results are flattering, the magic number may be remembered forever.

Psychology owes much to the efforts of Alfred Binet, a French physician, who undertook development of an instrument to assess the ability levels of Parisian children as a basis for selecting those low enough in general ability to require specialized schooling. His pioneering work drew the attention and admiration of Lewis Terman, an American psychologist, who pursued the creative leads offered by Binet and, in 1916, developed the first American version of the Binet-type scales at Stanford University — the Stanford-Binet Intelligence Scale. Revisions followed — one in 1937, another in 1960.

The ratio originally adopted as an index of general ability was one between mental age and chronological age, represented by the formula:

$$\frac{\text{mental age}}{\text{chronological age}} \times 100$$

(the multiplication simply helping to get rid of the decimal point). The person's chronological age was readily calculable; determination of the so-called mental age was the real problem.

With his collaborator Simon, Binet rose to the challenge. He explored all kinds of measures that held promise for discriminating between brighter and duller children, looking for those measures that correlated well with acceptable criteria of intelligence. For practical purposes, it was necessary that the tasks be ones that could be administered and scored in a standardized way, and ones on which performance correlated well with performance on the rest of the scale. The scale as a whole was arranged by year levels, with each test item placed at a point in the scale where experience had shown it could be passed by approximately half the subjects of that age. With six subtests at an age level, the subject is given two months' credit for each test passed.[2] The following typical items are representative of the differing orders of complexity as well as the variety of tasks contained in the 1960 version of the Stanford-Binet Intelligence Scale (Terman & Merrill, 1960).

Year II — Subtest #3: Identifying parts of the body

The examinee is presented with a large paper doll and is asked to point to various parts of it (for example, the doll's nose).

Scoring: To receive credit, the child must indicate clearly at least four of the parts specified.

Year VII — Subtest #5: Opposite analogies

The subject is asked to complete sentences on the order of the following: "The donkey's ears are long; the mouse's ears are _____."

Scoring: To pass, the subject must get two or more of the items correct, according to the scoring standards contained in the examiner's manual.

Year XIII — Subtest #3: Memory for sentences

The examiner asks the subject to listen carefully to a sentence, so that the latter will be able to repeat it exactly as it was said by the examiner.

Scoring: The examinee must get one of two sentences correct, that is, without omissions, substitutions, additions, changes in words, or in order of words.

Year XIII — Subtest #6: Copying a bead chain from memory

Using beads of various shapes from a box of 48, the examiner strings a standard chain of nine beads of various shapes in a particular order. The subject is asked to watch carefully while the chain is being made, since it will be taken away later, and he will be asked to reproduce one like it. On completion of the chain, the subject is allowed to look at it for five seconds, whereupon it is removed, and he is told to make one just like it.

Scoring: The subject must produce an identical chain within two minutes to receive credit.

---

[2] The interested reader will find more specific details of the test's makeup in Terman and Merrill (1960) and Cronbach (1960).

Clearly the items differ not only in difficulty but also in character. The subtest of Year II can be handled simply by pointing to the correct part; that of Year VII necessitates the use of abstract concepts. At Year XIII, subtest #3 requires the ability to hold verbal material correctly in memory for a short period; subtest #6 also taps retention, although here the memory test is for visual and concrete rather than verbal and symbolic material.

Terman and his collaborators successively refined their instrument through its several revisions. The technical problems were many, however. If, for example, mental age scores tend to level off around the age of 16, a simple ratio IQ runs into difficulty. Someone with a mental age of 14, who is now 14 years old would have an IQ of 100; at 30, if his mental age score proved to be 15, his IQ would technically have dropped to 50—an absurd situation. Hence, the test developers at first dealt with the problem by adjusting chronological age arithmetically, tapering it off gradually between the ages of 13 and 16 and using a mental age of 15 as the norm for all subjects 16 years of age or older. More recently, however, they have used the "deviation IQ," comparing the person's test performance with that of his age-mates (using a table of norms). The mental age score falling at a point one standard deviation above the mean of the particular age group is assigned an IQ of 116. [See Hays (1967) for a discussion of the standard deviation.]

In its present form the Stanford-Binet Intelligence Scale (generally regarded as best adapted to the range from preschool through early adolescence) is widely used for measuring the general mental ability of subjects who have been exposed to the normal opportunities of contemporary American life, in terms of schooling, social experience, and related aspects of development. Since the examiner wishes to establish the examinee's intellectual capacity, he begins testing at the age level at which he judges the subject capable of passing all of the items—the subject's basal age—and then takes him progressively through higher age levels of the scale to one at which the subject fails all of the subtests—his maximal age. His mental age score is derived by adding to his basal age all the extra credit he accumulates for items passed at the successive levels. The person's IQ is then readily determined by referring to that point in a table of the test manual where his mental age and chronological age scores intersect.

It is evident why the Stanford-Binet Intelligence Scale is called an age scale. Another widely used individual intelligence scale—the Wechsler Adult Intelligence Scale (1958)—is, in contrast, a "point scale." Its items are not arranged by ages but rather in unitary subtests in which each item increases in difficulty over the one preceding. Thus, in the information subtest a person would begin with such a question as "How many weeks are there in a year?," gradually come to a harder one like "Where is Syria?," and later find himself being asked even more difficult questions like "What is the Talmud?" (These questions are typical of but not identical to the actual questions.) An examinee is given each of the subtests in turn, six of them representing verbal ability, the other five performance ability. Among the verbal tests, for example, is such a subtest as "Similarities" which presumes, among other things, to get at the ability to form concepts through the use of such questions as "In what way are a pen and a pencil alike?" The reader will probably agree intuitively that such a subtest taps a different kind of ability than does one that asks the subject to repeat increasingly longer strings of digits, or one that asks him to define a series of vocabulary words, both of which tests are among those making up the "Verbal IQ."

On the other hand, the WAIS (as it is called for short) contains a set of different types of subtests, measuring the "Performance IQ." Among them is one which requires the subject to reproduce successively more complex designs with a set of colored cubes and another which presents various jigsaw-puzzle affairs that are to be assembled as rapidly as possible.

Wechsler's test calculates the intelligence quotient not by comparing a person's mental age with his chronological age but by comparing his performance with that of his peers. If he is 37 years old, his scores are evaluated in relation to the performance of the group of 37-year-old subjects who were in the population on which the test was standardized.

At least two features of this kind of format are of interest: (a) it is possible for several people to have the same IQ, yet be quite different in the way their abilities are patterned; (b) a set of scores representing a certain IQ at one age can represent a different IQ at another age. The situation described in (a) is shown in Table 1.

Each of the three subjects, all the same age, technically has the same IQ as the other two; yet it is obvious that, although equally "smart," they differ considerably in the way in which their various capacities are distributed. From such "scatter" patterns Wechsler had, in fact, hoped to derive information at least as valuable as the overall intelligence quotient. Could subjects with suspected brain damage, for example, be detected on the tests by significantly low scores on certain subtests? Would some types of neurotic adjustment (for example, anxiety reaction) be detectable by characteristically poor scores on some subtests? Psychologists continue to argue the merits and shortcomings of such scatter analysis, but that is not our concern at the moment. A test such as the WAIS is useful for depicting a person's distribution of abilities over almost a dozen types of tasks. The pattern of abilities thus revealed provides useful information beyond a simple figure indexing his general level of performance.

Table 1
Varying test records resulting in similar IQ scores on Wechsler Adult Intelligence Scale for persons of similar ages.

	Person A: Age 50	Person B: Age 50	Person C: Age 50
Information	15	13	16
Comprehension	10	12	12
Arithmetic	14	16	12
Similarities	12	14	15
Digit Span	14	12	11
Vocabulary	18	16	17
Sum of Scaled Scores (Verbal)	83	83	83
Digit Symbol	5	7	10
Picture Completion	11	11	10
Block Design	13	13	11
Picture Arrangement	10	9	9
Object Assembly	10	9	9
Sum of Scaled Scores (Performance)	49	49	49
Verbal IQ	125	125	125
Performance IQ	110	110	110
Full Scale IQ	120	120	120

Again, it is important to note that the IQ equivalent assigned a given score is a function of the performance registered by the person's age-mates on whom the test was standardized. Thus, the same overall score may represent various IQs, depending upon the age of the particular subject. Table 2 illustrates the situation.

As is evident, the three subjects of different ages achieve the same subtest totals; yet these totals represent different IQs. In general, subjects in the 60-year range tend to maintain lower scores than those of comparable subjects of age 20 (particularly on certain subtests, such as digit span, for example). Hence, a person who does hold his own with the 20-year-olds is given suitable credit, as reflected in the IQ represented by his score. Assessment of ability, in short, is a relative rather than absolute affair.

Thus, there is more to the measurement of ability than tallying right and wrong responses or fast and slow performance on a standard set of tasks. The technical aspects noted present problems in their own right. But even more complex, and more psychologically interesting, methodological problems arise out of the fact that in an individual intelligence test there is an interaction between two people—the examiner and the examinee. The next section will analyze this interaction.

Table 2
Similar test records resulting in varying IQ scores on Wechsler Adult Intelligence Scale for persons of different ages.

	Person A: Age 21	Person B: Age 41	Person C: Age 61
Information	15	15	15
Comprehension	18	18	18
Arithmetic	8	8	8
Similarities	13	13	13
Digit Span	7	7	7
Vocabulary	13	13	13
Sum of Scaled Scores (Verbal)	74	74	74
Digit Symbol	10	10	10
Picture Completion	13	13	13
Block Design	12	12	12
Picture Arrangement	12	12	12
Object Assembly	9	9	9
Sum of Scaled Scores (Performance)	56	56	56
Verbal IQ	114	114	118
Performance IQ	107	113	125
Full Scale IQ	112	114	122

Problems in Prediction

E. L. Thorndike once remarked that whatever exists, exists in some degree and can therefore be measured. For a variety of reasons, some practical, others theoretical, it would be nice if this were true of the measurement of ability. One could then lay the yardstick called an "intelligence test" alongside a person, read off the appropriate number, and use it as an index for everything from placement of students in special classes to determination of whether a person charged with a crime is mentally retarded.

The situation is not that simple, as is evident in the literature on the comparative intelligence test performances of people of varying cultural and experiential backgrounds. The problems are most dramatically evident and the lessons to be learned clearest in research such as that of Irwin Katz and his colleagues on the test performance of black subjects under various conditions.

Some of the difficulties are at once obvious. Little research is necessary to convince most of us that some test items that may differentiate ability *within* certain groups would hardly be considered appropriate *across* groups. The question "What is vichyssoise?" might discriminate among the adolescent children of upper-middle-class families; it would be of dubious validity as a test item for their ghetto age-mates, many of whom are glad to get soup of any kind, and none of whom has ever eaten in a fancy restaurant. For that matter, another question—"What are chitlings?"—might well put the upper-middle-class youngster at a similar disadvantage and even the score.

But how about items on which everyone would seem to have a fair chance? If students were asked, for example, to associate the number 2 with the symbol X, the number 3 with a triangle, and 5 with a square, we would think that social-class, ethnic, or racial differences should interfere minimally in forming such arbitrary associations. Even here there may conceivably be some extenuating factors giving one person, or even one group, an advantage over another. But let us assume, for purposes of further discussion, that such test items are relatively neutral and that they place all examinees on fairly even footing. Nonetheless, Katz and his collaborators suspected, there might still be features of the testing situation that could make for invalid measures of ability across groups of different cultural or racial background.

Is performance on a task simply a function of ability? Or can it be affected by the expectation of being evaluated against one set of norms rather than another? Does it matter, for example, whether a black student feels his score will be compared with that of black students or with that of white students? The investigators found some interesting outcomes.

The Role of Invidious Comparison

The work of some earlier psychologists had suggested that sociocultural aspects of the testing situation might well influence test performance. Preston and Bayton (1941) had found, for example, that, on a task in which they were told their scores equaled the scores of whites, black subjects subsequently set their level of aspiration lower on succeeding trials. More recently, Katz and Cohen (1962) noted that black college students did more poorly on a task when working with a white teammate than when working alone; in contrast, the performance of white students did not suffer in the presence of a black teammate.

In this day of emergent "Black Power," we might well be tempted to speculate about whether some of the relationships found earlier will continue to hold. In any case, Katz, Epps, and Axelson (1964) hypothesized that, when told their performance would be compared with that of whites, blacks might be expected to do less well than they really could, partly as a defensive measure and partly because of the effect of anxiety on performance. They hypothesized further that, if poorer performance were found, it would reflect not the effects of competition in general but rather the comparison with whites in particular. Finally, Katz and his team hypothesized that the differences in performance might be more pronounced on difficult than on easy tasks, inasmuch as earlier research had shown that anxiety (which they assumed would be present in the comparison situation) tended to facilitate performance on easy tasks but hinder it on hard ones.

Using 116 black male undergraduates of Florida Agricultural and Mechanical University and 96 white male undergraduates of Florida State University, Katz et al. set up an appropriate design. The task was the digit-symbol test, the form described above serving as the easy version, while flags in various positions (thus readily confused) constituted the hard form. The black students were tested by black examiners, the white students by white examiners. The race of the group with which they were told their performance would be compared was manipulated by suggesting, in one group, that "local" (own-college, that is, black) norms would be used, while, in the other, that "national" (or predominantly white) norms would serve the purpose. In order to be sure the findings were characteristic of black subjects rather than simply of southerners generally, the white students of Florida State University were used as a control group. The findings are shown in Figures 3 through 5.

The results are revealing. (1) The performance of black subjects *does* seem to be affected by whether they expect to be compared with blacks or with whites; they do better under the former condition than under the latter. (2) As hypothesized, in the black-white comparison situation the decline in the performance of the black subjects is more noticeable on the hard form than on the easy form of the test. (3) That the results reflect socio-racial (that is, black-white) rather than regional (that is, north-south) differences would seem to follow from the fact that the performance of the white Florida State University students shows no comparable decline when they expect to be evaluated by white norms in general. One could ask, Katz et al. point out, whether the results could not simply be attributable to lower motivation on the part of the black subjects. To answer this question, a self-rating scale had been built into the design. According to this measure of how much they "cared about doing well," the black students were, if anything, even more motivated than the whites.

Interesting as such findings are, Katz and his associates have no illusions about the difficulty of taking all relevant variables into account. They were led to wonder, for example, whether the foregoing results would obtain in a black college with higher admission standards, where the academic ability of the student body was comparable

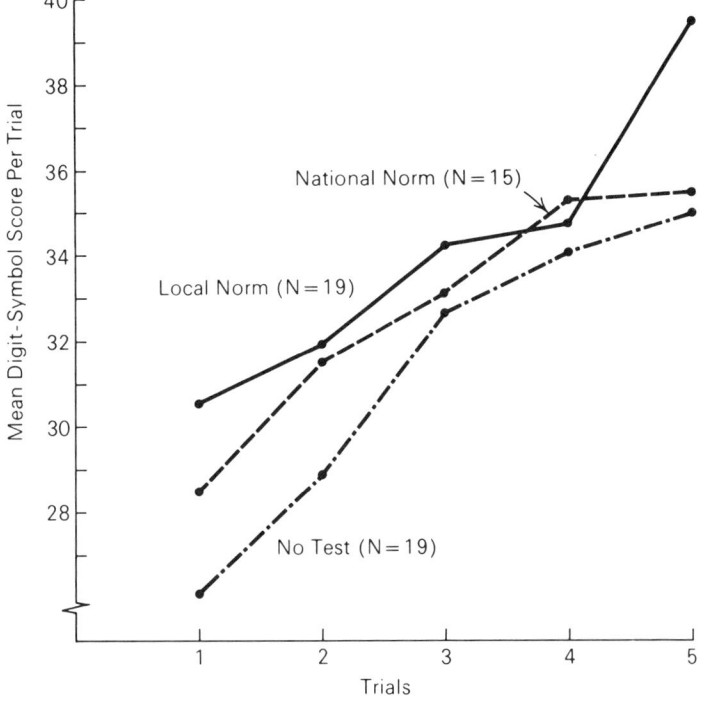

Figure 3
Mean digit-symbol scores of three matched groups of black subjects tested on an easy task and presumably being evaluated against various sets of norms. (Figure 1a of Katz et al., 1964. Copyright 1964 by the American Psychological Association and reproduced by permission.)

to that at predominantly white schools in the same state-supported system. Here comparison with whites would presumably have a different incentive value, and the assumed probability of success would also be different for these black students than for their more disadvantaged peers on less fortunate campuses. And, indeed, in a more recent study (Epps, Katz, Perry, and Runyon, in press), which replicated their earlier study in part, the results showed that students in black colleges with higher admission standards performed better when they felt the comparison group was white than when it was black.

The reader interested in pursuing these complicated interactions will do well to refer to a recent review by Sattler (1970) on "experimenter effects." His survey gives an impressive account of the influence of a race variable, whether of an experimenter, a

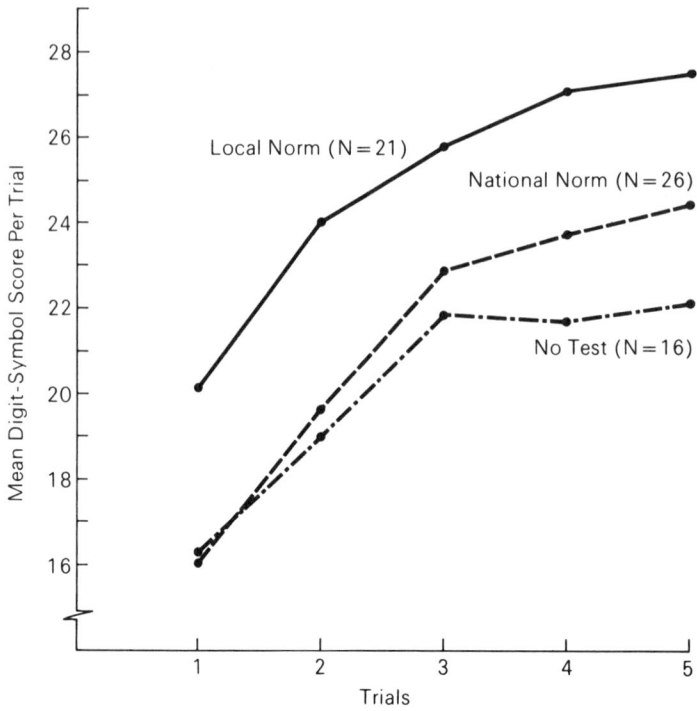

Figure 4
Mean digit-symbol scores of three matched groups of black subjects tested on a hard task and presumably being evaluated against various sets of norms. (Figure 1b of Katz et al., 1964. Copyright 1964 by the American Psychological Association and reproduced by permission.)

test administrator, an interviewer, or a psychotherapist. Katz and his colleagues decided to test one of these possible influences—how the race of an examiner might influence performance on a simple, objective task, especially in relation to how the task was presented to the examinee. Their findings are discussed in the following section.

Race of the Examiner and Examinee

In the previous study (Katz, Epps, & Axelson, 1964) the researchers had purposely used examiners of the same race as the subject. Suppose one manipulated the variable of race. Would performance be affected?

Earlier, Katz and Greenbaum (1963) had discovered the interesting fact that, under nonthreatening conditions, black subjects do better on a cognitive task when work-

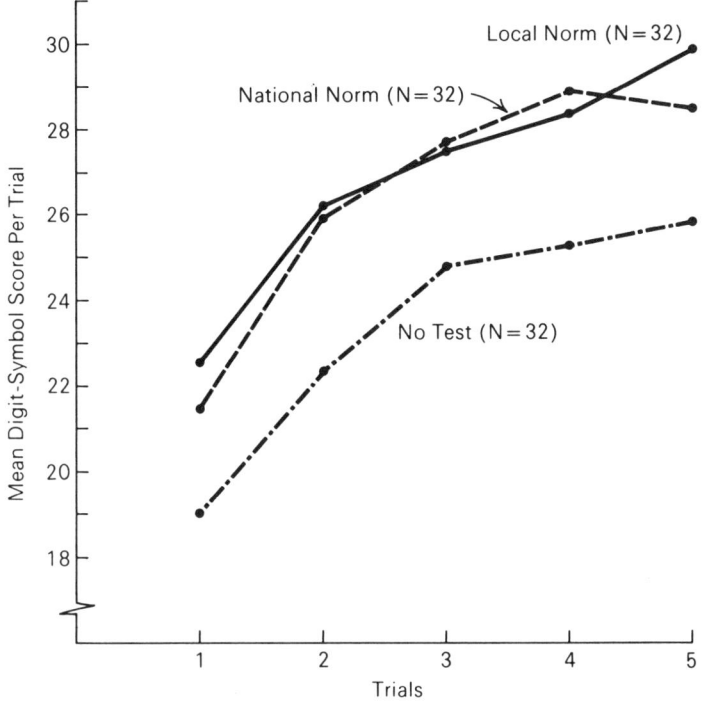

Figure 5
Mean digit-symbol scores of three matched groups of white subjects tested on a hard task and presumably being evaluated against various sets of norms. (Figure 2 of Katz et al., 1964. Copyright 1964 by the American Psychological Association and reproduced by permission.)

ing with whites than when working with blacks as partners; under conditions involving threat, however, they perform better when working with blacks. Speculating about such outcomes, one might well wonder whether the race of the examiner (which may or may not constitute a threat of some sort) could affect performance on intelligence tests as a function of level of arousal.

Taking their lead from earlier research, Katz, Roberts, and Robinson (1965) ventured two hypotheses: (1) on a test described as nonintellectual, black subjects might be expected to do better with a white examiner than with a black examiner; (2) on the same test, described as an intellectual task (hence presumably somewhat threatening), black subjects might be expected to do better with a black examiner than with a white examiner.

Using black male volunteers of Fisk University as paid subjects, the investigators again resorted to the digit-symbol test as a convenient, objectively scorable task appropriate to the testing of such hypotheses. However, this time they experimented with three forms—an easy, a moderately difficult, and a hard version. Three groups of 46 subjects each took the respective forms, assured by the black student assistants that the task had "... nothing to do with (your) course grades or (your) aptitude as a student." They were urged to do the best they could nonetheless. On the basis of their performance, each of the samples was subsequently divided into comparable groups by matching subjects with similar scores.

Several days later, each subgroup took its same test again, this time, however, with either a white or black adult male examiner unknown to them previously. Introducing himself as Dr. _____, the experimenter issued the following instructions:

> I am a psychologist and I am doing research on eye-hand coordination. I have the code task that you did the other day, and now you are going to do a code task for me, to give me a more complete picture of how you work on this type of task. This is not an intelligence test, and it has nothing to do with your course grades or your aptitude as a student. Nonetheless, it is important that you do the best that you can ... (p. 55).

As it turned out, the subjects taking the task with a white examiner did better than those with a black examiner, especially in the hard version of the task. Hence, this form was used for the next phase, during which 54 additional black subjects were pretested, then divided into two groups of 23 subjects each (8 subjects were not included), "... selected in a way that seemed to provide the closest equation of pretest means with one another, and with the pretest means of the previous two hard-task groups" (p. 55).

The two new groups were given their second sessions with the same black and the same white experimenters who had figured in the second testing of their predecessors—with one difference. This time, the task was described as follows:

> I am a psychologist and I am doing research on the measurement of intelligence. I have the code task that you did the other day, and now you are going to do a code task for me to give me a more complete picture of your ability on this type of mental test. This test measures the speed and accuracy of your intellectual processes, as well as how quickly you can learn abstract material. It also reveals your capacity for concentration. Eventually this test will be part of a new intelligence-test battery that will be used in colleges. Your score on this will not be shown to your teachers at Fisk. It will be used only for the purpose of developing the new intelligence-test battery ... (p. 55).

Some interesting results emerged. Figure 6 pictures the comparative performances of the four groups under two conditions—with a white or a black examiner and in the belief that the second task was either a motor or an intelligence test. (Note that the

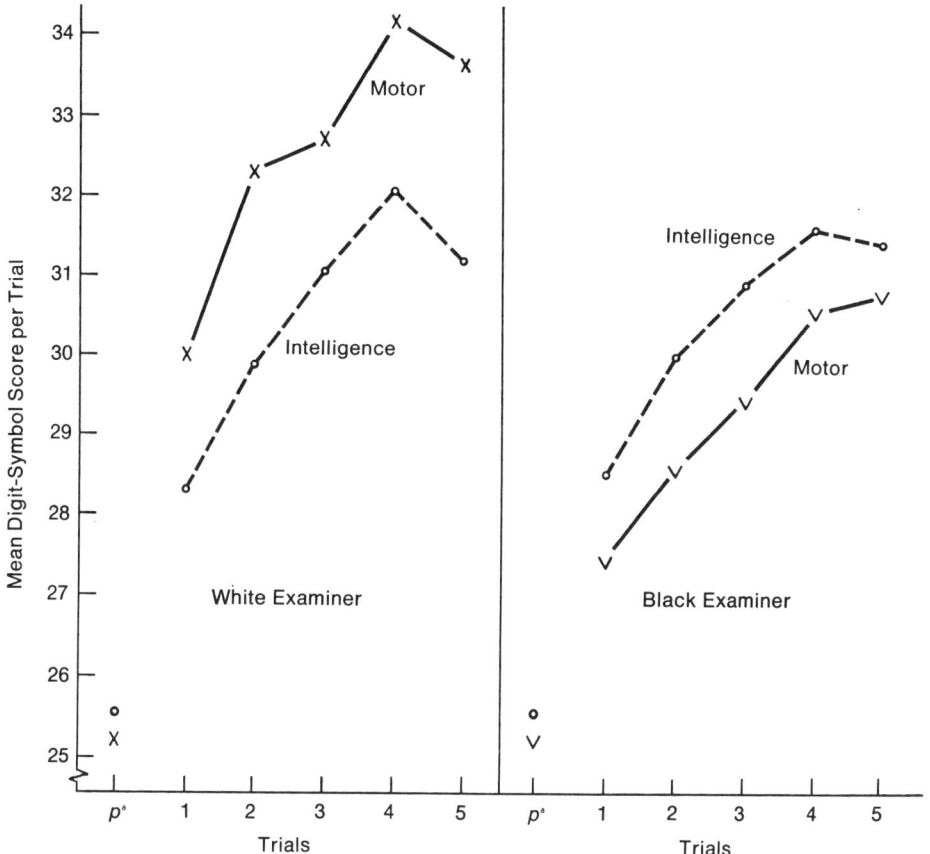

Figure 6
Mean digit-symbol scores (hard task version) on five one-minute trials for black subjects with a white or a black examiner under motor test or intelligence test instructions (N = 23 for each group). *Note:* The symbols above p^a represent the scores of the several groups on the third trial of the pretest, reflecting the degree to which they were matched. (Figure 1 of Katz, Roberts, & Robinson, 1965. Copyright 1965 by the American Psychological Association and reproduced by permission.)

p^a. Last trial of pretest

groups had been evenly matched, as shown in the figure above p^a, which represents their respective scores on the third trial of the pretest.)

The reader is reminded that in each of the four cases, subjects matched on the basis of their earlier performance were taking an identical test. Yet they performed differently, presumably as a result of the interaction between the way the test was described and the race of the person administering it. (All of the subjects, it must be remembered, were black.) In other words, whether a subject performed better when the task was described as an intelligence test than when described as a motor test depended on whether he was tested by a black examiner or a white examiner. Table 3, which shows "efficiency scores" (that is, second-session minus first-session performances), indicates the trends in another way.

Table 3
Mean "efficiency scores" (second-session minus first session performances) for black subjects with a white or a black examiner under motor-test or intelligence-test instructions on the hard version of the digit-symbol test.

		Presumed nature of task	
		Intellectual	Motor
Examiner	White	22.91	28.96
	Black	23.48	21.39

$N = 23$ in all cells.
(Adapted from Table 2 of Katz, Roberts, & Robinson, 1965. Copyright 1965 by the American Psychological Association and reproduced by permission.)

While only the mean score for the motor-test/white-examiner condition is significantly different from the other means statistically, the overall trend is interesting. Under the intelligence-test condition, the black examinees do better with a black examiner; under the motor-test condition, they do significantly better with a white examiner. In the white-examiner situation, black examinees do best when the test is presented as a motor test; with a black examiner, they do best when it is presented as an intelligence test.

In an effort to explain their provocative findings, Katz and his colleagues tried various theoretical notions on for size. They pointed out, for example, that, other things being equal, efficiency is optimal under conditions where arousal is neither excessively high nor excessively low and made several assumptions: ". . . first, that the white person [examiner] aroused more drive than did the black [examiner]; second, that intelligence-test instructions were more motivating than motor-test instructions; and third, that the increments of drive were additive" (p. 58).

While not all of the differences are statistically significant, the trends are in the expected direction. Thus, the black-examiner/motor-test condition should yield poor performance, since neither the race of the examiner nor the nature of the test would promote arousal; under conditions of excessively low arousal, performance should be poor. On the other hand, the white-examiner/intelligence-test condition should yield especially high arousal, since *both* the race of the examiner and the nature of the test promote arousal; again, a poor performance would be predicted, this time because of excessively high (rather than excessively low) arousal. The other two conditions—white-examiner/motor-test and black-examiner/intelligence-test—are more conducive to the moderate level of arousal under which performance is theoretically more efficient. This proves to be the case, as seen most graphically in the white-examiner/motor-test condition, which results in significantly superior performance.

Katz and his co-investigators do not propose a simple explanation. In fact, they suggest that such alternative possibilities as Atkinson's theory of the relation between incentive value and subjective probability of success (Atkinson & Feather, 1966) might provide equally good, perhaps better, explanations of the results. What they feel strongly about, however, is that, in presuming to measure ability of whatever kind objectively, psychologists need to pay considerably more attention to the influence of what might otherwise be considered extraneous factors—namely, such variables as race (of examiner and/or examinee), description of the test and its purposes, and supposed norms against which the examinee expects to be evaluated. Here, if anywhere, there would seem to be good reason for social psychologists and clinical psychologists to enter into a marriage of convenience.

The Structure of Intellect

The heading is borrowed from Guilford, who has been closely concerned with what he calls the "structure of intellect." Is intelligence composed of a collection of special abilities (memory, judgment, concept formation, sensory-motor skills, and the like) or a general level of ability that runs through almost everything one might attempt? Or is it a combination of both general (g factor) and special (s factor) abilities? Some (for example, Cattell, 1968) have gone so far as to speak of two g's, a crystallized general ability g_c, made up of "judgmental skills that have been acquired by cultural experience" (for example, vocabulary and mechanical knowledge) and a fluid general ability g_f, consisting of capacities such as classification or drawing analogies, which presumably are not dependent on cultural influences. His notions seem less academic as he describes some typical real-life examples:

> To find a person high in fluid ability, but low in crystallized, we should have to take someone who accidentally has missed schooling. I have measured deck-hands and farmers who scored much higher than average professors in fluid ability but who acquired no comparable level of crystallized ability because they had not systematically applied their fluid intelligence to what is usually called culture. Such men will astonish you in a game of chess, or by solving a wire puzzle with which you have struggled in vain, or in swift insights into men and motives. But their vocabularies may be arrested at a colloquial level, their knowledge of history negligible, and they never may have encountered algebra or geometry (p. 58).

A running dialogue continues between those, like McNemar (1964), who feel the "*g*-factor" is being given progressively less credit than it deserves and those, like Guilford (1966), who have spent considerable energy in extracting and analyzing statistically the factors they feel make up intelligence.

In an earlier paper, Guilford (1959) had made graphic his conviction, based on empirical investigation and statistical analysis, that intelligence is at least a three-sided affair. His "three faces of intellect" model, shown in Figure 7, depicts the operations (processes) that can be performed on various contents (figural versus semantic, for example) to yield different kinds of products (relationships as compared with implications, for example), as pictured in a later paper (Guilford, 1966).

The nature of Guilford's model of intelligence is best understood through his examples. If, for instance, one were studying the operation of cognition on symbolic content in ability to discern classes, one might ask such a question as:

> Which letter group does not belong?
> XECM   PVAA   QXIN   VIRO (Guilford, 1959, p. 471).

If, on the other hand, one wanted to test the same ability operating on semantic (rather than symbolic) content, an appropriate item would be:

> Which object does not belong?
> clam   tree   oven   rose (p. 471).

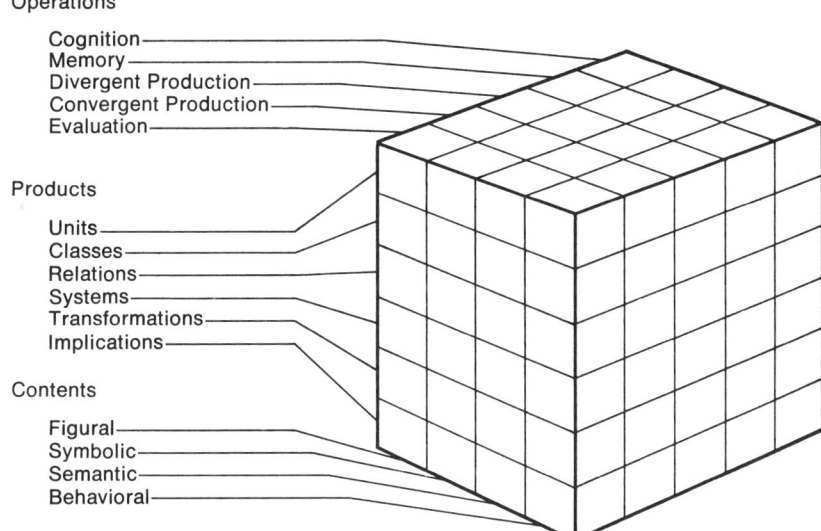

Figure 7
Model of the structure of intellect. (Figure 1 of Guilford, 1966. Copyright 1966 by the American Psychological Association and reproduced by permission.)

If one were interested in testing a person's ability to perform the operation of "convergent thinking" on symbolic content with respect to relationships, items of the following type would serve the purpose:

pots . . . . stop   bard . . . . drab   rats . . . . <u>?</u>   (p. 475).

In contrast to this ability to discern configurations, to conceptualize, is the process of "divergent thinking," which rests on the capacity to produce a *variety* of appropriate responses. Conceivably a person could be very good at convergent thinking but mediocre or poor in divergent thinking. Giving a person a set amount of time in which to think of as many possible uses for a brick as he can, would be a way of measuring divergent thinking. However, here again the many-sided nature of intelligence becomes apparent if one considers the qualitatively different types of performance two people might turn in on such a straightforward item; both could be technically correct, yet differ substantially on the dimension of flexibility. Guilford (1959) describes the situation well:

> If his responses are: build a house, build a barn, build a garage, build a school, build a church, build a chimney, build a walk, and build a barbecue, he would earn a fairly high score for ideational fluency but a very low score for spontaneous flexibility, because all these uses fall into the same class. If another person said: make a doorstop, make a paperweight, throw it at a dog, make a bookcase, drown a cat, drive a nail, make a red powder, and use for baseball bases, he would also receive a high score for flexibility. He has gone frequently from one class to another (p. 473).

It seems, then, that, unlike the case with hat sizes, which identify each of us quite adequately as a 7 or a 7 1/4, "head sizes" (in the form of ability levels) are not all that easily indexed. Intelligence turns out to be a multidimensional attribute (even though one of its dimensions may be a g-factor — or g-factors). Further, while for practical purposes it would have been nice to find that ability level remains constant, we seem to be dealing with a relative rather than an absolute condition. The interaction of genetic potential and environmental influence needs to be reckoned with, and while its effects may be more critical at certain stages of development than at others, they seem to be felt throughout.

It is not easy to render judgments about the comparative ability of people, let alone nations or races. In his book on *Intelligence and Experience,* Hunt (1961) makes some pointed observations on this score:[3]

> In view of the technological developments in Western culture during the past half century, which demand that a higher and higher proportion of the population have a high level of ability to manipulate symbols in the solution of problems, probably the most unfortunate consequences of the assumptions of fixed intelligence and genetically predetermined development lie, first, in the encouragement they have given to the policy of leaving infants essentially alone during their early months so that they can grow undisturbed by excessive stimulation, and second, in the discouragement they have given to the investigation of the effects of various programs of child-environment interaction during the full course of development from birth to maturity.
>
> It is fairly clear from the evidence surveyed . . . that impoverishments of experience during the early months can slow up the development of intelligence. In terms of the traditional measurement of intelligence, this means reducing the IQ. Various bits of the evidence have strongly suggested that such slowed development is permanent, that it may result not only in a permanently reduced IQ but in a failure of the basic criterion capacities of individuals to develop to the degree that they might have developed under other, more varied programs of encounters with the environment which were appropriately matched to the intellectual structures developing within the child. But much remains to be learned about

---

[3] From Hunt, J. McV. *Intelligence and experience.* New York: The Ronald Press Company, © 1961. Reprinted by permission of the author and publisher.

> the degree of permanence in such failures to develop and about the conditions under which these failures to develop become permanent (pp. 345–346).

Nonetheless, Hunt sees some promising possibilities in the last analysis:

> The hope of increasing the average level of intelligence by proper manipulation of children's developmental encounters with their environments, a hope which becomes reasonable with the evidences surveyed here and with relinquishing the assumptions of fixed intelligence and predetermined development, provides a challenge of the first order. It has great implications for human welfare as the growth of technology in Western cultures demands a higher and higher percentage of people who can manipulate symbols and solve complex problems. In this challenge the theory of man's nature and the fate of his welfare are obviously intertwined (p. 346).

If the IQ was once king, it should be clear by now that it no longer reigns supreme. Its infallibility has been questioned and its authority challenged. This is not a reflection on the efforts of measurement specialists but rather an indication that we have come to recognize the complexity of the problem they have set themselves. But if the measurement of ability is complicated, the study of personality is no less so, as will become evident in what follows.

Personality Dynamics

A Standardized Approach to Interviewing

Anyone who follows the pollsters in their attempts to predict election results is familiar with the criticisms they encounter about their interview techniques. While clinicians are professionally less interested in the outcome of elections than in the outcome of psychotherapy, the business of interacting most effectively with people is of particular interest to them.

There seem as many styles of interviewing as there are interviewers. Watch the efforts of the TV professionals, and one will note some who talk more than those being interviewed. Others seem to have difficulty getting the interviewee to say much beyond simple Yes's and No's, although they may continually ply him with questions. Fortunately, there are some who succeed admirably, having the knack for setting up a situation conducive to spontaneous, relevant responsiveness on the part of the interviewee. Commonplace as interviews are, it is clear that there is much to be learned about the interaction process involved, whether the situation be that of Eric Sevareid and Richard Nixon or Dr. X and Patient Y.

Since such interaction abounds in clinical work, Matarazzo and his colleagues decided to study interview behavior under controlled conditions. They devised a special methodology that would allow them not only to observe and record the interaction but also to manipulate the various parameters of the interview situation. The heart of their approach lies in what they call the "standardized interview."

Departing from the character of the usual clinical interview, Matarazzo's group deliberately (but as naturally as possible) arranged the situation so that certain conditions would exist during the interview, each following the other in a prescribed sequence and for a given duration. Each interview was purposely divided into five periods (without the interviewee's knowledge), with the interviewer behaving in prearranged ways in each period. During three of the five periods he promoted a free, easygoing exchange; during the remaining two he behaved in a way designed to be stressful to the interviewee—remaining silent during one period and repeatedly interrupting the interviewee during the other. Each of the five periods was held to a predetermined length by the interviewer (again without the interviewee's knowledge, except as he might become aware of changes in the interviewer's behavior at various points). Thus, the three free-exchange periods lasted 10, 5, and 5 minutes respectively, while the interspersed stress periods (silence or interruption) were held to either 15 minutes or to a predetermined number of silences and interruptions. The outline of such a standardized interview is pictured in Table 4.

Table 4
Characteristics of the standardized interview.

Period	Type of Interviewing	Duration of Period Fixed	Duration of Period Variable
I	Free interviewing	10 minutes	
II	Stress (via silence)		12 silences, or 15 minutes (whichever is shorter)
III	Free interviewing	5 minutes	
IV	Stress (via interruptions)		12 interruptions, or 15 minutes (whichever is shorter)
V	Free interviewing	5 minutes	
	Total time:	20 minutes plus a maximum of 30 minutes more	

Note: Interviewer behavior in Periods I, III, and V is essentially nondirective, with interviewer utterances being approximately 5 seconds long. In Period II, the interviewer fails to respond to interviewee statements a total of 12 times; at points where the interviewee himself does not break the silence, the interviewer makes another 5-second comment. In Period IV, during which the interviewee is interrupted a total of 12 times, such interruptions come about 3 seconds after an interviewee has begun an utterance. (Adapted from Table 1 of Matarazzo in Bachrach, 1962. Copyright 1962 by Basic Books and reproduced by permission.)

As noted, the interviewer decided in advance how he would behave vis-à-vis the interviewee at each stage. The dependent variable is thus the behavior of the interviewee, and the behavior of the interviewer is the independent variable. The investigators were impressed with the extent to which the effects of such planned manipulation of the interview situation manifested themselves in changes in the behavior of the interviewee. In the case of Period II (the silence phase), for example, it was noted that . . . "experimentally introduced changes in duration of interviewer silence behavior are followed by similar changes in interviewee silence behavior. In addition, for this (silence) interaction dimension at least, normals, neurotics, mixed neurotics and psychotics, and schizophrenics act similarly; i.e., are influenced by the interviewer's behavior in identical directions" (Matarazzo, 1962, p. 488).

It is understandable that Matarazzo and his colleagues were led to investigate further aspects of interview behavior. One might wonder, for example, whether the length of the interviewer's utterances affects the duration of the interviewee's responses. Thus, the interviewer might speak in 5-second lengths during one part of the interview, switch to 10-second lengths at some point, and revert to 5-second lengths again after a given interval. Or he might reverse the order to 10-5-10. Too, he could hold each of his comments to about 5-seconds. Would the interviewee's speech show corresponding (or other) changes? Figure 8 shows compelling results.

Apparently the simple device of controlling the length of one's own utterances significantly affects the duration of the interviewee's responses. If the interviewer talks in long bursts, so does the subject; shorter bursts elicit correspondingly short utterances from the subject. It is as if, without being aware of it, the interviewee mimics the interviewer — at least with respect to duration of speech.

Matarazzo (1962) sees some important implications for the clinician:

> . . . if one of the characteristics of some depressed patients is that they speak infrequently, and when they do, do so in utterances of short durations, then one might ask what would be the effect on their duration of utterances of an interviewer, himself, using only long utterances when interviewing them? Would there be a corresponding increase in the patient's own duration of utterance and, thus, along this one dimension, at least, less "depression"? Likewise, with patients who speak in unusually long utterances, e.g., the so-called manic patient, would the effect of an interviewer using unusually brief utterances (e.g., one or two words per communication unit) be to reduce these long patient utterances? . . . further research would then need to be undertaken to study whether or not, and with what persistence, such intra-interview-produced interviewee changes do, in fact, generalize to the patient's everyday behavior in a variety of life situations (pp. 491–492).

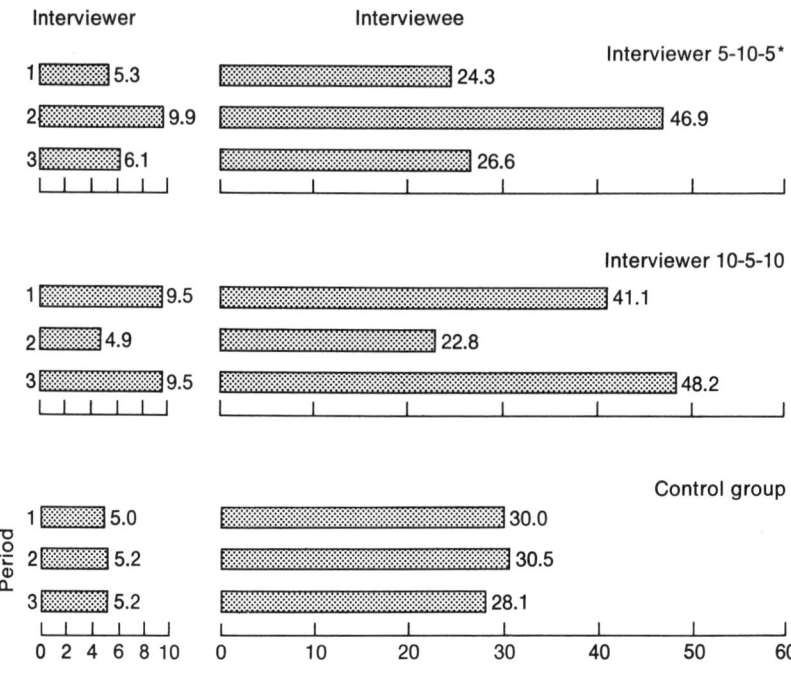

Mean Duration of Single Units of Speech, Seconds

Figure 8
Influence of length of interviewer's utterances on interviewee speech. *Note:* The top third of the figure shows the length of an interviewee's utterances (in seconds) as a function of the length of the interviewer's utterances, when the latter attempted to keep his utterances first to 5 seconds each, then changed to a 10-second length, and then reverted back to the 5-second period (as shown by the notation "Interviewer 5-10-5" in the upper right-hand corner). Actual lengths of the interviewer's utterances are shown in the left-hand column, those of the interviewee in the right-hand column. In the other two phases, the interviewer attempted the sequence 10-5-10 (middle third of the figure) and 5-5-5 (the control group shown in the lower third). [Figure 6 of Matarazzo in *Handbook of clinical psychology,* B. B. Wolman (Ed.), 1965. Used with permission of McGraw-Hill Book Company.]

More interestingly, it turns out that a subtle signal-exchange system (a term used by Rosenthal, 1963) may operate during the interview. That is, the interviewee seems to respond to peripheral, or even nonverbal, aspects of the communication between interviewer and interviewee, unwittingly altering his behavior as a result. Thus, without the interviewee's awareness (as attested by postinterview questioning), his pattern of verbal behavior can be molded by very slight, hardly noticeable changes in the interviewer's behavior. Figure 9 shows, for example, how so simple an act as slight head-nodding by the interviewer can significantly alter the volume of interviewee speech.

Dividing the interview period into thirds (without the interviewee's knowledge), the interviewer held his utterances to the same length throughout (approximately 5 seconds each). But during the second of the three periods he introduced, in addition, slight head-nodding responses to the interviewee's comments. As Figure 9 shows, the interviewee's utterances increase significantly in length during the latter period (as they do in a replication of the situation). Meanwhile, a control group, in

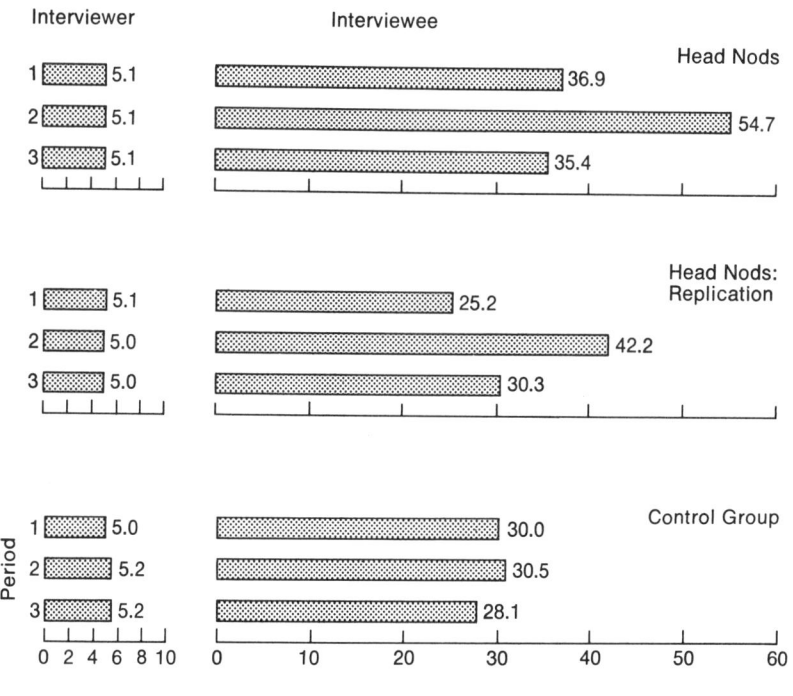

Mean Duration of Single Units of Speech, Seconds

Figure 9
Influence of interviewer's nonverbal communication on interviewee speech. [Figure 7 of Matarazzo from *Handbook of clinical psychology*, B. B. Wolman (Ed.), 1965. Used with permission of McGraw-Hill Book Company.]

which the interviewer again speaks in 5-second bursts throughout but does not resort to head-nodding during any part of the period, shows no such variation in the length of the interviewee's utterances.

The same consequences follow when the interviewer, instead of employing head-nodding, as in the sequence above, responds with "Mm hm." This simple comment significantly increases the length of the interviewee's utterances during the period in which it is used. Looking ahead to where these findings may lead us, Matarazzo observes: "It is clear . . . that careful study of non-content (as well as content) interaction measures may make it possible for us someday to pair (for psychotherapy) an interviewer, with his own unique interaction characteristics, with a selected patient with whom this interviewer's interaction pattern might best be suited" (p. 492).

If such a controlled approach holds merit, one might consider other types of objective intervention in the clinical process. The following section explores another such possibility.

An Actuarial Approach to Prediction

The capacity to predict outcomes in advance (especially such important outcomes as marital happiness or occupational success) is certainly to be sought. Psychologists in general and clinicians in particular continue to work hard not only at assessing how good their predictions are (whether about rats' ability to learn mazes, clients' ability to profit from psychotherapy, or pilots' ability to fly planes) but also at improving their "hit-and-miss" ratios. The problem is squarely in the lap of any clinician, whether called upon to make predictions concerning how safely a depressed patient can be granted a weekend pass at home or whether a student will fare better in a school of business administration than in a school of medicine. To enliven the discussion and provoke some healthy debate, Paul Meehl, himself an able clinician, several years ago published a little book (1954) that created a big storm.

Although Meehl stated the problem in his own way, let us begin by asking a question. If you had the job of selecting secretaries for a big company and had a choice between interviewing each applicant or having her take a written test devised by a psychologist experienced in personnel selection, which procedure would you adopt (assuming you could not use both)? Chances are you would feel more confident of selecting the right girls—that is, those who would make good secretaries—if you interviewed each one in turn and made some "clinical" judgment about her suitability. Understandable, Meehl would agree—but, he hastens to add, perhaps unfortunate.

Meehl's book, *Clinical versus Statistical Prediction,* presents some disturbing facts and comes to some unnerving conclusions. Looking back over published studies in which either clinical judgment (for example, impressions gained in an interview) or an actuarial method (for example, a paper-and-pencil personality inventory) figured, Meehl compared the predictive efficiency of the two approaches, only to discover results he felt should give clinicians some pause for thought. The actuarial (statistical) approach did as well as (in fact, slightly better than) the clinical in the particular studies reviewed. At the very least, Meehl suggested, the moral of the story was as follows: "Regardless of one's theory about personality and regardless of one's choice of data . . . ; regardless of how these data are fused for predictive purposes—by intuition, table, equation, or rational hypotheses developed in a case conference—the honest clinician cannot avoid the question: 'Am I doing better than I could by flipping pennies?' " (p. 136).

Meehl's fellow clinicians were quick to join the issue, sometimes as heatedly as Holt (1958), who stated in his opening remarks that: "Clinical students in particular complain of a vague feeling that a fast one has been put over on them, that under a great show of objectivity, or at least bipartisanship, Professor Meehl has actually sold the clinical approach up the river" (p. 1).

Recasting the problem in his own way, Holt suggested that Meehl was operating on an either-or basis which pitted the clinical and actuarial approaches against each other. Conceiving the situation in such a way was both oversimplified and unfortunate, according to Holt. Instead of talking about "clinical *versus* statistical prediction," why not talk of "clinical *and* statistical prediction"? After all, the two need not, indeed *should* not, be antithetical, he insisted. Thus, one could think of at least three approaches—the pure actuarial, the naive clinical, and the sophisticated clinical, to use his terms. In the third approach,

> All of the refinements of design that the actuarial tradition has furnished are employed, including job analysis, pilot studies, item analysis, and successive cross-validations. Quantification and statistics are used wherever helpful, but the clinician himself is retained as one of the prime instruments, with an effort to make him as reliable and valid a data-processor as possible; and he makes the final organization of the data to yield a set of predictions tailored to each individual case (p. 4).

He summarized the situation thus: "... we should try to find the optimal combination of actuarially controlled methods and sensitive clinical judgment for any particular predictive enterprise" (p. 12).

In the healthy hammer-and-tong debate that characterizes the development of clinical psychology, there has been further dialogue between protagonists and antagonists. More recently, Sawyer (1966), acting somewhat as mediator, has tried to step back from the problem a bit in order to get some useful perspective. The flavor of his conception is implicit in its title—"Measurement *and* Prediction, Clinical *and* Statistical." The problem, Sawyer argues, is that Meehl, Holt, and others have been looking at only one side of the coin—that is, whether data are best combined clinically or statistically. By concerning themselves solely with prediction and how data are best combined, they have ignored the problem of *measurement* and how data are best *collected*. For, just as data can be combined by either method in prediction, so can they be collected by either method in measurement.

One has, then, a more complex situation to consider—not two possibilities but at least four—and if one considers mixtures of the clinical and statistical (mechanical, as he calls it) approaches, actually eight possible combinations. Thus, Sawyer suggests, the fuller picture is represented by Table 5.

Table 5
Classification of prediction methods.

Mode of Data Collection	Mode of Data Combination	
	Clinical	Mechanical
Clinical	1. Pure clinical	2. Trait ratings
Mechanical	3. Profile interpretation	4. Pure statistical
Both	5. Clinical composite	6. Mechanical composite
Either or both[a]	7. Clinical synthesis	8. Mechanical synthesis

[a] Plus, for the clinical synthesis, the prediction of Method 2, 4, or 6; or, for the mechanical synthesis, the prediction of Method 1, 3, or 5. (Table 1 of Sawyer, 1966. Copyright 1966 by the American Psychological Association and reproduced by permission.)

The reader may find an illustration of one of the cells helpful. In the case of "profile interpretation," for example, the clinician would use a mechanical mode of measurement in data collection, then combine the data so collected in a clinical fashion for purposes of making his prediction. Thus, a subject might be given the MMPI—a set of 550 statements to which he replies "True," "False," or "Don't know"—and have his responses tabulated by a secretary familiar with the scoring system. The resulting profile might then be interpreted by a clinician who has actually never seen the person. The reader who balks at such a seemingly mechanistic approach would do well to read another of Meehl's (1956) controversial pieces whose title gives away its plot: "Wanted—a Good Cookbook."

Reviewing the literature in terms of his own broad schema, Sawyer comes to a conclusion not unlike Meehl's. As he describes it:

> Altogether, the findings of these 45 studies indicate that, whatever the data, clinical combination never surpasses mechanical combination. Nonetheless, clinical skills may contribute through data collection, by assessing characteristics that would not otherwise enter the prediction. Moreover, it seems likely that inaccurate prediction usually results less from inappropriate combination than from lack of valid predictors to start with. If this is so, then improvement should result from devising better ways for the clinician to report objectively the broad range of possibly relevant behavior he perceives (p. 193).

In his carefully reasoned piece, Sawyer nevertheless comes to feel ultimately that "the clinical-statistical problem is far from being solved . . ." (p. 198). Evidently Holt would agree, for he entitles a more recent article (Holt, 1970) "Yet Another Look at Clinical and Statistical Prediction." In it he takes a critical look at the 45 studies cited by Sawyer and finds the evidence unconvincing, pointing out various types of error that, according to him, "flaw" the studies. Only 15 of the studies approach Holt's criteria of adequacy, and after reassessing the overall problem, he feels justified in replying with a strong affirmative to the question in the subtitle of his article: "Is Clinical Psychology Worthwhile?"

It is in this spirit of healthy contentiousness that clinical psychology continues to develop. Its adherents thrive on the intellectual stimulation provided by lively dialogue on basic questions on which the evidence is not yet all in. Meanwhile, some find even greater satisfaction in striking out in new directions altogether, as the following section will attest.

A Computerized Approach to Psychotherapy

Psychotherapy being the complicated process it is, experienced teachers and practitioners struggle manfully to find new ways to teach its various techniques. Typical of training procedures is the practice of recording sessions between therapist and client (with the latter's knowledge and consent), so that they may later be replayed to a group of professional colleagues for the purpose of gaining needed criticism. Too, the experienced therapist can observe the novice through a one-way screen as the beginner interacts with a client and can comment later on aspects of the interaction. Or, the novice can observe the trained therapist under similar circumstances. Video taping of treatment sessions permits the interaction to be observed and evaluated later without having lost any of its nuances. Most recently, some (for example, Sanders, 1966, and Welsh, 1966) have even devised electromechanical devices (the "bug-in-the-ear") by which the teacher can communicate with the therapist-in-training during his interaction with a client (who does not hear the comments being received from the trainer).

Providing training in psychotherapy is not simple. Subjects cannot be chosen for therapy at random from large groups; they come of their own accord, seeking help. Further, once the therapeutic sessions begin, they cannot be terminated as readily as the usual experimental situation; the relationship, once established, must run its course. Again, despite the benefits accruing to such devices as the recording of sessions, the fact remains that while an actual session is in progress, the novice therapist is largely on his own. Even when "hooked up" with an experienced therapist who is communicating with him from a separate room, the teacher can hardly take over for him in the moment-to-moment interaction with the client.

As with the medical intern, the beginning therapist is to some extent learning at the expense of the client (although close supervision is meant to minimize, if not eliminate, any undesirable effects). Clearly, everyone would feel more comfortable, were it possible to arrange a situation in which the budding therapist might gain comparable experience without cost to anyone. Starkweather (1965) suggests that this is precisely where the computer comes in, provided we are sufficiently ingenious to make use of its capabilities.

The principles of computer programming, although technical, are straightforward. The reader seeking a somewhat lighthearted presentation of the kinds of decision making that can be written into a program is referred to an amusing flow chart (reprinted in Borko, 1962, p. 116) showing how a computer might approach various decisions on getting up in the morning, including everything from turning over for a few extra minutes' sleep to deciding whether to kiss its wife. In a more serious vein, Starkweather (1965) presents a computer program written by third-grade pupils, simple in conception but illustrative of the elements involved in constructing a computer program.

It took only some extra imagination to see the possibilities of "teaching" (that is, programming) a computer to act like a therapist or a client. That is to say, having obtained tapes documenting how an experienced therapist functions, it is possible to analyze them in terms of the strategies he employs—the kinds of questions he asks, the way he typically reacts to certain references by the client, how he decides among possible alternative things he can say in return, and so on. After studying the live therapist in detail, it should be possible to write a computer program incorporating the set of rules by which an experienced therapist seems to operate.

Assuming that the computer is now a therapist of sorts, the psychologist or psychiatrist in training can put himself in its hands, playing the role of client and observing how the computer treats him. This is readily accomplished by interacting with the computer via typewriter, the client typing out whatever he wishes to say, the computer, in turn, printing out its reply. The interaction, if a bit stilted, is intriguing, as the following sample (from Starkweather) illustrates.[4]

A programmed interviewer in conversation
with a human subject
(Computer typing is indented)

    PLEASE TYPE YOUR LAST NAME
MISS JONES RS
    WHAT YEAR WERE YOU BORN, MISS JONES
I DON'T LIKE TO THINK BACK THAT FAR. RS
    THAT DATE IS NOT CLEAR
    WILL YOU PLEASE TYPE THE YEAR YOU WERE BORN
WELL, IT WAS IN 1935. RS
    FINE, WE WILL GO ON
    WHAT IS THE REASON YOU ARE HERE TODAY
I GUESS I JUST HAVE TO SAY THAT I AM CONFUSED AND DISCOURAGED. RS
    JUST A MINUTE
    HOW BAD HAS IT BEEN
WELL, THIS WORLD SEEMS SO AWFUL. RS
    HAVE THINGS BEEN SO BAD THAT YOU FEEL YOU WOULD
    RATHER DIE THAN GO ON LIKE THIS . . .
I FEEL LOW MOST OF THE TIME. RS
    HOW CLOSE HAVE YOU COME TO HARMING YOURSELF
I WOULDN'T LOOK ON IT AS HARM REALLY. NO, I'M NOT CLOSE TO HARMING MYSELF. RS
    DESCRIBE ANY CHANGES IN YOUR EATING AND SLEEPING
    HABITS

[4]Reprinted from Starkweather, 1965b, with permission of the author and publisher, *Psychological Reports*.

I HAVEN'T HAD A GOOD APPETITE FOR A LONG TIME, AND IT GIVES ME TROUBLE TO GET TO SLEEP. SOMETIMES THOUGH, I JUST DON'T FEEL LIKE GETTING OUT OF BED. WHAT'S THE USE. RS
    HOW ABOUT CHANGES IN YOUR WEIGHT
NO, MY WEIGHT HASN'T CHANGED MUCH. RS
    DESCRIBE ANY CRYING SPELLS YOU HAVE HAD
SOMETIMES I JUST CAN'T HELP IT. RS
    ANYTHING ELSE ABOUT THAT
I TRY NOT TO. RS
    DO YOU HAVE TROUBLE WITH FEELINGS OF NERVOUSNESS OR TENSION
NO, I WOULDN'T CALL IT THAT. RS
    DESCRIBE ANYTHING UNUSUAL YOU HAVE NOTICED RECENTLY
I GUESS I'M NOT A VERY OBSERVANT PERSON. I CAN'T THINK OF ANY. RS

(Appendix, Table 1)

If the novice wishes to try his hand at "treating" the computer, it is possible to arrange the training situation accordingly, for a computer can be programmed to simulate an anxious client, or a depressed client, or a hostile one. Now the intern has his chance to use whatever therapeutic strategy he wishes, in order to observe its effectiveness in dealing with clients of various types. Such a dialogue has a somewhat lifelike quality, as demonstrated in the following selection (from Starkweather).

A programmed patient in conversation
with a human interviewer
(Computer typing is indented)

WHAT FOLLOWS IS AN EXPERIMENT IN COMPUTER SIMULATION OF AN INITIAL INTERVIEW WITH A PATIENT.
DO YOU KNOW HOW TO CONVERSE WITH A COMPUTER BY TYPEWRITER Q. IF SO TYPE YES, THEN R-S. IF NOT, PRESS THE R-S KEY ON THE KEYBOARD.
    YES RS
GOOD. THE ONLY OTHER THING YOU WILL NEED TO KNOW IS THAT TO RESPOND WITH SILENCE, YOU MERELY STRIKE S, THEN THE R-S KEY. TO BEGIN WITH, PLEASE TYPE YOUR LAST NAME, THEN PRESS R-S.
    DR. MISTYPE RS
GOOD, YOU HAVE THE IDEA. NOW THE INTERVIEW BEGINS. THE PATIENT ENTERS YOUR OFFICE. HE IS A SLENDER, CONVENTIONALLY-DRESSED MAN APPEARING ABOUT THIRTY YEARS OLD. HIS NAME IS JOHN SANDERS. YOU SEAT YOURSELF, AND ASK HIM TO BE SEATED. HE SITS DOWN AND SAYS—
    THANK YOU.

```
WHAT BRINGS YOU HERE, MR. SANDERS RS
          WELL, MY WIFE WANTED ME TO COME.
YES RS
          IT'S NOT MY IDEA, THAT'S FOR SURE.
          SHE JUST TOLD ME I OUGHT TO SEE A PSYCHIATRIST.
          SHE SAID . . .
          SHE SAID SHE WAS GOING TO LEAVE IF I DIDN'T GO.
HOW DO YOU FEEL ABOUT SEEING A PSYCHIATRIST RS
          YOU KNOW WHAT I THINK ABOUT PSYCHIATRISTS. I THINK
          THEY ARE THE BIGGEST BUNCH OF PHONIES THERE EVER
          WAS.
WHAT MAKES YOU THINK THAT RS
          I DIDN'T COME HERE TO DISCUSS PSYCHIATRISTS.
WHAT IS YOUR PROBLEM RS
          WELL, LIKE I SAID BEFORE, THAT'S WHY I CAME HERE—
          BECAUSE SHE SAID I HAD TO.
                                                  (Appendix, Table 6)
```

The possibilities offered by this new technological approach to training are obvious. First, the beginning (and even the advanced) student can practice and learn at the expense of the computer rather than at the expense of another human being. Too, he can try his hand at interacting with a whole gamut of "patients." Or, he can feel what it is like to be exposed as a client to a variety of "therapists." Perhaps most convenient of all is the opportunity to remake history. For example, having tried a certain strategy in interaction with his computer-client, the therapist-in-training may wonder what might have happened at a certain point had he made statement *B* rather than statement *A*. Unlike the real-life situation in which steps cannot be retraced, he can now take full advantage of the possibilities for erasing the preceding statements from the computer's memory, starting the interaction all over again to see what happens when he makes statement *B*.

We are not suggesting, of course, that the simulated client has the richness, subtlety, and complexity of its human counterpart. But this fact is to some extent the fault of programming technology and the state of knowledge at this time rather than the fault of the computer itself. At the rate the computer field is developing, however, the day may not be too distant when it will be hard, if not impossible, to distinguish what has been said (printed) by a computer from what has been said (typed) by a person.[5] Granted that while the millennium (or Armageddon, as some would have it) has not yet arrived, Starkweather's pioneering efforts suggest that the computer

---

[5] The interested reader is referred to Türing's test. By way of answering the question of whether computers can think, Türing (1956) suggested that one might, by teletype, ask a series of questions of a man, on the one hand, and of a computer, on the other. Both would type out their replies. If the interrogator were unable to distinguish between their responses, one might conclude that computers can, in fact, think.

may serve not only as slave but as teacher, ironically helping man to help his fellow man.

That the cynic may have the last word, we should add that some have pointed out that if technology continues its relentless march unchecked, we may look forward to the 1984 prospect of having a computerized client interact with a computerized therapist while their real counterparts go about the business of living—for better or worse.

Some Methodological Dilemmas

Lest it appear that we are trying to make clinical prediction seem the world's hardest, let us hasten to agree that prediction of *any* kind has its problems. Weather satellites and wind balloons notwithstanding, forecasting even so objective a fact as whether it will rain tomorrow is risky, as the much maligned weatherman will attest. But even if clinical prediction is not the most difficult of all, it does have problems unique to it, as we shall try to demonstrate.

The "Twisted Pear" Phenomenon

As Fisher (1959) has pointed out, it is helpful to distinguish between various kinds of hits and misses in prediction of any kind. We may be right or wrong in a number of ways. In a sample of 1000 men between the ages of 20 and 30, one might try to predict, for example, who would eventually die of cancer and who of some other natural cause. If records were then kept until no member of the sample of 1000 survived, one could examine the reasons listed as cause of death to learn how right or wrong the predictor had been.

It might turn out that a large number of the people who were tagged as prone to cancer did so die eventually. Similarly, many who were regarded as not cancer-prone (by whatever predictor was used) may prove to have died of some other natural cause. One could hardly expect the prediction to have been right in every case, but one would hope that it had identified most of them correctly. Ideally, of course, we would like to achieve the situation shown in Table 6.

The tallies in cell *C* represent "true positives"—that is, those identified as cancer-prone who subsequently did die of cancer. Conversely, the tallies in cell *B* represent the "true negatives"—the people who were not expected to die of cancer and didn't. A predictor would be happy if he found cells *A* and *D* completely empty, as in the idealized situation shown. There, in cell *D* we find no "false positives"—that is, peo-

Table 6
Idealized relationship between prediction and outcome.

	Cause of death	
Test prediction	Cancer	Other-than-Cancer
Not Cancer-prone	A	B (80 tallies)
Cancer-prone	C (45 tallies)	D

ple who, according to our test, were destined to die of cancer but died of other natural causes. Nor do we find in cell A any "false negatives," or people who, according to our test, were not cancer-prone but who nevertheless died from cancer.

The false negatives provide the clinician with his greatest difficulty, according to Fisher (1959), for they are hardest to spot accurately. The matter of detecting brain damage with the aid of psychological tests, he suggests, illustrates this problem. Assume, for example, that a test developed for this kind of prediction contains various "signs" suggestive of brain damage that may show up in a person's performance. Table 7 helps illustrate the situation.

Table 7
Relationship between prediction and actuality.

	Actual condition	
Test prediction	Brain-Damaged	Normal
Normal	A	B
Brain-Damaged	C	D

One would hope all cases fall in cells B and C (that is, prove to be true negatives and true positives respectively), with none in cells A and D. Were this the case, we would have available a faultless instrument—the test would be a perfect predictor. Unfortunately, the situation seldom approaches this ideal. Instead, if we use the shaded area to represent the proportion of cases in the respective cells, the picture looks more typically like the "twisted pear" (Fisher's term) pictured in Figure 10.

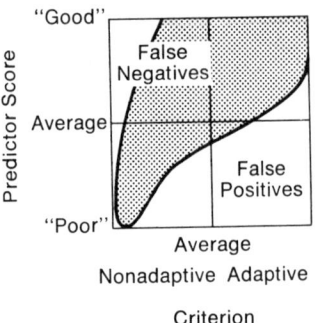

Figure 10
Schematic relationship of predictor and criterion. (From Figure 1 of Fisher, 1959. Copyright 1959 by the American Psychological Association and reproduced by permission.)

It would seem, then, that our tests have the most trouble with false negatives. That is, the test performance of these persons is within normal limits, yet in actuality they turn out to have pathological features (brain damage, or schizophrenia, or low ego strength, or whatever else is being investigated). It is not only psychological tests that encounter the "twisted pear" phenomenon. Medicine, for example, has to contend with the cases whose chest X-rays look normal but who show other signs suspicious of tuberculosis (and prove to have the disease). And many of us know of people who left their doctor's office with a sigh of relief because their electrocardiogram looked normal, only to fall dead of a heart attack that evening.

Since tests are imperfect predictors, and since they err mostly in the area of false negatives, the problem of prediction takes on some interesting features, of which Meehl and Rosen have made us aware. It is instructive to look at caveats they have urged, lest we lose sight of some of the complexities of clinical prediction.

The "Base Rate" Problem

There are fancy and not so fancy methods of prediction. "Experience" is in the second category, for it relies simply on past history rather than on any particular instrument or formal test. The farmer knows how thickly or thinly to sow his particular brand of winter rye, based on past experience with conditions in his area; the personnel officer can make a pretty good guess as to how many secretaries will "work out" (according to their bosses' evaluations) and how many will not; the commandant of a military post knows what percent of inductees usually get "washed out" in the course of their basic training.

Meehl and Rosen (1955) use this military illustration to make some telling points. Let us assume, they suggest, that on the basis of past experience it is possible for the commandant of Fort Ord to predict that 5 percent of the men inducted usually adjust so poorly during their initial basic training as to warrant a discharge from military service at that point. This figure is termed a "base rate." That is, it is a known statistic based on accumulated previous findings in a particular situation. As such—and this is the point Meehl and Rosen stress—it is a predictor that should be shown some respect. Even without any formal assessment device, the officers of Fort Ord can predict with reasonable confidence that, of a sizable group of recruits, 95 percent will adjust to military life and be retained, while 5 percent will adapt so poorly as to warrant discharge.

Small as the latter figure looks, it represents 500 out of 10,000 men who should never have been lifted out of civilian life, either for their sake or the army's. Hence, any test that would serve to cut down on the number of "misfits" inadvertently inducted would be a boon to all concerned. Let us assume, then, as Meehl and Rosen do, that an enterprising psychologist sets himself this task. After considerable pretesting of items, he comes up with a test that predicts correctly 55 percent of the men who actually turn out later to have made a poor adjustment in the army. These are certainly the cases (true positives) one would hope to be able to spot in advance, and this test correctly identifies a good number of them. Being far from perfect, however, it turns out also to label as poor risks some men who prove actually to make a good adjustment to the army. In the case of this particular test, 19 percent of the men in the good adjustment group turn out to be such "false positives." The situation existing in a sample of 10,000 inductees is thus shown in Table 8.

Table 8
Prediction of the adjustment of inductees on the basis of a screening inventory.

Predicted Adjustment	Actual adjustment				Total Predicted
	Poor		Good		
	No.	%	No.	%	
Poor	275	55	1,805	19	2,080
Good	225	45	7,695	81	7,920
Total	500	100	9,500	100	10,000

(Table 1 of Meehl & Rosen, 1955. Copyright 1955 by the American Psychological Association and reproduced by permission.)

By definition, the test predicts correctly for true negatives and true positives, but incorrectly for false negatives and false positives. In the present case, then, it made incorrect predictions in the case of 2,030 men, or 20.3 percent of the group of 10,000; it predicted correctly in the case of 7,970 men, or 79.7 percent of the total group. As Meehl and Rosen point out, if all 10,000 men had been accepted *without testing* and it turned out, as it usually had on the basis of past experience, that 9,500 made the grade, 95 percent of the total group would have been correctly identified. Ironically, using the test would have lowered the percentage of correct choices to less than 80 percent.

But suppose the test developer were to point out that if the army had accepted only those men for whom the test had predicted a good adjustment, it would have kept 7,920 (of the total group of 10,000), of whom 7,695, or 97.1 percent, would have been correct choices. In other words, by using the test in this way (that is, taking only inductees who score *above* a certain point), the army could have improved about 2 percent on its prediction over use of the base rate alone. While 2 percent is a seemingly small improvement, it must be remembered that such a figure can represent millions of dollars in savings if thousands of costly misfits can be screened out of the military early.

But, as Meehl and Rosen point out, the test did not simply spring into existence—its development and the administration of the subsequent testing program also cost money. Too, the 225 men it failed to screen out (the "false negatives" of cell *A*) also cost money—their unsuitability became apparent only after expensive training. Finally, using a cut-off point—that is, accepting only the 7,920 of the 10,000 men who scored above a certain point on the test—meant rejecting out of hand 2,080 men in every batch. One would need to be sure the manpower supply could afford such an extravagant rejection rate—which, in this case, would mean losing 1,805 men who would have adjusted well to the army.

Clearly, the psychologist as predictor has no easy job on his hands!

The Nature of Prediction

The clinical psychologist frequently faces the unenviable task of describing the inner workings and predicting the external behavior of people he has had little time to get to know. A patient enters a mental hospital weeping uncontrollably and accusing himself of being worthless. Perhaps a day later, when he has stopped crying but sits morosely in a corner, the psychologist is asked to do a psychological evaluation of him. The staff hopes to find out many things as a result. Is the patient suicidal? (If so, certain precautions need to be observed.) Does his feeling of being worthless represent severe guilt feelings about something he has done? Or, as is sometimes the case, is it the product of a delusional system ("God is giving me signs I'll go to hell")? Are hallucinatory experiences at work ("voices" telling the patient he is a sinner)? More generally, what is the patient like as a person? How does he typically cope with problems? What are his psychological strengths and weaknesses? How good or poor is his prognosis? To what kinds of treatment might he respond best?

Answers to these questions are sought through many channels, of which special tests are one. There is, for example, a whole series of "projective techniques" from which the psychologist can put together the particular "test battery" he feels most appropriate to the understanding of a particular patient. However he goes about the assessment process, in the last analysis he is expected to come up with an appraisal that adds appreciably to the staff's understanding of the patient and helps map the most effective treatment plan and rehabilitation program.

No one recognizes better than the clinical psychologist himself the hazards of making predictions and the necessity for refining present instruments and procedures while continuing to look for better ones. Studies of the effectiveness of psychological assessment are plentiful, and some basic questions typically recur, among them the following: (1) How effective are the current methods of clinical assessment? (2) How does the skilled clinician do the job—that is, by what process does he put together the data he gathers in order to reach his conclusions?

The first of the questions has certain subquestions, some of which have already been addressed in Chapter 8:
a. Are clinical psychologists better at this kind of assessment than some others not specially trained for the purpose (for example, physical scientists)?
b. Is the more experienced clinical psychologist (that is, the practicing professional) more skilled at it than the less experienced (for example, the psychological intern)?
c. Can the clinical psychologist's skill at assessment be improved by training?

Similarly, question 2 has subquestions as well:
a. Is it possible to describe objectively (even to quantify) the process by which the clinical psychologist reaches his conclusions and makes his predictions?
b. Can one "simulate" the process by, for example, feeding data into a computer and instructing it to make clinical decisions by means of a computer program derived from the manifest behavior of a live clinician?
c. Is it possible to devise mathematical models that represent the way in which the average clinician combines his data in reaching conclusions?

The Prediction of Behavior

For some years, clinicians like Paul Meehl ("When shall we use our heads instead of the formula?," 1957) have been speculating about, writing on, and making analyses of just such questions, while others have come to conclusions of their own. There are the loyalists, who point proudly to studies validating the clinician's skill, and the cynics, who chuckle when clinical psychology is found wanting. Most psychologists are, fortunately, some place in the middle, feeling their efforts will be vindicated by results but at the same time viewing with interest those findings that point up shortcomings or purport to show how the average clinician goes about the process of psychological assessment.

As Goldberg (1968) points out, many studies underscore the effectiveness of clinical prediction. Psychologists in World War II achieved considerable recognition for the way they improved on techniques previously in use for predicting success as an airplane pilot (Holtzman & Sells, 1954). Similarly, psychologists have been able to predict how well a patient would respond to such treatment as electroshock therapy (Winslow & Rapersand, 1964). More recently, good examples of the effectiveness of clinical prediction are to be found in the highly efficient job psychologists have been doing in selecting candidates for the Peace Corps (Goldberg, 1966).

On the other hand, evidence is all too abundant that the batting average of clinical psychologists is often much lower than they would like it to be. Again, Goldberg cites examples (Marks, 1961; Watley, 1967; Ringuette & Kennedy, 1966).

Interestingly, the granddaddy of all such studies (Kelly & Fiske, 1951) — the effort to predict which novices in training would later turn out to be good clinical psychologists — wound up with a frank admission that such prediction was not possible with any degree of confidence despite the fact that the investigators had "thrown the book at" the subjects by having them take an extensive battery of their own tests.

It is a healthy sign that it is largely clinical psychologists themselves who undertake the studies designed to evaluate how good (or poor) a job they are doing, to get a clearer picture of how they go about it, and, above all, to improve on their performance. For example, Goldberg and his associates at the Oregon Research Institute have had a special continuing interest in "modeling" the process by which the clinician arrives at his judgments. Does he look for certain cues and then weight each of them according to some *linear* equation, attaching the greatest weight, let us say, to cue number one, less to cue two, and least to cue three? Or does he use the cues in a *curvilinear* way — that is, predicting that persons who score either very high or very low on a certain test would not be suited for a certain job (for example, frogman in the navy) while those scoring in the middle range would do well? Or does he possibly combine his cues in an *interactive* or *configural* way, attaching much weight to cue number one if cue number two is present, but attaching little weight to cue one if cue two is absent?

Ask the clinician himself, and he may well feel he reaches his formulations in a fairly complicated way. While not denying the possibility, Goldberg (1968) chose to begin with a simple representation of the clinical process (that is, a linear rather than curvilinear or interactive model), being prepared to make the model more complicated, should this prove necessary. Thus, he tried to represent the clinical process in a form that read:

$$Z = b_1 X_1 + b_2 X_2 \cdots + b_k X_k$$

To be sure, such a lifeless equation seems at first blush a very synthetic way of representing the manner in which a flesh-and-blood clinician makes his predictions about another human being. Sentiment aside, however, the same clinician might find it interesting to discover how he really operates, if this were possible. In simple mathematical language, then, the above equation suggests that a particular clinician looks for various cues and attaches characteristic values to them. Cue X_1, for example, may be how freely the person relates to him; X_2 may represent the person's premorbid history (that is, how well or poorly he had adjusted up to the present); and so on through the ultimate cue (X_k) the particular clinician may utilize in his predictions.

The cues sought may well differ from clinician to clinician, as would the weights attached to them. Thus, for clinician A, cue X_1 (social responsiveness, let us say) may count a lot—its weight (b_1) would be high; clinician B, on the other hand, may weight its significance less. Similarly, whatever the cues, weights b_1 through b_k would vary from clinician to clinician; what seems very important to one might well seem to be of only average importance to another.

It is understandable that if clinicians themselves are asked how they reach their judgments, they are confident they behave in a more complex and elaborate fashion than a linear equation would indicate. They like to feel their approach is configural (as defined earlier). But, Goldberg pointed out, research studies have indicated that the linear model "... appeared to characterize quite adequately the judgmental processes involved" (p. 488).

So that he would not be oversimplifying the situation, Goldberg had considered three hypotheses, namely that:

(a) human judges behave in fact remarkably like linear data processors, but somehow they believe that they are more complex than they really are; (b) human judges behave in fact in a rather configural fashion, but the power of the linear regression model is so great that it serves to obscure the real configural processes in judgment; (c) human judges behave in fact in a decidedly linear fashion on most judgmental tasks (their reports notwithstanding), but for some kinds of tasks they use more complex judgmental processes (p. 488).

Nevertheless, on the basis of available evidence to date, he concludes that hypothesis (b) "... is, at this point, certainly the most compelling one." He goes on to add:

> While Meehl (1959) has suggested that one potential superiority of the clinician over the actuary lies in the human's ability to process cues in a configural fashion, it is important to realize that this is neither an inherent advantage of the human judge (i.e., the actuary can include nonlinear terms in his equations), nor is this attribute—in any case—likely to be the clinician's ace in the hole. If the clinician does have a long suit—and the numerous clinical versus statistical studies have not yet demonstrated that he has—it is extremely unlikely that it will stem from his alleged ability to process information in a complex configural manner (p. 491).

In fairness, Goldberg suggests that the process of clinical inference, like everything else, should be improvable through training, so that the judgments of clinicians can become more accurate, more valid, more refined, and perhaps more elaborate. In this effort, he suggests, training and research must go hand in hand.

It is this willingness to look at how one operates that characterizes the true behavioral scientist and distinguishes the clinician from the intelligent layman who fancies himself a sensitive observer. But while such methodological dilemmas remain to be resolved, there are also quandaries of another sort—those carrying ethical implications—which haunt the clinician at work. We look next at some representative ethical concerns.

Extracurricular Problems of Prediction

Let the U.S. Bureau of the Census ask citizens such questions as how many showers members of the family take per week and public indignation mounts in a hurry. If such factual information is considered a private matter, one can appreciate the consternation that attends being asked to answer "True," "False," or "Don't know" to such statements as "I go to church every week" or "I like to kiss attractive persons of the opposite sex." These happen to be two items from the 550-item Minnesota Multiphasic Personality Inventory, cited by a member of the House of Representatives Special Subcommittee on Invasion of Privacy (1965). His reaction can be judged by the following remarks made after his exchange with the administrator of a federal agency who defended the use of psychological tests in reaching personnel decisions:

> I will tell you what: I am impressed to the point where if the House were still in session today, and I don't think they are in session, I am prepared to offer a bill on Monday to prohibit the giving of psychological tests by any Federal agency, under any circumstances, at any place, and to make it a Federal crime for any Federal official to do it. That is how much I am impressed by the violation of privacy in the testimony we have had. Thank you, Mr. Chairman (p. 982).

It is important to note, however, that some witnesses appearing before a comparable committee of the Senate took an equally dim view of psychological tests. A prominent psychologist among them, K. U. Smith (1965), Professor of Industrial Psychology at the University of Wisconsin, put it this way:

> The American people have been fooled into believing that a few simple-minded, true-false or multiple-choice questions can be used to forecast the careers of the children in school and in the university, and to predict their own careers in work, because of two influences: fear of the pseudo-quantitative mental-medical mumbo jumbo of the psychiatrist and clinical psychologist, and the misleading propaganda of organized psychology in claiming that guesswork and statistical shotgun procedures have medical and scientific significance (p. 911).[6]

The profession itself was not simply reacting to the concern of others; it had long before been cognizant of the responsibilities of the test developer and user and had painstakingly developed and published a code intended to promote high standards in the development of tests and observance of ethical considerations in their use. A few excerpts from the *Standards* will help the reader appreciate the thought psychologists themselves have given the subject.

Standards for Educational and Psychological Tests and Manuals

Tests are hardly to be regarded as psychic divining rods to be used with impunity. The *Standards* (1966) make this point clear: "The test manual should state implicitly the purposes and applications for which the test is recommended. . . . The

---

[6] The reader who may wish a full account of the lively testimony before the congressional committees will find that a full issue of the *American Psychologist* (November 1965) was devoted to the panorama of views on the issue of "Testing and Public Policy." It would also be helpful to consult the *Standards for Educational and Psychological Tests and Manuals* (1966) developed and codified by a committee of the American Psychological Association, an earlier version of which appeared in 1954, long before congressional and public ire had been stirred.

test manual should indicate the qualifications required to administer the test and to interpret it properly" (p. 10).

Written for sophisticated readers (that is, those with training in education or psychology to at least a level between the master's and doctoral degree), the *Standards* spell out a long series of principles and their corollaries as guides to test users and test developers. Included is everything from a detailed description of what should be in the manual accompanying each test to such important test features as reliability and validity, the norms on which the test was standardized, procedures for administering and scoring the test, and scales used for reporting scores.

Further, the *Standards* make it clear that the profession takes its responsibilities seriously: "Almost any test can be useful for some functions and in some situations, but even the best test can have damaging consequences if used inappropriately. Therefore, primary responsibility for improvement of testing rests on the shoulders of test users" (p. 6).

So that these ideals may have some force, the code of ethics developed by the American Psychological Association deals explicitly with the issues.

Ethical Standards of Psychologists

"The psychologist believes in the dignity and worth of the individual human being." These are the opening words of the *Ethical Standards of Psychologists* (1963), the code that covers virtually all aspects of the psychologist's professional activities. Included, among others, are principles (and corollaries) relating to the maintenance of confidentiality in the interest of client welfare, precautions to be observed in research, rules governing the rendering of clinical services, and other features of the psychologist's responsibilities. In this interest, several principles deal with tests and their proper use:

> *Principle 13. Test Security.* Psychological tests and other assessment devices, the value of which depends in part on the naiveté of the subject, are not reproduced or described in popular publications in ways that might invalidate the techniques. Access to such devices is limited to persons with professional interests who will safeguard their use . . . (p. 59).
>
> *Principle 14. Test Interpretation.* Test scores, like test materials, are released only to persons who are qualified to interpret and use them properly . . . (p. 59).
>
> *Principle 15. Test Publication.* Psychological tests are offered for commercial publication only to publishers who present their tests in a professional way and distribute them only to qualified users . . . (p. 59).

Perhaps the injunctions contained in the code and the technical requirements set forth in the *Standards* will by now have combined to assure the reader that the psychologist, as well as the public, is concerned about the ethics of his profession. The reader will probably find a new set of disturbing thoughts, however, as we move into the next chapter "The Control of Behavior." Here, too, voices have been raised in protest; but here again psychologists themselves have been among the first to be concerned that each proceed with great respect for the dignity and worth of the individual human being.

The Prediction of Behavior

13
The Control of Behavior

For professional purposes it does not seem out of order to try to predict the behavior of a person, particularly when that person's behavior could have consequences for others. If young men are being selected for the diplomatic service, for example, one might well wish for a trustworthy measure of their ability to tolerate frustration, their capacity for performing under stress, their resistance to getting drunk (at future embassy parties), and other relevant characteristics. But articles like "The Tyranny of Testing" (Hoffman, 1962) and a host of other publications leave little doubt that there is considerable public concern, if not consternation, about decisions made on the basis of psychological tests. Given such reactions to the attempted prediction of behavior, it is little wonder that others find the *control* of behavior still more awesome a prospect.

Whatever satisfaction it may afford, the fact is that at this point the mental health professions are far from able to control the mind of man. As will be evident in the following sections, therapists struggle manfully just to help clients learn to live a little more comfortably. Yet as greater sophistication is reached through research, and as practice becomes more effective in implementing theory, the notion of being able to control behavior by psychological means becomes less farfetched. In the area of chemotherapy that day is already here, as thousands of psychotic patients are made more "manageable" through the use of tranquilizing drugs, while other thousands of neurotics keep functioning on the job with the help of antidepressants. When the medium of control becomes a psychological one, however, various social and philosophical issues become at once apparent.

The Issues

In a celebrated debate (1956) some years ago, Rogers and Skinner, two psychologists of comparable stature but divergent views, expressed some contrasting ideas on issues surrounding the control of human behavior.

Skinner, whose novel *Walden Two* described life in an "engineered" society planned and developed systematically by behavioral scientists, was concerned less with the dangers of control than with those of planlessness. Rogers, wary of scientists' temptation to jump into the breach, was more concerned with recognizing the costs of such intervention. As he put it: "We can choose to use the behavioral sciences in ways which will free, not control" (p. 1064). To which Skinner responded: "What Rogers seems to me to be proposing . . . is this: Let us use our increasing power of control to create individuals who will not need and perhaps will no longer respond to control. Let us solve the problem of our power by removing it. At first blush this seems to be as implausible as a benevolent despot" (p. 1065).

Rogers' set of values, as enunciated, included ". . . man as a process of becoming, as a process of achieving worth and dignity through the development of his potentialities; the individual human being as a self-actualizing process, moving on to more challenging and enriching experiences; the process by which the individual creatively adapts to an ever-new and changing world . . ." (p. 1063). Skinner finds Rogers' values understandable but unconvincing. He replies:

> What evidence is there that a client ever becomes truly *self*-directing? . . . Even though the psychologist does not do the choosing, even though he encourages "self-actualization"—he has not ceased to control as long as he holds himself ready to step in when occasion demands—when, for example, the client chooses the goal of becoming a more accomplished liar or murdering his boss. . . . The therapeutic situation is only a small part of the world of the client. From the therapist's point of view it may appear to be possible to relinquish control. But the control passes, not to a "self," but to forces in other parts of the client's world (p. 1065).

The reader who wishes the full treatment of pros and cons can turn to the original debate and decide for himself who, if anyone, has won the duel. In any case, the foregoing dialogue serves as a fitting backdrop against which to view a variety of efforts to modify behavior.

Psychotherapeutic Approaches

Anyone who gets his knowledge of psychotherapy from the *New Yorker* may well have developed the notion that the process consists of someone lying on a couch saying strange things to a strange-looking psychoanalyst, who is perhaps saying equally strange things in return. Cartoons, like caricatures, have a way of making their point by exaggerating some of the features of a situation at the expense of others. Suffice it to say that not all, or even most, psychoanalysts are bearded men with Viennese accents; nor do all therapists use a couch; and it is not a funny business.

It is, though, a complicated business. Schools of therapy are about as numerous as schools of painting—and probably as controversial. Interestingly, all of them get results. People come to Therapist *A* with problems that seem to them insuperable; nine months later they feel better. Meanwhile, Therapist *B,* who practices another brand of psychotherapy, is "curing" his own set of clients. So are Therapists *C* through *Z*. What interests the behavioral scientist is that, although the several types of psychotherapy seem so different, apparently all of them work!

Consider for a moment the flavor of each of the following transactions between therapist and client. Each originates with the same statement by the client but then soon travels its own distinctive route.

Therapy A
Client: That reminds me of when I was a little girl.
Therapist: Makes you feel kind of small and helpless.
C: Yes, like here I am so weak—and everyone else is so, so—
T: Powerful.
C: Exactly!
T: Mm hm.

Therapy B
Client: That reminds me of when I was a little girl.
Therapist: *Are* you a little girl?
C: No, but it reminds me of it!
T: But *are* you a little girl?
C: No, but—
T: How old are you?
C: Thirty.
T: Then you are *not* a little girl.
C: OK, I'm *not*!! [grumpily]

Therapy C
Client: That reminds me of when I was a little girl.
Therapist: In what way?
C: My father used to tease me all the time too.
T: Oh?
C: Yes, he always seemed to want to make me angry.
T: And what was your reaction?

C: I'd cry instead.
T: A trick for getting him to feel guilty maybe?
C: Well, maybe.

Therapy D
Client: That reminds me of when I was a little girl.
Therapist: Sopping up all the do's and don'ts.
C: Yes, probably.
T: The same kind of thing you hound yourself with now all the time—"I *must* do this"; "I *mustn't* do that."
C: It seems that way.
T: Hounding yourself all the time with a lot of moralistic nonsense that belongs back in the 1920's—instead of saying: "Heck, I'm entitled to my fling just like the next!"
C: That's so true.

The reader will doubtless agree that these four samples of just a few of the possible approaches are rather different in character. In *A* the therapist attempts to resonate to how the client feels, neither approving nor disapproving, nor leading her, questioning her, or interpreting possible hidden meanings. Therapist *B,* who is much more active, makes almost a frontal attack on what he sees as an issue. Although Therapist *C* behaves in a similar fashion, he and *B* differ in that, while *C* is quite willing to use past history as a clue to what is going on in the client's life at present, *B* feels that to talk about the past is simply to duck the real issue of present problems. Therapist *D* goes his own way, apparently feeling that maladjustment has its roots in meaningless taboos picked up earlier, which now are an unnecessary albatross around the client's neck. The sooner she learns this, the better, according to him; hence, he misses no opportunity to point out how the client is tying herself in moralistic knots.

To ask which of these (or yet other) approaches to psychotherapy is the best is to cloud the issue. None of them sprang full-blown from someone's brow; each has a plausible rationale. The behavioral scientist asks other kinds of questions. Can behavior be changed through talking with another person—in a particular way and in a unique relationship? If so, can we back off from the problem to consider the range of alternatives available? Can we classify the various approaches so as to make the psychotherapeutic relationship conceptually comprehensible? Let us look at the problem from these perspectives.

What can a therapist do? He can reassure, advise, preach, admonish, cajole, empathize, simply listen—in short, most of the things one human being can do with another. To bring some kind of order out of the possibilities, we might try stringing them out along a continuum—for example, from the extreme of unabashedly prescribing the client's course of action to the other extreme of being totally noncommittal. Such a dimension of therapist behavior might then be scaled somewhat as follows:

- Lecture: "You can't expect *all* the attention *all* the time!"
- Advise: "It would be good for you to join a church group."
- Encourage: "Why not try it once?"
- Reassure: "You'll feel better as we go on."
- Empathize: "I can imagine it's pretty rough on you now."
- Re-echo: "If I understand you correctly, you're saying you would rather wait to make a decision."
- Listen: "Mm hm."

If the student of clinical psychology wishes to retain his sanity as he reads a book by Rogers (1961), another by Ellis (1962), a third by Berne (1964), and so on, he is well advised to try to work out a conceptual scheme of his own by which to decode what might otherwise sound like a babble of tongues talking different languages at cross-purposes. Let us, therefore, consider some representative reference points, but merely by way of illustration, for the reader is strongly encouraged to define the area in the ways most meaningful to himself as he becomes more familiar with it.

Simply by looking at the short illustrative exchanges quoted previously, we might get the notion that one significant dimension could be the degree to which the therapist directs the interaction. Therapist *B* assumes an active role; therapist *A* studiously avoids taking over. It might be meaningful, then, as we study the major therapies now in vogue, to think of a dimension ranging like this:

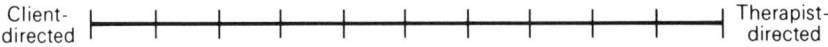

The idea makes some intuitive sense, enough at least to encourage us to speculate about other dimensions that might help differentiate one brand of therapy from another. How about noting that one therapist (*C*) seems to seize the opportunity to get the client to talk about the past, while another therapist (*B*) seems to nip such references in the bud? We might reasonably conclude (and, indeed, the writings of the respective therapists would state as much) that for therapist *C* references to the past constitute significant material for understanding the client's present behavior, the genesis of which is, so far as this therapist is concerned, very important. Therapist B, on the other hand, might state frankly that talking about the past is actually the client's way of avoiding getting down to the real problems of the present, that it is a dodge which the client uses consciously or unconsciously. While therapist C encourages such talk, therapist B cuts it short.

Who is right? As in many other areas, the better question is whether each of the schools can offer a suitable rationale for proceeding as it does. In any case, it would seem as though a conceptual model that could encompass the various approaches must take into account another dimension—a time dimension—that reflects where the therapist feels interaction should primarily be directed. Again, it is conceivable that some therapists would place considerable emphasis on the past, and others on the here and now, while still others feel that a perspective on the future is more important than either. At any rate, one might therefore see the need for at least a two-dimensional schema, such as the one shown in Figure 1, for the representation of the various therapies.

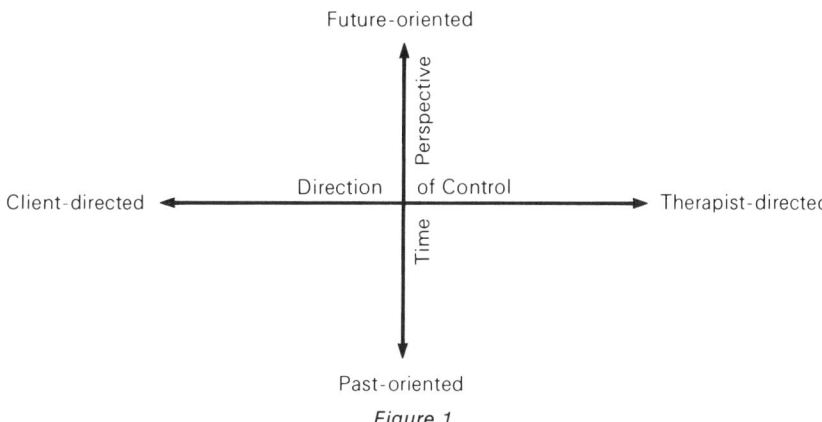

Figure 1

There are sophisticated statistical procedures for building such representations of conceptual space in which to plot the many therapies that exist, of which most (if not all) presumably share certain characteristics with others. Thus, by the methodology of factor analysis[1], we could arrive more systematically at the smallest set of relevant dimensions (factors) that would enable us to account for most of the difference (variance) among the many therapies. But we are at this point attempting to

---

[1] See Kelly, *Assessment of Human Characteristics*, 1967, pp. 32–34.

develop habits of hypothesizing about clinical theory and practice in our own way, in order to have them become as meaningful as possible for us. Let us assume, then, that in proceeding in this more rudimentary intuitive fashion we conclude that yet another dimension is needed. We observe, for example, that in some types of therapy the client and therapist are content to interact in purely verbal terms; that is, they sit and talk (or the client lies on a couch) hour after hour, the focus being largely on the words that pass between them (Greenson, 1967). Another school of therapy (Perls et al., 1951), however, repeatedly draws attention to the client's nonverbal behavior—the fact that he sits rigidly, seems to scowl without realizing it, constantly plays with his ear lobe, and so on. In fact, this same school, insisting that motoric behavior is as important as verbal behavior, actually arranges for the client to perform bodily exercises as part of psychotherapy—breathing deeply, clenching his fists, pounding a sofa cushion. Still another school (G. A. Kelly, 1955) insists that psychotherapy consists of, or at least requires as part of its procedure, having the client actually *practice* certain aspects of behavior in real life, with the therapy sessions being used to discuss the problems that arise as the client experiences the inevitable frustrations of learning more effective patterns of behavior.

We see, then, that here is a third dimension that might help plot the several therapies in some meaningful conceptual space. We now scan the psychological radar screen on which we have located blips 1 through 6, the major therapies we have heard and read about. If the reader can visualize (see Figure 2) the third dimension—motor involvement—rising up out of the page at right angles (dotted line) to the plane in which the other two dimensions intersect, and if he will recall the various approaches

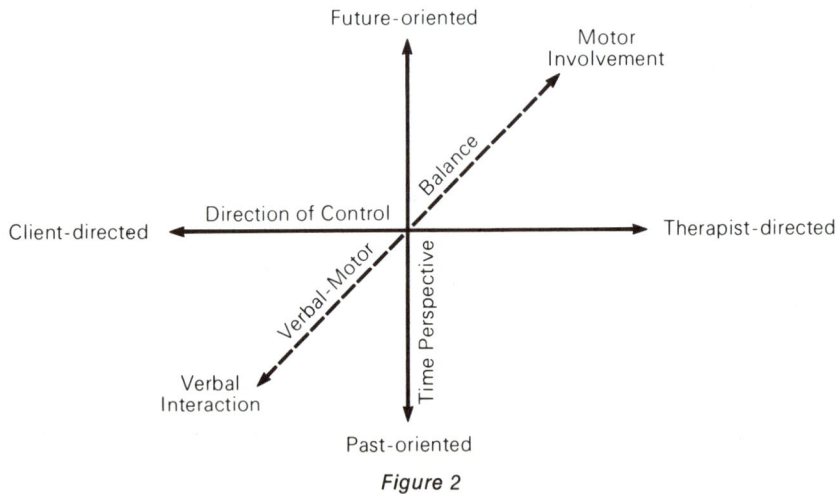

Figure 2

he knows about, then he may find himself plotting these approaches within the conceptual space in the way that is most meaningful to him.

There is no magic in the particular schema of Figure 2. There is, however, an important process represented—namely the propensity of the good clinician for thinking theoretically about his practices. Surely there are at least a dozen (perhaps a hundred) ways in which one can carry on the process called therapy. It takes no great imagination to think of a new way to do it. A group of well-read laymen brainstorming for a half hour might come up with three creative suggestions worth considering. What marks the clinician is his ability to evaluate whether Procedure 22 is (a) grounded in a respectable theoretical foundation and (b) consonant with some broad psychological principles. What characterizes the good clinician even more is his desire to submit his ideas to empirical test, letting the findings decide the issues. He takes faint hunches, turns them into testable hypotheses, and hopes that they will grow to become robust theories.

Suppose now that our inquisitive, intellectually restless, truth-seeking clinician is trying to bring some psychological order out of the chaos that seems to prevail as the advocates of six approaches to psychotherapy argue it out. As he listens, he hears some proclaiming that insight is crucial to change, others (Hobbs, 1962) arguing that it is incidental (or epiphenomenal). Some therapists talk about the importance of getting at the unconscious factors influencing behavior; others insist that one must stick to the analysis of purely conscious behavior. Again, some feel that one must look to the past, get back to the origins of the client's problems; others feel that one needs to focus on the client's aspirations (or lack of them), his perception of the future, and so on.

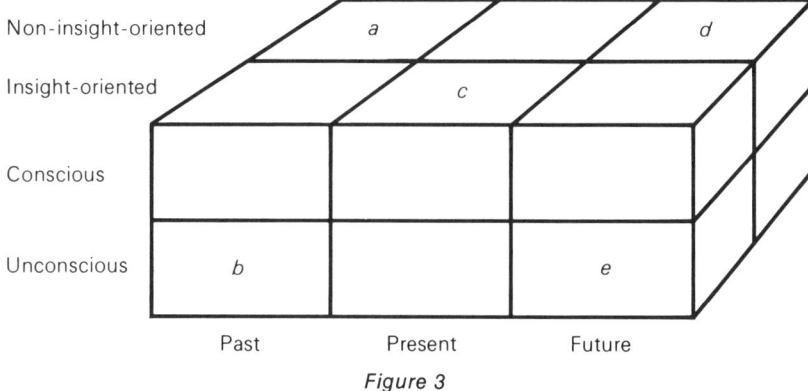

Figure 3

How can we represent such diverse points of view, each espoused by competent, effective clinicians? Perhaps as shown in Figure 3.

If the reader wants to slice the therapeutic pie in other ways, that is fine; the complicated business of psychotherapy cannot be digested if swallowed whole. The student of clinical psychology needs to be in the habit of carving the fare into a form conceptually appealing and intellectually assimilable.

There is no end of such food for thought. Clinical psychology is not learned in a professional school; it is a way of scientific life, an endless asking of questions that lend themselves to exploration in theory, implementation in practice, and confirmation or disconfirmation in research. How can it be, for example, the clinician must ask himself, that approaches to psychotherapy which, at least phenotypically, look so different all seem to be effective (perhaps even equally effective)? Is it that therapists of the different schools draw different populations of patients? In that case, the situation would look like this:

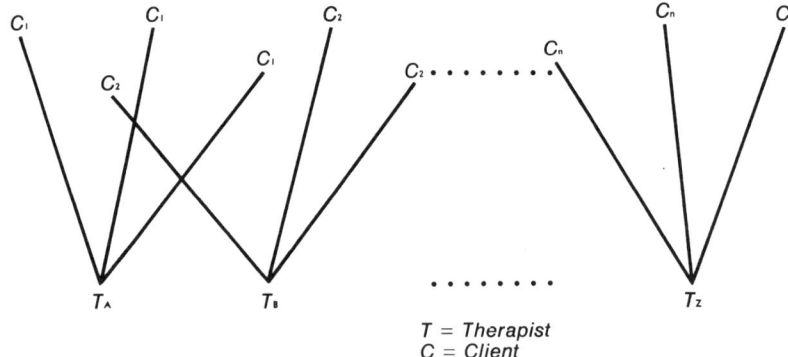

T = Therapist
C = Client

If, indeed, Therapist A (T_A) has clients (C_1) of a type different from those of Therapist B (who has C_2 types), an explanation for the success of such seemingly different approaches is at hand.

Or is it the case that the several schools of therapy treat clients from the same general population but get results because they have in common a basic characteristic (despite differences in technique) that is ultimately responsible for successful outcome in treatment? If so, the situation would look like this:

That is to say, one might speculate that, while phenotypically the various approaches (A, B, . . . Z) look very different, genotypically they share a certain characteristic (x) — perhaps the accepting attitude of the therapist or the conviction of the client that he will improve — that is basically responsible for a successful treatment outcome. Such a line of speculation assumes, of course, that we have a valid measure of outcome and, especially, that the several schools of therapy are agreed on what constitutes a successful outcome. Of course, if each defines a "cure" differently, then we have a problem of another sort. In any case, there is still room for conjecture and research, lest the process of psychotherapy remain more mysterious than it needs to be.

This discussion is not intended as an "answer" to anything. It *is* intended as an article of faith — namely, that the only good clinician is a thinking clinician. The practitioner, no matter how skillful, is otherwise a technician, not a clinician. From a technician we expect methodical performance, from a clinician we expect inquisitive exploration. The one does the world's work today and should be amply rewarded; the other is, we hope, striving toward the better world of tomorrow.

Psychotherapists are convinced that genuine change takes time; only superficial "cures" are achieved quickly and cheaply. Their newfound colleagues in "behavior therapy" argue that, contrary to long-held but (according to them) untested beliefs, there is nothing wrong with treating symptoms per se; the symptom, they insist, *is* the neurosis. The behavior therapist therefore works at the problem directly rather than indirectly, treating symptomatology unabashedly and hoping to shorten the period of treatment while still achieving lasting results.

Behavior Modification Approaches

One of my colleagues once narrated the following incident (possibly apocryphal). A well-known psychologist of Skinnerian persuasion was participating in a day-long committee meeting. As such meetings go, this one was inordinately dull, and our psychologist participant found it quite unbearable. During some of his mind-wandering moments he noted that the committee chairman had the habit of pounding the air with his right hand as he spoke, by way of emphasizing points. What would happen, our imaginative friend wondered, if he were to reinforce the hand waving of the chairman with interested looks and nods, while gazing away or looking bored whenever the hand waving was absent? According to the story, the latter hours of the day found the chairman in an almost incessant flurry of hand waving (with our friend having at least conducted an experiment, if not having contributed much to the committee meeting).

There are similar disquieting tales of students shaping a teacher's behavior, so that, for example, the teacher, who originally had a habit of standing in the right half of the room while lecturing, gets selectively reinforced by (planned) student attention whenever he moves to the left and extinguished (by student yawns and window gazing) whenever he moves to the right. Several weeks after the beginning of the term, the unsuspecting teacher finds himself, for some reason, delivering all of his lectures while squeezed into the front left corner of the classroom.

Our interest here is hardly in the game-playing aspects of conditioning. We wish instead to dwell on the possibilities for modifying abnormal behavior—the kind with which the clinician is so frequently asked to deal—in a planned, relatively systematic way. Let us first cite some examples of the attempted modification of pathological behavior.

Modification of Abnormal Behavior

Lindsley (1961, 1962) has made a series of exploratory efforts to see what can be done to modify the behavior of severely disturbed mental patients. A paraphrase of one of his accounts will illustrate an attempt to develop cooperation or competition among patients who had otherwise shown little responsiveness to others.

Take Patient A, for example. In the hospital for many years, he tends to stay by himself virtually all the time, perhaps sitting in a corner or lying on the floor. However, he did exhibit a willingness to respond in some experimental sessions in which he had the opportunity to receive pieces of candy as reinforcement for pulling a plunger on the laboratory apparatus. Let us say that on a "fixed ratio" schedule of reinforcement (15 pulls required for 1 piece of candy) he earned 12 pieces in 5 minutes. Let us assume a similar patient from another ward showed the same behavior, again remarkable in that such activity seemed incongruous in a patient who otherwise led a solitary, apathetic existence.

According to Lindsley, such reinforcement can be used to good advantage in modifying the behavior of the patients in a desired direction—for example, in promoting their willingness to cooperate with others. For the purpose, one might set up a situation in which both patients are able to earn reinforcements (candy in this instance, since both have been shown to work for it), but only under conditions in which they cooperate. The apparatus can be programmed (that is, arranged to function) in such a way that, if Patient *A* pulls his lever and Patient *B* follows by pulling his in one-half second or less (or vice versa), both receive a candy reinforcement. If, however, either pulls his lever and the other does not follow suit within one-half second, neither is reinforced. What happens? Cooperative behavior has a chance to develop, according to Lindsley. Admittedly it has a materialistic base, but it represents, at the very least, responsiveness to the behavior of another.

If it is felt that real life demands the ability to compete as well, Lindsley's procedure can handle that contingency too. Now we would simply program the apparatus so that if *A* pulls his plunger and *B* fails to pull his own within one-half second, *A* gets the candy; if *B* pulls his in time, *B* gets it (but not *A*). The reverse situation obtains if *B* pulls his first. The trick now is to catch one's partner off guard, since only one of the two can receive the reinforcement. What happens, Lindsley finds, is that under such an arrangement competitive behavior can be developed, in the same way that cooperative behavior was developed.

These simple demonstrations are not intended as quaint illustrations by the behavior modifiers but rather as evidence that, given enough ingenuity on the part of the professional people in charge, what we know about principles of learning may well be put to systematic use in the elimination of undesirable behavior and the cultivation of desirable behavior in its place. (The terms "desirable" and "undesirable" are admittedly value-laden. We will assume, for the sake of discussion, that society can agree in these matters and that its judgment is "right"—although that too can be debated.) Hence, if a given patient is in the habit of stuffing materials (such as magazines) into his clothing, so that, over the course of the last year, he has carried around an average of thirty magazines per day, one might well regard such behavior as undesirable, especially if the patient rarely reads them. If nothing else, it denudes the ward library, depriving other patients of reading matter.

In one such study (Ayllon & Michael, 1959), the investigators concerned themselves with the reduction or elimination of such behavior as the hoarding of magazines by mental patients. They noted at the outset that such behavior did not escape the attention of the nursing staff. Indeed, the nurses were very consistent in attending to the patients, remonstrating with them to desist from hoarding, and, in fact, "dejunking" them periodically. The fact that the behavior persisted suggested to Ayllon and Michael that such scolding, rather than being aversive, might actually be reinforcing. In other words, it was conceivable that the constant attention from the staff was the very factor that maintained the behavior they wished to eliminate. What to do?

Two procedures were invoked—stimulus satiation and extinction. Ayllon and Michael wanted first to be sure the patients' behavior was not an understandable reaction to magazine shortage. If the ward contained very few magazines, it might be sensible (if not nice) to hoard them. Hence, the experimenters flooded the ward with magazines before the start of the experimental project. That is, stimulus satiation was accomplished.

The nurses on the ward were instructed as follows: "During this program the patients ... must not be given reinforcement (attention) for hoarding. There will be a full supply of magazines in the dayroom. Every night, after all patients have gone to bed, check their clothes to record the amount of hoarding. Do not, however, take their hoarding from them" (p. 332). This, then, was the extinction procedure.

The dependent variable—that is, the measure of the effect of the experimental program—was to be the number of magazines hoarded by the patients over a period of time. The results for two of the patients are pictured in Figure 4.

According to the experimenters, "The results for all patients were essentially similar: a gradual decrease in hoarding. After 9 weeks of satiation and extinction, the program was terminated, since hoarding was no longer a problem. This improvement has been maintained for the last 6 months" (p. 332).

The issue might well be raised, as it was by one of the nurses, that "behavior has its roots in the personality of the individual. The fact that he hoards so much indicates that Harry has a strong need for security. I don't see how we are going to change this need, and I also wonder if it is a good thing to do that" (p. 332).

To this, Ayllon and Michael reply: "It would seem in this case that Harry transferred his security needs from hoarding rubbish and magazines to sitting in the dayroom

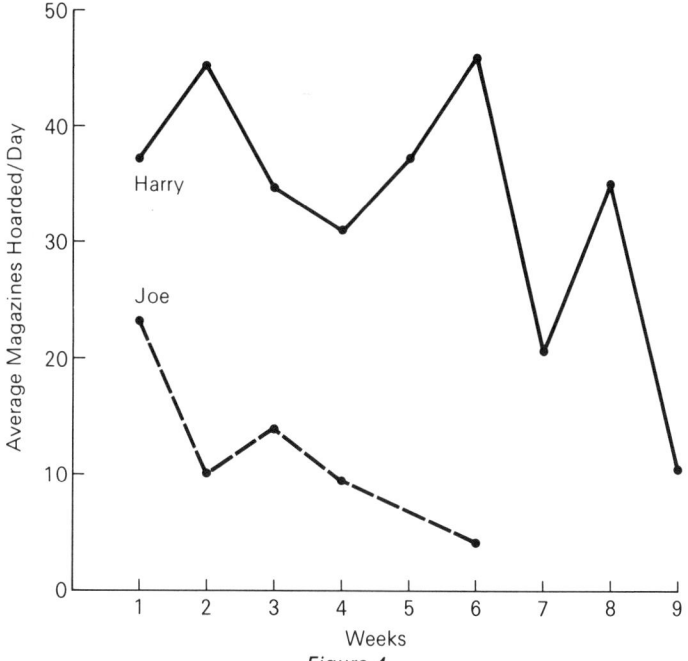

Figure 4
Change in magazine hoarding behavior as a function of satiation and extinction. (Adapted from Figure 5 of Ayllon and Michael, 1959. Copyright 1959 by the *Journal of Experimental Analysis of Behavior* and reproduced by permission.)

and looking at magazines, especially during TV commercials. The transfer occurred with no apparent signs of discomfort on his part" (pp. 332–333).[2]

By way of bringing the problem closer to home, we now turn to the efforts of the behavior therapists in dealing with the problems of people like ourselves—those we like to call "normal."

Modification of "Normal" Behavior

Ironically enough, the mental health professions may know more about abnormal behavior than about normal behavior, more about pathology than about adjustment.

---

[2] The reader may judge the pros and cons for himself. To do so properly, you will need to become acquainted with and evaluate the broad array of efforts being launched in the behavior therapy area. The great bulk of the literature can be found in two journals—*Behaviour Research and Therapy* and the *Journal of Applied Behavior Analysis*, although a number of other journals (as well as books) consistently carry latest developments in this field.

The situation is not unlike that in medicine, where it is sometimes facetiously said that the common cold still baffles the profession, but, should the patient have tuberculosis, the physician knows exactly what to do.

Few of us will probably ever experience delusions and hallucinations, but many of us will suffer what may seem equally intractable problems—inability to stop smoking, habitual overeating, possibly even a tendency to fight with one's wife. It is to the credit of behavior therapists that they have given considerable attention to the modification of such behavior. From a conventional standpoint, their methods seem at best unorthodox, and even peculiar. Let us look at some of their efforts and the results they have reported.

Breaking the Smoking Habit

Repeating a familiar point, Franks, Fried, and Ashem (1966) underscore the assumption that "irrespective of the question of physiological addiction or social pressures, a 'voluntary' act which provides an average of some 60,000 reinforcing puffs in each year of the subject's smoking life may well be a directly learned habit. The implications are that this habit will be amenable to extinction by appropriate procedures and that the resistance to such extinction will be considerable" (p. 302).

The "appropriate procedures" chosen by Franks et al. relied on aversive conditioning. Using the apparatus pictured in Figure 5 to dispense aversive reinforcing stimuli, the experimenters arranged the situation so that the subject sat in front of an aperture that could deliver either cigarette smoke or fresh air into his face. Mounted on the apparatus was a conveniently placed ashtray which, when a cigarette was stubbed out in it, operated a microswitch that would cut off delivery of the aversive stimulus (smoke) and start delivery of fresh air, the stimulus that was to reinforce the act of putting out a cigarette.

After the subjects had completed a personality inventory and been interviewed, the procedure was as follows:[3]

> The subject was then asked to leave the room briefly to allow time for six lighted cigarettes to be placed in the smoke chamber and the window fan set to run for 60 seconds. The subject was then brought back . . . , seated in front of the machine. . . . He was also told that he would be required to smoke in his normal fashion and preferably inhaling the brand of cigarettes of his choice. . . . The subject was shown which aperture would deliver the smoke, from where cool air would come and where the words "smoke" and "fresh air" would appear. He was instructed

[3]Copyright 1966 by Pergamon Press Ltd. Reprinted by permission of the authors and publisher.

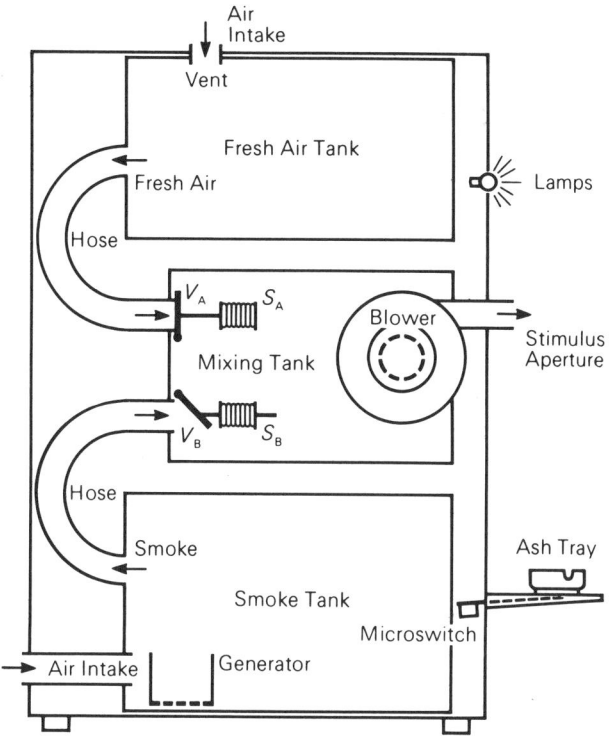

Figure 5
Apparatus used in the attempted reduction of cigarette smoking. (Figure 1 of Franks, Fried, and Ashem, 1966. Copyright 1966 by Pergamon Press Ltd. and reproduced by permission.)

to look at the word "smoke" and to continue puffing at his cigarette as long as he could bear the experience; when he could bear it no longer he was to stub out his cigarette in the special ashtray provided for him [whereupon, as mentioned above, the smoke would cease blowing in his face and be replaced by fresh air instead]. This procedure was repeated at irregular intervals, ranging from one to five minutes according to the whim of the subject, for as many as ten cigarettes per session (Franks et al., 1966, p. 305).

Of 23 smokers who had volunteered for the experiment, only nine completed the four-week program; the 14 who did not were lost for such reasons as lack of motivation, unavailability, or dislike of the method. On a six-month follow-up of the nine subjects who had completed the experiment, "four were not smoking (despite the consumption of twenty to forty a day prior to treatment), one was smoking less, two were smoking as much as ever, and one had switched to a pipe [with one subject not heard from]" (p. 306).

Powell and Azrin (1968) also attempted their own brand of therapy with cigarette smokers, using electric shock as the aversive stimulus. But, as noted in a subsequent paper (Azrin & Powell, 1968, p. 193), they found that "a major problem with using shock . . . was that very few smokers would wear the shock apparatus; those who did tended to abandon it as shock intensity was increased to the levels needed for suppression. . . ." Their conclusion: "It seemed necessary to find some other controlling event that would be effective and yet sufficiently non-aversive to permit usage by more smokers" (p. 193).

Such a controlling event, they felt, might well be built around the principle of extinction, which, while also possessing aversive properties, was much less noxious than smoke in the face or an electric shock to one's cigarette-grasping hand. Consequently, inveterate smokers would be less likely to abandon the treatment procedure before their smoking had been curtailed. Furthermore, in this instance Azrin and Powell set themselves the more modest goal of bringing the cigarette consumption of heavy smokers to the "medically safe level of about one-half of a package per day" (according to the Surgeon General's report of 1964) rather than eliminating the habit entirely.

Their apparatus was simple. A specially designed cigarette case would allow a cigarette to be taken from it, but, when released, its lid would snap shut and not be openable until a set period of time had elapsed. The time period could be predetermined, so that the case might be locked for a relatively short time (6 minutes, for example) or a relatively long time (such as 55 minutes). In this experiment, the case was originally locked for periods of only 6 minutes, about the time required to smoke one cigarette, and kept at that duration for a week in order to allow subjects to become accustomed to the apparatus.

There were further elaborations, as described by the experimenters:

> Distinctive stimuli signalled when the case was unlocked; at the moment when the case could be opened, a clicker ratchet-type noise sounded for about 0.5 sec. and a narrow rod projected about 0.25 in. from the top of the case. Additionally, a clock dial face on the side of the case showed how many minutes remained, if any, before the lid would be unlocked. . . . A non-resetable counter within the case recorded the number of times the lid was opened (Azrin & Powell, 1968, p. 195).

Subjects recorded each day the time at which they smoked their first and last cigarettes and the corresponding counter readings at both points. Their records were collected regularly by the experimenters. In addition, each subject was asked to designate one or more persons in his living and working areas who could report on any deviations from the treatment plan (for example, bumming a cigarette from someone else while one's own cigarette case was in its locked phase). The reports of these participant-observers were mailed to the experimenter daily in addressed envelopes supplied to the observers for that purpose.

The rationale for the overall procedure, as described by Azrin and Powell, was simply that "approach responses, such as reaching for the case and pushing the case lid, would be extinguished by the unavailability of the cigarettes during that period" (p. 194). The time period for which the case was locked was to be lengthened progressively by increments of no more than 5 minutes over the course of treatment, but only at the wish of the subject, who was asked every three days whether he wished the duration of the locked phase to be increased. In a control procedure, control subjects set their own durations by using a commercially available device. The durations used by the control subjects were not necessarily arranged to increase by regular increments, and the device they used did not provide any stimuli that indicated when the cigarette case was openable. In the two cases in which the commercial device was tried, it did not prove effective, as contrasted with the experimental device.

Unfortunately, as in many studies of behavior modification techniques, the number of subjects was very small—five in this case—so that the results are only suggestive. The data on these five subjects, shown in Figure 6, are nonetheless interesting.

At least in the case of the five subjects studied, the device seemed effective. As determined by the participant-observers, cases of "cheating" were almost nonexistent. Of 374 reports, only four mentioned instances of subjects smoking a cigarette obtained from a source other than his special cigarette case, and in each instance the subject had himself reported the irregularity. Each subject, then, showed significant decreases in his smoking behavior over the course of, at most, 13 weeks. True, when the investigators made "redeterminations" after the subjects had been at maximum duration for 1 to 3 weeks—that is, when they set the duration of the locked period back to 6 minutes for S–1, S–3, S–4, and S–5, and back to 30 minutes for S–2—then the incidence of smoking returned to about its original level. But the experimenters had set out neither to eliminate smoking altogether nor to free the subject from dependence on the special cigarette case. They had, instead, attempted to define a target behavior operationally (opening a cigarette case to obtain a cigarette), and they were interested in setting up certain behavioral contingencies, via the

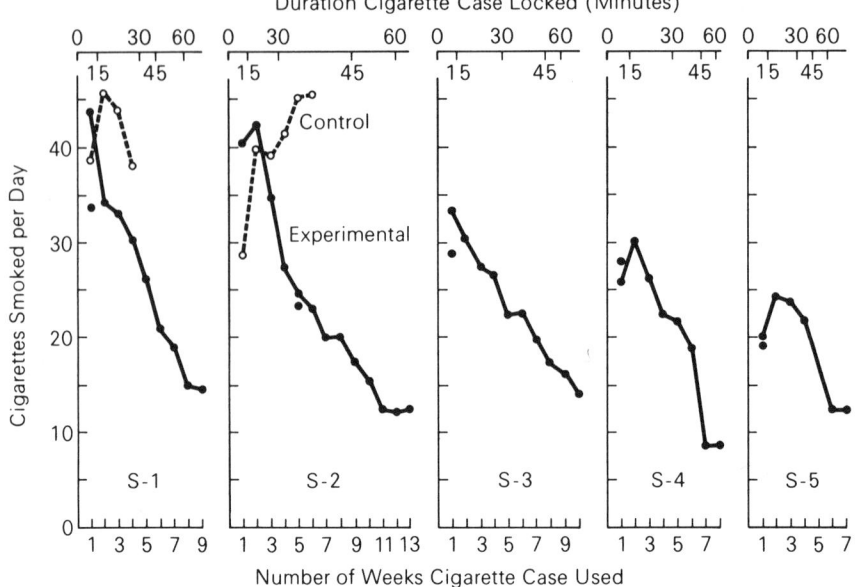

Figure 6
The number of cigarettes smoked per day while using a special cigarette case (solid circles, solid line) that locked automatically for a predetermined time after a cigarette was removed from it. Two control subjects used a control apparatus (open circles, dotted line) that required the subject himself to present the time for which the cigarette case would be locked. Each data point is a seven-day average except for the initial points, which included 4 to 10 days for different subjects. The lower horizontal axis shows the number of weeks each cigarette case was used; the upper horizontal axis shows the duration for which the experimental subjects' cigarette case was locked. The upper horizontal axis does not show the duration for which the control subjects' case was locked. The unconnected points on the graphs indicate the redeterminations. The lower of the two redetermination points for S–1 represents the first redetermination; the upper one represents a redetermination made four weeks later. (Figure 1 of Azrin & Powell, 1968. Copyright 1968 by the Society for the Experimental Analysis of Behavior, Inc., and reproduced by permission.)

mechanism of extinction, that could be programmed in an apparatus that was convenient and portable.

The results, as Azrin and Powell saw them, were that "the procedure reduced smoking for each of the subjects to one-half or less of the original rate and to the level of about 12 cigarettes per day that is considered medically safe" (p. 198). If this is considered a substantial accomplishment, and it may well be by heavy smokers, we might wonder about the applicability of behavior modification techniques to a similar addictive habit—overeating. In the experience of many otherwise normal people, this habit is equally as intractable as smoking. Let's take a look at what is happening in this area.

The Problem of Overeating

The dictum of Skinner and his followers is that behavior is controlled by its consequences. Break the particular behavior into its components, analyze the events that control its units, alter the contingencies that exist, and the behavior becomes modifiable.

As Goldiamond (1965a) put it, it helps little to urge a person who is trying to eliminate a bad habit to modify his behavior; rather, he needs to be "trained in the experimental analysis of behavior, and also in the variables which maintain it, or which he can recruit to modify it."

Stuart (1967), among others, has tried to follow this pattern to its logical conclusion in the case of overeaters, with encouraging results. A brief description of his procedure will help illustrate the conviction of behavior therapists that a habit like overeating, for which psychodynamic interpretations are readily available, may be brought under control without the subject (or therapist) having concerned himself with its underlying psychological meaning.

The initial interview that Stuart conducted with his subjects was aimed not at psychodynamic formulations of the problem but rather at (a) assessing the behavioral patterns that are centered in eating and (b) establishing a working relationship. Included in these initial procedures were Food Data Sheets that detailed the subject's eating habits and Weight Range Sheets on which the subject was instructed to record his weight at specified times during the day. Additional data secured during these interviews concerned weight-related fears (whether, for example, they were physical or social in nature) and a list of high-probability behaviors. The latter provided useful information about the kind of available behaviors that could serve as reinforcing events, for, according to "Premack's principle" (Premack, 1962), a behavior occurring with high frequency may be used as a reinforcing stimulus for a behavior occurring at lesser frequency.

With such data in hand, Stuart prescribed a straightforward "behavioral curriculum" that the subject was expected to master. Additional interviews were interspersed throughout the sequence, the better to consolidate gains and plan necessary steps in treatment. Stuart (1967) describes the procedure as follows, giving the rationale for each step:[4]

Step One: The first step in treatment, following introduction of the recording procedures, requires the patient to interrupt his meal for a predetermined period of time, usually two or three minutes, which is gradually increased to five minutes. He is instructed to put down his utensils and merely sit in his place at the table for a specified period of time.
Rationale: The logic of this maneuver is that the patient is given an early experience of control over one aspect of his eating, however small, and learns that eating is a response which can be broken down into components which can be successively mastered . . . (p. 359).

Step Two: The patient is instructed to remove food from all places in the house, other than the kitchen. He is also instructed to keep in the house only foods which require preparation. . . . *Rationale:* Much compulsive eating is "automatic," in the sense that the patient may be unaware of the fact that he is eating. If a series of actions is required prior to eating, the patient is forced to become aware of his behavior . . . (p. 360).

Step Three: The patient is instructed to make eating a "pure experience," that is, he is instructed to pair eating with no other activity, such as reading, listening to the radio, watching television, or talking on the telephone or with friends. *Rationale:* If the patient reads while he eats, he is mostly likely to want to eat while he reads . . . (p. 360).

Step Four: . . . To slow the process of ingestion, the patient is instructed to put a small amount of food in his mouth, and to replace his utensils on the table until he has swallowed. *Rationale:* This step is aimed directly at manipulation of the eating response, and success with this step is tantamount to direct control over the response. In addition to its control value, this step also helps the patient to derive more enjoyment from his food so that he can replace quantity with quality . . . (p. 361).

Step Five: The patient is instructed to engage in one of the previously identified high probability behaviors at times [between meals] when he would normally eat. . . . *Rationale:* Between-meal eating is understood to be an important source of positive reinforcement for patients who overeat. They cannot be expected to forego this reinforcement without a substitute. The substitute has inherent reinforcing value (it is a high probability behavior) and it implies the occurrence of self-control which is reinforcing . . . (p. 361).

[4]Copyright 1967 by Pergamon Press Ltd. Reprinted by permission of the author and publisher.

It should be noted again that, along with such treatment procedures, interviews are concomitantly conducted with the patient as necessary in order to "consolidate gains" and to provide "considerable discussion of ways of refining behavioral steps so as to maximize their effectiveness" (p. 362). As Stuart describes the treatment plan: "Treatment sessions are scheduled three times per week, usually last for approximately thirty minutes, and extend over a four to five week period. Subsequent sessions occur as needed, but usually at intervals of two weeks for the next twelve weeks. 'Maintenance sessions' are scheduled as needed, while follow-up sessions occur on a planned monthly basis" (p. 358).

In the present instance, two of the eight patients treated had some special difficulty with between-meal eating. For them a sixth step was included:

> *Step Six:* [This step employs] . . . the process of "coverant sensitization" [Cautela, 1966] in which the patient is trained to relax, then to imagine that he is about to indulge in a compulsion, then to imagine the occurrence of an aversive event . . . [as in the case of one patient who was instructed to imagine herself eating forbidden cookies, then to switch the image suddenly to a scene in which her husband was seducing another woman]. *Rationale:* . . . the image of a forbidden object (CS) is paired with the image of an aversive stimulus (also a CS). The imagined aversive CS then forestalls the occurrence of the forbidden CS and ultimately interferes with eating (p. 362).

It is true that only eight patients were involved in the treatment project reported by Stuart, but the results are nonetheless impressive. (See Figure 7.) In each case, the patient showed a significant reduction in weight over a 12-month period. What is more, according to Stuart, "seven of the eight patients reported having an increased range of social activities, and three of the six married patients reported more satisfying relationships with their husbands" (p. 365).

When the behavior therapist deals with helping stutterers eliminate their habit (Goldiamond, 1965b) or attempts to get mute patients to talk (Isaacs, Thomas, & Goldiamond, 1960), his efforts, though they may interest us, still seem far afield. When he begins to deal with smoking and overeating, the problems come closer to home. Perhaps this is the case too with Goldiamond's (1965a) stategy for promoting self-control, a talent of many uses that is also serviceable in maintaining marital harmony, as we shall see in the following section.

Development of Self-Control

Beware of the marriage counselor who offers to substitute bliss for unhappiness in three easy (but expensive) visits. This area attracts more than its share of quacks.

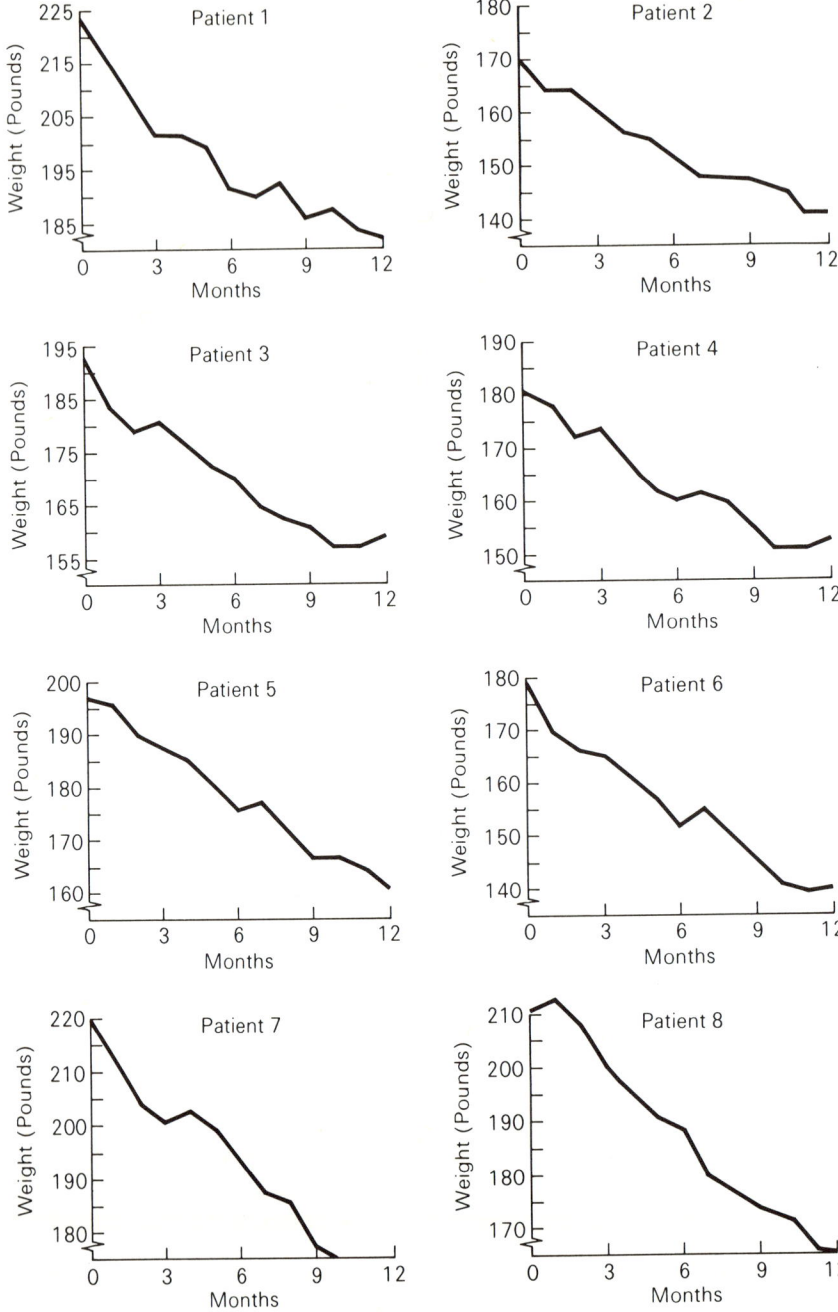

The legitimate, trained counselor makes no extravagant promises about guaranteed short-term miracles. A couple that enters psychotherapy with him can usually expect to be in treatment over a period of time. Problems which have been long in developing do not often yield to quick, prefabricated solutions. Understanding the interaction patterns of the couple involved takes time.

But suppose one were to conclude, as Goldiamond (1965a) does, that "the 'underlying' problem can still be considered as a behavioral one" (p. 852). Then a sophisticated analyst of behavior studying the contingencies that maintain the disadvantageous behavior should be able actually to help set up new contingencies that will eliminate the undesired behavior and replace it with more compatible interaction patterns. Goldiamond has tried his hand at just such situations.

An illustrative case is that of a 29-year-old husband working toward his master's degree, whose relationship with his wife alternated between yelling at her for hours at a time, subsequently feeling ashamed of himself, and lapsing into periods of sulking or brooding. This behavior pattern was of two years' standing, apparently having originated at the time his wife had committed the "ultimate betrayal"—with his best friend. Such an event would, indeed, have been grist for the mill of a skilled psychotherapist, particularly when, as it happened, the husband had urged his friend to keep his wife company while he, the husband, studied at the library. Goldiamond foreswore such interesting psychodynamic fare in order to focus on the more prosaic, but tangible, external behavior of the husband—his yelling and sulking.

Concerned with modifying such behavior, Goldiamond's treatment program comprised three phases—stimulus change, the establishment of new behavior, and stimulus control. Inasmuch as the husband's behavior furnished the stimuli which led his wife to behave in ways that made the marriage less than romantic, the first task was to provide different stimuli. Here is Goldiamond's description of this part of the treatment plan:[5]

> One of the most rapid ways to change behavior is by altering the conditions under which it usually occurs. This is called *stimulus change* or the effects of novel stimuli. If the novel stimuli are then combined with

[5]From Goldiamond, 1965a. Reprinted by permission of the author and publisher, *Psychological Reports*.

Figure 7
Weight profile of eight women undergoing behavior therapy for overeating. (Figure 1 of Stuart, 1967. Copyright 1967 by Pergamon Press Ltd. and reproduced by permission.)

new behavioral contingencies designed to produce different behavior, these contingencies are apt to generate the new behavior much more rapidly than they would in the presence of the old stimuli.

As part of the program of establishing new stimuli, S [the subject] was instructed to rearrange the use of rooms and furniture in his house to make it appear considerably different. His wife went one step further and took the occasion to buy herself a new outfit (p. 856).

The next step—establishing new behavior—consisted of the husband's actually carrying out a program discussed with the therapist, planned so that the husband and his wife would each succeeding evening find themselves in an environment (for example, eating out at a favorite restaurant) "where civilized chitchat can be maintained," in contrast to the kind of communication that had prevailed at home.

The third aspect of the treatment program—stimulus control—can be illustrated by the contingencies set up with respect to the husband's yelling and sulking. Goldiamond describes the arrangement thus:

> Since in the absence of yelling at his wife S sulked and since the program was designed to reduce yelling, S's sulking was in danger of increasing. S was instructed to sulk to his heart's content but to do so in a specified place. Whenever he felt like sulking, he was to go into the garage, sit on a special sulking stool, and sulk and mutter over the indignities of life for as long as he wished. When he was through with his sulking, he could leave the garage and join his wife (p. 857).

How successful was such a mechanical treatment plan? Figure 8 tells the story.

Arrangements with respect to romance itself were no less practical in character. As Goldiamond describes it, that situation was handled as follows:

> Since the bedroom had been the scene of both bickering and occasional lapses, the problem was presented of changing its stimulus value when conjugality was involved. If this could be done consistently, eventually the special stimuli might come to control such behavior. The problem was to find a stimulus which could alter the room entirely and would be easy to apply and withdraw. Finally, a yellow night light was put in, was turned on when both felt amorous, and was kept turned off otherwise. This light markedly altered the perceptual configuration of the room (p. 858).

The treatment period lasted through the school summer term, during which the husband met with the therapist three times weekly. The sessions were focused around "behavioral analysis." The kind of material that is usually discussed in con-

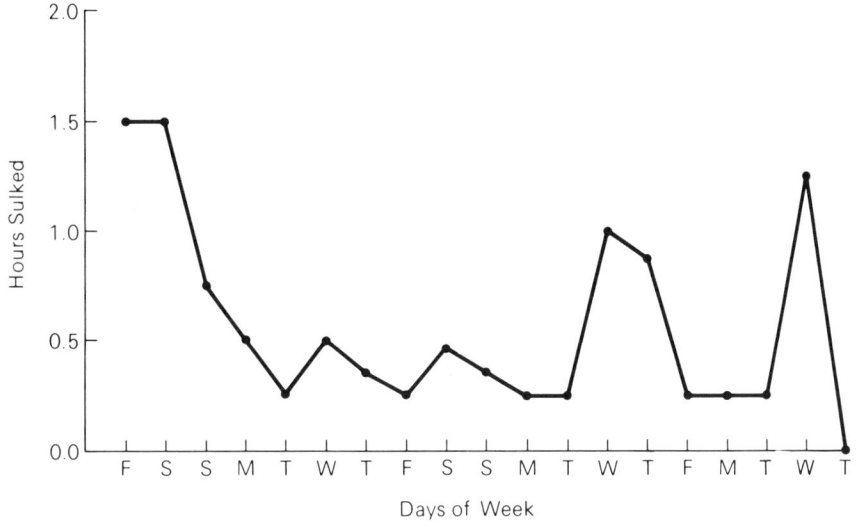

Figure 8
The course of sulking behavior of a subject undergoing behavior therapy. (Figure 1 of Goldiamond, 1965a. Copyright 1965 by Southern Universities Press and reproduced by permission.)

ventional psychotherapy—one's childhood experiences, for example—"was summarily cut off." Did the couple live happily ever after? Goldiamond reports that "at the end of the period there was no sulking in the garage and the partners were able to commune" (p. 859).

Whatever one thinks of techniques of this kind, the fact is that, like the mountain, behavior therapy is there. To some it represents the dawn of a new era, to others a flash in the pan. History will render the final judgment, as time and results determine whether the new techniques will replace psychotherapy, supplement it in some areas, or fall of their own weight.

Meanwhile there is plenty of room for debate—about both psychotherapy and behavior therapy—and we hope the dialogue will not only generate testable hypotheses and sharpen issues but also lead to further empirical work intended to settle some of them. The nature of this give-and-take on both fronts can be gathered from the following chapter.

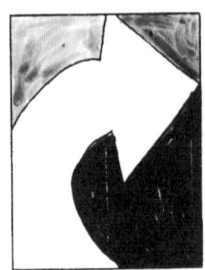

14
The Continuing Dialogue

Research is not invariably the open sesame to knowledge; often it provides definitive answers, but sometimes it opens as many new issues as it settles old ones. But meaningful and relevant controversy also helps advance the cause of knowledge. The area of psychotherapy and behavior modification is not without its share of this creative controversy.

Psychotherapy: Pro and Con

Shortly after midcentury, as research in psychotherapy was burgeoning, Eysenck (1952) made the iconoclastic statement that there "... appears to be an inverse relationship between recovery and psychotherapy; the more psychotherapy, the smaller the recovery rate" (p. 322). While he adds that "this conclusion requires certain qualifications," he nevertheless summarizes the results of an extensive survey on the improvement of neurotic patients as follows: "The figures fail to support the hypothesis that psychotherapy facilitates recovery from neurotic disorder" (p. 323).

Eysenck rested his case in large measure on the results of earlier studies by Landis and Denker. Landis (1937) had argued that the proper evaluation of the effects of psychotherapy required that one establish an appropriate baseline—that is, that one compare the results from a group of people who had received psychotherapy with the progress made by a comparable group that had received no psychotherapy. For the purpose, he decided to look at the recovery rate of psychoneurotics confined to state mental hospitals, where they received essentially custodial care rather than formal psychotherapy. Admitting that the two groups were less comparable than one might wish, but failing to find any existing studies that had included appropriate control groups, he found that the annual discharge rate of psychoneurotic state hospital patients fell within the very narrow range of 66–72 percent. To prove its mettle, then, psychotherapy would need to achieve recovery rates significantly higher than those of the "spontaneous remission" group—that is, those who had been discharged from the custodial care hospitals where they had presumably received little or no psychotherapy.

As another attempt to establish a baseline for recovery from psychoneurosis without psychotherapy, Eysenck cited the findings of Denker (1947), who had followed the cases of 500 consecutive disability insurance claims, defined as severe psychoneurotics in that they had not been able to hold a position for at least a 3-month period before submission of their claim. Of this group, treated (by general practitioners only) with sedatives, tonics, suggestion, and reassurance (most superficial psychotherapy at best, Eysenck contended), a total of 72 percent had recovered within a two-year period, as measured by (a) return to work, (b) no complaint of further difficulties or, if so, only of very slight ones, and (c) successful social adjustment.

Using these results as a baseline—that is, the rate of "spontaneous recovery" of psychoneurotic patients who had received no formal psychotherapy, Eysenck compiled figures from 24 studies of the results of psychotherapy. With psychotherapy of one kind or another, he discovered, from 44 percent to 64 percent of the patients fell in the category of "improved, much improved, or cured"—results inferior to those in the spontaneous remission (no therapy) group. Hence, he concluded, the data ". . . fail to prove that psychotherapy, Freudian or otherwise, facilitates the recovery of neurotic patients" (p. 322).

Needless to say, many were unwilling to accept Eysenck's proposition. New and further points were raised, some in a cogent paper by Bergin (1963), others in a more recent analysis by Kiesler (1966). Let us take note of some of the qualifications they introduce.

As Bergin pointed out, studies of process and outcome in psychotherapy indicate that it is hazardous, if not inexcusable, to speak of psychotherapy in the mass or of psychotherapists as a homogeneous group. Cartwright and Vogel (1960) found, for example, that when they divided therapists into experienced and inexperienced subgroups, patients improved under the former and remained the same, or even got worse, under the latter. Thus, with his simple "psychotherapy—no psychotherapy" dichotomy, Eysenck may have been washing out the very significant variable of therapeutic expertise by lumping all therapy in one category, regardless of the competence of the therapist. As Bergin described the result: "The effectiveness of one group of therapists is cancelled out by the negative effects of the other group when the two are combined into a single experimental group and compared with the control. . . . This may indeed be the answer to the series of negative findings on the generalized effectiveness of psychotherapy" (p. 246).

The series of negative findings to which Bergin refers includes not only Eysenck's, which Bergin hardly saw as a masterpiece of research design, but also six other studies which, he agrees, are among the "more adequately designed." What was troublesome for Bergin was that, of the six, only that of Shlien, Mosak, and Dreikurs (1962) showed "unequivocally positive results." That is, in the others, either there was no change as the result of psychotherapy, or, more usually, the experimental group (which had received the psychotherapy) showed improvement, but the control group (which had received no psychotherapy) showed equal improvement (in one case, even greater improvement).

On the basis of some other evidence (Gurin, Veroff, & Feld, 1960; Frank, 1961), Bergin eventually came upon a possible explanation. The latter two studies had made it clear that people in trouble do not necessarily enter psychotherapy as such; they do, however, seek help informally—from clergymen, family physicians, teachers, friends, and others. In short, the control groups in the series of studies referred to above may, according to Bergin, not have been control groups at all in the usual sense, but simply groups that were receiving informal rather than formal therapy. Further, he pointed out, research that has compared successful and unsuccessful therapists has found that it is not technique per se which distinguishes between them but, rather, certain personal qualities (warmth, understanding, ability to see the client's problems through his eyes, and so on). If, then, people in difficulty are found to seek help informally, if not formally, and if what makes a successful helper are personal attributes of various kinds, Bergin saw a possible resolution of the dilemma that Eysenck had raised. The situation, as Bergin described it, might well be the following:

> The therapists who produce positive results are those who have certain personal qualities and ways of responding to others rather than a well-trained armamentarium of techniques; therefore it is no vain stretch of the imagination to hypothesize that our so-called control subjects who change in spite of being controls are seeking help from and being influenced by people who have the same personal qualities as those therapists who produce positive personality change. The propositions tendered for consideration here suggest that not only have our control groups not been control groups, but that what we have called psychotherapy is not in fact the psychotherapeutic agent (p. 248).

The situation, it appears, is not as simple as Eysenck would have it. In fact, more recently Kiesler (1966), searching for a better paradigm, has pointed to some "myths" he feels have dogged research in psychotherapy to date. Discussing one of them—the "spontaneous remission myth"—he takes Eysenck particularly to task for having rested his case on the Landis (1937) and Denker (1947) reports. In connection with these studies, Kiesler cited the arguments of others on three counts.

Were the "untreated" patients in the Landis and Denker studies comparable to those receiving psychotherapy, with whom they were contrasted? Some of the Kiesler quotes suggest not:

> *Rosenzweig (1954):* "The insurance disability cases were, as a whole, in all likelihood less severely ill than any of the others. . . . To compare psychoneuroses of long standing, dating in many instances from early childhood (the typical case treated by psychoanalysis), with such disability neuroses is highly dubious . . ." (p. 300).
>
> *Luborsky (1954):* "Many of the 'insurance group' would probably never have visited the doctor if it were not required . . ." (p. 129).

Were the "untreated" patients really untreated? Hardly, says Kiesler, again citing Rosenzweig (1954):

> In Eysenck's words these patients were "regularly seen and treated by their own physicians with sedatives, tonics, suggestion, reassurance.". . . These various presumably nonpsychotherapeutic techniques mentioned include suggestion and reassurance—well known methods of psychotherapy; and psychiatrists regularly use sedatives and tonics as adjuncts to their practice . . . (p. 300).

Were the criteria of improvement used comparable for the "untreated" and treated groups? Again Kiesler expresses serious reservations, this time citing Cartwright (1955), who suspects that in the case of the Denker insurance company cases ". . . 'complaint of no further, or very slight, difficulties' [one of Denker's criteria] may represent little more than no further supportable claims against the company" (p. 291).

The notion of spontaneous remission of psychoneurosis seems to Kiesler, then, ". . . nothing more than a myth propagated by a popularized and naive interpretation of two research studies" (p. 119). Research on the effects of psychotherapy has been further obscured by additional myths, Kiesler argues—for example, the assumption that one patient is like another (the "patient uniformity myth") or that one therapist is like another (the "therapist uniformity myth"). All in all, Kiesler insists, the paradigms that have governed research in psychotherapy up to now are very inadequate.

In order to improve such research, Kiesler would take into account many factors that were previously overlooked or disregarded. To simplify his technical argument, one might point to some features that characterize his search for a new and better paradigm:

> (a) we need to recognize that the patient improves, if he does, not because of any single characteristic of the therapist or his technique but because of a combination of such characteristics;
>
> (b) at some stages of the psychotherapeutic process certain characteristics of the therapist and his behavior may be more important than at other points; hence, this must be taken into account when we study the therapeutic process by taking only samples of it;
>
> (c) using as subjects patients who are self-selected introduces various methodological problems, since patients of any diagnostic category, for example, psychoneurotic, differ on many dimensions, which, if not controlled, constitute confounding variables—". . . verbal intelligence, age, motivation for therapy, level of general anxiety, level of ego strength, type of disorder, severity of disorder, type of onset of disorder, socioeconomic background, patient expectancies, verbal expressive ability, level of occupational success, type of value system, and likely others" (p. 131).

It is obvious that psychotherapy, like politics, religion, and sex, provides fertile ground for argument. If so, behavior therapy is even more of a battleground. The behavior therapists, a vigorous new breed, do not hesitate to state their case emphatically—some would say dogmatically—occasionally twitting the psychotherapist, frequently arguing among themselves, but most often showing the kind of unrestrained enthusiasm that is refreshing in a relatively young science looking for new answers to old problems.

Behavior Therapy: Pro and Con

Behavior therapists as well as psychotherapists are sometimes chided about their facility in mustering theoretical arguments to justify almost anything they say or do. A recent addition to the armamentarium of behavior modification techniques—"implosive therapy" (Stampfl and Levis, 1967)—has received this kind of criticism.

As described in Chapter 2, the systematic desensitization procedure rests on the premise that if a person can be helped to tolerate a mild degree of anxiety in connection with something that is for him anxiety-producing (as in the case of a phobia), he can gradually learn to tolerate situations of a more traumatic kind until he can finally face and handle the specific object of his anxiety (dogs, for example, in the case of a fear of animals). The plausible rationale here is that one learns to deal with a traumatic situation by starting with milder doses of it in a situation incompatible with anxiety (a state of physical relaxation, as the reader will recall), then slowly works his way up the anxiety hierarchy while attempting to maintain a state of relaxation at each step.

However, Stampfl and Levis (1967), representing another school of thought, suggest that it is precisely the arousal and experiencing of a *high* level of anxiety that is a necessary condition for dispelling a phobia:

> The fundamental hypothesis is that a sufficient condition for the extinction of anxiety is to represent, reinstate, or symbolically reproduce the stimuli (cues) to which the anxiety response has been conditioned, in the absence of primary reinforcement. . . . Hypotheses are developed about the important cues involved, and these are presented to the patient in the most vivid or realistic manner possible. . . . The greater the degree of anxiety elicited, the greater the reason for continuing the presentations of anxiety-eliciting stimuli (p. 499).

As the authors point out, their technique rests primarily on the Pavlovian principle that ". . . presentation of the conditioned stimulus (cs) without the unconditioned stimulus (ucs) will lead to the extinction of the learned response [in this case, the phobia]" (p. 498).

The term "implosion" has been chosen by its practitioners for the form of therapy that involves having the patient place himself in a situation of high anxiety (but low risk in terms of any real outside harm befalling him). For a situation of the opposite kind—one in which an attempt is made to control any anxiety by such means as progressive relaxation—Wolpe (1958) had used the term "reciprocal inhibition," which he explained thus: "If a response antagonistic to anxiety can be made to occur in the presence of anxiety-evoking stimuli so that it is accompanied by a complete or partial suppression of the anxiety responses, the bond between these stimuli and the anxiety responses will be weakened" (p. 71). The process of "imploding oneself" can perhaps best be illustrated by excerpts from an actual session. Hogan and Kirchner (1967) had college students who were terrified of rats engage in the following imagery:

> The experimental group began with scenes such as imagining their touching a rat, having a rat nibble at their finger, or feeling one run across their hand. Then the rat might bite them on the arm. The subjects might next experience the rat's running rapidly over their body. The rodent could pierce them viciously in the neck, swish its tail in their face, or claw about in their hair. It might even devour their eyes. The subjects might be told to open their mouth. Suddenly, the rodent jumped in, and they swallowed it . . . (p. 107).

The foregoing will no doubt suffice to convince the reader that the imagined scenes are intended to produce anxiety. (The scenes, in fact, get more gruesome as they proceed). In contrast, a control group of subjects (presumably comparable in their fear of rats, as judged by failure to pass a pretest involving picking up a rat) was asked to imagine such relaxing cues as a vacation scene or a leisurely walk. Although the authors do not specify the length of treatment for the subjects, who had been assigned randomly to either the experimental group or the control group, it is indicated that the time spent in implosive therapy was very short (21 1/2 minutes in the case of one subject, 25 minutes in the case of another). The results, as measured behaviorally, are shown in Table 1.

Table 1
Behavior patterns of experimental and control subjects.

Group	N	Picked up Rat	Opened Cage	Stood in Room	Refused to Enter Room	Refused to Try Post-Test
Experimental	21	14	6	1	—	—
Control	22	2	1	12	4	3
Total	43					

(Table 1 of Hogan & Kirchner, 1967. Copyright 1967 by the American Psychological Association and reprinted by permission.)

Although certain details of the experiment about which one would like more information are unspecified, these preliminary results warrant notice. A more recent study by the same authors (Hogan and Kirchner, 1968) compared the results of implosive therapy, eclectic verbal therapy, and bibliotherapy, (self-help gained through reading psychological or other material). The experiment used 30 subjects with snake phobia—10 assigned randomly to each technique—and produced the results shown in Table 2.

Table 2
Comparative results obtained with three methods of treating fear of snakes, with ten subjects in each group.

	Therapy Employed		
	Implosive	Eclectic-Verbal	Bibliotherapy
Success	7	4	1
Failure	3	6	9
% Successful	70	40	10

(Table 1 of Hogan & Kirchner, 1968. Copyright 1968 by Pergamon Press Ltd. and reprinted by permission.)

To use an analogy, it is as if one treatment procedure (systematic desensitization) is akin to helping someone learn to swim by taking him slowly from shallow to deeper water as he manages to stay afloat, while the other (implosive therapy) shows him he can swim by throwing him into deep water from the outset, letting him prove to himself that, although he thrashes frantically about, he does not sink.

The contrast reminds one of the situation in psychotherapy, where a therapist of one school makes every effort to keep the therapeutic relationship minimally threatening, while a therapist of another school may feel that, unless the client gets stirred up as a result of the therapeutic interaction, nothing much is happening. But, again, progress often thrives on controversy, and behavior therapy, like psychotherapy, is not without its share. If its advocates are not debating among themselves, there is always outside criticism to be met. A case in point is the critique presented by Breger and McGaugh (1965).

They are bothered that behavior therapy is not as new as it is made out to be, but, more fundamentally, that its explanations are just too simple. "The behaviorist looks at a neurotic and sees specific symptoms and anxiety," they say. In contrast, ". . . the psychodynamicist looks at the same individual and sees a complex intra- and interpersonal mode of functioning which may or may not contain certain observable fears or certain behavioral symptoms such as compulsive motor acts" (p. 349). Furthermore, Breger and McGaugh assert, the behavior therapists have been ". . . focusing their attention on those neuroses that can be described in terms of specific symptoms (bedwetting, if this is a neurosis, tics, specific phobias, etc.) and have tended to ignore those conditions which do not fit their model, such as neurotic depressions, general unhappiness, obsessional disorders, and the kinds of persistent interpersonal entanglements that characterize so many neurotics" (p. 348).

Traditional S-R (stimulus-response) explanations, which the behavior therapists invoke, are inadequate for Breger and McGaugh. They argue that one cannot simply state, as behavior therapy does, that the symptom *is* the neurosis. For them ". . . what is learned in a neurosis is a set of central strategies (or a program) which guide the individual's adaptation to his environment. Neuroses are not symptoms (responses) but are strategies of a particular kind which lead to certain observable (tics, compulsive acts, etc.) and certain other less observable phenomena (fears, feelings of depression, etc.)" (p. 355).

It is not necessary to go into the more technical details of the arguments Breger and McGaugh present, and the interested reader is referred to the attempted rebuttal by

Rachman and Eysenck (1966), if he wishes to judge which team won. More recently, others have jumped into the fray (Wiest, 1967; Katahn & Koplin, 1968). Equally interesting, or perhaps more so, are the efforts of those who attempt to serve as peacemakers by taking the broader theoretical view. It may be well, therefore, to note some of the points made by such mediators as Marks and Gelder (1966) and Weitzman (1967).

Rapprochement

Psychology, like international affairs, can be said to have its hawks and its doves. Some would probably categorize McConnell (1968) among the hawks from the fact that he published an article in *Esquire* magazine entitled "Psychoanalysis Must Go." This article has as its frontispiece a cartoon of Sigmund Freud plummeting—couch and all—from an office window to the implied demise of psychoanalysis. At the same time, other psychologists carry a dialectic olive branch, feeling that their scientific mission is to gather the various theoretical clans around the therapeutic conference table. Marks and Gelder (1966) apparently enjoy this role of mediator.

Are psychodynamic therapy and behavior therapy mutually incompatible? Is one "better" than the other? These are questions that, according to Marks and Gelder, not only hamper progress but also distort the situation. To them, psychotherapy and behavior therapy share considerable common ground. Behavior therapy happens to favor a molecular approach, trying to show how learned habits can be used to explain complex behavior; psychotherapy, on the other hand, adopts a molar approach, attempting to come to grips with behavior as a whole by means of analyzing its components. Each is useful, according to Marks and Gelder; the two approaches "have a common meeting point where the language of each can be translated into the other" (p. 21). For some symptoms (simple phobias, for example) behavior therapy may be more effective. Other symptoms (for example, agoraphobia, the fear of open spaces) may require psychotherapy. Marks and Gelder conclude that "behaviour and psychodynamic theories are complementary, not conflicting. Character disorders require the first, others the second, and yet others require a combined approach" (p. 21).

Woody (1968) has more recently advocated that we not only recognize the kinship that exists between psychotherapy and behavior therapy, but also exploit it in practice. He urges the introduction of "psychobehavioral therapy," the integration of the two techniques, where practical. He sees at least three circumstances in which such integration would be appropriate: (1) to facilitate the progress of psychotherapy whenever psychotherapy meets certain barriers that cannot otherwise be used to good advantage (as, for example, in "analyzing the resistance"); (2) to eliminate uncomfortable symptoms of the kind that simply impede psychotherapeutic progress; (3) to make certain clients responsive to psychotherapy who would otherwise not be amenable to treatment.

Still other psychologists place their faith in data per se. They attempt to set up respectable research designs that will allow each mode of treatment a fighting chance, letting the results speak for themselves. In one such study, Paul (1967) found that clients who received either psychotherapy or behavior therapy improved significantly more than comparable untreated clients who served as a control group. However, while the clients treated by insight psychotherapy and attention-placebo treatment showed equal amounts of significant improvement (50%), those who were treated by behavior therapy techniques showed the greatest proportion of gain (85%).

So the lively controversy continues. But even while action proceeds on this front, other vistas are opening, and some of them provide the kind of perspective that makes it appear that the best strategy at this point might be one of disengagement rather than further locking of horns.

Reorientation

Science not only shapes history; history also shapes science. The search for newer, faster, more effective techniques of behavior modification is not motivated merely by the behavioral scientist's natural curiosity and his urge to improve his capability; it also arises from the need of the people for better mental health care. People no longer slink off to a psychiatrist or psychologist, hoping that no one will ever find out. They are urged to seek help with problems of adjustment, whether alcoholism, parent-child relationships, or overeating, much as they are urged to see their dentist regularly. This is "community psychology," as it has come to be called, and its first principle is that prevention is better than cure. Someone has remarked that if you are standing at a river watching bodies float by, it may be commendable to pull out one after the other, but it would be more appropriate to go upstream to find who is throwing them in. Every clinician knows that treating schizophrenics requires patience, special skill, and experience. These same qualities can be applied to discovering ways of preventing schizophrenia, or at least ways of helping the incipient schizophrenic to maintain a marginal level of adjustment.

In contrast to the forbidding, isolated, huge mental hospital of today—the "great stone mother," as Mendel calls it—the community mental health center of tomorrow will be close at hand, easily accessible, and intended especially to deal early with incipient problems rather than late with unmanageable ones. But as Carter (1968) pointed out in a symposium on the subject: "The crucial problems in developing some 2,000 community mental health centers in this country by 1980 will be to alleviate manpower shortages in the mental health disciplines and to develop new and more effective ways of delivering mental health services" (p. 1).

In the same symposium, Cowen and Zax described some ongoing projects intended to solve precisely the two problems that Carter cites, namely, enlarging the pool of mental health workers and devising new ways of dispensing services. Ideally, psychological disorders would be preventable altogether. Such "primary prevention" is, unfortunately, not yet possible, but efforts at "secondary prevention" can be amazingly effective. "High-risk" youngsters (those who are prone to serious later disorders) can be spotted early in school and can be given close ongoing treatment and follow-up by trained personnel. Such prophylactic treatment is immeasurably preferable to the delayed efforts of even the most skilled therapist, who, in fact, is consulted only after a long-standing problem of adjustment has grown to serious proportions. Cowen and Zax (1968) described some ongoing programs that combine an emphasis upon prevention with the need to develop new and more effective ways of delivering mental health services. Here is their description of some of these programs:[1]

> One of our "programs-in-action" has recruited and trained middle-aged housewives for roles as mental-health aides in the schools (Zax, Cowen, Izzo, Madonia, Merenda, & Trost, 1966). Such women, though they have been incorporated in a variety of volunteer programs in the past, have tended to be used for relatively trivial jobs such as chauffeuring, distributing books, cleaning blackboards, etc., when in fact they have much to offer in interpersonal relationships and as a resource in the mental health helping enterprise. . . . Several models for the functioning of the housewife aide have already been explored, each of which presumes at least half-time involvement to assure continuity and relatively stable relationships with the child. One such model "stations" the housewife directly in the classroom; the second has her in the school building, combining classroom observations and "on-call" service with children. The aide is oriented toward the educational and emotional needs of the disturbed child who, in many instances, cannot receive special attention from the teacher who is charged with the progress of her entire class. Through such efforts the child with withdrawal tendencies may be encouraged to come out of his shell and the over-active child who needs attention may get this plus intelligent guidance toward useful pursuits before either type becomes rigidified in a pathological pattern.
>
> A second program (Cowen, Zax, & Laird, 1966) utilizes undergraduate education majors as companions in after-school activity programs with

[1] Copyright 1968 by Behavioral Publications, Inc. Reprinted by permission of the authors and publisher.

children referred by their teachers because of emotional difficulties—particularly acting-out problems, problems of shyness, timidity, and withdrawal, and those of educational underachievement. This program also involves fourth-year clinical graduate students, hopefully providing for them a meaningful experience in the community and the schools, and a taste of functioning in a consultative-resource capacity. Our pattern of operation runs roughly as follows. Each graduate student works with a group of six undergraduate volunteers. Each volunteer is assigned specifically to an individual child or a pair of children. Twice a week volunteers and graduate student leaders go to the schools. Activities with the children take place between 3:30 and 4:45 p.m. Then the entire group returns to campus for a postmortem discussion between 5 and 6 p.m. These discussions range across topics such as trying to understand the child's behavior, considering the efficacy of varying types of actions and interventions, and trying to deal with the volunteer's concerns about his own role and function. . . .

The third group of nonprofessionals that we have trained to work as mental health aides with young children in the schools consists of retired people. . . . Independent objective data obtained from teachers and aides indicated that referred children profited significantly from their experience. Moreover, participation in the program was a gratifying experience for the retirees as well . . . (Cowen & Zax, 1968, pp. 54–56).

The new methods of mental health intervention, as typified by those described by Cowen and Zax, have emerged out of a considerable body of research and theory in the area of public health. Indeed, a paper by J. G. Kelly (1968) dwells essentially upon the theoretical underpinnings of community psychology. His "ecological conception of preventive interventions" lays the groundwork for research on social environments by drawing principles from empirical work in such areas as field biology. The more theoretically inclined reader, who wishes to convince himself that the adjustment of students in high school can be studied with as much scientific respectability as the Brownian movement of particles in physics, will find Kelly's background material reassuring.

It is not to be assumed that one simply takes out after clinical problems with scientific vengeance and that they then dutifully yield to solutions. One cannot "commission" behavioral scientists to solve problems as patrons once did the old masters to write symphonies (although the "Manhattan Project" of World War II proved that even atom-splitting can be hurried along with enough support). But what characterizes scientists of any stripe is not so much the ability to produce solutions à la carte as it is their insatiable inquisitiveness, and when the penchant for theorizing interacts with the relentless desire to try out ideas in practice, the science of behavior is the better for it.

15
Theory and Practice: Two Sides of the Coin

Theory: A Guide to Practice

Economy-minded congressmen are wont to kick up their heels periodically about federally supported research on things like the croaking of the Brazilian bullfrog or the shape of snowflakes. Whether called basic research or something else, such scientific investigations do not appeal to those whose criterion of worth is: "Of what *use* is it?"

Scientists, on the other hand, are more than simply pragmatic. Knowledge is valuable in its own right; not all of it needs to be put to immediate practical use. Yet clinicians are in many ways appliers of knowledge and *do* have an interest in whether ideas and findings generated in the laboratory can be harnessed for use. It matters little whose laboratory they come from; indeed, the research findings of a social psychologist may on occasion have broader theoretical relevance for the clinician than do some of his own.

Such is the relationship between the work of a couple of social psychologists, Schachter and Singer (1962), and a group of clinical investigators, Bandura et al. (1967). While there was no planned interaction between the two groups—"you produce the knowledge; I'll find ways to apply it"—the work of the two teams provides a fitting illustration of the kinship between basic and applied research.

Schachter and Singer were interested in the area of emotion, particularly its cognitive, social, and physiological determinants. The general problem has, of course, a long history, having been explored in depth by philosophers and by such early giants of psychology as William James (1890). Nevertheless, Schachter and Singer perceived some interesting possibilities for controlled laboratory research, whereby specific aspects of emotion might be manipulated experimentally.

The investigators had a general thesis: emotion is a function of physiological arousal and accompanying cognition. That is, without arousal there is no experience that can be called "emotion"; on the other hand, the emotion that is experienced depends on how the situation is "cognized"—that is, perceived and interpreted. Most of the time circumstances are such that the consequent emotion can be readily labeled. A young girl walks down a lonely street at night worrying for her safety, a shadowy figure suddenly darts from a dark alleyway, and she experiences "fear." The soldier returning from Vietnam, waiting impatiently to dash down the gangplank of his ship into the arms of his waiting wife, experiences "joy." In short, arousal under such circumstances is readily labeled as fear in one case, joy in the other, as a function of the cognitions at hand. Interestingly, when examined as it experiences different emotions, the organism does not look *physiologically* different under one experience or the other. In some typical research on the physiology of the respective emotions, Ax (1953) found, at best, only subtle differences among them.

As Schachter and Singer point out, earlier research by Cantril and Hunt (1932) had suggested that, when injected with a drug (epinephrine) that produced dramatic bodily reactions (pounding of the heart, flushing of the face, and so on), subjects frequently described themselves as ". . . ripe for *any* kind of emotional suggestion." All of this might tempt one to explore, under controlled conditions, the possibility of getting subjects to experience one emotion rather than another (for example, anger rather than euphoria) by influencing their cognition of the situation in which arousal occurred. Physiological arousal could readily be accomplished; an injection of epinephrine (adrenalin) would see to that. What interested Schachter and Singer was whether one could determine how the subject was to interpret the arousal emotionally—that is, which emotion he would wind up experiencing. Could one, in short, produce emotions à la carte?

Given a state of arousal (occasioned, for example, by the squeal of automobile tires and a loud thump) and a percept (a child lying limp in the street), there is little doubt that all of the bystanders would share the same cognition (an accident has occurred) and experience similar emotions (grief or horror). What would happen, however, were one highly aroused but found it difficult to interpret the situation so unambiguously? Given such arousal, would the emotion experienced be a function of how we were led to *label* the situation? That is, would our "evaluative needs," as Schachter and Singer call them, cause us to label the state of arousal either Emotion *A* or Emotion *B* in terms of the cognitions available to us at the moment? The investigators set up an experimental situation to test this hypothesis.

The drug epinephrine produces an unmistakable state of arousal. Assuming one had been told exactly what aftereffects to expect (palpitation, trembling, flushing), one should have no trouble labeling the sensations (as natural sequelae of the injection). If, however, one had been given no such forewarning, or if one had actually been deliberately misled as to the effects to be experienced, some interesting outcomes might ensue. If the thesis that emotion is a function of arousal and cognition is correct, then the latter subjects, in seeking ways in which to label their arousal, would be largely at the mercy of the external situation and how it might be perceived and interpreted. It would be the *experimenters* who determined what emotion subjects experienced by the way in which they had set up the external situation.

Was this really so? With a little ingenious stage-setting, it would be possible to find out. The true purpose of the experiment needed to be clothed in some plausible rationale, lest the subjects' knowledge of the question being studied confound the results. Consequently, subjects were told that the investigation dealt with the effects on vision of a new vitamin compound, "Suproxin" (an invented name for what was actually to be epinephrine). The experimenters obtained their subjects' consent (only one of 185 objected), and a physician administered the drug. Subjects in a control group received a placebo injection (neutral saline solution) in the belief that they were receiving "Suproxin."

Subjects in the experimental group were in one of three treatment conditions. The Epinephrine Informed (Epi Inf) group was told correctly what sensations they might expect from the injection of "Suproxin." Subjects in the Epinephrine Misinformed (Epi Mis) group were misled about the sensations to be experienced; instead of the heart palpitation, tremor, and flushing of the face that would actually occur, they were led to expect such sensations as numbness, itching, and headache (which epinephrine normally does not produce). Subjects in the Epinephrine Ignorant (Epi Ign) group were told nothing about what to expect; in administering the injection, the physician mentioned simply that it was harmless and would have no side effects.

So much for the arousal condition. Clearly, each of the experimental groups in actuality experienced physiological arousal as a result of the injection of epinephrine, yet each had different expectations. The task now was to arrange appropriate external situations in which the subjects would find themselves as they experienced the effects of the drug (usually felt from 3 to 5 minutes after injection and lasting from 10 minutes to an hour). For this purpose, the investigators enlisted the aid of a stooge, presented as a fellow subject, who was to foster one of two cognitions. In one case, he would behave in a way that would make euphoria seem appropriate; in the other, his behavior would be intended to suggest that anger was appropriate. Thus, in the euphoric setting, after the physician had administered the injection to the subjects (who had received one of the three types of explanations earlier) and left the room, the experimenter reappeared with the stooge, introducing him as a fellow subject; he then instructed them both as follows:

> Both of you have had the Suproxin shot and you'll both be taking the same tests of vision. What I ask you to do now is just wait for 20 minutes. The reason for this is simply that we have to allow 20 minutes for the Suproxin to get from the injection site into the bloodstream. At the end of 20 minutes when we are certain that most of the Suproxin has been absorbed into the bloodstream, we'll begin the tests of vision (p. 384).

Since the room had purposely been left in somewhat disorderly condition, the experimenter added: "The only other thing I should do is to apologize for the condition of the room. I just didn't have time to clean it up. So, if you need any scratch paper or rubber bands or pencils, help yourself. I'll be back in 20 minutes to begin the vision tests" (p. 384).

While the drug was taking effect and the two were ostensibly killing time before the vision test, the other "subject" went through a standard series of maneuvers calculated to create a situation in which it was appropriate to feel euphoric. He used the scratch paper to fashion small basketballs with which he then shot baskets, encouraging the subject to try a few, made paper airplanes which he flew, encouraging the subject to do likewise, built a tower of manila folders which he jubilantly shot down, played with a hula hoop, offering another to the subject. In short, in a prescribed sequence, he attempted to create an atmosphere conducive to euphoria, encouraging the subject to get into the spirit of the situation.

Subjects in the other condition—the anger situation—underwent an analogous experience. Their waiting was to be used in filling out a questionnaire. In this case (regardless of which of the three instructions subjects had received earlier) the job of the stooge was to create a situation in which anger seemed an appropriate reaction. In this he was abetted by the nature of the questionnaire to be filled out—one which seemed, indeed, to get unduly personal, to the point where questions pried into such matters as "How many times each week do you have sexual intercourse?"

or even "With how many men (other than your father) has your mother had extra-marital relationships?" By his exclamations as he proceeded, the stooge left no doubt as to his increasing anger, which culminated in his eventually leaving the room with "I'm not wasting any more time. I'm getting my books and leaving" (p. 385).

Given subjects who had experienced the same physiological arousal but who differed in their expectations about sensations they would experience, how might the three groups be influenced by these external situations? If the general assumptions of Schachter and Singer were correct, the Epi Inf subjects, who had ample knowledge of the arousal sensations they were experiencing (on the basis of their correct previous instructions) should need to depend least on the external situation for an explanation. The Epi Ign group, in contrast, had little basis for the internal sensations being experienced, hence should be much more dependent on their cognition of the external situation for an explanation; presumably they should label the arousal state "euphoria" if they were in that group, or "anger" if in the other. The Epi Mis group, with misleading information, should experience greatest difficulty, searching as they must for some way in which to label sensations at variance with those expected. Cognizing the external situation as euphoria-inducing in one case, anger-inducing in the other, provided such a label.

For Schachter and Singer, the test of their hypothesis was the degree to which the respective subjects would either join in the spirit of the occasion (twirl a hula hoop, for example, as observed through a one-way vision mirror) and/or report on subsequent questionnaires that they had experienced euphoria or anger in greater or lesser degree. Having established that subjects in the three experimental groups had indeed experienced significantly greater arousal following the injection than those in the control group (by such measures as pulse rate and self-ratings of tremor), the investigators were interested in the differential influences which the stooge's experimental manipulation had exerted on the emotions experienced in the respective conditions.

Let us look at the results for the several groups in the euphoria setting. (The anger situation produced essentially similar findings.) One could investigate how euphoric the subjects felt on the basis of their self-reports; in addition, one could look at their actual behavior in terms of euphoric acts initiated by them. Table 1 shows the results.

On the basis of both self-report and behavioral measures the trend was in the directions predicted. The Epi Inf group, having ready-made explanations for sensations experienced, seemed least dependent on alternative cognitions for labeling the feel-

Table 1
Behavioral indications of emotional state in the euphoria setting.

Condition	N	Activity Index	Mean Number of Acts Initiated
Epi Inf	25	12.72	.20
Epi Ign	25	18.28	.56
Epi Mis	25	22.56	.84
Placebo	26	16.00	.54

Note: The score under "Activity Index" is a weighted index combining credits assigned for various activities (for example, 5 for hula hooping, 2 for shooting paper basketballs, etc.) and time spent in those activities. The figure under "Mean Number of Acts Initiated" represents the degree to which subjects departed from the stooge's routine and initiated activities of their own. (Table 3 of Schachter & Singer, 1962. Copyright 1962 by the American Psychological Association and reproduced by permission.)

ings being experienced. The Epi Ign and Epi Mis groups, whose subjects were respectively without adequate explanations or with misleading ones, were heavily dependent on their cognition of the external situation for labeling the arousal being experienced. But what about the control group? Presumably these subjects had not been aroused at all by their saline solution, yet they scored between the Epi Inf and Epi Ign groups in each case. As an afterthought, it occurred to the experimenters that having a hypodermic needle jabbed into one's arm might well result in arousal, regardless of the fluid it contained. Clearly, future investigations of this type would need to produce the placebo condition in nonarousing ways.

In any case, some interesting propositions emerged—propositions with clinical implications and applications, as we shall show in the work of Bandura et al. to follow. Schachter and Singer state them thus:

> 1. Given a state of physiological arousal for which the individual has no immediate explanation, he will label this state and describe his feelings in terms of the cognitions available to him. . . .
>
> 2. Given a state of physiological arousal for which an individual has a completely appropriate explanation, no evaluative needs will arise and the individual is unlikely to label his feelings in terms of the alternative cognitions available.
>
> 3. Given the same cognitive circumstances, the individual will react emotionally or describe his feelings as emotions only to the extent that he experiences a state of physiological arousal (p. 398).

Here, in theory, lay the germ of an idea for clinical practice. Bandura and his colleagues were not ones to let it lie fallow. In the following year, Bandura and Walters (1963), referring to the Schachter and Singer study, wrote: "These results suggest that the influence of models may be potent when the observers are emotionally aroused and cannot rationally attribute their feelings to stimuli other than the model's behavior" (p. 88).

Indeed, they went on at the time to explain, on this basis, such observations as the tendencies of children to show aggressive behavior themselves when their parents are aggressively punitive toward them. In what follows, we are concerned with how the findings of Schachter and Singer might be turned to good advantage in the treatment and modification of behavior.

Practice: The Implementation of Theory

Bandura et al. (1967) do not make specific reference to the theoretical work of Schachter and Singer described above. Nevertheless, the reader is urged to take special note of how theory may be translated into practice. Bandura and his team had a specific problem to handle—children's fear of dogs—and a specific treatment procedure to test—a form of behavior therapy making use of modeling. Here is how it went.

Using nursery-school children, ages 3 to 5, the investigators asked parents to rate the degree to which their children showed fear of dogs. Children who were regarded as fearful were then observed in a standardized situation, where their actual behavior in relation to a dog could be rated objectively. A female experimenter brought each child individually to a testing room in which a brown cocker spaniel was confined in a playpen. Here the child was asked (although, of course, not forced) to go through a series of interactions with the dog, ranging from such relatively innocuous tasks as walking up to the playpen to such intimate contact as sitting in the playpen with the dog and scratching its belly. As the child performed (or did not perform) the various tasks suggested, he could be rated on each according to whether it had been performed willingly (two credits), with reluctance (one credit), or not at all (zero credit). On the basis of these measures, the 24 boys and 24 girls who were to serve as subjects could then be divided into three groups—those most fearful (who had earned 0–7 points in the behavioral test), those next most fearful (8–17 points), and those least fearful (18–20 points). Each group contained approximately the same number of children, divided equally by sex. Subjects were then assigned randomly to one of four conditions, so that four groups, comparable in age, sex, and fear of dogs, could be exposed to four different procedures in order to see which might prove effective in reducing their fear.

Bandura and his colleagues were interested in combinations of two variables. In some cases, the treatment procedure was to involve a party, in the other not. (The reader may wish at this point to reflect on the Schachter and Singer notions concerning modes of arousal.) In addition, two groups were to witness the behavior of a model (a four-year-old boy) interacting fearlessly with a dog; the other two were not. (Again, we invite the reader to recall the role which the stooge had played in the Schachter and Singer study in creating a situation that subjects could "cognize" in one way or another.) At least four conditions were thus possible, labeled as follows by the experimenters: (1) a modeling-positive context (model and dog plus party); (2) a modeling-neutral context (model and dog minus party); (3) an exposure-positive context (party and dog minus model); and (4) a positive context (party without either dog or model).

Each group experienced eight sessions of 10 minutes' duration each on four consecutive days. Two experimenters were involved, one to create the party situation, the other to carry in the dog, as the situation required. The four-year-old model, a boy totally unafraid of dogs, went through a prearranged series of interactions with the dog in those situations where his presence was indicated, beginning with mild forms of interaction in the early sessions (calling "Hi, Chloe!" and petting the dog) and increasing in intimacy in later sessions (sitting in the playpen with Chloe while hugging her and feeding her milk from a baby bottle). In the third condition—the exposure-positive context—the dog was confined in a playpen during the parties in the first four sessions and allowed to roam about the room in the last four. The fourth condition—the positive context—provided opportunity for the children to experience the presence of the friendly experimenters so that one could determine to what extent such interaction alone (without either dog or model) might have reduced the fear of dogs in the later test.

Following the experimental sessions, the comparative results of the four treatment conditions were to be evaluated by the same behavioral test administered originally. Bandura et al. included the following methodological precautions. (1) Lest the experimenter unwittingly introduce some bias into the situation, the same female experimenter who had administered the pretreatment behavioral test administered the posttreatment test, but without knowledge of which treatment procedure any of the children had undergone. (2) As a check on her ratings, a second judge rated a randomly selected 25 percent of each group of children, observing them in the behavioral test through a one-way vision mirror; the two raters agreed on 97 percent of the items. (3) The degree of activity displayed by the animal might influence the reactions of the children and thus should be taken into account. In 81 percent of the test trials, the raters were in agreement as to whether the animal was passive, moderately active, or vigorous. In terms of the distribution of the activity level of the dog across the four treatment conditions, there were no significant differences among the groups. Hence, these variables seemed to have been adequately controlled.

Keeping in mind the theoretical implications of the Schachter and Singer study, it would be interesting for the reader to speculate as to the relative effectiveness of the four treatment conditions. The findings are shown in Figure 1.

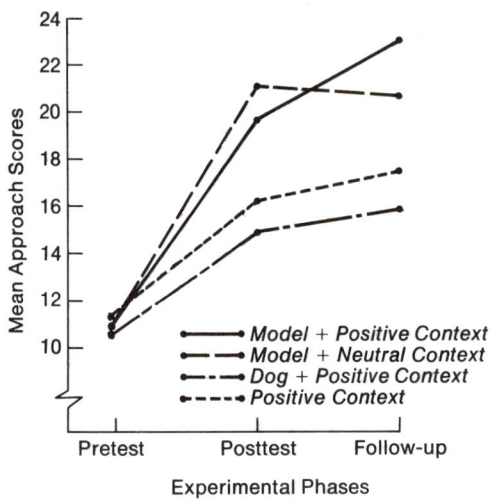

Figure 1
Mean approach scores of children in different treatment conditions at three assessment periods. (Figure 1 of Bandura, Grusec, & Menlove, 1967. Copyright 1967 by the American Psychological Association and reproduced by permission.)

"Vicarious extinction of avoidance behavior," as Bandura et al. call it, does indeed seem possible, with the various treatment conditions having differential effects. But was the lessened fearfulness a lasting thing and would reduction in fear of Chloe generalize to another dog? One month after the posttest, the experimenters conducted a follow-up test, this time with "Jenny," a white mongrel of approximately the same size and of about the same activity level of Chloe (as determined by the behavior of a separate set of children reacting to both Chloe and Jenny). As seen in

Table 2, the approach scores of the children in the two modeling situations either held up or improved, both conditions remaining superior to the results obtained with children in the two control groups.

Table 2
Mean increases in approach responses as a function of treatment conditions, assessment phases, and test animals.

Phases	Treatment Conditions			
	Modeling— Positive Context	Modeling— Neutral Context	Exposure— Positive Context	Positive Context
Posttreatment				
Spaniel	10.83	9.83	2.67	6.08
Mongrel	5.83	10.25	3.17	4.17
Follow-Up				
Spaniel	10.83	9.33	4.67	5.83
Mongrel	12.59	9.67	4.75	6.67
Combined data	10.02	9.77	3.81	5.69

(Table 1 of Bandura, Grusec, & Menlove, 1967. Copyright 1967 by the American Psychological Association and reproduced by permission.)

Bandura and his co-workers suggest one might try to determine whether improvement was due to the information value contained in the modeling contexts or to the extinction of the conditioned emotional reactions experienced vicariously. In any case, they add, reduction in avoidance behavior through such vicarious procedures can be further supplemented. As they put it: "Once approach behaviors have been restored through modeling, their maintenance and further generalization can be effectively controlled by response-contingent reinforcement administered directly to the subject. The combined use of modeling and reinforcement procedures may thus serve as a highly efficacious mode of therapy for eliminating severe behavioral inhibitions" (p. 22).

Thanks to the theoretical propositions offered by Schachter and Singer, one has a better basis for explaining the practical applications tested by Bandura and his colleagues. Theory and practice make good bedfellows in the eternal triangle of theory, practice, and research.

If the reader comes away from this book with the feeling that psychologists do not know all the answers yet and that they disagree among themselves on many issues, he will be quite correct. Science, like democracy, is founded upon the right to dissent, the willingness to countenance opposing views, and the determination to pursue truth wherever it may be found. The struggle for knowledge has no easy victories.

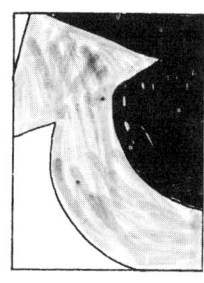

References

American Psychiatric Association, Committee on Nomenclature and Statistics. *DSM-II Diagnostic and statistical manual of mental disorders.* (2nd ed.) Washington, D. C., 1968.

American Psychological Association. *Standards for educational and psychological tests and manuals.* Washington, D. C., 1966.

Antrobus, J., Dement, W., & Fisher, C. Patterns of dreaming and dream recall: An EEG study. *Journal of Abnormal and Social Psychology,* 1964, **69**, 341–344.

Aserinsky, E. & Kleitman, N. Regularly occurring periods of eye motility and concomitant phenomena during sleep. *Science,* 1953, **118**, 273–274.

Atkinson, J. W. & Feather, N. T. (Eds.) *A theory of achievement motivation.* New York: Wiley, 1966.

Ax, A. F. Physiological differentiation of emotional states. *Psychosomatic Medicine,* 1953, **15**, 433–442.

Ayllon, T., Haughton, E., & Hughes, H. B. Interpretation of symptoms: Fact or fiction? *Behaviour Research and Therapy,* 1965, **3**, 1–7.

Ayllon, T. & Michael, J. The psychiatric nurse as a behavioral engineer. *Journal of the Experimental Analysis of Behavior,* 1959, **2**, 323–334.

Azrin, N. H. Pain and aggression. *Psychology Today,* 1967, **1**, 27–33.

Azrin, N. H., Hutchinson, R. R., & Hake, D. F. Attack, avoidance, and escape reactions to aversive shock. *Journal of the Experimental Analysis of Behavior,* 1967, **10**, 131–148.

Azrin, N. H. & Powell, J. Behavioral engineering: The reduction of smoking behavior by a conditioning apparatus and procedure. *Journal of Applied Behavior Analysis,* 1968, **1**, 193–200.

Bach, G. R. & Wyden, P. *The intimate enemy: How to fight fair in love and marriage.* New York: Morrow, 1969.

Bachrach, A. J. *Psychological research: An introduction.* New York: Random House, 1962.

Bandura, A., Grusec, J. E., & Menlove, F. L. Vicarious extinction of avoidance behavior. *Journal of Personality and Social Psychology,* 1967, **5**, 16–23.

Bandura, A. & Walters, R. H. *Social learning and personality development.* New York: Holt, Rinehart and Winston, 1963.

Barber, T. X. & Hahn, K. W., Jr. Physiological and subjective responses to pain producing stimulation under hypnotically-suggested and waking-imagined "analgesia." *Journal of Abnormal and Social Psychology,* 1962, **65**, 411–418.

Barber, T. X. & Silver, M. J. Fact, fiction, and the experimenter bias effect. *Psychological Bulletin Monograph,* 1968, **70**, Part 2, 1–29. (a)

Barber, T. X. & Silver, M. J. Pitfalls in data analysis and interpretation: A reply to Rosenthal. *Psychological Bulletin Monograph,* 1968, **70**, Part 2, 48–62. (b)

Barry, W. A. Conflict in marriage: A study of the interactions of newly wed couples in experimentally induced conflicts. Unpublished doctoral dissertation, University of Michigan, 1968.

Barry, W. A. Marriage research and conflict: An integrative review. *Psychological Bulletin,* 1970, **73**, 41–54.

Bateson, G., Jackson, D. D., Haley, J., & Weakland, J. Toward a theory of schizophrenia. *Behavioral Science,* 1956, **1**, 251–264.

Baumrind, D. Some thoughts on ethics of research: After reading Milgram's "Behavioral study of obedience." *American Psychologist,* 1964, **19**, 421–423.

Becker, H. W. History, culture and subjective experience: An exploration of the social bases of drug-induced experiences. *Journal of Health and Social Behavior,* 1967, **8**, 163–176.

Bergin, A. E. The effects of psychotherapy: Negative results revisited. *Journal of Counseling Psychology,* 1963, **10**, 244–250.

Berkowitz, L. Impulse, aggression and the gun. *Psychology Today,* 1968, **2**, 19–22.

Berkowitz, L. & Geen, R. G. Film violence and the cue properties of available targets. *Journal of Personality and Social Psychology,* 1966, **3**, 525–530.

Berkowitz, L. & LePage, A. Weapons as aggression-eliciting stimuli. *Journal of Personality and Social Psychology,* 1967, **7**, 202–207.

Berkun, M. M., Bialek, H. M., Kern, R. P., & Yagi, K. Experimental studies of psychological stress in man. *Psychological Monographs,* 1962, **76**(Whole No. 534).

Berne, E. *Games people play.* New York: Grove Press, 1964.

Bettelheim, B. *The informed heart.* New York: Free Press, 1960.

Blank, P., Flint, A., & Goodrich, D. W. *Married couples in experimentally induced conflict situations.* Film, 1962, Child Research Branch, National Institute of Mental Health, Bethesda, Md.

Bleuler, E. *Dementia praecox or the group of schizophrenias.* New York: International Universities Press, 1950.

Blum, G. S. *Psychodynamics: The science of unconscious mental forces.* Belmont, Calif.: Brooks/Cole, 1966.

Bonime, W. *The clinical use of dreams.* New York: Basic Books, 1962.

Borko, H. (Ed.) *Computer applications in the behavioral sciences.* Englewood Cliffs, N. J.: Prentice-Hall, 1962.

Bowers, K. Hypnotic behavior: The differentiation of trance and demand characteristic variables. *Journal of Abnormal Psychology,* 1966, **71**, 42–51.

Braginsky, B. M. & Braginsky, D. D. Schizophrenic patients in the psychiatric interview: An experimental study of their effectiveness at manipulation. *Journal of Consulting Psychology,* 1967, **31**, 543–547.

Braginsky, B. M., Grosse, M., & Ring, K. Controlling outcomes through impression management: An experimental study of the manipulative tactics of mental patients. *Journal of Consulting Psychology,* 1966, **30**, 295–300.

Bramel, D. A dissonance theory approach to defensive projection. *Journal of Abnormal and Social Psychology,* 1962, **64**, 121–129.

Breger, L. Function of dreams. *Journal of Abnormal Psychology,* Monograph, 1967, **72**(5, Part 2 of 2 parts, Whole No. 641).

Breger, L. & McGaugh, J. L. Critique and reformulation of "learning-theory" approaches to psychotherapy and neurosis. *Psychological Bulletin,* 1965, **63**, 338–358.

Broadbent, D. E. *Perception and communication.* London: Pergamon Press, 1958.

Brown, R. Models of attitude change. In T. M. Newcomb (Ed.), *New directions in psychology.* New York: Holt, Rinehart and Winston, 1962.

Buss, A. H. *The psychology of aggression.* New York: Wiley, 1961.

Buss, A. H. *Psychopathology.* New York: Wiley, 1966.

Butter, C. M. *Neuropsychology: The study of brain and behavior.* Belmont, Calif.: Brooks/Cole, 1968.

Cameron, N. *Personality development and psychopathology: A dynamic approach.* Boston: Houghton Mifflin, 1963.

Campbell, D., Miller, N., Lubetsky, J., & O'Connell, E. Varieties of projection in trait attribution. *Psychological Monographs,* 1964, **78**(15, Whole No. 592).

Cannon, W. B. "Voodoo" death. *American Anthropologist,* 1942, **44**, 169–181.

Cantril, H. & Hunt, W. A. Emotional effects produced by the injection of adrenalin. *American Journal of Psychology,* 1932, **44**, 300–307.

Carter, J. W., Jr. (Ed.) *Research contributions from psychology to community mental health.* New York: Behavioral Publications, 1968.

Cartwright, D. S. Effectiveness of psychotherapy: A critique of the spontaneous remission argument. *Journal of Counseling Psychology,* 1955, **2**, 290–296.

Cartwright, R. D. & Vogel, J. L. A comparison of changes in psychoneurotic patients during matched periods of therapy and no-therapy. *Journal of Consulting Psychology,* 1960, **24**, 121–127.

Cattell, R. B. Are I. Q. tests intelligent? *Psychology Today,* March 1968, 56–62.

Cautela, J. R. Treatment of compulsive behavior by covert sensitization. *Psychological Record,* 1966, **16**, 33–41.

Chapman, L. J. The problem of selecting drug-free schizophrenics for research. *Journal of Consulting Psychology,* 1963, **27**, 540–542.

Chapman, L. J. & Chapman, J. P. Genesis of popular but erroneous psychodiagnostic observations. *Journal of Abnormal Psychology,* 1967, **72**, 193–204.

Chassan, J. B. *Research design in clinical psychology and psychiatry.* New York: Appleton-Century-Crofts, 1967.

Cleckley, H. *The mask of sanity.* (3rd ed.) St. Louis: C. V. Mosby, 1955.

Colby, K. M. Computer simulation of a neurotic process. In S. S. Tomkins & S. Messick (Eds.), *Computer simulation of personality.* New York: Wiley, 1963.

Cowen, E. L. & Zax, M. Early detection and prevention of emotional disorder: Conceptualizations and programming. In J. W. Carter, Jr. (Ed.), *Research contributions from psychology to community mental health.* New York: Behavioral Publications, 1968.

Cowen, E. L., Zax, M., & Laird, J. D. A college student volunteer program in the elementary school setting. *Community Mental Health Journal,* 1966, **2**, 319–328.

Cronbach, L. J. The two disciplines of scientific psychology. *American Psychologist,* 1957, **12**, 671–684.

Cronbach, L. J. *Essentials of psychological testing.* New York: Harper, 1960.

Cronbach, L. J. Heredity, environment, and educational policy. *Harvard Educational Review,* 1969, **39**, 338–347.

Crow, J. F. Genetic theories and influences: Comments on the value of diversity. Harvard Educational Review, 1969, **39**, 301–309.

Davison, G. C. Systematic desensitization as a counterconditioning process. *Journal of Abnormal Psychology,* 1968, **73**, 91–99.

Deering, G. Affective stimuli and disturbance of thought processes. *Journal of Consulting Psychology,* 1963, **27**, 338–343.

Delgado, J. M. R. Aggression and defense under cerebral radio control. In C. D. Clemente & D. B. Lindsley (Eds.), *UCLA Forum in Medical Sciences,* **5**(7), 171–193. Berkeley, Calif.: University of California Press, 1967.

Dement, W. C. An essay on dreams: The role of physiology in understanding their nature. In T. M. Newcomb (Ed.), *New directions in psychology II.* New York: Holt, Rinehart and Winston, 1965.

Dement, W. C. & Kleitman, N. Cyclic variations of EEG during sleep and their relation to eye movements, body motility, and dreaming. *Journal of Electroencephalography and Clinical Neurophysiology,* 1957, **9**, 673–690.

Dement, W. & Wolpert, E. The relation of eye movements, body motility, and external stimuli to dream content. *Journal of Experimental Psychology,* 1958, **55**, 543–553.

Denker, P. G. Results of treatment of psychoneuroses by the general practitioner: A follow-up study of 500 cases. *Archives of Neurology and Psychiatry,* 1947, **57**, 504–505.

Deutsch, M. Happenings on the way back to the forum: Social science, IQ, and race differences revisited. *Harvard Educational Review,* 1969, **39**, 523–557.

Dollard, J., Doob, L. W., Miller, N. E., Mowrer, O. H., & Sears, R. R. *Frustration and aggression.* New Haven: Yale University Press, 1939.

Draguns, J. G. Responses to cognitive and perceptual ambiguity in chronic and acute schizophrenics. *Journal of Abnormal and Social Psychology,* 1963, **66**, 24–30.

Edlow, D. & Kiesler, C. Ease of denial and defensive projection. *Journal of Experimental Social Psychology,* 1966, **2**, 56–69.

Elkind, D. Piagetian and psychometric conceptions of intelligence. *Harvard Educational Review,* 1969, **39**, 319–337.

Ellis, A. *Reason and emotion in psychotherapy.* New York: Lyle Stuart, 1962.

English, H. B. & English, A. C. *A comprehensive dictionary of psychological and psychoanalytical terms.* New York: Longmans, Green and Co., 1958.

Epps, E. G., Katz, I., Perry, A., & Runyon, E. Effect of race of comparison referent and motives on Negro cognitive performance. (In press.)

Epstein, S. The measurement of drive and conflict in humans: Theory and experiment. In M. R. Jones (Ed.), *Nebraska Symposium on Motivation 1962.* Lincoln, Nebraska: University of Nebraska Press, 1962.

Erickson, M. H. An experimental investigation of the hypnotic subject's apparent ability to become unaware of stimuli. *Journal of General Psychology,* 1944, **31**, 191–212.

Ethical Standards of Psychologists. *American Psychologist,* 1963, **18**, 56–60.

Eysenck, H. J. The effects of psychotherapy: An evaluation. *Journal of Consulting Psychology,* 1952, **16**, 319–324.

Eysenck, H. J. *Crime and personality.* London: Routledge and Kegan Paul, 1964.

Farina, A. Patterns of role dominance and conflict in parents of schizophrenic patients. *Journal of Abnormal and Social Psychology,* 1960, **61**, 31–38.
Fenichel, O. *The psychoanalytic theory of neurosis.* New York: Norton, 1945.
Feshbach, S. & Singer, R. The effects of fear arousal and suppression of fear upon social perception. *Journal of Abnormal and Social Psychology,* 1957, **55**, 283–288.
Festinger, L. *A theory of cognitive dissonance.* New York: Row, Peterson, 1957.
Fisher, C. Psychological significance of the dream-sleep cycle. In H. A. Witkin & Helen B. Witkin (Eds.), *Experimental studies of dreaming.* New York: Random House, 1967.
Fisher, J. The twisted pear and the prediction of behavior. *Journal of Consulting Psychology,* 1959, **23**, 400–405.
Flint, A. A. & Ryder, R. G. Interpersonal disagreements in marriage: The stereognosis test. Paper presented at the annual meeting of the American Psychiatric Association, 1963.
Fontana, A. F. Familial etiology of schizophrenia: Is a scientific methodology possible? *Psychological Bulletin,* 1966, **66**, 214–227.
Forer, B. R. The fallacy of personal validation: A classroom demonstration of gullibility. *Journal of Abnormal and Social Psychology,* 1949, **44**, 118–123.
Foulkes, D. *The psychology of sleep.* New York: Scribner's, 1966.
Frank, J. D. *Persuasion and healing.* Baltimore: Johns Hopkins Press, 1961.
Franks, C. M., Fried, R., & Ashem, B. An improved apparatus for the aversive conditioning of cigarette smokers. *Behaviour Research and Therapy,* 1966, **4**, 301–308.
Freud, S. *Die Traumdeutung.* Vienna, Austria: F. Deuticke, 1900.
Freud, S. *Jokes and their relation to the unconscious.* (Ed. & trans. by J. Strachey) (Orig. publ. 1905) New York: Norton, 1960.
Freud, S. Psychoanalytic notes upon an autobiographical account of a case of paranoia. *Jahrbuch für psychoanalytische und psychopathologische Forschungen,* Vol. III, 1911.
Freud, S. The interpretation of dreams. In A. A. Brill (Ed.), *The basic writings of Sigmund Freud.* New York: Random House, 1938.
Fromm, E. *The forgotten language.* New York: Grove Press, 1957.
Fulcher, J. H., Gallagher, W. J., & Pfeiffer, C. C. Comparative lucid intervals after amobarbitol, CO_2, and arecoline in chronic schizophrenics. *Archives of Neurology and Psychiatry,* 1957, **78**, 392–395.
Garmezy, N. The prediction of performance in schizophrenia. In P. H. Hoch & J. Zubin (Eds.), *Schizophrenia.* New York: Grune & Stratton, 1965.
Geiwitz, P. J. *Non-Freudian personality theories.* Belmont, Calif.: Brooks/Cole, 1969.
Gilbert, G. M. *Nuremberg diary.* New York: Farrar, Straus, 1947.
Gittelman, M. Behavior rehearsal as a technique in child treatment. *Journal of Child Psychology and Psychiatry,* 1965, **6**, 251–255.
Goffman, E. *The presentation of self in everyday life.* New York: Doubleday, 1959.
Goffman, E. *Asylums.* New York: Doubleday, 1961.
Goldberg, L. R. Reliability of Peace Corps selection boards: A study of interjudge agreement before and after board discussions. *Journal of Applied Psychology,* 1966, **50**, 400–408.
Goldberg, L. R. Simple models or simple processes?: Some research on clinical judgments. *American Psychologist,* 1968, **23**, 483–496.

Goldiamond, I. Self-control procedures in personal behavior problems. *Psychological Reports,* 1965, **17** (Monogr. Suppl. 3). (a)

Goldiamond, I. Stuttering and fluency as manipulatable operant response classes. In L. Krasner and L. P. Ullmann (Eds.), *Research in behavior modification: New developments and implications.* New York: Holt, Rinehart and Winston, 1965. (b)

Gollob, H. F. & Levine, J. Distraction as a factor in the enjoyment of aggressive humor. *Journal of Personality and Social Psychology,* 1967, **5**, 368–372.

Goodrich, D. W. & Boomer, D. S. Experimental assessment of modes of conflict resolution. *Family Process,* 1963, **2**, 15–24.

Gordon, J. E. Personal communication, 1970.

Greenson, R. R. *The technique and practice of psychoanalysis.* Vol. 1. New York: International Universities Press, 1967.

Guilford, J. P. Three faces of intellect. *American Psychologist,* 1959, **14**, 469–479.

Guilford, J. P. Intelligence: 1965 model. *American Psychologist,* 1966, **21**, 20–26.

Gurin, G., Veroff, J., & Feld, S. *Americans view their mental health.* New York: Basic Books, 1960.

Hall, C. *The meaning of dreams.* New York: McGraw-Hill, 1966.

Harary, F., Norman, R. Z., & Cartwright, D. *Structural models: An introduction to the theory of directed graphs.* New York: Wiley, 1965.

Hare, R. D. Psychopathy, autonomic functioning, and the orienting response. *Journal of Abnormal Psychology,* Monograph Supplement, June 1968, **73**, No. 3, Part 2, 1–24.

Haughton, E., & Ayllon, T. Production and elimination of symptomatic behavior. In L. P. Ullmann & L. Krasner (Eds.), *Case studies in behavior modification.* Holt, Rinehart and Winston, 1965.

Hays, W. L. *Basic statistics.* Belmont, Calif.: Brooks/Cole, 1967.

Heath, R. G. & Mickle, W. A. Evaluation of seven years' experience with depth electrode studies in human patients. In Estelle R. Ramey & D. S. O'Doherty (Eds.), *Electrical studies on the unanesthetized brain.* New York: Hoeber, 1960.

Heath, R. G., Monroe, R. R. et al. Addendum A: Case history of the patient operated upon in June, 1952. In R. G. Heath (Ed.), *Studies in schizophrenia.* Cambridge, Mass.: Harvard University Press, 1954.

Hertel, R. K. The Markov-modeling of experimentally induced conflict. Unpublished doctoral dissertation, University of Michigan, 1968.

Hess, E. H. Attitude and pupil size. *Scientific American,* 1965, **212**, 46–54.

Hilgard, E. R. *Hypnotic susceptibility.* New York: Harcourt, Brace & World, 1965.

Hobbs, N. Sources of gain in psychotherapy. *American Psychologist,* 1962, **17**, 18–34.

Hoch, E. L. *Clinical psychology: An empirical approach.* Belmont, Calif.: Brooks/Cole, 1971.

Hoffman, B. *The tyranny of testing.* New York: Crowell-Collier, 1962.

Hogan, R. A. & Kirchner, J. H. Preliminary report of the extinction of learned fears via short-term implosive therapy. *Journal of Abnormal Psychology,* 1967, **72**, 106–109.

Hogan, R. A. & Kirchner, J. H. Implosive, eclectic verbal and bibliotherapy in the treatment of fears of snakes. *Behaviour Research and Therapy,* 1968, **6**, 167–171.

Hollingshead, A. B. & Redlich, F. C. *Social class and mental illness: A community study.* New York: Wiley, 1958.

Holmes, D. S. Dimensions of projection. *Psychological Bulletin,* 1968, **69**, 248–268.

Holt, R. R. Clinical and statistical prediction: A reformulation and some new data. *Journal of Abnormal and Social Psychology,* 1958, **56**, 1–12.

Holt, R. R. Yet another look at clinical and statistical prediction: Or, is clinical psychology worthwhile? *American Psychologist,* 1970, **25**, 337–349.

Holtzman, W. H. & Sells, S. B. Prediction of flying success by clinical analysis of test protocols. *Journal of Abnormal and Social Psychology,* 1954, **49**, 485–490.

Hornberger, R. The projective effects of fear and sexual arousal on the ratings of pictures. *Journal of Clinical Psychology,* 1960, **16**, 328–331.

Houston, J. P. & Mednick, S. A. Creativity and the need for novelty. *Journal of Abnormal and Social Psychology,* 1963, **66**, 137–141.

Hunt, J. McV. *Intelligence and experience.* New York: Ronald Press, 1961.

Hunt, J. McV. Has compensatory education failed? Has it been attempted? *Harvard Educational Review,* 1969, **39**, 279–300.

Inhelder, B. & Piaget, J. *The growth of logical thinking: From childhood to adolescence.* New York: Basic Books, 1958.

Isaacs, W., Thomas, J., & Goldiamond, I. Application of operant conditioning to reinstate verbal behavior in psychotics. *Journal of Speech and Hearing Disorders,* 1960, **25**, 8–12.

Jacobson, E. *Progressive relaxation.* Chicago: University of Chicago Press, 1938.

James, W. *The principles of psychology.* New York: Holt, 1890.

Jensen, A. R. How much can we boost IQ and scholastic achievement? *Harvard Educational Review,* 1969, **39**, 1–123. (a)

Jensen, A. R. Reducing the heredity-environment uncertainty. *Harvard Educational Review,* 1969, **39**, 449–483. (b)

Jones, Mary C. The elimination of children's fears. *Journal of Experimental Psychology,* 1924, **7**, 382–390.

Kadushin, A. Diagnosis and evaluation for (almost) all occasions. *Social Work,* January 1963, 12–19.

Kagan, J. S. Inadequate evidence and illogical conclusions. *Harvard Educational Review,* 1969, **39**, 274–277.

Kahneman, D. & Beatty, J. Pupil diameter and load on memory. *Science,* 1966, **154**, 1583–1585.

Kamiya, J. Conscious control of brain waves. *Psychology Today,* 1968, **1**, 57–60.

Kasanin, J. S. *Language and thought in schizophrenia.* Berkeley: University of California Press, 1946.

Katahn, M. & Koplin, J. H. Paradigm clash: Comment on "Some recent criticisms of behaviorism and learning theory with special reference to Breger and McGaugh and to Chomsky." *Psychological Bulletin,* 1968, **69**, 147–148.

Katz, I. & Cohen, M. The effects of training upon cooperative problem-solving in biracial teams. *Journal of Abnormal and Social Psychology,* 1962, **64**, 319–325.

Katz, I., Epps, E. G., & Axelson, L. J. Effect upon Negro digit-symbol performance of anticipated comparison with whites and with other Negroes. *Journal of Abnormal and Social Psychology,* 1964, **69**, 77–83.

Katz, I. & Greenbaum, C. Effects of anxiety, threat, and racial environment on task performance of Negro college students. *Journal of Abnormal and Social Psychology,* 1963, **66**, 562–567.

Katz, I., Roberts, S. O., & Robinson, J. M. Effects of task difficulty, race of administrator, and instructions on digit-symbol performance of Negroes. *Journal of Personality and Social Psychology,* 1965, **2**, 53–59.

Kelley, H. H., Condry, J. C., Jr., Dahlke, A. E., & Hill, A. H. Collective behavior in a simulated panic situation. *Journal of Experimental Social Psychology,* 1965, **1,** 20–54.

Kelly, E. L. *Assessment of human characteristics.* Belmont, Calif.: Brooks/Cole, 1967.

Kelly, E. L. & Fiske, D. W. *The prediction of performance in clinical psychology.* Ann Arbor: University of Michigan Press, 1951.

Kelly, G. A. *The psychology of personal constructs.* New York: Norton, 1955.

Kelly, J. G. Toward an ecological conception of preventive interventions. In J. W. Carter, Jr. (Ed.), *Research contributions from psychology to community mental health.* New York: Behavioral Publications, 1968.

Kidd, A. H. & Walton, N. Y. Dart throwing as a method of reducing extra-punitive aggression. *Psychological Reports,* 1966, **19,** 88–90.

Kiesler, D. J. Some myths of psychotherapy research and the search for a paradigm. *Psychological Bulletin,* 1966, **65,** 110–136.

Korte, C., & Milgram, S. Acquaintance networks between racial groups: Application of the small world method. *Journal of Personality and Social Psychology,* 1970, **15,** 101–108.

Kraepelin, E. *Psychiatrie.* Leipzig: Barth, 1915.

Krapfl, J. E. & Nawas, M. M. Differential ordering of stimulus presentation in systematic desensitization. *Journal of Abnormal Psychology,* 1970, **75,** 333–337.

Landis, C. A. Statistical evaluation of psychotherapeutic methods. In L. E. Hinsie (Ed.), *Concepts and problems of psychotherapy.* New York: Columbia University Press, 1937.

Lang, P. J. & Buss, A. H. Psychological deficit in schizophrenia: II. Interference and activation. *Journal of Abnormal Psychology,* 1965, **70**(2), 77–106.

Lang, P. J. & Lazovik, A. D. Experimental desensitization of a phobia. *Journal of Abnormal and Social Psychology,* 1963, **66,** 519–525.

Lang, P. J., Lazovik, A. D. & Reynolds, D. J. Desensitization, suggestibility, and pseudotherapy. *Journal of Abnormal Psychology,* 1965, **70,** 395–402.

Latané, B. & Schachter, S. Adrenalin and avoidance learning. *Journal of Comparative and Physiological Psychology,* 1962, **55,** 369–372.

Lazarus, A. A., Davison, G. C., & Polefka, D. A. Classical and operant factors in the treatment of a school phobia. *Journal of Abnormal Psychology,* 1965, **70,** 225–229.

Lazarus, R. S. A laboratory approach to the dynamics of psychological stress. *American Psychologist,* 1964, **19,** 400–411.

Lerner, B. Dream function reconsidered. *Journal of Abnormal Psychology,* 1967, **72,** 85–100.

Levine, S. Stimulation in infancy. *Scientific American,* 1960, **202,** 80–86.

Lewinsohn, P. M., Nichols, R. C., Pulos, L., Lomont, J. F., Nickel, H. J., & Siskind, G. The reliability and validity of quantified judgments from psychological tests, *Journal of Clinical Psychology,* 1963, **19,** 64–73.

Lidz, T. & Fleck, S. Schizophrenia, human integration, and the role of the family. In D. D. Jackson (Ed.), *The etiology of schizophrenia.* New York: Basic Books, 1960.

Light, R. J. & Smith, P. V. Social allocation models of intelligence: A methodological inquiry. *Harvard Educational Review,* 1969, **39,** 484–510.

Lindsley, O. R. Experimental analysis of cooperation and competition. Paper presented at a meeting of the Eastern Psychological Association, Philadelphia, April 1961.

Lindsley, O. R. Operant conditioning methods in diagnosis. In Lea & Febiger, *The first Hahnemann symposium on psychosomatic medicine,* 1962. Pp. 41–54.

Lorr, M. Multidimensional scales for rating psychiatric patients. Veterans Administration Bulletin, TB 10–507, 1953.

Luborsky, L. A note on Eysenck's article "The effects of psychotherapy: An evaluation." *British Journal of Psychology,* 1954, **45**, 129–131.

Lykken, D. T. A study of anxiety in the sociopathic personality. *Journal of Abnormal and Social Psychology,* 1957, **55**, 6–10.

Machover, K. *Personality projection in the drawing of the human figure.* Springfield, Ill.: Charles C Thomas, 1948.

Maher, B. *Principles of psychopathology: An experimental approach.* New York: McGraw-Hill, 1966.

Marks, I. M. & Gelder, M. G. Common ground between behaviour therapy and psychodynamic methods. *British Journal of Medical Psychology,* 1966, **39**, 11–23.

Marks, P. A. An assessment of the diagnostic process in a child guidance setting. *Psychological Monographs,* 1961, **75**(Whole No. 507).

Maslow, A. H. Deprivation, threat, and frustration. *Psychological Review,* 1941, **48**, 364–366.

Maslow, A. H. *Toward a psychology of being.* Princeton, N. J.: Van Nostrand, 1962.

Matarazzo, J. D. Prescribed behavior therapy: Suggestions from interview research. In A. J. Bachrach (Ed.), *Experimental foundations of clinical psychology.* New York: Basic Books, 1962.

Matarazzo, J. D., Wiens, A. N., & Saslow, G. Studies in interview speech behavior. In L. Krasner & L. P. Ullmann (Eds.), *Research in behavior modification: New developments and implications.* New York: Holt, Rinehart and Winston, 1965.

Maury, A. Le sommeil et les rêves. Paris: 1861.

McClelland, D. C. & Apicella, F. S. A functional classification of verbal reactions to experimentally induced failure. *Journal of Abnormal and Social Psychology,* 1945, **40**, 376–390.

McConnell, J. V. Psychoanalysis must go. *Esquire,* 1968, **70**, 176ff.

McGhie, A. & Chapman, J. Disorders of attention and perception in early schizophrenia. *British Journal of Medical Psychology,* 1961, **34**, 103–116.

McGrath, J. E. *Social psychology: A brief introduction.* New York: Holt, Rinehart and Winston, 1964.

McGuigan, F. J. The experimenter: A neglected stimulus object. *Psychological Bulletin,* 1963, **60**, 421–428.

McNeil, T. F. The relationship between creative ability and recorded mental illness. Unpublished doctoral dissertation, The University of Michigan, 1969.

McNemar, Q. Lost: Our intelligence? Why? *American Psychologist,* 1964, **19**, 871–882.

McReynolds, P. Anxiety, perception, and schizophrenia. In D. D. Jackson (Ed.), *The etiology of schizophrenia.* New York: Basic Books, 1960.

Mednick, S. A. A learning theory approach to research in schizophrenia. *Psychological Bulletin,* 1958, **55**, 316–325.

Mednick, S. A. The associative basis of the creative process. *Psychological Review,* 1962, **69**, 220–232.

Mednick, S. A. & Halpern, S. *Remote Associates Test* (Form 1). Berkeley, Calif.: Institute of Personality Assessment and Research, University of California, 1959.

Mednick, S. A. & McNeil, T. F. Current methodology in research on the etiology of schizophrenia: Serious difficulties which suggest the use of the high-risk-group method. *Psychological Bulletin,* 1968, **70**, 681–693.

Mednick, S. A. & Mednick, M. T. An associative interpretation of the creative process. In C. W. Taylor & F. Barron (Eds.), *Widening horizons in creativity.* New York: Wiley, 1964.

Mednick, S. A. & Mednick, M. T. The associative basis of the creative process. Cooperative Research Project No. 1073, Cooperative Research Program, U.S. Office of Education, 1965.

Mednick, S. A. & Schulsinger, F. A longitudinal study of children with a high risk for schizophrenia: A preliminary report. In S. Vandenberg (Ed.), *Methods and goals in human behavior genetics.* New York: Academic Press, 1965.

Meehl, P. E. *Clinical versus statistical prediction.* Minneapolis, Minn.: University of Minnesota Press, 1954.

Meehl, P. E. Wanted—a good cookbook. *American Psychologist,* 1956, **11**, 263–272.

Meehl, P. E. When shall we use our heads instead of the formula? *Journal of Counseling Psychology,* 1957, **4**, 268–273.

Meehl, P. E. A comparison of clinicians with five statistical methods of identifying psychotic MMPI profiles. *Journal of Counseling Psychology,* 1959, **6**, 102–109.

Meehl, P. E. The cognitive activity of the clinician. *American Psychologist,* 1960, **15**, 19–27.

Meehl, P. E. Schizotaxia, schizotypy, schizophrenia. *American Psychologist,* 1962, **17**, 827–838.

Meehl, P. E. & Rosen, A. Antecedent probability and the efficiency of psychometric signs, patterns, or cutting scores. *Psychological Bulletin,* 1955, **52**, 194–216.

Mendel, W. M. Effect of length of hospitalization on rate and quality of remission from acute psychotic episodes. *Journal of Nervous and Mental Diseases,* 1966, **143**, 226–233.

Mendel, W. M. Tranquilizer prescribing as a function of the experience and availability of the therapist. *American Journal of Psychiatry,* 1967, **124**, 16–22.

Mendel, W. M. Personal communication, 1969.

Mendel, W. M. & Rapport, S. Determinants of the decision for psychiatric hospitalization. *Archives of General Psychiatry,* 1969, **20**, 321–328.

Menninger, K., Mayman, M., & Pruyser, P. *The vital balance.* New York: Viking Press, 1963.

Milgram, S. Behavioral study of obedience. *Journal of Abnormal and Social Psychology,* 1963, **67**, 371–378.

Milgram, S. Group pressure and action against a person. *Journal of Abnormal and Social Psychology,* 1964, **69**, 137–143. (a)

Milgram, S. Issues in the study of obedience: A reply to Baumrind. *American Psychologist,* 1964, **19**, 848–852. (b)

Milgram, S. Liberating effects of group pressure. *Journal of Personality and Social Psychology,* 1965, **1**, 127–134.

Milgram, S. The small-world problem. *Psychology Today,* 1967, **1**, 61–67.

Miller, N. E. The frustration-aggression hypothesis. *Psychological Review,* 1941, **48**, 337–342.

Miller, N. E. Liberalization of basic S-R concepts: Extensions to conflict behavior, motivation, and social learning. In S. Koch (Ed.), *Psychology: A study of a science.* Vol. 2. New York: McGraw-Hill, 1959.

Miller, N. E. Learning of visceral and glandular responses. *Science,* 1969, **163**, 434–445.

Miller, N. E. & Banuazizi, A. Instrumental learning by curarized rats of a specific visceral response, intestinal or cardiac. *Journal of Comparative and Physiological Psychology,* 1968, **65**, 1–7.

Miller, N. E. & Carmona, A. Modification of a visceral response, salivation in thirsty dogs, by instrumental training with water reward. *Journal of Comparative and Physiological Psychology,* 1967, **63**, 1–6.

Mintz, A. Non-adaptive group behavior. *Journal of Abnormal and Social Psychology,* 1951, **46**, 150–159.

Mishler, E. G. & Scotch, N. A. Sociocultural factors in the epidemiology of schizophrenia. *Psychiatry,* 1963, **26**, 315–351.

Moss, C. S. *The hypnotic investigation of dreams.* New York: Wiley, 1967.

Münsterberg, H. *On the witness stand.* New York: McClure, 1908.

Murray, H., et al. *Explorations in personality.* New York: Oxford University Press, 1938.

Murstein, B. I. Studies in projection: A critique. *Journal of Projective Techniques,* 1956, **20**, 418–428.

Newcomb, T. M. An approach to the study of communicative acts. *Psychological Review,* 1953, **60**, 393–404.

Nunnally, J. C., Knott, P. D., Duchnowski, A., & Parker, R. Pupillary response as a general measure of activation. *Perception and Psychophysics,* 1967, **2**, 149–155.

Olds, J. & Milner, P. M. Positive reinforcement produced by electrical stimulation of septal area and other regions of rat brain. *Journal of Comparative and Physiological Psychology,* 1954, **47**, 419–427.

Orne, M. T. On the social psychology of the psychological experiment: With particular reference to demand characteristics and their implications. *American Psychologist,* 1962, **17**, 776–783.

Osgood, C. E. & Tannenbaum, P. H. The principle of congruity in the prediction of attitude change. *Psychological Review,* 1955, **62**, 42–55.

Osgood, C. E. & Walker, Evelyn G. Motivation and language behavior: A content analysis of suicide notes. *Journal of Abnormal and Social Psychology,* 1959, **59**, 58–67.

Overmier, J. B. & Seligman, M. E. P. Effects of inescapable shock upon subsequent escape and avoidance responding. *Journal of Comparative and Physiological Psychology,* 1967, **63**, 28–33.

Page, H. A. & Markowitz, G. The relationship of defensiveness to rating scale bias. *Journal of Psychology,* 1955, **40**, 431–435.

Panel on Privacy and Behavioral Research. Preliminary summary of the report of the panel. *American Psychologist,* 1967, **22**, 345–349.

Paterson, D. G. Character reading at sight of Mr. X according to the system of Mr. P. T. Barnum. (Mimeographed, unpublished.)

Paul, G. L. Insight versus desensitization in psychotherapy two years after termination. *Journal of Consulting Psychology,* 1967, **31**, 333–348.

Perls, F. S., Hefferline, R. F., & Goodman, P. *Gestalt therapy.* New York: Julian Press, 1951.

Peters, F. *The world next door.* New York: Farrar, Straus & Giroux, 1949.
Pierce, A. H. The subconscious again. *Journal of Philosophy, Psychology, and Scientific Method,* 1908, **5**, 264–271.
Powell, J. & Azrin, N. H. The effects of shock as a punisher for cigarette smoking. *Journal of Applied Behavior Analysis,* 1968, **1**, 63–71.
Premack, D. Reversibility of the reinforcement relation. *Science,* 1962, **136**, 255–257.
Preston, M. G. & Bayton, J. A. Differential effect of a social variable upon three levels of aspiration. *Journal of Experimental Psychology,* 1941, **29**, 351–369.
Rachman, S. & Eysenck, H. J. Reply to a "critique and reformulation" of behavior therapy. *Psychological Bulletin,* 1966, **65**, 165–169.
Rapaport, D., Gill, M. M., & Shafer, R. *Diagnostic psychological testing.* (Revised edition by R. R. Holt.) New York: International Universities Press, 1968.
Raush, H. L., Dittmann, A. T., & Taylor, T. J. Person, setting, and change in social interaction. *Human Relations,* 1959, **12**, 361–378.
Raush, H. L., Goodrich, D. W., & Campbell, J. D. Adaptation to the first years of marriage. *Psychiatry,* 1963, **26**, 368–380.
Reik, T. *Listening with the third ear.* New York: Farrar, Straus, 1948.
Richter, C. P. On the phenomenon of sudden death in animals and man. *Psychosomatic Medicine,* 1957, **19**, 191–198.
Ringuette, E. L. & Kennedy, T. An experimental study of the double bind hypothesis. *Journal of Abnormal Psychology,* 1966, **71**, 136–141.
Rodnick, E. H. & Garmezy, N. An experimental approach to the study of motivation in schizophrenia. In M. R. Jones (Ed.), *Nebraska Symposium on Motivation.* Lincoln: University of Nebraska Press, 1957.
Roffwarg, H. P., Muzio, J. N., & Dement, W. C. Ontogenetic development of the human sleep-dream cycle. *Science,* 1966, **152**, 604–619.
Rogers, C. R. *On becoming a person.* Boston: Houghton Mifflin, 1961.
Rogers, C. R. & Skinner, B. F. Some issues concerning the control of human behavior: A symposium. *Science,* 1956, **124**, 1057–1066.
Rorschach, H. *Psychodiagnostics: A diagnostic test based on perception.* (Trans. by P. Lemkau & B. Kronenberg.) Bern: Verlag Hans Huber, 1921. (Republished: New York: Grune & Stratton, 1942.)
Rosenthal, R. On the social psychology of the psychological experiment: The experimenter's hypothesis as unintended determinant of experimental results. *American Scientist,* 1963, **51**, 268–283.
Rosenthal, R. Experimenter expectancy and the reassuring nature of the null hypothesis decision procedure. *Psychological Bulletin Monograph,* 1968, **70**, Part 2, 30–47.
Rosenthal, R. & Fode, K. L. Three experiments in experimenter bias. *Psychological Reports Monograph,* 1963, **12**(3).
Rosenthal, R., Kohn, P., Greenfield, P. M., & Carota, N. Data desirability, experimenter expectancy, and the results of psychological research. *Journal of Personality and Social Psychology,* 1966, **3**, 20–27.
Ross, S., Krugman, A. D., Lyerly, S. B., & Clyde, D. J. Drugs and placebos: A model design. *Psychological Reports,* 1962, **10**, 383–392.
Rosenzweig, S. An outline of frustration theory. In J. McV. Hunt (Ed.), *Personality and the behavior disorders.* New York: Ronald Press, 1944.

Rosenzweig, S. A transvaluation of psychotherapy; A reply to Hans Eysenck, *Journal of Abnormal and Social Psychology,* 1954, **49**, 298–304.

Ruesch, J. *Therapeutic communication.* New York: Norton, 1961.

Sanders, R. A. The "Bug-in-the-ear": A device for training of clinical psychologists. Paper presented at the meeting of the Midwestern Psychological Association, Chicago, May 1966.

Sarbin, T. R. Hypnosis as a behavior modification technique. In L. Krasner & L. P. Ullmann (Eds.), *Research in behavior modification: New developments and implications.* New York: Holt, Rinehart and Winston, 1965.

Saslow, G. A case history of attempted behavior manipulation in a psychiatric ward. In L. Krasner & L. P. Ullmann (Eds.), *Research in behavior modification: New developments and implications.* New York: Holt, Rinehart and Winston, 1965.

Sattler, J. M. Racial "experimenter effects" in experimentation, testing, interviewing, and psychotherapy. *Psychological Bulletin,* 1970, **73**, 137–160.

Sawyer, J. Measurement *and* prediction, clinical *and* statistical. *Psychological Bulletin,* 1966, **66**, 178–200.

Schachter, S. & Latané, B. Crime, cognition, and the autonomic nervous system. In D. Levine (Ed.), *Nebraska symposium on motivation 1964.* Lincoln: University of Nebraska Press, 1964.

Schachter, S. & Singer, J. E. Cognitive, social, and physiological determinants of emotional state. *Psychological Review,* 1962, **69**, 379–399.

Schuham, A. I. The double-bind hypothesis a decade later. *Psychological Bulletin,* 1967, **68**, 409–416.

Schwitzgebel, R. L. Survey of electromechanical devices for behavior modification. *Psychological Bulletin,* 1968, **70**, 444–459.

Scott, J. P. Discussion section of Delgado, J. M. R. Aggression and defense under cerebral radio control. In C. D. Clemente and D. B. Lindsley (Eds.), *UCLA Forum in Medical Sciences,* 1967, **5**, 171–193.

Scott, W. A. & Wertheimer, M. *Introduction to psychological research.* New York: Wiley, 1962.

Sears, R. R. Experimental studies of projection: I. Attribution of traits. *Journal of Social Psychology,* 1936, **7**, 151–163.

Sears, R. R. Survey of objective studies of psychoanalytic concepts. *Social Science Research Council Bulletin,* 1943.

Seligman, M. E. P. & Maier, S. F. Failure to escape traumatic shock. *Journal of Experimental Psychology,* 1967, **74**, 1–9.

Seligman, M. E. P., Maier, S. F., & Geer, J. H. Alleviation of learned helplessness in the dog. *Journal of Abnormal Psychology,* 1968, **73**, 256–262.

Selye, H. *The stress of life.* New York: McGraw-Hill, 1956.

Shakow, D. Psychological deficit in schizophrenia. *Behavioral Science,* 1963, **8**, 275–305.

Shlien, J. M., Mosak, H. H., & Dreikurs, R. Effect of time limits: A comparison of two psychotherapies. *Journal of Counseling Psychology,* 1962, **9**, 31–34.

Shneidman, E. S. The NIMH Center for Studies of Suicide Prevention. *Bulletin of Suicidology,* July 1967, 2–7.

Shneidman, E. S. & Farberow, N. L. (Eds.), *Clues to suicide.* New York: McGraw-Hill, 1957.

Shneidman, E. S. & Mandelkorn, P. *How to prevent suicide.* Public Affairs Pamphlet No. 406. New York: Public Affairs Pamphlets, 1967.

Silverman, J. Scanning-control mechanism and "cognitive filtering" in paranoid and nonparanoid schizophrenia. *Journal of Consulting Psychology,* 1964, **28**, 385–393. (a)

Silverman, J. The problem of attention in research and theory on schizophrenia. *Psychological Review,* 1964, **71**, 352–379. (b)

Silverman, J., Berg, P. S. D., & Kantor, R. Some perceptual correlates of institutionalization. *Journal of Nervous and Mental Disease,* 1965, **141**, 651–657.

Singer, D. L. Aggression arousal, hostile humor, catharsis. *Journal of Personality and Social Psychology,* 1968, **8**(Monogr. Suppl. 1, Part 2), 1–14.

Singer, J. L. & Opler, M. K. Contrasting patterns of fantasy and motility in Irish and Italian schizophrenics. *Journal of Abnormal and Social Psychology,* 1956, **53**, 42–47.

Skeels, H. M. Adult status of children with contrasting early life experiences. *Monographs of the Society for Research in Child Development,* 1966, **31**(Serial No. 105), 1–65.

Skodak, M. & Skeels, H. M. A follow-up study of children in adoptive homes. *Journal of Genetic Psychology,* 1949, **75**, 85–125.

Smith, K. U. Testimony before the Senate Subcommittee on Constitutional Rights of the Committee on the Judiciary. *American Psychologist,* 1965, **20**, 907–915.

Solomon, R. L., Kamin, L. J., & Wynne, L. C. Traumatic avoidance learning: The outcomes of several extinction procedures with dogs. *Journal of Abnormal and Social Psychology,* 1953, **48**, 291–302.

Soskin, W. F. Bias in postdiction from projective tests. *Journal of Abnormal and Social Psychology,* 1954, **49**, 69–74.

Soskin, W. F. Influence of four types of data on diagnostic conceptualization in psychological testing. *Journal of Abnormal and Social Psychology,* 1959, **58**, 69–78.

Stampfl, T. G. & Levis, D. J. Essentials of implosive therapy: A learning-theory-based psychodynamic behavioral therapy. *Journal of Abnormal Psychology,* 1967, **72**, 496–503.

Stanton, A. H. & Schwartz, M. S. *The mental hospital.* New York: Basic Books, 1954.

Starkweather, J. A. Computest: A computer language for individual testing, instruction, and interviewing. *Psychological Reports,* 1965, **17**, 227–237. (a)

Starkweather, J. A. Programming strategies in computer-assisted interviewing. Paper presented at meetings of American Association for the Advancement of Science, Berkeley, California, December 1965. (b)

Stoyva, J. & Kamiya, J. Electrophysiological studies of dreaming as the prototype of a new strategy in the study of consciousness. *Psychological Review,* 1968, **75**, 192–205.

Stuart, R. B. Behavioral control of overeating. *Behaviour Research and Therapy,* 1967, **5**, 357–365.

Sullivan, H. S. *Conceptions of modern psychiatry.* Washington, D. C.: William Alanson White Psychiatric Foundation, 1947.

Surgeon General's Directives on Human Experimentation. *American Psychologist,* 1967, **22**, 350–355.

Swain, M. A. Husband-wife patterns of interaction at three stages of marriage. Unpublished doctoral dissertation, University of Michigan, 1969.

Taffel, C. Anxiety and the conditioning of verbal behavior. *Journal of Abnormal and Social Psychology,* 1955, **51**, 496–501.

Terman, L. M. & Merrill, M. A. *Stanford-Binet intelligence scale: Manual for the third revision, Form L-M.* Boston: Houghton Mifflin, 1960.

Testimony before House Special Subcommittee on Invasion of Privacy of the Committee on Government Operations, June 1965, Washington, D. C. *American Psychologist,* 1965, **20**, 955–988.

Thorson, M. The development of several criteria for assessing changes in the prediction of human behavior. Unpublished master's thesis, State University of Iowa, 1962.

Tilker, H. A. Socially responsible behavior as a function of observer responsibility and victim feedback. *Journal of Personality and Social Psychology,* 1970, **14**, 95–100.

Tsushima, W. T. Responses of Irish and Italian patients of two social classes under preoperative stress. *Journal of Personality and Social Psychology,* 1968, **8**, 43–48.

Türing, A. M. Can a machine think? In J. R. Newman (Ed.), *The world of mathematics.* New York: Simon and Schuster, 1956.

Valins, S. Psychotherapy and physiological reactivity under stress. Unpublished master's thesis, Columbia University, 1963.

Valins, S. Emotionality and information concerning internal reactions. *Journal of Personality and Social Psychology,* 1967, **6**, 458–463.

Vandenberg, S. G. Contributions of twin research to psychology. *Psychological Bulletin,* 1966, **66**, 327–352.

Venables, P. H. Input dysfunction in schizophrenia. In B. A. Maher (Ed.), *Progress in experimental personality research.* Vol. 1. New York: Academic Press, 1964.

Venables, P. H. & Wing, J. K. Level of arousal and the subclassification of schizophrenia. *Archives of General Psychiatry,* 1962, **7**, 114–119.

Vernon, P. E. Ability factors and environmental influences. *American Psychologist,* 1965, **20**, 723–733.

Versace, J. Personal communication, 1968.

Walker, E. L. *Conditioning and instrumental learning.* Belmont, Calif.: Brooks/Cole, 1967.

Walster, E., Berscheid, E., Abrahams, D., & Aronson, V. Effectiveness of debriefing following deception experiments. *Journal of Personality and Social Psychology,* 1967, **6**, 371–380.

Watley, D. J. Counselor predictive skill and differential judgments of occupational suitability. *Journal of Counseling Psychology,* 1967, **14**, 309–313.

Watson, J. B. & Rayner, R. Conditioned emotional reactions. *Journal of Experimental Psychology,* 1920, **3**, 1–14.

Webb, W. B. *Sleep: An experimental approach.* New York: Macmillan, 1968.

Wechsler, D. *The measurement and appraisal of adult intelligence.* Baltimore: Williams & Wilkins, 1958.

Weil, A. T., Zinberg, N. E., & Nelson, J. M. Clinical and psychological effects of marihuana in man. *Science,* 1968, **162**, 1234–1242.

Weiss, J. H. Effect of professional training and amount and accuracy of information on behavioral prediction. *Journal of Consulting Psychology,* 1963, **27**, 257–262.

Weitzman, B. Behavior therapy and psychotherapy. *Psychological Review,* 1967, **74**, 300–317.

Welsh, R. S. A highly efficient method of parental counseling: A mechanical third ear. Paper presented at the meeting of the Rocky Mountain Psychological Association, Denver, June 1966.

Wiest, W. M. Some recent criticisms of behaviorism and learning theory: With special reference to Breger and McGaugh and to Chomsky. *Psychological Bulletin,* 1967, **67**, 214–225.

Winslow, C. N. & Rapersand, I. Postdiction of the outcome of somatic therapy from the Rorschach records of schizophrenic patients. *Journal of Consulting Psychology,* 1964, **28**, 243–247.

Witkin, H. A. & Lewis, H. B. (Eds.) *Experimental studies of dreaming.* New York: Random House, 1967.

Wolberg, L. R. Hypnotic experiments in psychosomatic medicine. *Psychosomatic Medicine,* 1947, **9**, 337–342.

Wolman, B. B. (Ed.) *Handbook of clinical psychology.* New York: McGraw-Hill, 1965.

Wolpe, J. *Psychotherapy by reciprocal inhibition.* Stanford: Stanford University Press, 1958.

Woody, R. H. Toward a rationale for psychobehavioral therapy. *Archives of General Psychiatry,* 1968, **19**, 197–204.

Zajonc, R. B. Social facilitation. *Science,* 1965, **149**, 269–274.

Zax, M., Cowen, E. L., Izzo, L. D., Madonia, A., Merenda, J., & Trost, M. A. A teacher-aide program for preventing emotional disturbance in young school children. *Mental Hygiene,* 1966, **50**, 406–415.

References

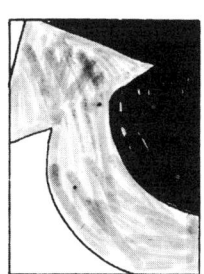

Name Index

Abrahams, D., 55 n
Antrobus, J., 30
Apicella, F. S., 96
Aronson, V., 55 n
Aserinsky, E., 20, 21
Ashem, B., 328-330
Atkinson, J. W., 285
Ax, A. F., 353
Axelson, L. J., 277-281
Ayllon, T., 35-37, 37 n, 37-39, 326-327
Azrin, A. H., 97, 98-103, 330-333
Bach, G. R., 130
Bachrach, A. J., 33, 60
Bandura, A., 46, 352, 358-361
Banuazizi, A., 157-159
Barber, T. X., 73, 145-147
Barron, F., 215
Barry, W. A., 132, 135
Bateson, G., 219
Baumrind, D., 55 n
Bayton, J. A., 277
Beatty, J., 139
Becker, H. W., 75
Berg, P. S. D., 63, 220
Bergin, A. E., 341-342
Berkowitz, L., 96, 104-109
Berkun, M. M., 56-59
Berne, E., 241, 318
Berscheid, E., 55 n
Bettelheim, B., 89
Bialek, H. M., 56-59
Binet, A., 271
Blank, P., 131
Bleuler, E., 89-90, 92, 195
Blum, G. S., 13, 26 n, 201, 242 n
Bonime, W., 13-14
Boomer, D. S., 130
Borko, H., 298
Bowers, K., 148-152
Braginsky, B. M., 258-260, 260-261
Braginsky, D. D., 260-261
Bramel, D., 242-248
Breger, L., 15-17, 28, 347
Broadbent, D. E., 209
Brown, R., 187-192
Buss, A. H., 95, 201-202, 209-210, 212-214, 218
Butter, C. M., 156, 211
Cameron, N., 201
Campbell, D., 132, 249-250
Cannon, W. B., 93
Cantril, H., 353
Carmona, A., 156-157
Carota, N., 70-71
Carter, J. W., Jr., 349-350
Cartwright, D. S., 186
Cartwright, R. D., 341, 343
Cattell, R. B., 285-286
Cautela, J. R., 335
Chapman, J. P., 174-181
Chapman, L. J., 61-62, 174-181, 209
Chassan, J. B., 65
Cleckley, H., 229, 235
Clyde, D. J., 65-67
Cohen, M., 277
Colby, K. M., 251-254
Condry, J. C., 122-123
Cowen, E. L., 350-351

Cronbach, L. J., 12, 17, 264, 268, 272
Crow, J. F., 268
Dahlke, A. E., 122-123
Davison, G. C., 40, 45
Deering, G., 204-205
Delgado, J. M. R., 109-111
Dement, W. C., 22, 27-28, 30-31
Denker, P. G., 341, 343
Deutsch, M., 269-270
Dittmann, A. T., 132
Dollard, J., 95
Doob, L. W., 95
Draguns, J. G., 210
Dreikurs, R., 342
Duchnowski, A., 139-140
Edlow, D., 250
Elkind, D., 268
Ellis, A., 318
English, A. C., 7, 242
English, H. B., 7, 242
Epps, E. G., 277-281
Epstein, S., 119-121
Erickson, M. H., 144
Eysenck, H. J., 235, 340-343, 348
Farberow, N. L., 116-117
Farina, A., 220
Feather, N. T., 285
Feld, S., 342
Fenichel, O., 201
Feshbach, S., 250
Festinger, L., 152, 242
Fisher, C., 30-31
Fisher, J., 302-304
Fiske, D. W., 308
Fleck, S., 201, 220
Flint, A. A., 130-131
Fode, K. L., 68-69
Fontana, A. F., 220
Forer, B. R., 164
Foulkes, D., 28-30
Frank, J. D., 342
Franks, C. M., 328-330
Freud, S., 11, 24, 26, 26 n, 127, 162, 249
Fried, R., 328-330
Fromm, E., 26 n
Fulcher, J. H., 205
Gallagher, W. J., 205
Garmezy, N., 218-219
Geen, R. G., 96, 104-106
Geer, J. H., 86, 89-92
Geiwitz, P. J., 242 n
Gelder, M. G., 348
Gilbert, G. M., 53

Gill, M. M., 115
Gittelman, M., 96
Goffman, E., 258
Goldberg, L. R., 308-310
Goldiamond, I., 333, 335-339
Gollob, H. F., 127-130
Goodman, P., 320
Goodrich, D. W., 130-132
Gordon, J. E., 152-153
Greenbaum, C., 280-281
Greenfield, P. M., 70-71
Greenson, R. R., 320
Grosse, M., 258-260
Grusec, J. E., 46, 352, 358-361
Guilford, J. P., 285-288
Gurin, G., 342
Hahn, K. W., Jr., 145-147
Hake, D. F., 98-103
Haley, J., 219
Hall, C., 26 n
Halpern, S., 214
Harary, F., 186
Hare, R. D., 235-236
Haughton, E., 35-37, 37 n
Hays, W. L., 58, 273
Heath, R. G., 112-113
Hefferline, R. F., 320
Hertel, R. K., 134-135
Hess, E. H., 137-140
Hilgard, E. R., 143-144, 147
Hill, A. H., 122-123
Hobbs, N., 40, 321
Hoch, E. L., vii
Hoffman, B., 314
Hogan, R. A., 345-346
Hollingshead, A. B., 119
Holmes, D. S., 248-250
Holt, R. R., 295-297
Holtzman, W. H., 308
Hornberger, R., 250
Houston, J. P., 216-217
Hughes, H. B., 35-37
Hunt, J. McV., 268, 288-289
Hunt, W. A., 353
Hutchinson, R. R., 98-103
Inhelder, B., 33
Isaacs, W., 335
Izzo, L. D., 350
Jackson, D. D., 219
Jacobson, E., 41
James, W., 353
Jensen, A. R., 267-270
Jones, M. C., 41

Kadushin, A., 164–167
Kagan, J. S., 268
Kahneman, D., 139
Kamin, L. J., 80–85, 92
Kamiya, J., 32–33, 154–155
Kantor, R., 63, 220
Kasanin, J. S., 182
Katahn, M., 348
Katz, I., 276–285
Kelley, H. H., 122–123
Kelly, E. L., 259, 308, 319
Kelly, G. A., 320
Kelly, J. G., 351
Kennedy, T., 308
Kern, R. P., 56–59
Kidd, A. H., 96
Kiesler, D. J., 250, 341, 343–344
Kirchner, J. H., 345–346
Kleitman, N., 20–22
Knott, P. D., 139–140
Kohn, P., 70–71
Koplin, J. H., 348
Korte, C., 184
Kraepelin, E., 161, 195
Krapfl, J. E., 45
Krugman, A. D., 65–67
Laird, J. D., 350
Landis, C. A., 340–341, 343
Lang, P. J., 7, 40–45, 213–214
Latané, B., 229–235
Lazarus, A. A., 40
Lazarus, R. S., 123–127
Lazovik, A. D., 7, 40–45
LePage, A., 107–108
Lerner, B., 28
Levine, J., 127–130
Levine, S., 114
Levis, D. J., 344–345
Lewinsohn, P. M., 172–174
Lewis, H. B., 31
Lidz, T., 201, 220
Light, R. J., 268
Lindsley, O. R., 324–325
Lomont, J. F., 172–174
Lorr, M., 173
Lubetsky, J., 249–250
Luborsky, L., 343
Lyerly, S. B., 65–67
Lykken, D. T., 225, 229–230
McClelland, D. C., 96
McConnell, J. V., 348
McGaugh, J. L., 347
McGhie, A., 209

McGrath, J. E., 186
McGuigan, F. J., 69–70
McNeil, T. F., 217, 220–224
McNemar, Q., 286
McReynolds, P., 206–209
Machover, K., 175
Madonia, A., 350
Maher, B., 210–211
Maier, S. F., 86–92
Mandelkorn, P., 117
Markowitz, G., 250
Marks, I. M., 308, 348
Maslow, A. H., 95
Matarazzo, J. D., 290–294
Maury, A., 24
Mayman, M., 161
Mednick, M. T., 215, 217
Mednick, S. A., 211–217, 220–224
Meehl, P. E., 12, 17, 181, 211, 294–295, 297, 304–306, 308, 310
Mendel, W. M., 254–258, 261–263
Menlove, F. L., 46, 352, 358–361
Menninger, K., 161
Merenda, J., 350
Merrill, M. A., 272
Michael, J., 37–39, 326–327
Mickle, W. A., 112–113
Milgram, S., 53–55, 183–184
Miller, N., 249–250
Miller, N. E., 95, 114, 155–160
Milner, P. M., 109
Mintz, A., 121–123
Mishler, E. G., 220
Mosak, H. H., 342
Moss, C. S., 144
Mowrer, D. H., 95
Münsterberg, H., 5
Murray, H., 250
Murstein, B. I., 250
Muzio, J. N., 28
Nawas, M. M., 45
Nelson, J. M., 73–75
Newcomb, T. M., 185
Nichols, R. C., 172–174
Nickel, H. J., 172–174
Norman, R. Z., 186
Nunnally, J. C., 139–140
O'Connell, E., 249–250
Olds, J., 109, 156
Opler, M. K., 119
Orne, M. T., 44, 67–68, 145
Osgood, C. E., 117, 189–192
Overmier, J. B., 85, 89

Page, H. A., 250
Panel on Privacy & Behavioral Research, 55 n
Parker, R., 139–140
Paterson, D. G., 164
Paul, G. L., 349
Perls, F. S., 320
Perry, A., 279
Peters, F., 193–195
Pfeiffer, C. C., 205
Piaget, J., 33
Pierce, A. H., 68
Polefka, D. A., 40
Powell, J., 330–333
Premack, D., 333
Preston, M. G., 277
Pruyser, P., 161
Pulos, L., 172–174
Rachman, S., 348
Rapaport, D., 115
Rapersand, I., 308
Rapport, S., 254–256
Raush, H. L., 130, 132, 134–135
Rayner, R., 34, 212
Redlich, F. C., 119
Reik, T., 11, 12
Reynolds, D. J., 44
Richter, C. P., 93–95
Ring, K., 258–260
Ringuette, E. L., 308
Roberts, S. O., 281–285
Robinson, J. M., 281–285
Rodnick, E. H., 218–219
Roffwarg, H. P., 28
Rogers, C. R., 315, 318
Rorschach, H., 162
Rosen, A., 304–306
Rosenthal, R., 68–71, 73, 292
Rosenzweig, S., 95, 343
Ross, S., 65–67
Ruesch, J., 182
Runyon, E., 279
Ryder, R. G., 130
Sanders, R. A., 298
Sarbin, T. R., 144
Saslow, G., 40, 292–293
Sattler, J. M., 279–280
Sawyer, J., 296–297
Schachter, S., 111, 119, 229–235, 352–361
Schuham, A. I., 219
Schulsinger, F., 221, 224
Schwartz, M. S., 182–183
Schwitzgebel, R. L., 112

Scott, J. P., 111–112
Scott, W. A., 12, 15
Sears, R. R., 95, 249
Seligman, M. E. P., 85–92
Sells, S. B., 308
Selye, H., 56, 114
Shafer, R., 115
Shakow, D., 193, 195–200, 209
Shlien, J. M., 342
Shneidman, E. S., 116–117
Silver, M. J., 73
Silverman, J., 63, 182, 209–210, 220
Singer, D. L., 130
Singer, J. E., 111, 119, 352–358, 359, 360, 361
Singer, J. L., 119
Singer, R., 250
Siskind, G., 172–174
Skeels, H. M., 265–267
Skinner, B. F., 315
Skodak, M., 265
Smith, K. U., 311
Smith, P. V., 268
Solomon, R. L., 80–85, 92
Soskin, W. F., 164, 167–169, 171–172
Stampfl, T. G., 344–345
Stanton, A. H., 182–183
Starkweather, J. A., 254, 298–302
Stoyva, J., 32–33
Stuart, R. B., 333–335
Sullivan, H. S., vii, 201
Swain, M. A., 135
Taffel, C., 149
Tannenbaum, P. H., 189–192
Taylor, C. W., 215
Taylor, T. J., 132
Terman, L. M., 271–272
Thomas, J., 335
Thorson, M., 172
Tilker, H. A., 55
Trost, M. A., 350
Tsushima, W. T., 118–119
Türing, A. M., 301
Valins, S., 225–229
Vandenberg, S. G., 219
Venables, P. H., 203, 205
Vernon, P. E., 270
Veroff, J., 342
Versace, J., 60
Vogel, J. L., 341
Walker, E. G., 117
Walker, E. L., 34, 40, 84, 90, 156, 212
Walster, E., 55 n

Walters, R. H., 358
Walton, N. Y., 96
Watley, D. J., 308
Watson, J. B., 34, 212
Weakland, J., 219
Webb, W. B., 21, 23, 28
Wechsler, D., 273–276
Weil, A. T., 73–75
Weiss, J. H., 164, 169–172
Weitzman, B., 348
Welsh, R. S., 298
Wertheimer, M., 12, 15
Wiens, A. N., 292–293
Wiest, W. M., 348

Wing, J. K., 203
Winslow, C. N., 308
Witkin, H. A., 31
Wolberg, L. R., 141–143
Wolpe, J., 41
Wolpert, E., 27
Woody, R. H., 348–349
Wyden, P., 130
Wynne, L. C., 80–85, 92
Yagi, K., 56–59
Zajonc, R. B., 80
Zax, M., 350–351
Zinberg, N. E., 73–75

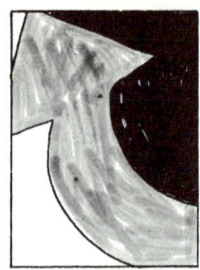

Subject Index

Abstraction, levels of, 5–6
Actuarial approach to psychopathology, 261–263
Aggression:
  animal, 97–103, 109–112
  and frustration, 95–97
  human, 95–97, 104–109
  research on, 95–112
  treatment, 96–97
Alpha rhythm, control of, 153–155
Animal research, 79–95, 97–103, 109–112
  effects of prior experience, 88
  escapable/inescapable shock, effects of, 85–90
  escape/avoidance behavior, 80–85
    theoretical explanation, 84–85
  extinction of avoidance learning, 82–84
  human parallels, clinical, 82, 89–90, 92
  implications for psychosomatic disorders, 159–160
  learned helplessness, 85–90
    treatment of, 90–92
  shuttlebox training, 80–81
  traumatic avoidance learning, 80–85
Assessment, clinical, study of, 161–181
Associational processes:
  associative hierarchies, 215–216
  creativity, 216–217
  Remote Associates Test, 215
  schizophrenia, 204–205, 213–214
Autonomic nervous system, 155
Autonomic processes, 153–160
  alpha rhythm, control of, 153–155
  brain waves, control of, 153–155
  classical conditioning, 156

Autonomic processes (*continued*)
  clinical implications, 159–160
  control of:
    conscious, 153–155
    unconscious, 155–160
  heart rate, control of, 157–159
  intestinal motility, control of, 157–159
  operant conditioning, 155–160
  salivation, control of, 156–157
  specificity of conditioned responses, 157–158

Base rate problem, 304–306
Behavior modification, 33–47, 325–339
  aversive stimulation, 328–330
  classes treated:
    abnormal behavior, 324–327
    "normal" behavior, 327–339
  conditioned emotional reaction, 34
  conditioned reinforcer, 36
  counterconditioning, 35
  eating, treatment of:
    overeating, 333–335
      behavioral curriculum, 333–336
      high probability behaviors, 334
      personal data, 333
      weight reduction, 335–336
    refusal to eat, 38–39
  establishment of new behavior, 335–339
  experimental treatment program, 40–45
  extinction of response, 36
  hoarding behavior, treatment of, 326–327
  imaginal item hierarchy, 41, 45
  implosive therapy, 345–347
  journals, 327

Behavior modification (continued)
   Applied Behavior Analysis, 327
   Behaviour Research and Therapy, 327
   modeling technique, 358–361
   phobia, treatment of, 40–45
   reciprocal inhibition, 41
   reconciliation with psychotherapy, 348–349
   reinforcement contingencies, 38
   self-control, development of, 335–339
   shaping, 35–36, 324
   smoking, treatment of, 328–333
      apparatus, 328–330
      extinction, 328–333
      stimulus change, 337–338
      stimulus control, 338–339
   systematic desensitization, 41–42
      evaluation of effectiveness, 344–348
Brain, electrostimulation, 109–113, 157–159
Brain waves:
   control of, 153–155
   recording of, 20–22
   of Yoga practitioners, 155
   in Zen meditation, 155

Client-oriented approach to psychopathology, 258–261
Clinical analysis of dreams, 13–17
Clinical assessment:
   phenomena:
      "Aunt Fanny" statements, 164–167
      "Barnum effect," 164
   study of, 161–181
Clinical decision making:
   hospitalization, 254–256
   adjustment following discharge, 262–263
   length of stay, 261–263
Clinical inference, 3–5
Clinical prediction:
   effect of:
      background training, 169–172
      familiarity with population, 172–174
      fund of information, 169–172
      self-devised instrument, 169–172
   illusory correlates, 174–181
   implications for training, 169–172, 173–174, 180–181
   studies of, 167–181
Clinical psychology:
   dictionary definition, 7
   expanded definition, 7
Clinician as generalist, 9
Clinician-oriented approach to psychopathology, 254–258

Coding of human interaction:
   categorization, 133–134
   phase demarcation, 134
Community psychology, 349–351
   reorientation, 349–350
   secondary prevention, 350
   students as "therapists," 350–351
Computerization:
   simulation of neurotic process, 251–254
   therapeutic interaction, 253, 297–302
Conditioning:
   classical, 156
   operant, 156
Conflict, interpersonal:
   coding of marital interaction, 133–134
   improvisation of conflict, 131–132
   interaction patterns of spouses, 135
      changes during marriage cycle, 135
      happy vs. unhappy marriages, 135
   laboratory study of, 130–135
   Markov process analysis, 134–135
Conflict, role of stress, 114
Construct, hypothetical, 32
Constructs, theoretical, 242–251
Control of behavior, 314–339
Control group, yoking, 86
Correlation, dream content and personality variables, 17–19
Correlational psychology, 12, 17

Defense mechanisms:
   laboratory analysis of, 123–130
   simulation of, 252–253
Diagnostic nomenclature, manual of, 193, 229
Dissonance reduction:
   as defense mechanisms, 242–243
   relation to projection, 242–243
Draw-a-Person Test, 172–181
Dreaming, study of, 11–33 (*see also* Sleep)
   amount, 23
   animals, 28, 31
   clinical analysis, 13–17
   conceptual model of, 32
   deprivation, 25
   dream length, 24
   dreams:
      hypothetical relationships, 18–19
      interpretation, 13–14, 15–17
      symbols, 13
      types, 18
   experimental analysis, 19–33
   external inputs, effect of, 23–24
   functions presumed:
      repression, 29–30

Dreaming, study of (continued)
　　sexual expression, 30–32
　　sleep preservation, 28–29
　　wish fulfillment, 26–27
　hypnotic induction, 144
　infants, 28
　nondreamers, 29–30
　nonrecallers, 29–30
　parameters of sleep cycle, 21–23
　preprogramming subjects, 23
　questions for research, 25
　recall, 22 n, 23–24
　recall rate:
　　forgetting, 23–24
　　repression, 23–24, 29–30
　research paradigms for study of, 23–24
　statistical analysis, 17–19
　symbols, 13–17
　time spent in, 23
Dream laboratory:
　apparatus, 20
　procedure, 20
　research paradigms, 23–24

Electroencephalograph (EEG):
　in dream research, 20
　as indicator of stages of sleep, 21
Electromyograph (EMG):
　in dream research, 20
Electrooculograph (EOG):
　apparatus, 20
　patterns, 21–22
　rapid eye movement, 21–22
Electrostimulation, 109–113, 157–158
Emotion:
　assumptions underlying, 357
　function of arousal and cognition, 353–354
　laboratory manipulation, 352–358
Emotionality, 225–229
　classification, 225
　feedback, 226
　measures of, 225
　physiological reactivity, 228
　questionnaire, 225–230
　responsiveness to "internal" cues, 226–229
Escape/avoidance behavior, 80–90
Ethical Standards of Psychologists, 312–313
Experimental analysis of dreaming, 19–33
Frustration and aggression, 95–97

General ability:
　heredity-environment controversy, 265–271
　problems of measurement, 270–271, 277
　　effects of race of examiner and examinee, 280–285
　　role of invidious comparison, 277–280
　types:
　　crystallized, 285–286
　　fluid, 285–286
Halo effect in projection, 246–248
Hospital:
　communication processes, 182–185
　as social system, 182–191
Hospitalization:
　effect of length, 261–263
　role of drugs, 256–258
Humor as mechanism of defense, 127–130
Hypnosis:
　analgesia, test of, 145–147
　conflict induction, 141–143
　controversy, 144–145, 152–153
　dream induction, 144
　surgical applications, 143–144
　trance state, research on, 148–152
　unconscious behavior, study of, 141–153

Implosive therapy, 345–347
Impression management, 258–261
Inference, clinical, 3–5
Institutionalization:
　confounding effects, 63
Intellect, theoretical model, 286–288
Intelligence, nature of, 288–289
Intelligence quotient, 271–275
Intelligence scales:
　Stanford-Binet Intelligence Scale, 271–273
　Wechsler Adult Intelligence Scale, 273–275
Interpersonal conflict, laboratory study of, 130–135
Interpersonal interaction, models:
　A-B-X, 185–186
　congruity, 189–192
Interview:
　research on, 290–294
　standardized, 290–294

Labeling, 3–5
Learned helplessness:
　in animals, 85–89

Learned helplessness (continued)
  in humans, 89-90, 93-95
  treatment of, 90-92, 94
Levels of awareness, research on, 136-160

Marital interaction patterns, 130-135
Methodology, approaches to study of dreaming, 12-33
MMPI, 225, 243, 259, 310-311
Modeling, 46, 358-361

Naturalistic observation, 12, 15
Neurotic process, simulated, 251-254
Non-rapid eye movement (see NREM)
NREM (non-rapid eye movement):
  role in sleep cycle, 21-22

Observation:
  of behavior, 241-263
  naturalistic, 12, 15
Overeating, treatment of, 333-335

Patients, study of types, 258-261
Performance (see also Testing, psychological):
  effects of various factors:
    comparison group, 277-280
    difficulty of task, 278-280
    level of aspiration, 277
    threat, 280-281
Persistent nonadaptive behavior, 81
Phobia, treatment of, 40-45, 358-361
Physiology of sociopathy (see Sociopathy)
Placebo effects, 63-67
Postdiction, clinical, 167-172
Prediction:
  base rate problem, 304-306
  clinical and actuarial, 167-172, 294-297
  errors:
    false negatives, 302-304
    false positives, 302-304
  modeling:
    configural, interactive, 308-309
    curvilinear, 308
    linear, 308-309
  nature of process, 306-310
Prediction of behavior, 264-313
Projection:
  as dissonance reduction, 242-243
  experimental induction, 242-251
  role of halo effect, 246-248
  types, 248-251
    attributive, 250

Projection (continued)
  complementary, 250
  Panglossian-Cassandran, 250
  similarity, 249
Psychodynamics, 5-6
Psychopathology, 193-237, 254-263 (see also Schizophrenia; Sociopathy)
  actuarial approach, 261-263
  client-oriented approach, 258-261
  clinician-oriented approach, 254-258
  patients, differences between:
    "old-timers," 258-261
    "short-timers," 258-261
  schizophrenia:
    performance, 195-200
    thought processes, 194-195
  sociopathy, 229-236
Psychopathy, 235-236 (see also Sociopathy)
  primary, 235
  secondary, 235
Psychosomatic disorders, implications of animal research, 159-160
Psychotherapy:
  approaches, 315-323
  computerization, 297-302
  conceptualization of approaches, 317-321
  evaluation of effectiveness, 340-344
  insight, role of, 321
  motor involvement, 320
  myths:
    patient uniformity, 343
    therapist uniformity, 343-344
  question of spontaneous remission, 340-344
  reconciliation with behavior therapy, 348-349
  therapist responses, 318
  time dimension, 319
Psychotic behavior, treatment of, 324-327
Punishment (see Animal research, traumatic avoidance learning)
Pupillometrics, 136-141
  and cognition, 138-139
  and perception, 137-138, 139-140

Rapid eye movement (see REM)
Reinforcement, differential, 157-159
REM (rapid eye movement):
  as dream index, 21-22
  incidence, 23

REM (rapid eye movement) (continued)
  relation to dream recall, 22 n
  relation to EEG pattern, 21
Remote Associates Test, 215
Research:
  artifacts:
    experimenter bias, 68–72
    perceived demand characteristics, 67–68
    subjects' expectancies, 73–75
  clinically relevant examples:
    field, 53–55
    socioclinical, 56–59
  drugs, clinical aspects, 65–67, 73–75
  ethical dilemmas, 51–59
  methodological considerations, 60–75
  problems:
    artifacts with human subjects, 67–75
    confounding of variables, 63
    constraints of field studies, 61–62
    placebo effects, 63–67
  relation between rigor and meaningfulness, 6
Research paradigms:
  dream experience, 24
  effects of prior experience, 88
Role playing, 131–132
Rorschach inkblots, 115, 162

Schizophrenia, 193–225 (see also Psychopathology)
  association processes, 204–205, 213–214
  attentional difficulty, 210–211
  double-bind hypothesis, 219
  effect of practice on performance, 196–197
  family influence, 219–220
  high-risk-group research design, 220–224
  interference theory, 210–211
  longitudinal paradigm, 220–224
  "normalizing trends," 196
  performance, solitary, cooperative, competitive, 198–199
  physiological/behavioral relationships, 203–204
  reaction time, typical vs. self-paced, 197
  social censure theory, 218–219
  theoretical models:
    interpersonal, 217–220
    learning, 211–214
    motivational, 202–206
    perceptual/cognitive, 206–211
  regression, 201

Schizophrenia (continued)
  thought processes, 194–195
Self-control, development of, 335–339
Self-esteem, experimental manipulation of, 243–244
Sleep, study of, 11–33 (see also Dreaming)
  body shifts, 22
  non-rapid eye movement, 22 ff
  physiological function, 28–29
  preservation via dreaming, 28–29
  psychological function, 28–29
  rapid eye movement, 22 ff
  REM time, 23
  REMPs, number of, 23
  stages:
    Stage 1 "emergent," 22 n
    Stage 1–REM, 22 ff
Small-world problem, 183–184
Smoking, treatment of, 328–333
Sociopathy, 229–236
  anxiety, role of, 235
  autonomic reactivity, 233–236
  characteristics, 229
  clinical implications:
    physiological, 234–236
    psychodynamic, 234–236
  definition, 229–230
  emotionality, 234–235
  learning ability:
    with adrenalin, 231–233
    avoidance learning, 231–233
    with placebo, 231–233
    positive learning, 231
  orienting response, 235–236
  psychopathy:
    primary, 235
    secondary, 235
  relation to neurosis, 234–235
Standards for Educational and Psychological Tests and Manuals, 311–312
Statistical analysis of dreaming, 17–19
Stress:
  laboratory simulation:
    defense mechanisms, 123–127
    panic behavior, 121–123
  methods of investigation:
    clinical data, 115
    experimental manipulation, 121–127
    study of natural events, 115–121
      parachuting, 119–121
      suicide, 116–117
      surgery, 118–119
Symbolism, 11–12

Taxonomy, 162–163
Taylor Manifest Anxiety Scale, 243
Testing, psychological, 264–285 (*see also* Performance)
    effects of:
        comparison group, 277–280
        race of subject, 280–285
        task difficulty, 278–281
    experimenter effects, 279–280
    general ability, 265–271
    intelligence, 265–271
    maximal performance, 264
    typical performance, 264
Thematic Apperception Test, 115, 250

Therapy (*see* Psychotherapy)
Tranquilizing drugs, prescription of, 256–258
Trauma, animal and human analogues, 89–90
Traumatic avoidance learning, 80–85
Treatment, animal behavior, 90–92
    clinical parallels, 92
    by forcible exposure, 91
    by immunization, 90
"Twisted pear" phenomenon, 302–304

Voodoo death, 93